The CHRONICLES *of* LONDON

The CHRONICL

ST. MARTIN'S

ES *of* LONDON

Andrew SAINT and
Gillian DARLEY

PRESS · NEW YORK

Text © Andrew Saint and Gillian Darley 1994

All rights reserved. For information, write:
Scholarly and Reference Division,
St. Martin's Press, 175 Fifth Avenue,
New York, NY 10010

First published in Great Britain in 1994 by
George Weidenfeld & Nicolson Limited

First published in the United States of America in 1994

Printed in Italy

ISBN 0-312-12213-6

Library of Congress Cataloging in Publication Data
Saint, Andrew.
    The chronicles of London/by Andrew Saint and Gillian
Darley.
       p.   cm.
    Includes bibliographical references (p.   ) and index.
    ISBN 0-312-12213-6
    1. London (England)–History. I. Darley, Gillian. II. Title.
DA677.S25   1994
942.1—dc20
                                 94-9977
                                 CIP

DESIGNER Harry Green
PICTURE RESEARCHER Annette Balfour-Lynn

Typeset by Keyspools Ltd, Newton le Willows, Lancs
Printed and bound in Italy

ENDPAPERS *Covent Garden, 1754.*

TITLE PAGE *Detail of a letter from Henry VIII
to Anne Boleyn, 1528.*

CONTENTS PAGE *(clockwise from left) London, c.1500;
London from Westminster Abbey, 1857;
The Royal Exchange, c. 1900; London Bridge
in the seventeenth century, by Claude de Jong.*

The authors and publishers would like to thank the following for permission to reprint copyright material: Alison & Busby for Colin MacInnes, *Absolute Beginners* (1959): The extract from *Testament of Youth* by Vera Brittain is included with the permission of Paul Berry, her literary executor, Victor Gollancz, and the Virago Press; Chatto & Windus (1954) and Viking Penguin, a division of Penguin USA Inc. (Copyright © 1954, renewed 1982 by Iris Murdoch) for Iris Murdoch, *The Net*; Victor Gollancz and Rogers, Coleridge & White Ltd for Jessica Mitford, *Hons and Rebels* (1960); The Hogarth Press for Virginia Woolf, *The Early Journals, 1897–1909*, ed. Mitchell A. Leaska (1990); The Hogarth Press and Harcourt Brace Jovanovich Inc. for *The Diary of Virginia Woolf, 1915–19*, vol. I, ed. Anne Olivier Bell (1977); The Hogarth Press and Harcourt Brace Jovanovich Inc. for *The Diary of Virginia Woolf, 1925–30*, vol. II, ed. Anne Olivier Bell (1980); King's College, Cambridge, The Society of Authors as the literary representatives of the E. M. Forster Estate, and Harcourt Brace Jovanovich Inc. for E. M. Forster, *Marianne Thornton*, Hodder Headline/Harcourt Brace Jovanovich (1956); Kingsley Martin and Martin Secker and Warburg for Kingsley Martin, *Critic's London Diary* (1960); John Murray (Publishers) Ltd for Arthur Munby, *Man of Two Worlds*, ed. Derek Hudson (1972); Nigel Nicolson for Harold Nicolson, *Diaries and Letters*, 1930–9, 1939–45, Collins (1966, 1967); The Estate of the late Sonia Brownell Orwell, Martin Secker and Warburg, and Harcourt Brace Jovanovich Inc. for George Orwell *Down and Out in Paris and London* (1933); The Estate of the late Sonia Brownell Orwell, Martin Secker and Warburg, and Harcourt Brace Jovanovich Inc. for *Collected Essays, Journalism and Letters of George Orwell*, vols I and II, ed. Sonia Orwell and Ian Angus (1968); *The Spectator*; Virago Press for *The London Journal of Flora Tristan*, translated, annotated and introduced by Jean Hawkes (1982); A. P. Watt on behalf of H. C. Robbins Landon for *The Collected Correspondence and London Notebooks of Joseph Haydn* by H. C. Robbins Landon (1959); A. P. Watt on behalf of The Literary Executors of the Estate of H. G. Wells for *An Experiment in Autobiography* by H. G. Wells (1937); Yale University Press for Karl Friedrich Schinkel, *The English Journey*, ed. David Bindman and Gottfried Riemann (1993). The publishers have endeavoured to contact all copyright holders and apologise for any inadvertent errors or omissions.

Strong be thy walles that about thee standes,

Wise be the people that within thee dwells,

Fresh is thy river with his lusty strands,

Blythe be thy churches, well sounding be thy bells,

Rich be thy merchants that in substance excels,

Fair be their wives, right lovesome, white and small,

Clear be thy virgins, lusty under kells:

London, thou art the flower of cities all.

WILLIAM DUNBAR 1465?–1530?

List of CONTENTS

INTRODUCTION

History written long after the events it describes too often lacks immediacy and impact. Partial or obscure though they may be, contemporaries convey the heat, the sensation and the freshness of the moment far better. This book is devoted to making the past of one of the world's great cities vivid once again. It aims to bring London's long history to life through the testimony of those that were closest to the events that shaped the city – chroniclers, journalists, visitors and, above all, Londoners themselves.

Their record allows us to reach back through the centuries, to feel the past as part of ourselves and of the city we know. A sympathetic understanding of the history of a great city such as London and of the experiences of its citizens is surely needed if we are to grapple with its present and future. At heart, the concerns and struggles, the delights and entertainments of city-dwellers have changed little over the years. It is in the hope that *The Chronicles of London* may help people to understand and love London better that this book has been compiled.

The wealth of source material and fine writing upon London is inexhaustible, at least from the sixteenth century onwards. In our selection, we have had two principal aims in mind. Firstly, we have wanted to describe the most momentous and critical events in London's history in the words of those who either shaped, witnessed or endured them. And secondly, we have tried to convey the special flavour of the metropolis, the strong characteristics which have emerged during the successive stages of its growth and development. In each section of the book, we have attempted to keep a balance between historic events and the atmosphere, texture and feeling of London – positive and negative – at that particular time.

For the sake of liveliness and interest, we have had recourse to a wide variety of sources, from inscriptions, deeds, legal records and statistics to diaries, letters and poems. We have included fiction only where its roots are self-evidently in the close observation of reality and when it conveys an immediate sense of the moment. Untapped riches lie among the published but half-forgotten diaries and memoirs by visitors to London; where possible, we have chosen unfamiliar writers, or figures known in other spheres who remark on the city as *they* discover it. But we have not hesitated to use such famous accounts as those of Pepys or Evelyn for the Great Fire of London; it would have been perverse, we felt, to omit such wonderful though familiar passages entirely.

A short introduction precedes every extract, or on occasion a group of extracts, in each section. Wherever possible, we have excerpted a passage entire, without abbreviation; where something is left out, the omission is clearly marked. Spelling in older passages has been modernized, with the exception of proper names, though some old spelling has been left in Dunbar's poem on London so as to make it easier to scan. Archaic words have not been explained, on the grounds that most can be found in a good dictionary

The list of sources at the back of the book will allow readers to trace the passages to their original sources, should they so desire. We have not included a bibliography, but we would like to record our debt to two equally outstanding, equally human encyclopaedias devoted to London: William Kent's of 1937, and Ben Weinreb and Christopher Hibbert's of 1983. Anyone curious about London cannot fail to be diverted, educated and stimulated by these two evergreen books.

We have had help from many friends in drawing our attention to writers about London of especial fascination or obscurity. We are particularly grateful to Nicholas Jacobs for telling us about and translating Theodore Fontane's account of disabled cricket at the Oval, and to Allen Synge for kindly loaning us his picture; to Michael Hunter for referring us to Samuel Jeake's diary; to Peyton Skipwith and Andrew Patrick of the Fine Art Society; and to Robert Thorne for sundry helpful suggestions. Many extracts have been happy discoveries, chanced upon through the open-shelf system of the London Library. May librarians and archivists everywhere come likewise to appreciate the value of scholarly serendipity! To the staff of that library, as to librarians and archivists at the Bishopsgate Institute, Holborn Library and the Institution of Civil Engineers, we owe thanks. We are grateful also to Annette Balfour-Lynn for her work on the pictures, and Coralie Hepburn for efficient editing in the face of exacting deadlines.

ANDREW SAINT

GILLIAN DARLEY

43–1066

ROMAN

and

SAXON

LONDON

Archaeologists have dug and antiquaries have dreamed. But no one has been able to disprove the proud and plain truth that London was by foundation Roman – the direct outcome of the Claudian invasion of AD 43. Not only was London a Roman city, but it was a port that soon showed exceptional vigour at the confluence of ancient maritime trade routes. Its first chronicler is Tacitus, a historian and stylist of suitable distinction; he speaks of London as *copia negotiatorum et commeatuum maxime celebre* – 'famous for its crowd of traders and a great centre of commerce'. Six and a half centuries later, in its nebulous, post-Roman phase of eclipse, Bede still calls London *multorum emporium populorum terra marique venientium* – 'an emporium for many nations who come to it by land and sea'.

These words, twelve in all, are our most precious key to the character of early London. Modern excavation has added inestimably to our understanding of the city. We know where London's great forum lay, and now also its amphitheatre. Inscriptions tell us who lived and died in Roman London, what parts of the empire they came from, how they worshipped and what their jobs were. But without the invaluable phrases of Tacitus and Bede, we would hardly know what sort of a city London was, or recognize the almost uncanny similarities to the London of today.

All too often, ancient history means compressed accounts of particular episodes having largely to do with war. We have snippets of this kind about London. We know something about its destruction by Boudicca in AD 60, its repossession in 296 by Constantius Chlorus after a spasm of semi-independence for Britain under Carausius and Allectus, and the efforts made at the end of the fourth century by Count Theodosius to shore up its defences in the face of the first Saxon incursions. The gaps between these episodes are grievous. Archaeology suggests a city-port that careered ahead rapidly for the first seventy years of its existence, was checked by a bad fire in about AD 120, then recovered a quieter rhythm and continued without radical upsets until the decline of Roman power in the fourth century. But our lack

ABOVE *Edward the Confessor is borne to his grave in the newly completed Westminster Abbey. A scene from the Bayeux Tapestry.*

OPPOSITE *Boadicea or Boudicca: destroyer of London, but Britain's first symbol of freedom.*

Coin of Nero, Emperor at the time of Boudicca's rebellion.

of documentation means that there is much we do not know. In particular, we cannot say whether London went into gentle decline after AD 400, or whether some savage incident or incidents precipitated the depopulation of what by then had become a well-walled and presumably well-guarded city. One thing it is hard to believe: that when Christianity came to London in 604 and King Ethelbert built the first St Paul's Cathedral for Bishop Mellitus, it was raised amid empty streets. Recent digging in the Guildhall Yard confirms there was more continuity between Roman and Saxon London than it was once fashionable to believe. The presence of a now strongly attested Saxon settlement outside the wall, further west along the Strand, need not mean that the Roman city was abandoned.

Despite St Paul's and Mellitus, Christianity in London was precarious until about 675. For the next two centuries the city and region were mostly under the control of the Mercian kings. Around 800 the first monastery at Westminster was established, but its pedigree is mired in forged charters and mythical lives of the saints. The fog begins to clear only after 886, when the power of Wessex and King Alfred reaches London and the Anglo-Saxon Chronicle starts to mention the city. There is a sense hereafter of a fresh start: new roads, new

buildings, better prospects for trade, growing population and power and perhaps a new constitution. By the time of Ethelred a century later, London was a regular seat of government and of kings, though we are not sure where they lived. Its security, however, was doubtful. Lying as it did between two spheres of influence, those of Wessex and Mercia, and easily reached from the sea, it became vulnerable in the violent and complex power-play of the early eleventh century, when Danish and Norse kings took a longer-term interest in southern England. Until 1016 the Saxon kings and their bishops managed to hang on. If we are to believe the chroniclers, London and its citizens were largely on their side. But there were awkward moments: the celebrated breaking of London Bridge in 1014 was the upshot of a campaign in which Danes and Londoners were actually defending the city against an alliance of Saxons and Norsemen.

This period of violence and instability all but ended when Cnut took the throne in 1016. London then enjoyed fifty years of comparative stability, first under Cnut and his sons, then under Edward the Confessor. The most memorable episode of Edward's reign, the founding of Westminster Abbey, with which must be linked the transfer of the royal seat to the embryonic Palace of Westminster, required peace for its accomplishment. But hardly had the abbey been consecrated and Edward gone to his grave, than the last successful invasion of England took place.

60

Boudicca's revolt

The first years of every settlement are the most precarious; so it was to prove for Londinium. A short time after Aulus Plautius's invasion of AD 43, some thirty acres on a shallow stretch of the Thames, to the east of the Walbrook stream, were designated for the deep-water port of a new Roman province. Scarcely had the first London Bridge been thrown across from the marshy south bank, scarcely too had a main street been laid out and wharves and houses been erected, when disaster struck. Prasutagus of the Iceni in Norfolk had struck a treaty with the Roman invaders, but had failed to grasp that his territory would revert to Rome after his death. This took place in AD 60, during the Emperor Nero's reign. A tactless procurator piled insult upon injury by dispossessing and flogging the widow Boudicca and condoning the rape of her daughters. East Anglia was soon in uproar. Colchester – Camulodunum, the provincial capital – was viciously sacked, a Roman legion overwhelmed, and Boudicca with thousands of followers headed for London. The troops of the tough governor, Suetonius Paulinus, were meanwhile engaged in a far-away campaign against Anglesea. Outnumbered, they started a forced march back. Tacitus takes up the story – and London for the first time enters the history books.

With a fine show of steadiness and courage, Suetonius now marched straight through enemy territory to reach London, a place without the distinguishing name of 'colony' but important on account of its large number of traders and its commerce. There he considered whether he should stand and fight on the spot. He was aware that the number of his troops was small, and that Petilius Cerealis had been defeated because of his rashness. He therefore decided to sacrifice this one town in order to preserve the whole. The weeping and wailing of those who besought his help did not deter him from giving the order for departure. He did allow those who were prepared to leave to accompany his formation. Those who stayed behind because of their gender, their decrepitude or their attachment to the place were overwhelmed by the enemy. The same disaster overtook the *municipium* of Verulamium, since

ABOVE *London's Roman wall: a section at Tower Hill. The masonry dates from many periods, but the lowest courses are Roman.*

BELOW *Plan of Roman London according to present archaeological scholarship.*

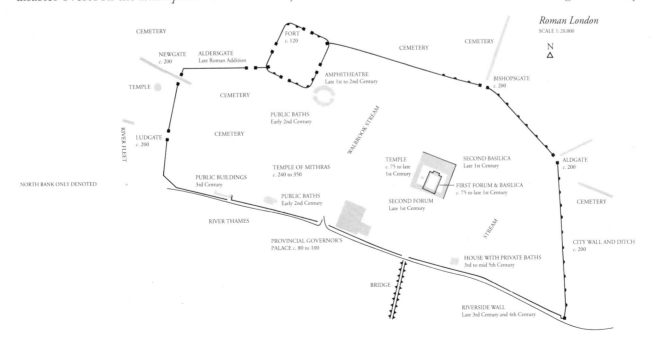

the rebels, eager for plunder and undisciplined, shunned forts and military strongholds and made only for what was easy to pillage and lacked defenders. In the places I have mentioned [Camulodunum, Londinium, Verulamium], it is estimated that no fewer than 70,000 Roman citizens and allies perished. The enemy neither took captives nor bartered them, nor did they observe any of the usual conventions of warfare. Instead they massacred, hanged, burned and crucified with an energy that suggested they were aware that retribution would soon be visited upon them, and so hastened to exercise vengeance while they could.

60–400
The Roman city

Tacitus got much of his knowledge about Britain from his father-in-law, Julius Agricola, governor of the province during the years AD 77–84. By then, Roman authority had long been restored and was in the process of extending up into Scotland. Tacitus, however, never again mentions London by name. For the city's reconstruction and spectacular growth over the sixty years following Boudicca's Revolt, we have to rely on archaeology. Occasionally, an inscription comes to light that secures or transforms our understanding of Roman London. Of these,

the most remarkable is the tombstone of Julius Classicianus, found in two pieces and at two dates on the site of a cemetery on Tower Hill, and now in the British Museum. Classicianus too is mentioned by Tacitus, as the procurator who put the finances and administration of Britain to rights after the destruction of AD 60–61. That the procurator, the highest imperial official, lived and was buried in London leaves us in no doubt that London was already the foremost city of Roman Britain, in practice if not yet in constitutional theory.

<blockquote>
TO THE GODS OF THE DEPARTED JULIA PACATA INDIANA, DAUGHTER OF INDUS, THE [sorrowing?] WIFE OF GAIUS JULIUS ALPINUS CLASSICIANUS, SON OF GAIUS, OF THE FABIAN VOTING TRIBE, PROCURATOR OF THE PROVINCE OF BRITAIN [caused this to be erected].
</blockquote>

More than a hundred other Roman inscriptions have been unearthed in London. Most come from funerary monuments. With the effigies of those they commemorate and the context in which they are found, they help us to piece together a picture of Roman London as a large, restless, cosmopolitan port populated by Romanized Britons and by soldiers and traders from every outpost of the empire. They were drawn there by the benefits of

LEFT *Tombstone of C. Julius Classicianus, the procurator who restored the province of Britain and city of London after Boudicca's rebellion.*

RIGHT *Roman altar commemorating the restoration of the Temple of Isis.*

OPPOSITE ABOVE *Tombstone of Vivius Marcianus, from Ludgate Hill.*

OPPOSITE BELOW *Tile with graffito immortalizing the work-shy Austalis.*

Roman civilization: prosperity, security, religious toleration
and diversity, the cult of games and of bathing, and the
sophisticated Latin tongue, however rudely some spoke it.

AULUS ALFIDIUS OLUSSA, OF THE POMPTINE TRIBE, BORN
AT ATHENS, LIES HERE, AGED 70. THIS STONE WAS SET UP
BY HIS HEIR IN ACCORDANCE WITH HIS WILL.
> Found at Tower Hill, first century AD

TO THE GODS OF THE DEPARTED, ANENCLETUS,
PROVINCIAL OFFICIAL, SET THIS UP IN MEMORY OF HIS
MOST DEVOTED WIFE, CLAUDIA MARTINA, AGED 19, WHO
LIES HERE.
> Found on Ludgate Hill, *c.* AD 100. Anencletus would have been
> a superior, literate slave on the staff of the Provincial Council,
> which was responsible for maintaining the Imperial Cult.

ULPIANUS SILVANUS, VETERAN OF THE 2nd AUGUSTAN
LEGION, PAID HIS VOW MADE AT ORANGE [Arausio].
> A second-century AD relief with carvings showing Mithraic
> symbolism.

IN HONOUR OF THE IMPERIAL HOUSE, MARCIUS
MARTIANNUS PULCHER, GOVERNOR APPOINTED BY THE
TWO EMPERORS, ORDERED THE TEMPLE OF ISIS,
DILAPIDATED THROUGH OLD AGE, TO BE RESTORED.
> An altar of *c.* AD 255, found at Blackfriars in 1975.

TO THE GODS OF THE DEPARTED, JANUARIA MARTINA,
THE MOST DEVOTED WIFE OF VIVIUS MARCIANUS OF THE
2nd AUGUSTAN LEGION, SET UP THIS MONUMENT.
> Found at Ludgate Hill, third century AD. Marcianus is shown
> holding a scroll, indicating he had both bureaucratic and
> military duties.

AUSTALIS HAS BEEN GOING OFF BY HIMSELF EVERY DAY
FOR THIRTEEN DAYS.
> Scratched on the back of a roofing tile found in Warwick Lane.
> It may refer to absenteeism on the part of a worker in a tile
> factory, but it could be the first recorded British joke.

RUFUS, SON OF CALLISUNUS: GREETINGS TO EPILLICUS
AND ALL HIS COLLEAGUES. YOU KNOW THAT I AM WELL, I
BELIEVE. IF YOU HAVE THE LIST, PLEASE SEND IT. LOOK
AFTER EVERYTHING CAREFULLY. SEE THAT YOU TURN
THE GIRL INTO MONEY.
> Britain's earliest business letter, written on a wooden writing
> tablet and probably addressed from a master on business
> outside London to his slaves.

Roman London had its ups and downs, like every ancient city. Its first impetus was checked by a fire in about AD 125. But it remained one of the empire's largest and most successful cities for the next two hundred years. It was walled only in about AD 200. As Roman power began to fragment in civil wars between bickering emperors, the fortifications proved their worth. In 296, during one such war, London enters written history again. Carausius, the governor of Britain, had declared his independence of Rome. He fared very well until he was assassinated and supplanted by one of his staff, Allectus. The emperor in whose sphere Britain fell, Constantius Chlorus, then sailed from Boulogne and managed to recapture the island, despite fog at sea. In a panegyric to Constantius, the writer Eumenius offers a flowery account of what ensued. The 'relief' of London in 296 was important enough for a medal to be struck which gives us our first – albeit idealized – depiction of the city.

crumbling. It might have continued, had the emperors been able and willing to commit legions to the permanent defence of the island. The last coherent glimpse of Roman London comes from the pages of Ammianus Marcellinus. He chronicles the efforts of Theodosius, a general acting for the Emperor Valentinian and father of the emperor who bore his name, to shore up the province in the years 367–9. For a time London was even renamed 'Augusta', but this desperate public-relations exercise seems to have been of little avail. London's defensive wall was strengthened at about this time, a measure that it is tempting to ascribe to Theodosius.

At that time the Picts ... and likewise the Attacotti, a very warlike people, and the Scots were roving all over different parts of the country and committing great ravages ...

To put a stop to this, should fortune allow him a

Invincible Caesar, by the favour of all the immortal Gods it was granted to you to inflict such slaughter upon the enemy, especially the Franks, that those also of your troops who had been led astray by the sea fog to which I have referred and had at last reached the town of London, found the remnants of the barbarian mercenaries who had survived the battle plundering the place, and when these thought to take flight, slew them throughout the city. Not only did they bring safety to your subjects by destroying the enemy, but in addition they induced a sentiment of satisfaction at the sight. O manifold victory!

By the later fourth century, under the impact of sea raids from the German and Scandinavian coasts and incursions from the north, the Roman pattern of life in Britain was

The Medallion of Arras, showing Constantius Chlorus on one side and the personification of London welcoming him on the other, to commemorate his 'relief' of the city in AD 296.

favourable occasion, this most energetic general [Theodosius] set out for the end of the earth. Reaching the sea at Boulogne . . . he crossed the strait in a leisurely manner and arrived at Richborough, a sheltered harbour on the coast opposite. Once the Batavian and Herulian troops had arrived, as well as the Jovian and Victorian legions, he felt confident of his strength and made for London, an ancient town subsequently named 'Augusta'. He then split his army into several detachments and attacked the enemy, who were straggling in separate predatory bands, weighed down with plunder and driving chained prisoners and cattle along with them. They were rapidly routed and deprived of the booty which the poor tribute payers had surrendered to them. He restored it all to them apart from a small portion which he allotted to his weary troops. Then, as if in a triumph, he joyfully entered the city that had so recently been overwhelmed by disasters but now had been restored to safety almost before such a thing could have been hoped.

604

St Paul's founded

It is through the testimony of Bede, chronicling the history of the early church in Britain and Augustine's mission to 'restore' Christianity in Saxon England from 597 onwards, that London first emerges from the mists of the fifth and sixth centuries. By 601 Augustine had set up the headquarters of the English Church in Canterbury. But Pope Gregory, writing from distant Rome, evidently still expected London and York to be the chief seats of the new ecclesiastical authority, as they had been of Roman secular government.

Three years later Augustine established a London bishopric, and the first St Paul's Cathedral was built by Ethelbert, the Saxon king of Kent. Mellitus, London's first bishop, was an Italian monk who stood second in authority on the English expedition after Augustine. In the event, he proved unable to maintain a base in London after Ethelbert's death and withdrew to Canterbury, becoming archbishop himself in 619. The state of London when St Paul's was founded is a puzzle. For trading purposes, the Roman city seems to have been all but abandoned for a Saxon settlement further west, along the Strand. The founding of a church in the half-ruinous old city seems to have been a device to claim Roman authority and legitimacy on behalf of the Pope.

Since Bishop Augustine had advised him that the harvest was great and the workers were few, Pope Gregory sent more colleagues and ministers of the word together with his messengers. First and foremost among these were Mellitus, Justus, Paulinus and Rufinianus . . . He also sent a letter in which he announced that he had despatched the pallium to him and at the same time directed how he should organize the bishops in Britain. Here is the text of this letter:

To the most reverend and holy brother Augustine, our fellow-bishop, Gregory, servant of the servants of God:

. . . Because the new church of the English has been brought into the grace of Almighty God through the bounty of the Lord and by your labours, we grant to you the use of the pallium in the church . . . so that you may ordain twelve bishops in various places who are to be subject to your jurisdiction: the bishop of London shall however for the future always be consecrated by his own synod and receive the honour of the pallium from that holy and apostolic see which by the guidance of God I serve. We wish to send as bishop to the city of York one whom you yourself shall decide to consecrate . . . but after your death, he should preside over the bishops he has consecrated, being in no way subject to the authority of the bishop of London.

In the year of our Lord 604, Augustine, archbishop of Britain, consecrated two bishops, namely Mellitus and Justus. He consecrated Mellitus to preach in the province of the East Saxons, which is divided from Kent by the river Thames and borders on the sea to the east. Its chief city is London, which is on the banks of that river and is an emporium for many nations who come to it by land and sea. At that time Sebert, nephew of Ethelbert and son of his sister Ricule, ruled over the nation although he was under the dominion of Ethelbert, who . . . held sway over all the English nations as far as the Humber. After this province had accepted the word of truth through the preaching of Mellitus, King Ethelbert built the church of the apostle St Paul in the city of London, in which Mellitus and his successors were to have their episcopal seat.

886–994

From Alfred to Ethelred

Of London under the great Mercian kings of the eighth century, Ethelbald and Offa, we know little. The city existed and in 811 was described as a 'famous place and royal city'. Digging has revealed rather more about the settlement west of the city wall, along the Strand; at about this time, too, the

A royal charter granting land at Aldenham, Hertfordshire, to the monastery at Westminster, from the reign of King Offa, AD *785.*

first Christian settlement and monastery at Westminster were founded. The real revival of London's fortunes has a definite date, however: 886, when it came into King Alfred's power. It was entrusted to his son-in-law Ethelred, lord of the Mercians. A new era now begins, with London acting as a delicate pivot between Wessex and Mercia. The city is replanned on a fresh road system. Soon, the Anglo-Saxon Chronicle refers more to London than Winchester, the Wessex capital. By 1000 London is indisputably the country's main city once again, and its citizens begin to act with a measure of independence. But a renewed period of Viking intervention after 980 proves them vulnerable to aggression.

886 In this year ... King Alfred occupied London; and all the English people that were not under subjection to the Danes submitted to him. And he then entrusted the borough to the control of Ealdorman Ethelred.

895 In the same year the aforesaid army [the Danes] made a fortress by the Lea, 20 miles above London. Then afterwards in the summer a great part of the citizens and also of other people marched till they arrived at the fortress of the Danes, and there they were put to flight and four king's thegns were slain. Then later in the autumn, the king [Alfred] encamped in the vicinity of the borough while they were reaping corn, so that the Danes could not deny them that harvest. Then one day the king rode up along the river and examined where the river could be obstructed, so that they could not bring the ships out. And then this was carried out: two fortresses were made on the two sides of the river. When they had just begun that work and had encamped for that purpose, the enemy perceived that they could not bring the ships out. Then they abandoned the ships and went overland till they reached Bridgnorth on the Severn and built that fortress. Then the English army rode after the enemy, and the men from London fetched the ships and broke up all which they could not bring away, and brought to London those which were serviceable.

962 ... During the year there was a very great mortality, and the great and fatal fire occurred in London and St Paul's minster was burnt, and was rebuilt the same year.

992 In this year ... the King [Ethelred the Unready] and all his councillors decreed that all the ships that were any use should be assembled at London. And the king then entrusted the expedition to the leadership of Ealdorman Aelfric and Earl Thored and Bishop Aelfstan and Bishop Aescwig, and they were to try if they could entrap the Danish army anywhere at sea ... And then the Danish army encountered the ships from East Anglia and from London, and they made a great slaughter there and captured the ship on which the ealdorman was.

994 In this year Olaf and Swein came to London on the Nativity of St Mary with 94 ships, and they proceeded to attack the city stoutly and wished also to set it on fire; but there they suffered more harm and injury than they ever thought any citizens would do to them. But the holy mother of God showed her mercy to the citizens that day and saved them from their enemies. And these went away from there, and did the greatest damage that ever any army could do, by burning, ravaging and slaying, both along the coast and in Essex, Kent, Sussex and Hampshire.

1014

London Bridge destroyed

The breaking of London Bridge has been immortalized in English folklore. It was the most dramatic episode in a confused set of events centred on London between 1013 and

1017. Ethelred, the Saxon king, by now seems to have had his principal seat in London. But he had been weakened by the duplicity of his ealdorman Edric, the *bête noire* of the Anglo-Saxon Chronicle, who in 1012 went so far as to put a Bishop of London to death for not paying tribute. The next year, Sven or Swein of Denmark initiated one of the last great Viking campaigns, capturing London. Ethelred fled abroad, but in 1014 he teamed up with King Olaf of Norway. Together they sailed up the Thames with a fleet to help Ethelred repossess his kingdom. What followed is told, with fascinating technical detail, in the *Saga of St Olaf*.

First they made their way to London, and so up into the Thames, but the Danes held the city. On the other side of the river is a great market town called Southwark. There the Danes had entrenched themselves strongly; they had dug a great dike and barricaded the inside of the wall with timber and stones and turf, and inside it they had a large force. King Ethelred ordered a great attack to be made, but the Danes repulsed it and King Ethelred made no headway. There was a bridge over the river between the city and Southwark, broad enough for carts driven from opposite directions to pass each other. The bridge was fortified both by strongholds and by a covering of planks facing downstream and reaching up to a man's middle, and under the bridge there were stakes fixed into the river-bed. When an attack was made, the host stood ranged along the bridge and defended it. King Ethelred was much troubled how he should win the bridge. He called all the leaders of the host to speak with him, and sought counsel from them how they were to bring down the bridge. Then King Olaf said that he would try to attack with his host if the other captains would also attack, and it was agreed at this council that they were to press forward with their forces up under the bridge. Then each made ready his host and his ships.

King Olaf had made great wicker shields of tough roots and soft wood and had taken to pieces wattled houses, and had all this placed over his ships wide enough to stretch beyond the sides. He had stakes placed underneath at such a distance from one another and at such a height as to afford both a convenient place to fight from and ample strength to withstand any stones which might be thrown from above. Now when the host was arrayed, they made an attack by rowing up the river, and when they drew near the bridge both missiles and stones were hurled upon them from above so fiercely that nothing withstood them, neither helmets nor shields, and the ships themselves were severely damaged. Many then drew back. But King Olaf, and with him the Norwegian host, rowed right up under the bridge, and wound cables round the stakes that supported the bridge and, taking the cables, they rowed all the ships downstream as hard as ever they could. The stakes were dragged along the bottom until they were loosened under the bridge, and because there was an armed force ranged thick along the bridge with a quantity of stones and many weapons, and moreover the stakes were broken from under it, the bridge came crashing down and many fell into the river, but all the rest of the host fled from the bridge, some into the city and some into Southwark. After that they made an attack on Southwark and won it. Now when the citizens saw that the River Thames was won, so that they could no longer prevent the ships from pressing up inland, they were stricken with terror at the advance of the ships and gave up the city and accepted King Ethelred.

1017–1042

From Cnut to Hardacnut

The return of Ethelred was by no means the end of things. In 1016 Swein's son Cnut came back, in alliance with Edric. Ethelred was ageing and probably ill, so the defence of England fell mainly to his son and heir, Edmund 'Ironside'. The invading army was repulsed several times, but Ethelred died and, after a crushing defeat at Ashingdon in Essex, Edmund was compelled to make peace. He in his turn died in the same year, leaving Cnut as undisputed king of England. Cnut was merciless to Edric in victory, having him murdered and, as Florence of Worcester's Chronicle alleges, thrown over London's city wall. Some scholars take this as suggesting that the royal palace or castle was on the edge of the City against the wall; the Barbican area is the favoured location.

1017 In this year King Cnut received the dominion of the whole of England, and divided it into four parts: Wessex for himself, East Anglia for Earl Thorkel, Mercia for Ealdorman Edric, Northumbria for Earl Eric ... In the month of July, King Cnut married the widow of King Ethelred, Queen Aelfgifu. And at the Lord's Nativity, when he was in London, he gave orders for the perfidious ealdorman Edric to be killed in the palace, because he feared to be at some time deceived by his treachery, as his former lords Ethelred and Edmund had frequently been deceived; and he

ordered his body to be thrown over the wall of the city and left unburied. Along with him were killed, though guiltless, Ealdorman Northman, son of Ealdorman Leofwine and thus brother to Earl Leofric, Aethelweard, son of Ealdorman Aethelmaer, and Brihtric, son of the Devonshire magnate Aelfheah.

Under 1042, Florence of Worcester records another sudden death, though not apparently a violent one: that of Hardacnut, the son and successor to Cnut, at a wedding feast in Lambeth.

1042 At a feast at the place called Lambeth, at which Osgod Clapa, a man of great power, was giving his daughter Gytha in marriage to Tofi, surnamed the Proud, a Dane and an influential man, with much rejoicing, Hardacnut, king of the English, while he stood cheerful, in health and high spirits, drinking with the aforesaid bride and certain men, fell suddenly to the ground by a sad fall in the midst of his drinking, and remained thus speech-

RIGHT *The* Gesta Cnutonis *is given to Queen Emma, Cnut's wife, by the Monk of St Omer, an eleventh-century chronicler.*

OPPOSITE *A ship of Cnut's fleet. From a medieval manuscript.*

less, expired on Tuesday 8 June, and was borne to Winchester and buried next his father, King Cnut. And his brother Edward was raised to the throne in London, chiefly by the exertions of Earl Godwine and Lifing, bishop of Worcester. His father was Ethelred, whose father was Edgar, whose father was Edmund, whose father was Edward the Elder, whose father was Alfred.

1042–1066

Westminster Abbey rebuilt

The most far-reaching act of the Saxon kings to affect London was also their last one: the rebuilding of Westminster Abbey. At about the same time, their royal house or palace nearby became incontestably the English monarch's most important seat. These decisions, crucial to the history of London and of the country, were personal ones taken by Edward the Confessor (1042–66). So it is fitting that Edward's shrine still occupies the very heart of the abbey, as the venerated site of English nationhood and kingship. He lived just long enough to see the unfinished abbey's consecration, which seems to have been hurried up because of his impending death. Within a year, his successor Harold was defeated, and William the Conqueror was crowned in the great church Edward had so piously built and sat safe upon his throne. The story of why and how he rebuilt the abbey comes down to us in a life written in his memory by a contemporary and friend of the royal family, probably a Flemish monk from St Omer connected with the English court.

Outside the walls of London, upon the river Thames, stood a monastery dedicated to St Peter, but insignificant in buildings and numbers, for under the abbot only a small community of monks served Christ. Moreover the endowments from the faithful were slender, and provided no more than their daily bread. The king, therefore, being devoted to God, gave his attention to

that place, for it both lay hard by the famous and rich town and also was a delightful spot, surrounded with fertile lands and green fields and near the main channel of the river, which bore abundant merchandise of wares of every kind for sale from the whole world to the town on its banks. And especially because of his love of the prince of the apostles, whom he worshipped with uncommon and special love, he decided to have his burial place there.

Accordingly he ordered that out of the tithes of all his revenues should be started the building of a noble edifice, worthy of the prince of the apostles; so that, after the transient journey of this life, God would look kindly upon him, both for the sake of his goodness and because of the gift of lands and ornaments with which he intended to ennoble the place. And so the building, nobly begun at the King's command, was successfully made ready; and there was no weighing of the costs, past or future, so long as it proved worthy of, and acceptable to, God and St Peter.

The princely house of the altar, noble with its most lofty vaulting, is surrounded by dressed stone evenly

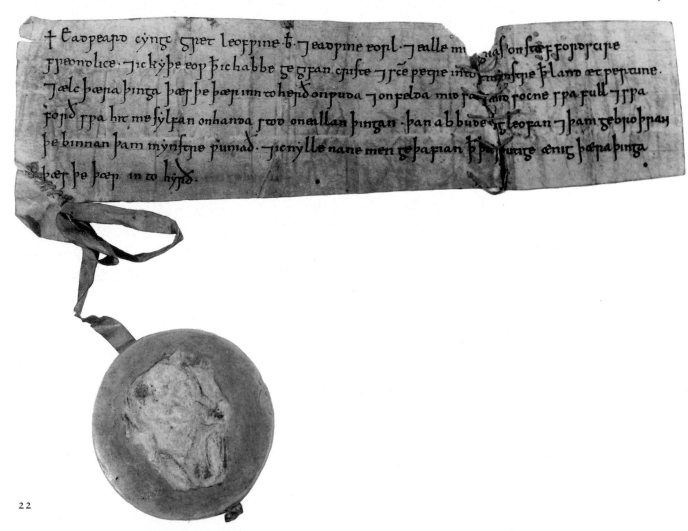

RIGHT *The shrine of Edward the Confessor in Westminster Abbey.*

OPPOSITE *Writ and seal of Edward the Confessor, on a document concerning Westminster Abbey.*

jointed. Also the passage round that temple is enclosed on both sides by a double arching of stone with the joints of the structure strongly consolidated on this side and that. Furthermore the crossing of the church, which is to hold in its midst the choir of God's choristers and to uphold with like support from either side the high apex of the central tower, rises simply at first with a low and sturdy vault, swells with many a stair spiralling up in artistic profusion, but then with a plain wall climbs to the wooden roof which is carefully covered with lead. Above and below are built out chapels methodically arranged, which are to be consecrated through their altars to the memory of apostles, martyrs, confessors and virgins. Moreover, the whole complex of this enormous building was started so far to the east of the old church that the brethren dwelling there should not have to cease from Christ's service and also that a sufficiently spacious vestibule might be placed between them.

1066–1485

MEDIEVAL
LONDON

From the Norman Conquest to the founding of the Tudor dynasty is a vast span in London's history. In 1066 the city was still quite small, having been all but refounded less than two centuries earlier. It had barely recovered from incursions by the Vikings and Norsemen, of which William the Conqueror's was the crowning example. Thereafter, the traffic in aggression was to be in the opposite direction. By the time Henry Tudor settled the dynastic squabbles of the fifteenth century, London was in a different class of city – the equal of Florence, Milan, Amsterdam or Antwerp, bigger than Bruges, and creeping up behind Naples, Venice and Paris. Counting in Westminster, Southwark and the suburbs, London's population lay somewhere in the region of 50000. It had two great Gothic centres of worship, several abbeys and convents not much inferior, and over a hundred tiny parishes and

churches within the City. It boasted a powerful mayor presiding over twenty-four aldermen in a newly rebuilt Guildhall; proud companies and guilds (many with their own halls) and a well-established apprenticeship system: adequate provision for law and order; thorough byelaws regulating construction and markets, as well as a fair supply of fresh water; inns of court where lawyers learned their trade; and above all an abundantly flourishing international commerce. The City of London was in its heyday of power and independence, to which subsequent regimes at the Guildhall have never ceased to look back.

How was all this achieved? The first need was safety. This William the Conqueror supplied, both through the guarantees of his charters and by building the Tower of London. The Tower reminded Londoners of their military insufficiency – of how much they needed the king's might, just as he

ABOVE *Reconstruction of London as it was in about 1400. Painting by A. Forestier.*

OPPOSITE *Edward I rides into London on his return from the Crusades, 1274.*

Marginal drawing of St Paul's Cathedral and the City of London. From Matthew Paris, 1252.

needed their money. The issue was how far they could run their own affairs without incurring royal jealousy. Had the kings lived far away, London might have won fairly full independence, as cities all over Europe were trying to do in the twelfth and thirteenth centuries. But their frequent presence, along with their barons, at the Tower and at Westminster made symbiosis the only alternative. When kings were weak and in financial need, London took what advantage it could. One notable example occurred during the reigns of Richard I and King John, when the City acquired first a mayor and then the trappings of self-government. This worked well in peaceable times. When war loomed, London made little bones about ingratiating itself with who ever was winning. Its inability to defend itself, despite the symbolism of its walls, was demonstrated as early as Stephen and Matilda's reign, when London had to change sides quickly. It was proved anew by the events of the Peasants' Revolt of 1381, Jack Cade's Rebellion of 1450, and various episodes during the Wars of the Roses. London was a commercial city, never a stronghold.

Under the indirect protection of the Plantagenets, London's port and trade developed by leaps and bounds, just as it had done under the Romans. Though no single good dominated its commerce, the key in the later Middle Ages was wool and cloth, commodities closely connected with the growth of banking. At first wool was exported raw, but in the fourteenth and fifteenth centuries a burgeoning trade in finished textiles undercut the continental weaving centres in Flanders and elsewhere and brought increased prosperity in which kings and merchants shared alike. Churches and houses were rebuilt and enriched, and the wills of rich Londoners like Richard Whittington and John Crosby show a strong consciousness of the public weal. From the jaunty, secular poetry of Chaucer and Hoccleve, as well as from official enquiries into goings-on in places like the nunnery of St Helen's Bishopsgate, we begin to get an inkling of an altogether more luxurious style of life, at least for those Londoners who had money. Cities of course were proverbial for licence; already by the end of the twelfth century we have from the pen of a Winchester monk a jaundiced account of the viciousness of London to balance the charming but clichéd adulation of William Fitzstephen. But the sophistication of fifteenth-century London feels quite new. Rightly or wrongly, the ageing William Caxton in the 1480s felt that the city was not doing as well as it had been. At the same time, he sensed a selfishness that had not been around in his prentice days – surely the concomitant of greater comfort.

Our sources for medieval London vary more than for any period of its history. Up until the mid-fourteenth century we depend much on charters, deeds, building agreements, accounts and statutes. To supplement these there are the rather lapidary chronicles of Latin-writing monks like Matthew Paris, whose stress tends to be on matters royal, national and ecclesiastical rather than civic. The chronicling tradition, whereby England's history is set out year by year, continues. But from about the time of the Peasants' Revolt the chroniclers shift into French or English, grow livelier, and show regular interest in civic affairs; at least one of them, William Gregory, was himself a Lord Mayor of London. A curiosity about personalities begins dimly to appear in, for instance, accounts of Wat Tyler and Jack Cade. There is still a huge gap between this kind of history and the powerful sense of individualism that emerges in such writings as Caxton's prefaces, where he expresses opinions that can only be his own, or Thomas More's life of Richard III, in which for the first time an English monarch is portrayed as a recog-

nizable, living personality – and a terrifying one at that. Documents like these are among the first fruits of the Renaissance, and of its profound literary effect on London's culture. They point to the sharper, more personal style of history that we take for granted from Tudor times onwards.

1066–1135

Citizens' charters

The Norman kings were well aware of the power and pride of London. The city had to be both protected and controlled. That was the dual purpose behind the Tower of London, when it was erected by William the Conqueror. It was also the thinking behind the various charters that the new dynasty granted to the citizens and that became the basis of the City of London's claim to self-rule. The first of these, issued by the king soon after 1066 and written in Anglo-Saxon, is addressed to the existing bishop (who was not dispossessed), the portreeve or chief magistrate, and the burgesses. It briefly reassures the citizens of William I's good intentions and confirms their existing privileges. The charter that follows, from the early years of Henry I's reign (1100–35), is a much fuller document. It shows that kings were already keen to curry favour from Londoners in return for their support – in this case, perhaps, against the claims of Henry's older brother Robert to the English throne.

William the king friendly salutes William the bishop, and Godfrey the portreeve, and all the burgesses within London, both French and English. And I declare that I grant you all to be law-worthy, as you were in the days of king Edward; and I grant that every child shall be his father's heir, after his father's days; and I will not suffer any person to do you wrong. God keep you.

Henry, by the Grace of God, king of England, to the archbishop of Canterbury, and to the bishops and abbots, earls and barons, justices and sheriffs, and to all his faithful subjects of England, French and English, greeting.

Know ye that I have granted to my citizens of London, to hold Middlesex to farm for three hundred pounds, upon accompt for them and their heirs; so that the said citizens shall place as sheriff whom they will of themselves; and shall place whomsoever or such a one as they will of themselves for keeping of the pleas of the crown, and of the pleadings of the same, and none other shall be justice over the same men of London; and the

LEFT *The wedding feast of Matilda, daughter of Henry I.*

OPPOSITE *William Fitzstephen's panegyric upon London, transcribed into a fourteenth-century book on City laws and costumes.*

citizens of London shall not plead outside the walls of London for any plea. And they shall be free from scot and lot and danegeld, and of all murder; and none of them shall wage battle . . .

And all the men of London shall be quit and free, and all their goods, throughout England and the ports of the sea of and from all toll and passage and lestage and all other customs; and the churches and barons and citizens shall and may peaceably and quietly hold their sokes with all their customs . . . And all debtors which do owe debts to the citizens of London shall pay them in London, or else discharge themselves in London, that they owe none . . . And the citizens of London may have their chaces to hunt, as well and fully as their ancestors have had, that is to say in Chiltre and in Middlesex and in Surrey.

1141

Matilda expelled from London

The years that followed Henry I's death in 1135 were a prolonged muddle, while his daughter Matilda, the Countess of Anjou, disputed the throne with his nephew Stephen. Having at first recognized Stephen, London was forced to acknowledge Matilda after he was captured in 1141 by forces loyal to her. But her arrogance and demands for money so greatly upset the citizens, says the author of the *Gesta Stephani*, that they took advantage of overtures from Stephen's wife – confusingly, also called Matilda – and precipitately ejected the countess. Eventually a compromise was reached, so that it was Countess Matilda's son who succeeded in 1153 as Henry II.

So when the countess, confident of gaining her will, was waiting for the citizens' answer to her demand, the whole city, with the bells ringing everywhere as the signal for battle, flew to arms, and all with the common purpose of making a most savage attack on the countess and her men, unbarred the gates and came out in a body, like thronging swarms from beehives. She, with too much boldness and confidence, was just bent on reclining at a well-cooked feast, but on hearing the frightful noise from the city and getting secret warning from someone about the betrayal on foot against her, she with all her retinue immediately sought safety in flight. They mounted swift horses and their flight had hardly taken them further than the suburbs when behold, a mob of citizens, great beyond expression and

calculation, entered their abandoned lodgings and found and plundered everywhere all that had been left behind in the speed of their unpremeditated departure.

1170s/80s

Splendid city or den of vice?

Thomas à Becket, the Archbishop of Canterbury murdered by Henry II in 1170, was the son of a portreeve of London. So when William Fitzstephen, a close companion of Becket's and one of very few present at his murder, set out a few years later to write the life of the martyr, he began with London. Fortunately for us, his enthusiastic pen ran away with him. The result is a preface that contains a picture of the city out of all proportion to the biography that follows. Fitzstephen's famous description of the city is at times preposterously flattering. But it has a fullness and freshness unique in medieval urbanistic literature of its date.

Amid the noble cities of the world, the City of London, throne of the English kingdom, is one which has spread its fame far and wide, its wealth and merchandise to great distances, raised its head on high. It is blessed by a wholesome climate, blessed too in Christ's religion, in the strength of its fortifications, in the nature of its site, the repute of its citizens, the honour of its matrons; happy in its sports, prolific in noble men . . .

On the east lies the royal citadel, of very notable size and strength; its court and wall rise from very deep foundations, where mortar mingles with animal's blood . . . On the west are two keeps strongly fortified . . . The whole way round the north of the city the wall, tall and wide, strengthened with turrets at intervals, links the seven gates of the city, each double-faced . . . Once London was walled and towered on the south side too; but that great river, the Thames, well-stocked with fish, with tidal flow and ebb, has lapped against the walls over the years and undermined and destroyed them . . . Two miles to the west of the City, with a populous faubourg in between, the royal palace rises on the bank, a building of the greatest splendour with outwork and bastions. Everywhere outside their houses are the citizens' gardens, side by side yet spacious and splendid, and set about with trees. To the north lie arable fields, pasture land and lush, level meadows, with brooks flowing amid them, which turn the wheels of watermills with a happy sound . . . There are also in the northern suburbs of London splendid wells and springs with sweet, healing, clear water . . . Holywell, Clerkenwell and St Clement's Well are especially famous and often visited; and crowds of schoolboys and students and young men of the City take the air there on summer evenings. A good city indeed – if it should have a good lord . . .

The citizens of London are universally held up for admiration and renown for the elegance of their manners and dress, and the delights of their tables. Other cities have citizens, London's are called barons. Among them an oath-swearing ends every dispute. The matrons of the City are very Sabines . . . London like Rome is divided into wards; has sheriffs annually appointed for consuls; has a senatorial order, and lesser magistracies; sewers and aqueducts in its streets; deliberative, demonstrative, judicial cases have their distinct places, their individual courts; London has its assemblies on fixed days. I can think of no city with customs more admirable, in the visiting of churches, ordaining of festivals to God's honour and their due celebration, in almsgiving, in receiving guests, in concluding betrothals, contracting marriages, celebrating weddings, laying on ornate feasts and joyful occasions, and also in caring for the dead and burying them. The only plagues of London are the immoderate drinking of fools and the frequency of fires. Added to all this almost all the bishops, abbots and great men of England are as it were citizens and dwellers in the City of London, having their own noble edifices, where they stay and lay out lavish expenditure when they are summoned to the City by the king or their archbishop to councils or other large gatherings, or to attend to their own affairs.

The pinch of salt needed to balance Fitzstephen's praise of London is supplied by Richard of Devizes, a monk from Winchester writing not much later. This is the jaundiced verdict on the city pronounced by a character in Richard's *Chronicle*. Winchester was then still in competition with London; so generosity from a writer there towards the more powerful city was not to be looked for.

I do not at all like that city. All sorts of men crowd together there from every country under the heavens. Each race brings its own vices and its own customs to the city. No one lives in it without falling into some sort of crimes. Every quarter of it abounds in grave obscenities ... Whatever evil or malicious thing that can be found in any part of the world, you will find in that one city. Do not associate with the crowds of pimps; do not mingle with the throngs in the eating-houses; avoid dice and gambling, the theatre and the tavern. You will meet with more braggarts there than in all France; the number of parasites is infinite. Acots, jesters, smooth-skinned lads, Moors, flatterers, pretty boys, effeminates, pederasts, singing and dancing girls, quacks, belly-dancers, sorceresses, extortioners, night-wanderers, magicians, mimes, beggars, buffoons: all this tribe fill all the houses. Therefore, if you do not want to dwell with evil-doers, do not live in London.

1215

King John's Charter

The critical moment in the City of London's early history came in 1215, the same year as the Magna Carta. The expense of Richard I's many foreign wars had led him to rely on loans from London merchants, in exchange for which the City gained rights of control over the Thames and acquired its first mayor, Henry Fitzailwin. Aware of the movement of cities all over Europe towards independent communes, Fitzailwin and his supporters pressed for self-rule. Complete civic independence on the continental model

could never be achieved; English kings were too powerful for that. But when Richard's successor King John became mired in difficulties with his barons, the City forced out of him a charter conceding an elective mayoralty. It was to be the basis of the City of London's whole constitutional arrangement. Elaborated over the years, the system has – through a series of flukes and anomalies – survived down to the present day.

John, by the grace of God, king of England, duke of Normandy, Aquitaine and earl of Anjou, to his arch-

Royal Charter of King John, recognizing the City of London's right to elect its mayor, 1215.

bishops, bishops, abbots, earls, barons, justices, sheriffs, rulers and to all his faithful subjects, greeting.

Know ye that we have gained and by this our present writing confirmed to our barons of our city of London, that they may choose to themselves every year a mayor, who to us may be faithful, discreet and fit for the government of the city, so as, when he shall be chosen, to be presented unto us or our justice (if we shall not be present); and he shall swear to be faithful to us; and that it shall be lawful to them at the end of the year to remove him and substitute another if they will, or to retain the same, so as he be presented to us or our justice if we shall not be present ... Wherefore we will and strictly command that our aforesaid barons of our aforesaid city of London may choose unto themselves a mayor of themselves, in manner and form aforesaid, and that they may have all the aforesaid liberties well and in peace, wholly and fully, with all things appertaining to the same liberties as is aforesaid.

1238/1303

The troublesome Thames

Medieval London relied on the Thames both for its economy and as a means of getting about. Its great houses were all riparian, having easy access to the water from inlets or landing stages; the Tower of London and Lambeth Palace still give an idea of how this worked. The river was a good deal broader than it is now, its edge marshier and its current more sluggish. Now and then, as in Venice today, high waters flooded the low-lying houses. This happened twice in the early part of Henry III's reign, in February 1238, and again in November 1242. Matthew Paris records the former occasion.

At the new moon at the festival of St Scolastica, the tide meeting the torrents from the river, their streams swelled so that fords became impassable; banks were burst, bridges were concealed by floods, mills with their weirs were damaged, and arable land and meadows were overwhelmed. Among other singular circumstances, the river Thames, transgressing its accustomed limits, flowed into the great Palace of Westminster, and spreading itself, so covered the area that the middle of the hall might be passed in boats, and persons rode through it on horseback to their chambers. The water, bursting into cellars, could scarcely be drawn out again.

Another body that evidently had trouble with the Thames was the Augustinian Priory of St Mary Overie, whose

church survives as the current Southwark Cathedral. Southwark, or so much of it as lies near the southern foot of London Bridge, is as old as London, but was never walled and therefore always depended on the City. It was going through a difficult phase in the early fourteenth century. In a curiously cheeky letter, couched in the politest Latin, the priory parries a request by Edward I in 1303 to pension off one of his servants on them by pleading poverty and asking for a subsidy in return. A generation later, in 1327, the young Edward III put Southwark formally under the City's jurisdiction because of disorders there.

To the most serene prince and their revered Lord Edward, by the grace of God king of England etc., his most humble and devoted priests, the prior and convent of the Blessed Mary in Southwark offer all they can to their sovereign, the suffrages of their prayers. It hath pleased Your Excellency to command that we should make provision as to living and necessaries for William le Fishere your servant during his life ... Your highness knows that we would with all humbleness obey your commands, if our abilities were equal to the task. But, noble prince, ought not our poverty to excuse us to Your Majesty from undertaking this burden, inasmuch as the whole of our goods, rents and possessions cannot afford enough for our own maintenance unless the pious gifts of the faithful through the grace of God assist us to supply our own necessities? Our church too, which now for the thirty years last past – alas – has been a ruin, we have laboured our utmost to repair since the beginning of that time. But, hindered by vexatious and burdensome exactions, both spiritual and temporal, we have only been able so far to proceed in its restoration as to raise our bell tower. Moreover, we are obliged to battle continuously against the violence of the river Thames, on whose banks our tiny house is situated, in order to safeguard our church and ourselves, and our strength for the task would be insufficient to remove the danger did we not have some help to assist our own efforts. In fine, most excellent Lord, let your own magnificence be brought to the subject, since in your provisions of this kind for servants your court has customarily addressed the rich, great and superabundant manors and other possessions of the sumptuous princes, your progenitors, the kings of England, the fragments and crumbs from whose tables are likely to be more than our whole substance – not the means of brethren living in modest cells founded by the simple generosity of good men out of their small portions: of which kind is this, our small house, to

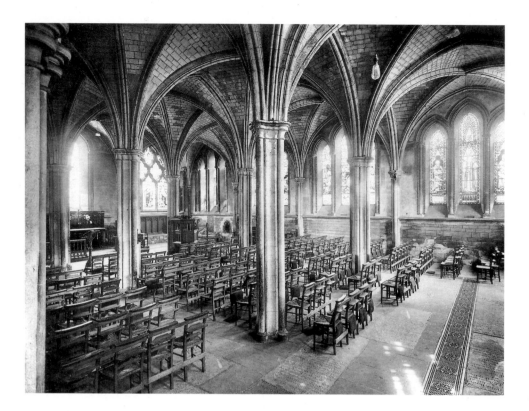

which you refer. For in truth if, as it has pleased you to write to us, we should take such a one into our society, we should be obliged to dismiss one of our own, which may seem to you grievous, nay inhuman. Forgive us, therefore, pious prince, we beg you, if we cannot obey your stated commands as we would like to; for truly not without blushing have we made you acquainted with the smallness of our means. May the Most High long keep you and prosper you etc.

1307/1378

Noise and pollution

After 1300, decrees, deeds, municipal regulations and records of law disputes give us a better grasp of commercial and everyday life in medieval London. There was, for example, a commission of 1307 about cleaning up the Fleet River, then navigable up to Fleet Street and beyond, but now long lost beneath the course of New Bridge Street and Farringdon Street.

Commission to Roger le Brabazon, Ralph de Sandwych and John le Blund, mayor of the city of London, to associate with themselves the more discreet of the aldermen and survey the watercourse of the Fleet running under the bridge of Holborn to the Thames which is said to be obstructed and straitened by mud

and filth being thrown into it and by the new raising of a quay by the master and brethren of the New Temple, London, for their mills by Castle Baynard, so that boats with corn, wine, firewood and other necessaries cannot go from the Thames by means of the watercourse as they have been accustomed, and to cause the obstructions to be removed by those they think liable and the watercourse to be as broad and deep as anciently it used to be. The jury to be of the city and the suburb.

In 1378 a case is recorded of noise, pollution and structural damage resulting from the workshop built by an armourer near St Paul's.

Thomas Yonge and Alice his wife complain by Richard Foster, their attorney, that the above-named Geoffrey Chadenesfeld, Walter and William with Stephen atte Fryth, armourer, on Monday 5 October 1377 built a forge of earth and timber 40 feet from the road in the close of their tenement adjoining the plaintiff's messuage in the parish of St Augustine by Paul's Gate on the south side of Watling Street, on which the chimney is lower by 12 feet than it should be and not built of plaster and stone as the custom of the City requires; and the blows of the sledgehammers when the great pieces of iron called *osmond* are being wrought into breastplates, cuirasses and jambs and other pieces of armour shake the stone and earthen party walls of the plaintiff's house so that they are in danger of collapsing, and disturb the rest of the plaintiffs and their servants day and night, and spoil the wine and ale in their cellar, and the stench of the smoke from the sea-coal used in the forge penetrates their hall and chambers, so that whereas formerly they could let the premises for ten marks a

term of years which has not yet expired, and that he has set up his anvil in what was formerly the kitchen at a sufficient distance from the plaintiffs' messuage, and strengthened the chimney with mortar and clay and raised it by six feet or more. They maintain that the plaintiffs cannot in any case complain of the chimney or of the noise of the hammers or the smoke, because their messuage was built as recently as 1349–50 and is much higher than the house it replaced, and has windows facing the forge, which its predecessors had not.

1388

Foreign merchants

The status of the many foreign merchants and traders in London was always a touchy issue. Occasionally things flared up, as in the following case recorded in 1388 and concerning members of the Hanseatic League.

Writ, dated at Westminster 14 July 1388. Whereas the merchants of the cities of London and Norwich and the boroughs of Lynn, Great Yarmouth, St Botolph

year, they are now worth only 40 shillings ... Geoffrey, Walter and William answer as tenants. They deny the plaintiffs' contention that chimneys ought to be built of stone and plaster and high enough to cause no nuisance to the neighbouring tenements, and declare that good and honest men of any craft, viz. goldsmiths, smiths, pewterers, goldbeaters, grocers, pelters, marshals and armourers are at liberty to carry on their trade anywhere in the City, adapting their premises as is most convenient for their work, and that according to ancient custom any feoffor may give, bequeath or lease his property as well to craftsmen using great hammers as to others. They add that they have let the premises against which the nuisance is alleged to Stephen Fryth for a

[Boston] and Kingston on Hull had complained that the men of Lubeck, Rostock, Wismar, Stralsund and Hamburg in Germany had arrested their servants and goods in the town of Stralsund, threatening to keep them in prison and their goods under arrest until they received redress for certain alleged wrongs done to them on the sea and elsewhere by Englishmen, whereof the said merchants were innocent, the King commanded the mayor and sheriffs of London to arrest all the men, goods and merchandise of the towns of Lubeck, Rostock, Wismar, Stralsund and Hamburg and other parts of Germany being in the ports of London or elsewhere within their bailiwick or district, and to detain them until they find sufficient security not to depart from the country without leave and to answer to such charges as may be made against them on behalf of the King or the said merchants.

Writ, dated at Cambridge 20 September 1388. Whereas it has been granted by the King's predecessors to the merchants of the Hanse of Germany that they should not be arrested for debts in which they were not sureties or principals or for trespasses committed by

Bond of John Kelsey, William Bonauntre, Ralph Spayne, Thomas Wade, Robert Hebbe and William Bullok, tapissers, and John Port and Philip Tayllour, parishioners of St Dionis Backchurch, for their good behaviour towards the mistery of Cordwainers, and that none of them would in future collect money for a football, or money called cock-silver for a cock, hen, capon, pullet or other bird or for any other use, and that

OPPOSITE *Extract from the* Liber Albus, *codifying the City of London's customs and regulations.*

LEFT *Medieval building craftsmen at work.*

others, and recently the King had ordered that the merchants and goods of Lubeck etc in London should be arrested, nevertheless the King, in consideration of the above liberties and because Hermann Vynthorpe, John Pape, William de Borne, Hermann Husman and Mathias Walkemole had entered into a pledge before the King and his council that English merchants at Lubeck, Rostock, Wismar and Hamburg should come and go freely without molestation, commands that the Hanse merchants be allowed to go at large with their goods.

1409

Sporting regulations

To judge from the following extract, the national games of football and blood sports were well established in the London of 1409, and already attracting the concern of the authorities.

they would not thrash any hen or capon or any other bird in the streets and lanes of the city, under penalty of £20.

1384

A building agreement

The earliest known London building agreement in the English language, as opposed to the French or Latin usually used for legal documents before then, dates from 1384. It concerns the erection of a timber house and warehouse between Lower Thames Street and the river.

Marked that John Chirteseye of the shire of Hertford gentleman made a statt by deed indented unto Richard Wyllysdon and to Anneys his wife of all his wharf called Pakemann's Wharf with all the land and tenements and pertinents in the parish of St Dunstan's in the East in London ... Richard Wyllysdon shall upon his own

place above stage that is to wit a hall of 40 foot of length and 24 foot of breadth, a parlour, kitchen and buttery as to such a hall should [be]long, and the remnant of the soil except the cartway and the said wharf of forty feet to do build chambers and house for the merchandise, sufficiently forseeing that as well under the said hall, parlour, kitchen and buttery and all the said chambers be cellared under the ground 7 foot in height.

1419

City customs and dues

Finally in this selection, some extracts from the *Liber Albus*, compiled by the town clerk, John Carpenter, in 1419 but incorporating material about city customs and dues that had prevailed in earlier centuries.

OF THE CUSTOMS PAYABLE UPON VICTUALS

Every load of poultry that comes upon horse shall pay three farthings, the franchise excepted. Every man who brings cheese or poultry, if the same amounts to four pence halfpenny, shall pay one halfpenny, the franchise excepted. If a man on foot brings one hundred eggs or more, he shall give five eggs, the franchise excepted ...

Every basket of bread shall pay one halfpenny per day. The basket of bread of the baker who brings it towards the west of Walbrook, entering the market on a Sunday, shall pay three halfpence, and upon other days but one halfpenny. Every foreign butcher who sells flesh in the market shall pay upon Sunday one penny for stallage.

Every cart that brings corn into the City for sale, shall pay one halfpenny; and if it enters by way of Holborn or by the Fleet it shall pay one penny, the franchise excepted ... Every cart of Bromley or Stepney that comes into the City with bread, shall pay each day one halfpenny. A cart that brings bread into the City from another town, shall pay each day one halfpenny or a loaf, of whatever franchise the owner may be. A cart that brings earthen pots shall pay one halfpenny, of whatever franchise. A cart that brings charcoal for sale, shall pay one farthing where such charcoal is sold, of whatever franchise. A cart that brings wood of alder for sale, shall pay one halfpenny. A cart that brings timber, with the bark or without the bark, shall pay one halfpenny. A cart that brings boards for sale, if it brings a quarter of a hundred or more, shall give one board ... The cart that brings buts or cheese shall pay two pence; and if it enters by the Fleet or by Holborn, it shall pay twopence halfpenny.

proper costs within ten year next following after the date of the said indenture enlarge stretching in the Thames-ward the said wharf four [?] foot of assize and wall all only of Maidstone stone. Also the said Richard Wyllysdon shall within the term of the said ten year to take down all manner of housing at the time of the said lease bearing upon all the said soil and build all the soil all only with new timber putting to nothing to of the old timber. And that to be performed in the form after written, that is to wit all the front of the said soil against the high street and 40 foot inward of three storeys of height, the first storey of 12 foot of height, the second of 10 foot, the third of 7 foot proportioned of sufficient timber all only of heart of oak as sufficiently [be]longeth to such manner of building, with all manner of dividing, garnishing and covering that should belong to the said building. Also the said Richard Wyllysdon shall within the said term of ten year to build up on the said soil inward a chief dwelling

The cart that brings fish or poultry into Westcheap shall pay twopence. The hired cart that comes into the City with wool or hides or other merchandise shall pay twopence. And if it enters by Holborn or by the Fleet or by Aldersgate, it shall pay two pence halfpenny. For every dead Jew buried in London, three pence halfpenny ... Every cart that brings leeks in Lent, shall pay one halfpenny and one fesselet of leeks. The cart that carries woad out of the City, if it carries four quarters or more, shall pay seven pence halfpenny ... The cart that brings melwels, herrings or other manner of fish shall pay one halfpenny for such cart. If a man or woman brings bread for sale from St Albans of the value of four pence halfpenny, such persons shall pay one farthing.

1381

The Peasants' Revolt

Much the most terrifying episode in fourteenth-century London history was the Peasants' Revolt of 1381. The rebellion grew out of rural discontent over the poll tax, allied with religious radicalism. It owed little or nothing to Londoners, who bore the brunt of the incursion, the sacking of many houses and the murder of Archbishop Sudbury. The courage of the young Richard II in meeting and calming the rebels was universally admired. But the slaying of Wat Tyler in the king's presence at Smithfield by Lord Mayor Walworth, given a heroic slant by the chroniclers, seems to modern readers a treacherous act. The best account of the Peasants' Revolt is given by a Westminster monk, writing soon afterwards; but Tyler's death, which marked the beginning of the end for the uprising, comes over graphically in the courtly prose of Froissart, as translated by Lord Berners in the 1520s.

On 12 June in this same year the peasants of Essex and Kent gathered together in very large numbers ... Growing ever denser, they went rampaging far and wide, declaring that Master Simon Sudbury, at that time archbishop and also chancellor of England, was a traitor and that he richly deserved to die. Swooping upon his manor at Lambeth they set fire to most of its abandoned contents, including books, clothes and linen; stove in wine-barrels and drained them, pouring what wine was left on the floor; banged together and smashed all the kitchenware; and all the while accompanied this behaviour as if in self-congratulation on some praiseworthy feat, with shouts of 'A revel! A revel!' ...

About four in the afternoon on the following day the peasantry, wrought up to a state of sheer frenzy, attacked the Duke's [John of Gaunt's] palace of the Savoy, where they burst through every barrier and spared no article of value from destruction either by burning or by being flung out to sink in the Thames ... They now started a fire at several points and reduced to ashes all the beauty of that noble dwelling. After this, as the evening twilight drew on, they made their way to the priory of St John at Clerkenwell and killing everybody who offered any opposition burned down the entire structure ...

In view of their aggressive temper and their gross effrontery, the King fell in with their request and went to the place known as Mile End, where the assembled throng of rustics insistently demanded of him that they should be given every kind of liberty and an amnesty for all offences committed up to that time, whether in connection with the insurrection or not. Fearing that if he did not give in to these demands mischief would follow from his refusal, the King bowed to the importunity of the raging mob ...

While these events were going forward, a sinister section of the horde of serfs moved on to the Tower of London, from which they dragged out the archbishop, the treasurer and a friar minor who was surgeon to the Duke of Lancaster, brought them to Tower Hill and there beheaded them together with a royal sergeant at arms named John Legg and another victim ... These executions took place on 14 June at eleven o'clock. The heads of the archbishop and the rest were stuck on poles and carried through the city streets before being set up on London Bridge. The hallowed head of the archbishop they set in the middle and higher than the others and to make it especially recognisable among them they nailed on it a scarlet cap.

The same proper morning Wat Tyler, Jack Straw and John Ball had assembled their company to commune together in a place called Smithfield, where as every Friday there is a market of horses. And there were together all of affinity more than 20,000, and yet there were many still in the town, drinking and making merry in the taverns and paid nothing, for they were happy that made them best cheer ... And therewith the King came the same way unwary of them, for he had thought to have passed that way without London, and with him 40 horses; and when he came before the abbey of St Bartholomew and beheld all these people, then the King rested and said how he would go no farther till he knew what these people ailed ...

Richard II confronts the mob, and Wat Tyler is slain in his presence. From Froissart's account of the Peasants' Revolt, 1381.

When Wat Tyler saw the King tarry, he said to his people, 'Sirs, yonder is the King, I will go and speak with him' ... And therewith he spurred his horse and departed from his company and came to the King, so near him that his horse's head touched the crop of the King's horse ... Wat Tyler cast his eyes on a squire that was there with the King, bearing the King's sword; and Wat Tyler hated greatly the same squire, for the same squire had greatly displeased him before for words between them. 'What,' said Tyler, 'art thou there? Give me thy dagger.' The King beheld the squire and said, 'Give it him, let him have it.' And when this Wat Tyler had it he began to play therewith and turned it in his hand, and said to the squire, 'Give me also that sword'. 'Nay,' said the squire, 'it is the King's sword; thou art not worthy to have it, for thou art but a knave; and if there were no more here but thou and I, thou durst not speak those words, for as much gold in quantity as all yonder abbey.' 'By my faith,' said Wat Tyler, 'I shall never eat meat till I have thy head.' And with those words the Lord Mayor of London came to the King

with twelve horses, well armed under their coats, and so broke the press and saw and heard how Wat Tyler demeaned himself, and said to him, 'Ha, thou knave, how art thou so hardy in the King's presence to speak such words? It is too much for thee so to do.' Then the King began to chafe, and said to the mayor, 'Set hands on him.' And while the King said so, Tyler said to the Mayor, 'In God's name, what have I said to displease thee?' 'Yes, truly,' quoth the Mayor, 'thou false stinking knave, shalt thou speak thus in the presence of the King my natural lord? I commit thee never to live without thou shalt dearly abye it.' And with those words the Mayor drew out his sword and struck Wat Tyler so great a stroke on his head that he fell down at the feet of his horse; and as soon as he was fallen, they environed him all about, whereby he was not seen of his company. Then a squire of the King's alighted, called

John Standish, and he drew out his sword and put it into Wat Tyler's belly, and so he died.

Then the ungracious people there assembled, perceiving their captain slain, began to murmur among themselves and said, 'Ah, our captain is slain; let us go and slay them all.' And therewith they arranged themselves on the place in manner of battle and their bows before them. Thus the King began a great outrage; howbeit, all turned to the best, for as soon as Tyler was on the earth, the King departed from all his company and all alone he rode to these people, and said to his own men, 'Sirs, none of you follow me, let me alone.' And so when he came before these ungracious people, who put themselves in ordinance to revenge their captain, then the King said unto them, 'Sirs, what aileth you, ye shall have no captain but me: I am your King, be all in rest and peace.' And so the most part of the people that heard the King speak and saw him among them were shamefaced, and began to wax peaceable and to depart.

1380s/1430s

The convent of St Helen's

One of the outstanding medieval survivals in the City of London is the church of St Helen's, Bishopsgate. It was formerly attached to a Benedictine nunnery, which used one side of the church as a private 'nuns' quire'. Situated in the heart of London, patronized by rich merchants and populated by their daughters, the convent could hardly expect to escape worldly influence; and so it proved. Official visitations by deans of St Paul's in the 1380s and again in the 1430s found much that was amiss, especially in the behaviour of the prioress. Injunctions were imposed.

Visitation of the 1380s

It is to be enjoined on the nuns publicly in chapter that they shall sing and say divine service day and night, and especially *Placebo* and *Dirige*, fully and distinctly, and not too fast as up to now they have been accustomed to do; nay rather with due and proper pauses.

It is to be enjoined on them that henceforth they abstain from kissing secular persons, a custom to which they have hitherto been too prone.

The prioress is to give up little dogs and to be content with one or two.

The nuns are to wear veils according to the rules of that order and not such as are unduly ostentatious unless necessity so demands.

Margaret Senior, one of the prioress's maids, is to be removed from the service and company of the prioress owing to certain causes moving the Dean and Chapter, and this for the better reputation of the prioress.

Visitation of the 1430s

The prioress was enjoined to keep her dormitory and lie therein at night according to the rule, except when the rule permits otherwise.

The prioress and convent were not to allow secular persons to be locked within the bounds of the cloister, nor to enter after the compline bell, except women servants and little girls at school there.

The prioress and sisters were not to frequent any place within the priory through which evil suspicion and slander might arise, such places to be notified later by the Dean to the prioress; and there was to be no looking out of the convent through which they might fall into 'worldly dilectation'.

They were not to speak or commune with secular persons; they were also not to send letters or gifts to secular persons nor receive such from them without permission of the prioress ...

They were to choose one of the sisters, upright, competent and tactful, who could undertake the task of training the nuns who were ignorant, so that they might be taught their service and the rule of their religion.

All dancing and revelry in the priory were forbidden except at Christmas and other proper times of recreation, and then only in the absence of seculars.

The prioress alone was to have keys to the postern door leading from the cloister to the churchyard, 'for there is much coming and going out at unlawful times'.

These injunctions were to be observed in their entirety and were to be read four times a year in the nuns' chapel before them.

1399

Henry IV's coronation

Exulting in his power and sure of his kingdom, Richard II in 1394 set about reconstructing the great public heart of his Westminster palace as the grandest royal hall in Europe. Westminster Hall and its wonderful roof – 'the masterpiece of English medieval carpentry', it has been called – are still there, having escaped the fire that destroyed the rest of the palace in 1834. But Richard never saw its completion. Instead, it was his usurper cousin, Henry IV, who held the first great coronation feast there in 1399, with the hall not quite finished and Richard captive in prison, soon to die. Henry's coronation and banquet, including the customary challenge by the King's Champion, are described by an anonymous English-language chronicler. He is the first of several such writers who interpolate much London material into their chronicles of England under the later Plantagenet and early Tudor kings. Doubtless he was a London citizen, for he makes a point of telling us how prominently the merchants and magistrates were seated at the banquet.

The Monday next after in the feast of St Edward, the same King Henry lay upon a cloth of gold before the high altar in Westminster Church. And there in four parts of his body his clothes were open, and there he was anointed, with *Veni Creator Spiritus* y-sungen. And after this anointing his body was lifted up into another place. And there with great solemnity was crowned, and *Te Deum Laudamus* was royally sungen. And

Thomas Arundell, Archbishop of Canterbury, did the solemnity. And when all was done, all the people went to Westminster Hall to meet.

And there the King was set in his see ... Harry Prince of Wales, Duke of Cornwall and Earl of Chester was on the right hand of the King with a new sword in his hand, pointless, the which betokeneth peace. The Constable of England was on the other side with another sword. And the sceptres were held in each part of the King, one sceptre on the one side and another on that other, alder next the swords. And on the right side of the hall at the second table sat the Cinque Ports well arrayed in scarlet. And at that other side table in the hall, at the second table, sat the Mayor, Recorder and Aldermen of London in one suit, also in scarlet. And the Dukes of Aumerle, Surrey, Exeter, March, Warwick and others stood before the King at meat. And in the same time came one Thomas Dymock knight, well armed, riding on the second best horse of the King's, for to do his service for his tenor, with two knights riding with him, the one bearing his spear and the other his shield. And an herald of arms went by him on his feet and had words for the same Dymock and said thus: 'If there be any man high or low, of what estate or condition he be, that will say that Harry King of England that here is and was this day crowned, that he is not rightful king nor rightfully crowned, right or else at what day our lord the King will assign, I will deraign battle with my body and prove that he lieth falsely.' The

The coronation of Henry IV in Westminster Abbey, 13 October 1399, following the usurpation of the throne from the hapless Richard II.

which proclamation was made through the hall in four places of the hall at this meat, by the same herald of arms both in English and in French. And after he voided the hall, and the revel ended.

And the Tuesday next then following ... began the Parliament in great hall of Westminster, and certain lords came and made their homage. And Sir John Cheyne speaking for the Commons made protestation in manner as it is used of old time, praying the King furthermore that he would grant them their liberties, franchises and customs 'in time of your old progenitors granted and used, the which were granted them and [have] been profitable to the realm'.

1451

The slaying of Jack Cade

Jack Cade's uprising of 1450 was in some ways a repeat of the Peasants' Revolt, with Kentish and Essex yeomen converging on London under a mysterious leader (the 'Captain of Kent') to vent grievances and demand the King's protection. Henry VI left the suppression of the rebellion to soldiers and courtiers, who at first made a mess of it. When tidings of their defeat came, Henry and the nobility decamped to the Midlands. Cade's forces were thus able to enter London, where his injunctions against looting made him at first welcome. But things turned ugly when the insurgents and local sympathizers started to execute people and rob merchants. There was stiff fighting, perhaps the stiffest London saw in the later Middle Ages, before the rebels could be ejected and the mayor and magistrates got the situation under control. The pardon granted did not extend to the ringleaders. The grisly aftermath, when Cade's body was ritually quartered and exhibited, is narrated by William Gregory, Lord Mayor in 1451-2 and a certain eye-witness.

And that day [12 July] was the false traitor the Captain of Kent y-taken and slain in the Weald in the county of Sussex, and upon the morrow he was brought in a car all naked, and at the Hart in Southwark there the car was made stand still, the wife of the house might see him if it were the same man or no that was named the Captain of Kent, for he was lodged within her house in his peevish time of his misrule and rising. And then he was had in to the King's Bench, and there he lay from Monday at even until the Thursday next following at even. And within the King's Bench the said captain was beheaded and quartered; and the same day y-drawn upon a hurdle in pieces with the head between his breast from the King's Bench throughout Southwark and then over London Bridge, and then through London to Newgate, and then his head was taken and set upon London Bridge.

1461

Edward IV claims the throne

London prospered in the fifteenth century, despite the spasmodic turbulence of the Wars of the Roses. There were factions among Londoners, as everywhere else, but in general the Yorkists were favoured. The welcome recorded by the so-called 'Vitellius A chronicler' as given to Edward IV when he claimed the throne was no doubt a genuine one. The merchants wanted secure government, which Henry VI and his Queen had failed to supply. After their northern army's victory at St Albans in 1461, London was threatened. But the City spun negotiations out for long enough until Edward (still the Earl of March) and 'Warwick the Kingmaker' came to the rescue, whereupon Henry and Queen Margaret withdrew north.

In this season the prickers or foreriders of the northern men came unto London and would have come in, but the Mayor and Commons would not suffer them; and many of them went into Westminster and disported there, and three of them were slain at Cripplegate. And the Wednesday before, the Duchess of Bedford and the Lady Scales with divers clerks and curates of the City went to St Albans to the King, Queen and Prince for to entreat for grace for the City. And the King and his Council granted that four knights with 400 men should go to the City and see the disposition of it and make an appointment with the Mayor and aldermen. Whereupon certain aldermen were appointed to ride to Barnet for to fetch in the said knights. And upon this, certain carts were laden with victuals to have gone to St Albans by the Queen's commandment. But when they came at Cripplegate the commons of the City would not suffer the carts to depart.

And anon upon this, tidings came that the Earl of Warwick in the aid of the Earl of March were coming toward London. Wherefore the King with the Queen and the Prince with all their people drew northward, and so into Northumberland. And the Thursday next after the Earl of March and the Earl of Warwick came to London with a great people. And upon the Sunday after, all the host mustered in St John's Field, where was read among the people certain articles and points that King Henry had offended in. And then it was demanded of the people whether the said Henry were worthy to reign still; and the people cried 'Nay! Nay!'. And then they asked if they would have the Earl of March to be their king; and they said 'Yea! Yea!'. And then certain captains were sent to the Earl of March's place at Baynards Castle and told to the Earl that the people had chosen him king; whereof he thanked God and them, and by the advice of the bishops of Canterbury and of Exeter and the Earl of Warwick with others, he took it upon him.

1470

The Inns of Court

London enjoyed no great medieval university. Instead, it developed, along the routes of communication between the merchant city and the royal centre of government, the system we now know as the Inns of Court. Half ecclesiastical and half secular, the legal inns were like Oxbridge colleges in their rules and arrangements. There were once far more than survive today, the smaller inns or Inns of Chancery having withered away. The difference between Oxford and Cambridge and the legal inns of the later Middle Ages is set out by Sir John Fortescue, a prominent Lancastrian and judge, in his treatise on English law written in exile around 1470.

In the universities of England, the sciences are not taught unless in the Latin language. But the laws of that land are learned in three languages, namely English, French and Latin ... Since the laws of England are learned in these three languages, they could not be conveniently learned or studied in the universities, where the Latin language alone is used. But those laws are taught in a certain public academy, more convenient and suitable for their apprehension than any university. For this academy is situated near the King's courts where these laws are disputed and pleaded from day to day, and judgements are rendered in accordance with them by the judges, who are grave men, mature, expert and trained in these laws. So those laws are read and taught in these courts as if in public schools, to which students of the law flock every day in term-time. That academy also is situated between the site of those courts and the City of London, which is the richest of all the cities and towns of that realm in all the necessaries of life. And that academy is not situated in the city, where the tumult of the crowd could disturb the student's quiet, but is a little isolated in a suburb of the city and nearer to the aforesaid courts, so that the students are able to attend them daily at pleasure without the inconvenience of fatigue ...

There are in this academy ten lesser inns and sometimes more, which are called inns of chancery. To each of them at least a hundred students belong, and to some of them a much greater number, though they do not always gather in them all at the same time. These students are indeed for the most part young men learning the originals and something of the elements of law, who, becoming proficient as they mature, are absorbed into the greater inns of the academy which are called Inns of Court, of which there are four in number and to the least of which belong 200 students or more.

1478

William Caxton's London

In September 1476, William Caxton set up his famous shop – the documents call it 'una shopa' – between two of the buttresses of the Westminster Abbey Chapter House. His presses were not far away at the sign of the Red Pale, near the Almonry Gate. Hence until Caxton's death in 1491 poured forth the flood of indulgences, romances, miscellanies, school texts, books of advice, books of devotion, books about games and translations of the classics that are the legacy of the founding father of English printing. He had learnt his revolutionary new trade abroad, in Cologne, and first practised it in Bruges. But he would never have been in these places had he not been apprenticed as a City mercer and gone as a trader to Bruges. Caxton never forgot his old loyalty to London. He expressed it in his quirky way, with an old man's sharp criticisms of the state that the City had got into under Richard III, in the preface to his *Disticha* of 1484, a schoolbook of moral couplets in Latin.

I, William Caxton, citizen and conjury of the same and of the fellowship and fraternity of the Mercery owe of right my service and good will and of very duty am bounden to assist, aid and counsel as far forth as I can to my power, as to my mother of whom I have received my nurture and living ... and shall pray for the good prosperity and policy of the same during my life, for as me seemeth it is of great need, by cause I have known it

WILLIAM CAXTON
Who first practiced the Art of Printing in England in 1471.
Engd. & publd. accordg. to the Act by J. Lockington, Shug Lane. Price 6d

in my young age much more wealthy, prosperous and richer than it is at this day, and the cause is that there is almost none that intendeth to the common weal but only every man for his singular profit ... By cause I see that the children that be born within the said City increase and profit not like their fathers and olders, but for the most part after that they be come to their perfect years of discretion and ripeness of age, how well that their fathers have left to them great quantity of goods, yet scarcely among ten two thrive. I have seen and known in other lands in divers cities that of one name and lineage successively have endured prosperously many heirs, yea a five or six hundred year, and in this noble city of London it can unnethe [hardly] continue unto the third heir or scarcely to the second. O blessed Lord, when I remember this I am all abashed, I cannot judge the cause. But fairer nor wiser nor better bespoken children in their youth be nowhere than there be in London, but at their full riping there is no kernel nor good corn founden but chaff for the most part.

1483

Lord Hastings denounced

All hopes of Edward IV setting up a lasting Yorkist dynasty foundered upon his death in 1483. Once installed as Protector of young Edward V, his brother Richard usurped the throne but proved unable to hold the state together, so offering Henry Tudor his opportunity. The arguments over Richard III's character and whether he had Edward IV's sons murdered in the Tower may never be settled. The problem is that those who wrote about his reign when memories of it were green were agents of the Tudors and had no motive to flatter Richard. Yet there is no substitute for their witness. Pre-eminent among them is Sir Thomas

More, whose *History of King Richard III* was epitomized by Holinshed and hence absorbed by Shakespeare. Not everything that More says need be taken as gospel. But he writes with such freshness and psychological conviction that one episode from his black biography must be given: the tale of the shocking denunciation and execution of Richard's erstwhile ally, Lord Chamberlain Hastings, just before young Edward V was due to be crowned. More must have heard it from the shrewd John Morton – then Bishop of Ely, afterwards Henry VII's chief minister, Archbishop of Canterbury and More's own patron.

On the Friday the —day of— many lords assembled in the Tower, and there sat in council devising the

OPPOSITE *Portrait of William Caxton. From an eighteenth-century engraving.*

RIGHT *The earliest accurate depiction of London, showing the Tower and London Bridge, c.1500. From a later manuscript copy of a volume of poems by Charles, Duke of Orleans, who was held captive in the Tower of London after the Battle of Agincourt.*

43

Ricardus texcius dei gra Rex
amalie o ffracie o dns hibnie

Dna Anna filia dni comitis warwici
dei gra Regina amalie o ffracie o dna hib

LEFT *Richard III and his queen, Anne Neville. From a Tudor chronicle.*

OPPOSITE *The opening page of Sir Thomas More's black biography of Richard III.*

honourable solemnity of the King's coronation, of which the time appointed then so near approached that the pageants and subtleties were in making day and night at Westminster, and much victual therefore that was afterward cast away. These lords so sitting together communing of this matter, the Protector came in among them first about nine of the clock, saluting them courteously and excusing himself that he had been from them so long, saying merely that he had been asleep that day. And after a little talking with them, he said unto the Bishop of Ely, 'My Lord, you have very good strawberries at your garden in Holborn, I require you let us have a mess of them'. 'Gladly, my Lord,' quoth he, 'would God I had some better thing as ready to your pleasure as that.' And therewith in all haste sent his servant for a mess of strawberries. The Protector set the lords fast in communing, and thereupon praying them to spare him a little while departed thence.

And soon, after one hour, between ten and eleven he returned into the chamber among them, all changed,

The tragical doynges of Kyng Richard the thirde.

Fol. xxb.

OThe I am to remembze, but moze I abhoze to wzite the miferable tragedy of this infoztunate pzince, which by fraude entered, by tyrannye pzoceded and by fodayn deathe ended his infoztunate life: But yf I fhould not declare the flagicious factes of the euyll pzinces, afwell as I haue done the notable actes of vertcous kinges, I fhoulde neither animate, noz incourage rulers of royalmes, Countreyes and Seignozies to folowe the fteppes of their pzofitable pzogenitozs, foz to attayne to the type of honour and wozldly fame: neither yet aduertife pzinces being pzoane to vice and wickednes, to aduoyde and expell all fynne and mifchiefe, foz dread of obloquy and wozldly fhame: foz contrary fet to contrary is moze apparaunt, as whyte iopned with black, maketh the fayzer fhewe: Wherfoze, I will pzocede in his actes after my accuftomed vfage.

RICHARD the third of that name, vfurped ý croune of Englãd & openly toke vp on hym to bee kyng, the nyntene date of June, in the yere of our lozd, a thoufand foure hundred lxxiii. and in the xxb. pere of Lewes the leuenth then beeyng french kyng: and the mozow after, he was pzoclaymed a kyng and with great folempnite rode to Weftminfter, and there fate in the feate total, and called befoze him the iudges of ý realme ftraightely commaundynge them to execute the lawe with out fauoure oz delate, with many good exhoztacios (of the which he folowed not one) and then he departed towarde the Abbaye, and at the churche dooze he was mett with pzoceffion, and by the abbot to hym was deliuered the fcepter of faincte Edwarde, and fo went and offered to faincte Edwarde his fhzine, while the Monkes fang Te deum with a faint courage, and from the churche he returned to the palace, where he lodged till the cozonacion. And to be fure of all enemies (as he thoughte) he fent foz fiue thoufand men of the Nozth againft his cozonacio, whiche came vp euill apparelel and woze harneiffed, in rufty harneys, neither defenfable noz fkoured to the fale, whiche muftered in Finefbury felde, to the great difdain of all the lookers on.

The fourth date of July he came to the tower by water with his wife, and the fifth date he created Edward his onely begotten fonne, a childe of x. pere olde, pzince of wales, and Jhon haward, a man of great knowlege and vertue (afwell in counfaill as in battaill) he created duke of Norffolke.

CC.i.

with a wonderful sour and angry countenance, knitting the brows, frowning and frotting and gnawing on his lips, and so sat him down in his place, all the lords much dismayed and sore marvelling of this manner of sudden change, and what thing should him ail. Then when he had sitten still awhile, thus he began: 'What are they worthy to have, that compass and imagine the destruction of me, being so near of blood unto the King and Protector of his royal person and his realm?' At this question, all the lords sat sore astonished, musing much by whom this question should be meant, of which every man wist himself clear. Then the Lord Chamberlain, as he that for the love between them thought he might be the boldest with him, answered and said that they were worthy to be punished as heinous traitors, whatsoever they were. And all the others affirmed the same. 'That is', quoth he, 'yonder sorceress, my brother's wife and others with her' (meaning the Queen).

At these words many of the other lords were greatly abashed that favoured her. But the Lord Hastings was in his mind better content that it was moved by her than by any other whom he loved better. Albeit his heart was somewhat grudged that he was not afore made of counsel in this matter, as he was of the taking of her kindred and of their putting to death, which were by his assent before devised to be beheaded at Pontefract this self same day, in which he was not ware that it was by others devised that himself should the same day be beheaded in London ... Nevertheless the Lord Chamberlain answered and said, 'Certainly, my Lord, if they have so heinously done, they be worthy heinous punishment.' 'What?', quoth the Protector, 'thou servest me, I wean, with "ifs" and "ands"; I tell thee they have so done, and that I will make good on thy body, traitor.'

And therewith as in a great anger, he clapped his fist upon the board a great rap. At which token given, one cried 'Treason' without the chamber. Therewith a door clapped, and in come there rushing men in harness, as many as the chamber might hold. And anon the Protector said to the Lord Hastings, 'I arrest thee traitor.' 'What, me, my Lord?', quoth he. 'Yea, thee, traitor,' quoth the Protector. And another let fly at the Lord Stanley, which shrank at the stroke and fell under the table, or else his head had been cleft to the teeth; for as shortly as he shrank, yet ran the blood about his ears. Then were they all quickly bestowed in divers chambers, except the Lord Chamberlain, whom the Protector bade speed and shrive him apace, 'for by Saint Paul,' quoth he, 'I will not to dinner till I see thy head off.' It booted him not to ask why, but heavily he took a priest at adventure and made a short shrift, for a longer would not be suffered, the Protector made so much haste to dinner, which he might not go to till this were done, for saving of his oath. So was he brought forth into the green beside the chapel within the Tower and his head laid down upon a long log of timber and there stricken off, and afterward his body with the head entered at Windsor beside the body of King Edward, whose both souls Our Lord pardon.

1485–1558

LONDON
under the
EARLY
TUDORS

The turbulent reign of Henry VIII dominates the early Tudor period. When Henry took the throne in 1509, the timber houses of London were set off with proud monastic foundations and little parish churches replete with roods and other precious fittings. The Lady Chapel begun by his father behind Westminster Abbey was still under way and promised to be the acme of English Gothic. At his death, unlamented, in 1547, London's churches were still intact, for Henry was a liturgical conservative. Iconoclasm was unleashed only during his son Edward VI's short reign (1547–53), coinciding with the triumph of extreme Protestantism. But the religious houses were already in the hands of courtiers or speculators, destined for conversion or destruction.

Against this must be set the rise in status that London and England achieved under the early Tudors' absolutist direction. The open feuding of the fifteenth century having been quashed by Henry VII, his son was able to enter upon a game of intricate diplomatic poker with monarchs stronger than himself. Because its *raison d'être* lay in sea trade, London had always been cosmopolitan. Now it became a centre also for this increased international activity, under the aegis of Henry VIII's great minister and manipulator, Cardinal Wolsey. Foreign embassies came and went; their permanent envoys, housed in greater grandeur, were kept busy trying to explain London, England, and the twists of Tudor policy, as the bulletins of the Venetian ambassadors reveal. 'Magnificence' was the means to all this. No English king grasped better than Henry the connection between image and power. Banquets, processions and ceremonies – still before the onset of the Reformation an unrestrained side of court and civic life – took on a new extravagance, with the open purpose of impressing visitors. Great sums were spent, and the luxury trades flourished.

Not all of this was impermanent. At Deptford and Woolwich, close to the Tudors' favourite palace of Placentia at Greenwich, Henry set up the ship-building yards which were to be the basis of the British navy and the kernel of the second and greater Port of London, far east of the crammed City wharves. Henry was also a great builder – but only in the second half of his reign, when confiscations allowed him to indulge his restlessness and greed. He seems to have picked up the building bug from Wolsey, whose York Place and Hampton Court were palaces in all but name before Henry took them over from his disgraced minister at the end of the 1520s. Wolsey in his turn had

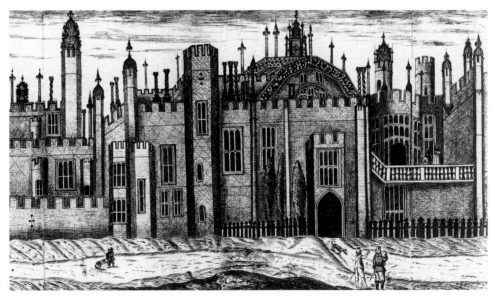

ABOVE *Part of the east front of Hampton Court. From an engraving,* c.1650.

OPPOSITE *The family of Henry VIII (detail)* c.1545.

learnt the knack of building from his own patron Cardinal Morton, Henry VII's canny minister and archbishop, whose gatehouse at Lambeth Palace is London's earliest surviving monument in the new brick style. Such projects were undertaken not just out of personal vanity, but also because they stimulated skills and trade. Since Henry VIII rarely stirred far from London, it was the capital that gained most from his palace-building spree. In London and Westminster he transformed Bridewell, Whitehall (Wolsey's York Place), and St James'; on its fringes, Greenwich (Placentia),

Eltham, Richmond and Hampton Court. Soon, the court style began to be diffused. Lord Protector Somerset had time during his short heyday as Edward VI's minister to build a great stone house on the Strand. At a humbler level of craftsmanship, overhangs and high gables, occasionally adorned with strange grotesques, frets and mouldings, began to creep into London's timber mansions as merchants grew wealthier.

If you were close to power under the Tudors, London was a dangerous place to be. William Dunbar, court poet to the Scottish kings, may have called it 'the flower of cities all', but his English equivalent, John Skelton, was bitingly outspoken about court abuses, follies and perils. The succession of political executions at Tower Hill and religious burnings at Smithfield was not a pretty business. The pursuit and punishment of heresy intensified up to the unhappy reign of Mary (1553–8), when a tit-for-tat policy of persecution attempted to reverse the equally bloody Protestantism of the previous six years. This intolerance went back to the first stirrings of the Reformation, not least under the lord chancellorship of Thomas More (1529–32), who himself fell victim to the axe in 1535. Two of Henry VIII's queens ended their lives on the block, and after the failure of Sir Thomas Wyatt's rebellion against Mary in 1554, there was a danger that his other daughter Elizabeth would follow suit. Her obduracy and guile enabled her to survive her brief imprisonment, and to guide the country and city into comparatively settled waters after 1558.

1498

A Venetian's impression of London

Throughout its history the most vivid descriptions of London have been written by visitors. In medieval and Tudor times these were rarely motivated by pure curiosity; they also had a practical purpose. Merchants and ambassadors were expected to report back to their governments with political and commercial information on the cities they traded with. The Venetian government was particularly keen to keep abreast of the rising commercial power of England and London. Andrea Trevisan, visiting in 1498, stresses the status and dignity of the Lord Mayor and Corporation and is remarkably impressed by London's gold and silversmiths.

All the beauty of this island is confined to London; which, although sixty miles distant from the sea, possesses all the advantages to be desired in a maritime town; being situated on the river Thames, which is very much affected by the tide, for many miles (I do not know the exact number) above it: and London is so much benefited by this ebb and flow of the river, that vessels of 100 tons burden can come up to the city, and ships of any size to within five miles of it; yet the water in this river is fresh for twenty miles below London.

Although this city has no buildings in the Italian style, but of timber or brick like the French, the Londoners live comfortably, and, it appears to me, that there are not fewer inhabitants than at Florence or Rome. It abounds with every article of luxury, as well as with the necessaries of life: but the most remarkable thing in London, is the wonderful quantity of wrought silver. I do not allude to that in private houses, though the landlord of the house in which the Milanese ambassador lived, had plate to the amount of 100 crowns, but to the shops of London. In one single street, named the Strand, leading to St Paul's, there are fifty-two

goldsmith's shops, so rich and full of silver vessels, great and small, that in all the shops in Milan, Rome, Venice, and Florence put together, I do not think there would be found so many of the magnificence that are to be seen in London. And these vessels are all either salt cellars, or drinking cups, or basins to hold water for the hands; for they eat off that fine tin, which is little inferior to silver (pewter). These great riches of London are not occasioned by its inhabitants being noblemen or gentlemen; being all, on the contrary, persons of low degree, and artificers who have congregated there from all parts of the island, and from Flanders, and from every other place. No one can be mayor or alderman of London, who has not been an apprentice in his youth; that is, who has not passed the seven or nine years in that hard service described before. Still, the citizens of London are thought quite as highly of there, as the Venetian gentlemen are at Venice, as I think your Magnificence may have perceived.

The city is divided into several wards, each of which has six officers; but superior to these, are twenty-four gentlemen who they call aldermen, which in their language signifies old or experienced men; and, of these aldermen, one is elected every year by themselves, to be a magistrate named the mayor, who is in no less estimation with the Londoners, than the person of our most serene lord (the Doge) is with us, or than the Gonfaloniero at Florence; and the day on which he enters upon his office, he is obliged to give a sumptuous entertainment to all the principal people in London, as well as to foreigners of distinction; and I, being one of the guests, together with your Magnificence, carefully observed every room and hall, and the court, where the company were all seated, and was of opinion that there must have been 1000 or more persons at table. This dinner lasted four hours or more; but it is true that the dishes were not served with that assiduity and frequency that is the custom with us in Italy; there being long pauses between each course, the company conversing the while.

A no less magnificent banquet is given when two other officers named *sheriffs* are appointed; to which I went, being anxious to see every thing well ... At this feast, I observed the infinite profusion of victuals, and of plate, which was for the most part gilt; and amongst other things, I noticed how punctiliously they sat in their order, and the extraordinary silence of every one, insomuch that I could have imagined it one of those public repasts of the Lacedemonians that I have read of.

1501–2

The visit of the Scottish Ambassadors

A visitor of another kind was William Dunbar, author of the first famous English-language poem about London. This beautiful panegyric was composed to order as an element in the formalities surrounding the Scottish embassy of 1501–2 to London. The outcome of the embassy was the dynastic marriage between James IV of Scotland and Margaret, the eldest daughter of Henry VII, through which after a century the crowns of the two kingdoms were to be united.

This year [1501] in the Christmas week the Mayor had to dinner the Ambassadors of Scotland, whom accompanied my Lord Chancellor and other lords of his realm; where sitting at dinner one of the said Scots giving attendance upon a bishop, ambassador, the which was reported to be a protonotary of Scotland and servant of the said bishop, made this ballad following:

London, thou art of towns A per se,
Sovereign of cities, seemliest in sight,
Of high renown, riches and royalty;
Of lords, barons and many goodly knight,
Of most delectable lusty ladies bright;
Of famous prelates in habits clerical;
Of merchants full of substance and might,
London, thou art the flower of cities all.

Gladdeth anon thou lusty Troy novant,
City, that some time cleped was new Troy,
In all the earth, imperial as thou stant,
Princess of towns of pleasure and of joy,
A richer resteth under no Christian roy,
For manly power with craftes natural,
Formeth none fairer since the flood of Noy;
London, thou art the flower of cities all.

Gem of all joy, jasper of jocundity,
Most mighty carbuncle of virtue and valour;
Strong Troy in vigour and in strenuity,
Of royal cities rose and giraflower,
Empress of towns, exalt in honour;
In beauty bearing the throne imperial,
Sweet paradise precelling in pleasure.
London, thou art the flower of cities all.

Above all rivers thy river hath renown,
Whose boreal streams pleasant and preclare,
Under thy lusty walles runneth down,
Where many a swan doth swim with winges fair,
Where many a barge doth sail and row with oar,
Where many a ship doth rest with top royal,
O! town of towns, patron and not compare,
London, thou art the flower of cities all.

Upon thy lusty bridge of pillars white
Been merchantes full royal to behold,
Upon thy streets goeth many a seemly knight
In velvet gownes and chaines of gold,
By Julius Caesar thy tower founded of old
May be the house of Mars victorial,
Whose artillery with tongue may not be told:
London, thou are the flower of cities all.

Buttresses and side chapels of Henry VII's Chapel, Westminster Abbey.

Strong be thy walles that about thee stands,
Wise be the people that within thee dwells,
Fresh is thy river with his lusty strands,
Blythe be thy churches, well sounding be thy bells,
Rich be thy merchants that in substance excels,
Fair be their wives, right lovesome, white and small,
Clear be thy virgins, lusty under kells:
London, thou art the flower of cities all.

Thy famous mayor, by princely governance,
With sword of justice thee ruleth prudently;
No lord of Paris, Venice or Florence
In dignity or honour goeth to him nigh,
He is exemplar, lodestar and guide,
Principal patron and rose original,
Above all mayors as master most worthy:
London, thou are the flower of cities all.

1502–3

The death of Elizabeth of York

William Dunbar's poem on London is uniquely recorded by the anonymous London chronicler known to scholars by the name of the manuscript that preserves his work, 'Vitellius A. XVI'. His year-by-year entries are one of the best sources for the London of Henry VII's reign. Under the dates 1502–3 the writer refers to two of the most important building projects of the reign: the completion of the Guildhall, which henceforward was to be the venue for the Lord Mayor's annual banquets rather than the livery halls; and the commencement of Henry VII's Chapel at Westminster. The new chapel – rich, romantic and architecturally adventurous – set the seal on the dynastic legitimation and triumph of the Tudors. It was intended as a shrine in memory of Henry VI. But coinciding as it did with the death of the Queen, Elizabeth of York, it became instead the memorial chapel of the early Tudors. It was finished in 1512, crowning three centuries of Gothic achievement.

This year [1502] began by the provision of the Mayor the new work of the Guildhall, four houses of office and other necessaries for the keeping of the Mayor and Sherriff's feasts; for the which, and towards the charge of which work, the Mayor had of the boxes of fellowships of the City by their own agreements certain sums of money, as of the Mercers £40, the Grocers £20, the Drapers £30. And so of all the other fellowships through the City, as their powers and havours were. And over that, the said Mayor by his providence gat of widows, and other well disposed persons, certain sums of money, as of the Lady Hill £10, the Lady Astrey £10, and so of many other.

This year [1503] in the month of January was the Chapel of Our Lady, standing at the east end of the high altar of Westminster, pulled down; and the tavern of the Sun, there also standing, with other housing; and the foundation begun of another chapel at the costs of the King.

And upon Candlemas Day, in the night following the day, the King and Queen then being lodged in the Tower of London, the Queen that night was delivered of a daughter; where she intended to have been delivered at Richmond; and upon the Saturday following was the said daughter christened within the parish church of the Tower, and named Katherine. And upon that day sevennight, or upon the Saturday, being the 11th day of February, in the morning, died the noble and virtuous Queen Elizabeth in the said Tower; upon whose soul and all Christians Jesu have mercy! Amen!

And the Wednesday, being the 22nd day of February, was the Queen's corpse conveyed from the Tower unto Westminster in a chair, with seven coursers trapped all in black velvet, and an image like the Queen lying upon the corpse; with six chairs following trapped with black cloth, with divers ladies and gentlewomen riding upon palfreys, between the first chairs eight, the next seven, and the other six. And before her chair next the lords and after the knights rode the aldermen, with mourning hoods as knights rode; and the Mayor, with a baron's hood, bore the mace next before the chair; and after the last chair rode a hundred of the citizens of divers fellowships in long black gowns. And the streets from Blanch Chapilton to Temple Bar were fulfilled upon the one side with burning torches, whereof Cheap and

ABOVE *Elizabeth of York, consort of Henry VII, from the tomb by Torrigiani in Henry VII's Chapel.*

RIGHT *Anthony van den Wyngaerde's panorama of Greenwich Palace and the Thames from Greenwich Hill, with London in the distance.*

Cornhill were garnished with new torches, and the bearers in white gowns of blanket and white frieze, which were found of divers fellowships, and the rest of churches and men's devotion. The number of torches was about two thousand, besides two hundred or more that went forth with the corpse, which were at the King's cost.

1515

May Day at Greenwich

Greenwich, or Placentia as it was fancifully called, was the favourite palace of the Tudors. Its position downstream from London allowed Henry VIII to keep an eye on the development of a national navy at Deptford and Woolwich – one of his early enthusiasms. It also fostered his love of sport and outdoor life. There were first-rate tiltyards at Greenwich, and plenty of hunting and coursing country up the hill in the direction of the subsidiary palace at Eltham. The following episode of 1515 from Hall's *Annals* gives a happy picture of an as-yet carefree young king.

The King and the Queen accompanied with many lords and ladies rode to the high ground of Shooters Hill to take the open air, and as they passed by the way, they espied a company of tall yeomen, clothed all in green with green hoods and bows and arrows, to the number of two hundred. Then one of them which called himself Robin Hood came to the King desiring him to see his men shoot, and the King was content. Then he whistled, and all the 200 archers shot and loosed at once, and then he whistled again, and they likewise shot again; their arrows whistled by craft of the head, so that the noise was strange and great and much pleased the King, the Queen and all the company.

made of boughs with a hall and a great chamber and an inner chamber very well made and covered with flowers and sweet herbs, which the King much praised. Then said Robin Hood, 'Sir, outlaws' breakfast is venison, and thereafter you must be content with such fare as we use.' Then the King and Queen sat down and were served with venison and wine by Robin Hood and his men, to their great contentation.

1527

Wolsey receives the French embassy

George Cavendish was Thomas Wolsey's usher and confidant during the heyday of the great cardinal's power in the late 1520s. After Wolsey's disgrace he wrote an elegant biography in justification of his master, not published until 1815. The extract below describes from personal witness the pomp and theatrical panache with which Wolsey received the French delegation in London, first at St Paul's, then at Hampton Court – which he had not yet ceded to Henry VIII – after the conclusion of peace in 1527.

This great embassade long looked for was now come over which were in number above forty persons of the most noblest and worthiest gentlemen in all the court of France, who were right honourably received from place to place after their arrival . . . and for the performance of

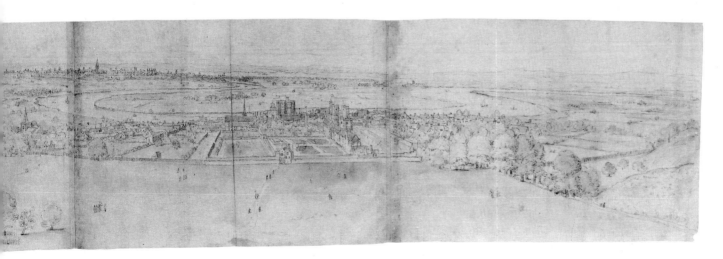

Then Robin Hood desired the King and Queen to come into the greenwood and see how the outlaws lived. The King demanded of the Queen and her ladies, if they durst adventure to go into the wood with so many outlaws. Then the Queen said that if it pleased him she was content. Then the horns blew till they came to the wood under Shooters Hill, and there was an arber

this noble and perpetual peace it was concluded and determined that a solemn mass should be sung in the cathedral church of Paul's by the Cardinal, against which time there was prepared a gallery made from the west door of the church of Paul's unto the choir door railed upon every side upon the which stood vessels full of perfumes burning. Then the King and my Lord

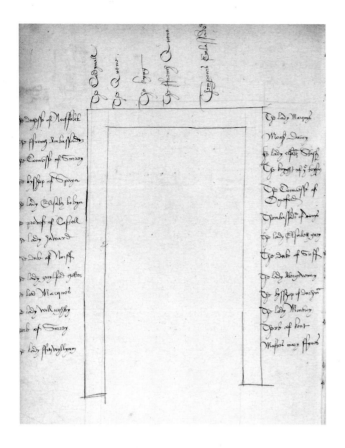

at Hampton Court for this assembly. Against the day appointed, my Lord called for his principal officers of his house as his steward, controller and the clerks of his kitchen, whom he commanded to prepare for this banquet at Hampton Court and neither to spare for expenses or travail to make them such triumphant cheer as they may not only wonder at it here but also make a glorious report in their country to the King's honour and of this realm. His pleasure once known, to accomplish his commandment they sent forth all their

LEFT *Seating plan for a banquet at Greenwich, 1517. Cardinal Wolsey sits at the top alongside Henry VIII, Catherine of Aragon, the King's sister and the Imperial Ambassador.*

OPPOSITE *Hampton Court from the river. A drawing by Wyngaerde.*

BELOW *Royal musicians at a reception or pageant, c.1530.*

Cardinal and all the French with all other noblemen and gentlemen were conveyed upon this gallery unto the high altar into their traverses. Then my Lord Cardinal prepared himself to mass associated with twenty-four mitres of bishops and abbots attending upon him and to serve him in such ceremonies as to him (by virtue of his legantine prerogative) was due. And after the last Agnus the King rose out of his traverse and kneeled upon a cushion and carpet at the high altar and the Grand Monsieur of France, the chief ambassador that represented the King his master's person, kneeled by the King's majesty, between whom my Lord divided the sacrament as a firm oath and assurance of this perpetual peace. That done the King resorted again unto his traverse and the Grand Monsieur in like wise to his. This mass finished (which was sung with the King's chapel and the choir of Paul's) my Lord Cardinal took the instrument of this perpetual peace and amity and read the same openly before the King and the assembly both of English and French, to the which the King subscribed with his own hand and the Grand Monsieur for the French King in like wise, the which was sealed with seals of fine gold engraven and delivered to each other as their firm deeds . . .

Then was there no more to do but to make provision

caters, purveyors and other persons to prepare of the finest viands that they could get either for money or friendship among my Lord's friends. Also they sent for all the expertest cooks besides my Lord's that they could get in all England where they might be gotten, to serve to garnish this feast. The purveyors brought in and sent in such plenty of costly provision as ye would wonder at the same. The cooks wrought both night and day in divers subtleties and many other crafty devices where lacked neither gold, silver ne any other costly thing meet for their purpose. The yeomen and grooms of the wardrobes were busied in hanging of the chambers with costly hangings and furnishing the same with beds of silk and other furniture apt for the same in every degree. Then my Lord Cardinal sent me being gentleman usher with two other of my fellows to Hampton Court to forsee all things touching our rooms to be nobly garnished accordingly; our pains were not

whose coming they would have risen and give place with much joy, whom my Lord commanded to sit still and keep their rooms. And straightway (being not shifted of his riding apparel) called for a chair and sat him down in the midst of the table, laughing and being as merry as ever I saw him in all my life. Anon came up the second course with so many dishes, subtleties and curious devices, which were above an hundred in number, of so goodly proportion and costly, that I suppose the Frenchmen never saw the like; the wonder

small or light but travailing daily from chamber to chamber . . .

The day was come that to the Frenchmen was assigned and they ready assembled at Hampton Court (something before the hour of their appointment). Wherefore the officers caused them to ride to Hanworth, a place and park of the King's within two or three miles of there, to hunt and spend the time until night, at which time they returned again to Hampton Court . . . Now was all things in a readiness and supper time at hand. My Lord's officers caused the trumpets to blow to warn to supper, and the said officers went right discreetly in due order and conducted these noble personages from their chambers unto the chamber of presence, where they should sup, and they being there, caused them to sit down. Their service was brought up in such order and abundance, both costly and full of subtleties with such a pleasant noise of divers instruments of music, that the Frenchmen (as it seemed) were rapt into an heavenly paradise. Ye must understand that my Lord was not there ne yet come, but they being merry and pleasant with their fare, devising and wondering upon the subtleties, before the second course my Lord Cardinal came in among them booted and spurred (all suddenly) and bade them preface. At

was no less than it was worthy in deed. There were castles with images in the same, Paul's church and steeple in proportion for the quantity, as well counterfeited as the painter should have painted it upon a cloth or wall. There were beasts, birds, fowls of divers kinds and personages most lively made and counterfeit in dishes, some fighting (as it were) with swords, some with guns and crossbows, some vaulting and leaping, some dancing with ladies, some in complete harness jousting with spears, and with many more devices than I am able with my wit to describe. Among all, one I noted; there was a chess board subtly made of spiced plate with men to the same. And for the good proportion because that Frenchmen be very expert in that play, my Lord gave the same to a gentleman of France commanding that a case should be made for the same in all haste to prevent it from perishing in the conveyance thereof into his country. Then my Lord took a bowl of gold (which was esteemed at the value of 500 marks) and filled with hippocras (whereof there was plenty), putting off his cap, said, 'I drink to the King, my sovereign lord and master, and the King your master,' and therewith drank a good draught. And when he had done, he desired the Grand Monsieur to pledge him cup and all, the which cup he gave him, and so caused all the other lords and gentlemen in other cups to pledge these two royal princes. Then went cups merrily about that many of the Frenchmen were fain to be led to their beds.

1533

Londoners welcome Anne Boleyn

Very different from Wolsey's display of pomp was the political mood in the spring of 1533, when, with Wolsey dead and Catherine of Aragon disgraced, Henry VIII commanded the citizens of London to convey Anne Boleyn, four months pregnant with the future Elizabeth, upstream by river from Greenwich to the Tower in preparation for her impending coronation. Whatever Londoners may privately have thought, they put on a loyal and noisy good show, records John Stow.

The Mayor and his brethren, all in scarlet, and such as were knights having collars of esses, and the residue having great chains, and the Council of the City assembled with them at St Mary Hill, and at one of the clock descended to the new stair to their barge which was garnished with many goodly banners and streamers, and richly covered, in which barge was shawms, sackbuts, and divers other instruments of music, which played continually ... First, before the mayor's barge was a foist for a wafter [a barge as convoy] full of ordnance, in which foist was a great red dragon continually moving and casting wild fire, and round about the said foist stood terrible, monstrous and wild men, casting fire and making hideous noise; next after the foist, at a good distance, came the Mayor's barge; on whose right hand was the bachelors' barge, in the which were trumpets, and divers other melodious instruments ... On the left hand of the Mayor was another foist, in the which was a mount, and on the mount was a white falcon crowned upon a root of gold, environed with white roses and red, which was the Queen's device; about which mount sat virgins singing and playing melodiously ... At Greenwich town they cast anchor, making great melody: at three of the clock (29th of May), the Queen, apparelled in rich cloth of gold, entered into her barge, accompanied with divers ladies and gentlewomen, and incontinent the citizens set forward in order, their minstrelsy continually playing, and the bachelors' barge going on the Queen's right hand, which she took great pleasure to behold ... She thus being accompanied rowed towards the Tower; and in the mean way the ships which were commanded

to lie on the shore for letting of the barges, shot divers peals of guns, and ere she landed, there was a marvellous shot out of the Tower, I never heard the like; and at her landing there met with her the Lord Chamberlain with the officers of arms, and brought her to the King, which received her with loving countenance at the postern by the water side and kissed her, and then she turned back again and thanked the Mayor and the citizens with many goodly words, and so entered into the Tower. To speak of the people that stood on every shore to behold this sight, he that saw it not will not believe it.

1530–59

Churches reformed/monasteries dissolved

By the 1530s, with Henry VIII bent on absolutism and the Reformation gathering momentum, England and London were heading into a period of turbulence and terror, as well as of bewildering inconsistency in politics and religion alike. The best that an ordinary citizen could do was to keep his head down. Yet the changes affected everyone's life and habits. How far they did so may be gleaned from the very complete early Tudor accounts of one City church, St Mary at Hill. Banal accounts for cleaning out cesspools and repairing windows give way in the 1540s and 1550s to bills concerning wholesale removals of prized and precious fittings – and then their reinstatement.

1500–1 First, paid to Donyng, gong farmer, the 30th day of January for farming of a siege in George Gysborow the clerk's chamber wherein was five ton at 2s the ton   10s

1501–2 Item, for making of a lectern in the rood loft and mending of desks in the choir   12d

Item, for mending of the best antiphoner's covering the which the rats had hurt   12d

1523–4 Paid to Northfolke and his company and ye children when that Mr parson gave to them a playing week to make merry   3s 4d

Paid for milk and ratsbane for the rats in the church   1d

Paid for a basket for the church for dust   2d

1529–30 Paid to Michael Greene for a quire of paper royal for ye pricked song book and for mouth glue   7d

	Paid for mending of the glass windows in the church and the chapels that were broken	5s
	Paid to Baleham for a year blowing the organs, for every week 2d, summa	8s 8d
1536–7	Item, for ringing of the great bell six hours for Queen Jane, and for ringing of ye bells divers peals to the same	2s 6d
	Item, paid to two men for bearing of ye copes to Paul's, and home again at the birth of Prince Edward	12d
1547–8	Item, for taking down the rood loft	5s
	Item, paid by great for taking down of the tabernacle over the vestry door, being all stone, and other stonework in the church, and for making up thereof, and for lime and sand	13s 4d
	Item, for six new psalters in English for the choir	6s
	Item, for removing of the organs	20d
1549–50	Paid to Lusheby for taking down of the high altar and for paving of the choir and church	22s 6d
1553	Paid for the sewing together of the best altar clothes for to lay on the communion board	6d
1554	Item, paid for mending of the canopy over the high altar wherein the sacrament hangs and for the silk	6s
1559	Paid for taking down ye rood, ye Mary and the John	16d
	Paid to Mr North, bricklayer, and three labourers with him for five days to take down the altars and for pointing the steeple above round about, and for mending of ye walls betwixt the lead and ye glass, and for lime and sand and for whiting where the altars were	17s
	Paid for bringing down the images to Romeland and other things to be burnt	12d

Liturgical change did not much affect parish churches until after Henry VIII's death in 1547. But the dissolution of the monasteries had an immediate impact on the stability of London. Dispossessed monks, friars and nuns had to fend for themselves; the whole future of social provision came into question, since such schools, hospitals and almshouses as existed had largely been run by the monastic orders. The end of the religious houses also brought swathes of valuable property into the market. The beneficiaries were generally the Protestant-sympathizing merchants and courtiers who identified themselves with Henry VIII's new order. Greatest of these was Thomas Cromwell, architect of the dissolution policy, one of whose high-handed tricks in the 1530s with City property still aggrieved John Stow, author of the *Survey of London*, sixty years later.

On the south side, and at the west end of this church, many fair houses are built; namely, in Throgmorton street, one very large and spacious, built in the place of old and small tenements by Thomas Cromwell, master of the king's jewel-house, after that master of the rolls, then Lord Cromwell, knight, lord privy seal, vicar-general, Earl of Essex, high chamberlain of England, etc. This house being finished, and having some reasonable plot of ground left for a garden, he caused the pales of the gardens adjoining to the north part thereof on a sudden to be taken down; twenty-two feet to be measured forth right into the north of every man's ground; a line there to be drawn, a trench to be cast, a foundation laid, and a high brick wall to be built. My father had a garden there, and a house standing close to his south pale; this house they loosed from the ground, and bare upon rollers into my father's garden twenty-two feet, ere my father heard thereof; no warning was given him, nor other answer, when he spake to the surveyors of that work, but that their master Sir Thomas commanded them so to do; no man durst go to argue the matter, but each man lost his land, and my father paid his whole rent, which was 6s 6d, the year, for that half which was left. Thus much of mine own knowledge have I thought good to note, that the sudden rising of some men causeth them to forget themselves.

It took time to close London's monasteries and find uses for their sites. Some were converted for private or institutional use; others were pulled down completely. Cromwell's commissioners tended to take the roof off the habitable portions to prevent their reoccupation, but the degree of destruction varied. It gathered pace in the last years of Henry VIII, turning into outright iconoclasm in all churches under Edward VI, as extracts from the *Chronicle of the Greyfriars* show. The church of the Greyfriars was converted into a parish church which survived until the

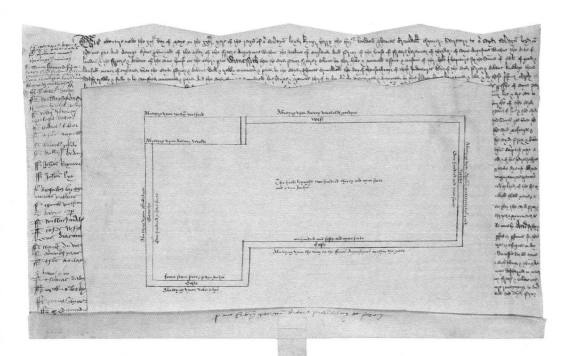

Deed and plan showing City property belonging to the Austin Friars acquired by Thomas Cromwell.

Great Fire, while the monastery itself was to become the site of Edward VI's refounded school of Christ's Hospital; so not all the changes were negative. Under 1547, the Greyfriars chronicle also records an abseiling spectacle, put on for the young king as part of the coronation festivities.

1544 Before Christmas was much wine taken of France with their ships and laid in the church sometime the Greyfriars, all the church full in every place of it, and at the Austin Friars and the Blackfriars with herring and other fish that was taken on the sea going into France that came from Antwerp.

1545 And this year was the church of the Whitefriars pulled down, and the steeple of the Blackfriars.
Item, this same year in the same month [September] was the Charterhouse pulled down, and the water turned to divers places there to gentlemen's places.

1547 Item, the 3rd day of January was set open the church again that was sometime the Greyfriars, and mass said at the altars with divers priests, and it was named Christ Church of the foundation of King Henry the VIIIth.
Item, the 20th day of the same month the said King Edward came from the Tower of London through London, and in divers places pageants, and all the streets hanged richly, with all the crafts standing in Cheap, presenting them as loving subjects unto their King, and so to Paul's; and at the west end of Paul's steeple was tied a cable rope, and the other end beside the Dean's place at an anchor of a ship, and a man running down on the said rope as swift as an arrow out of a bow down with his hands and feet abroad not touching the rope; and when the King had seen the said thing went forth unto the Palace of Westminster; and the next day came from thence unto Westminster Church, and there was crowned, and kept his feast in Westminster Hall. God of his mercy send him good luck and long life, with prosperity! And this was done in the ninth year of his age and birth.
Item, the 5th day after in September began the King's visitation at Paul's, and all images pulled down.
Item, at this same time was pulled up all the tombs, great stones, all the altars, with the stalls and walls of the choir and altars in the church that was sometime the Greyfriars, and sold, and the choir made smaller.
Item, the 17th day of the same month [November] at night was pulled down the rood in Paul's with Mary and John, with all the images in the church, and two of the men that laboured at it was slain and divers others sore hurt.

Item, after Easter began the service in English at Paul's ... and also in divers other parish churches. Item, also at Whitsuntide began the sermons at St Mary Spital. Item, also this year was Barking chapel at the Tower Hill pulled down, and St Martin's at the shambles end, St Nicholas in the Shambles, and St Ewins [?], and within the gate of Newgate these were put into the church that sometime was the Greyfriars; and also Strand church pulled down to make the Protector Duke of Somerset's place larger.

1551

Edward VI entertains Mary of Guise

Edward VI was a precocious boy. Amidst all his duties, Protestant devotions and studies he managed to keep a diary, which we have no reason to doubt is the work of the King's own person. Its entries, though often brief, shed much light on his eventful reign. One of the lighter episodes it records is Edward's chivalric entertainment at Hampton

Court and Westminster in 1551 of Mary of Guise, the strongly Catholic Queen Dowager of Scotland and mother of Mary Queen of Scots. The dowager had been forced ashore at Portsmouth by bad weather while en route from France to Scotland.

31 October She came to Hampton Court, conveyed by the same lords and gentlemen aforesaid; and two miles and a half from thence, in a valley, there met with her the Lord Marquess of Northampton, accompanied by the Earl of Wiltshire, son and heir to the Lord High Treasurer; Marquess of Winchester; the Lord Fitzwater, son to the Earl of Sussex; the Lord Evers, the Lord Bray, the Lord Robert Dudley, the Lord Garet, Sir Nicholas Throgmorton, Sir Edward Rogers, and divers other gentlemen, besides all the gentlemen pensioners, men of arms and ushers, sewers and carvers, to the number of 120 gentlemen, and so she was brought to Hampton Court. At the gate thereof met her the Lady Marquess of Northampton, the Countess of Pembroke, and divers other ladies and

gentlewomen, to the number of sixty; and so she was brought to her lodging on the Queen side, which was all hanged with arras, and so was the hall, and all the other lodgings of mine in the house very finely dressed; and for this night, and the next day, all was spent in dancing and pastime, as though it were a court, and great presence of gentlemen resorted thither.

4 November The Duke of Suffolk, the Lord Fitzwater, the Lord Bray, and divers other lords and gentlemen, accompanied with his wife the Lady Francis, the Lady Margaret, the Duchesses of Richmond and of Northumberland, the Lady Jane daughter to the Duke of Suffolk; the Marquess of Northampton and Winchester; the Countess of Arundel, Bedford, and Huntingdon, and Rutland; with 100 other ladies and gentlewomen went to her, and brought her through London to Westminster. At the gate there received her the Duke of Northumberland, Great Master, and the Treasurer, and Comptroller, and the Earl of Pembroke, with all the sewers, and carvers, and cup-bearers, to the number of

thirty. In the hall I met her, with all the rest of the Lords of my Council, as the Lord Treasurer, the Marquis of Northampton, etc., and from the outer gate up to the presence chamber, on both sides, stood the guard. The court, the hall, and the stairs, were full of serving men; the presence chamber, great chamber, and her presence chamber, of gentlemen. And so having brought her to her chamber, I retired to mine. I went to her to dinner; she dined under the same cloth of state, at my left hand; at her rearward dined my cousin Francis, and my cousin Margaret; at mine sat the French Ambassador. We were served by two services, two sewers, cupbearers, carvers, and gentlemen. Her master hostel [Maître d'hôtel] came before her service, and my officers before mine. There were two cupboards, one of gold four stages high, another of massy silver six stages: in her great chamber dined at three boards the ladies only. After dinner, when she had heard some music, I brought her to the hall, and so she went away.

1553–8

London under a Catholic queen

The Reformation and the Marian reaction brought persecution and terror to London, as well as physical destruction of the city's fabric. Heresy trials, denunciations and burnings intensified. These were all a familiar element in London life. But the contenders for religious supremacy and martyrdom were more literate than before, so we know more about them. In particular, Protestants who suffered for their beliefs during the short reign of Mary (1553–8) gloried in their endurance and loyalty to the Reformation after Elizabeth's accession. One such intransigent was Thomas Mountain or Mowntayne, a City rector and self-confessed supporter of Lady Jane Grey. Summoned before the formidable Bishop Gardiner of Winchester, Mountain was briefly imprisoned but escaped abroad, to be reinstated to his living when Elizabeth restored Protestantism.

In the year of Lord God a thousand five hundred and fifty three, Queen Mary was crowned Queen of England, such a day of the month being Sunday; and the next Sunday after, I Thomas Mowntayne, parson of St Michaels in the Tower Royal, otherwise called Whittington College in London, did there minister all kind of service according to the godly order then set forth by that most gracious and blessed prince King Edward the Sixth; and the whole parish, being then gathered together, did then and there most joyfully communicate together with me the holy supper of the

Lord Jesus, and many other godly citizens were then partakers of the same ... Now, while I was even a-breaking of the bread at the table, saying to the communicants these words, 'Take and eat this' etc., and 'Drink this' etc., there were standing by to see and hear, certain serving men belonging to the Bishop of Winchester, among whom, one of them most shamefully blasphemed God, saying 'Yea, God's blood, standst thou there yet saying "take and eat, take and drink"? Will not this gear be left yet? You shall be made to sing another song within these few days, I trow, or else I have lost my mark.'

The next Wednesday following, the Bishop of Winchester sent one of his servants for me to come and speak with my Lord his master; to whom I answered, that I would wait on his lordship after that I had done Morning Prayer. 'Nay,' saith his man, 'I may not tarry so long for you. I am commanded to take you wheresoever I find you, and to bring you with me; that is my charge given unto me by my Lord's own mouth.' ...

Now when I came unto the great chamber at St Mary Overies, there I found the bishop standing at a bay window with a great company about him, and many suitors both men and women, for he was going to the court ... Then the Bishop called me unto him and said, 'Thou heretic! how darest thou be so bold to use that schismatical service still, of late set forth? Seeing that God hath sent us now a Catholic Queen, whose laws thou has broken, as the rest of thy fellows hath done, and you shall know the price of it if I do live. There is such abominable company of you, as is able to poison a whole realm with your heresies.' 'My Lord,' said I. 'I am none heretic, for that way that you count heresy, so worship we the living God; and as our forefathers hath done and believed, I mean Abraham, Isaac, and Jacob, with the rest of the holy prophets and apostles, even so do I believe to be saved, and by no other means.' 'God's passion!', said the Bishop, 'did I not tell you, my Lord Deputy, how you should know an heretic? He is up with the "living God", as though there were a dead God. They have nothing in their mouths, these heretics, but "the Lord liveth, the living God ruleth, the Lord, the Lord", and nothing but the Lord.' Here he chafed like a bishop, and, as his manner was, many times he put up his cap and rubbed to and fro, up and down, the fore part of his head, where a lock of hair was always standing up ... Then stood there one by much like unto Doctor Martyn, and said, 'My Lord, the time passeth away; trouble yourself no longer with this heretic, for he is not only an heretic, but a traitor to the Queen's majesty, for he was one of them that went forth with the Duke of Northumberland and was in open field against her Grace; and therefore as a traitor he is one of them that is exempt out of the general pardon, and hath lost the benefit of the same.' 'Is it even so?', saith the Bishop, 'fetch me the book that I may see it.' Then was the book brought him, wherein he looked as one ignorant what had been done, and yet he being the chief doer himself thereof. Then asked he of me what my name was. I said my name was Thomas Mowntayne. 'Thou hast wrong,' saith he. 'Why so, my lord?' 'That thou has not *mounted* to Tyburn, or to such a like place.'

Edward Underhill was another zealot active in the cause of extreme Protestantism in the 1540s and 1550s. An East End firebrand, he boasted of his iconoclastic risk taking. But he

is now Hyde Park and Westminster. Underhill's mordant account may be exaggerated, but the element of farce and shambles has the ring of authenticity.

At Stratford on the Bow, I took the pyx off the altar, being of copper, stored with copper goods, the curate being present, and a popish justice dwelling in the town, called Justice Tawe. There was commandment it should not hang in a string over the altar, and then they set it upon the altar. For this act the justice's wife with the women of the town conspired to have murdered me; which one of them gave me warning of, whose good will to the Gospel was unknown unto the rest. Thus the Lord preserved me from them, and many other dangers more; but specially from hellfire, but that of his mercy he called me from the company of the wicked . . .

The manner of burning Anne Askew, Iohn Lacels, Iohn Adams, & Nicolas Belenian, with certane of y counsell sitting in Smithfield.*

Preparations for burning Protestants at Smithfield during the Marian persecution. From John Foxe's Book of Martyrs, *1684 edition.*

also claimed a measure of loyalty to Queen Mary and was proud of his part in the defence of Whitehall Palace during the Wyatt Rebellion of 1554. The rebellion, which came close to unseating Mary, reached an anticlimactic end when Sir Thomas Wyatt failed to organize his forces properly for an assault on London and the rebels straggled all over what

When Wyatt was come about, notwithstanding my discharge from the watch by Mr Norris, I put on my armour and went to the court [Whitehall Palace], where I found all my fellows armed in the hall, which they were appointed to keep that day. Old Sir John Gage was appointed without the outer gate, with some of the guard and his servants and others with him; the rest of the guard were in the great court, the gates standing open. Sir Richard Southwell had the charge of the backsides, as the woodyard and that way, with 500 men. The Queen was in the gallery by the gatehouse. Then came Knevett and Thomas Cobham, with a company of the rebels with them, through the gatehouse, from Westminster, upon the sudden, wherewith Sir John Gage and three of the judges, that were mainly armed in old brigandines, were so frighted that they fled in at the gates in such haste that old Gage fell down in the dirt and was foul arrayed; and so shut the gates. Whereat the rebels shot many arrows. By means of this great hurlyburly in shutting of the gates, the guards that were in the court made as great haste in at the hall door, and would have come into the hall amongst us, which we would not suffer. Then they went thronging towards the watergate, the kitchens, and those ways. Mr Gage came in amongst us all dirty, and so frighted that he could not speak to us; then came the three judges, so frighted that we could not keep them out except we should beat them down. With that we issued out of the hall into the court to see what the matter was; where there was none left but the porters, and, the gates being fast shut, as we went towards the gate, meaning to go forth, Sir Richard Southwell came forth of the back-yards into the court. 'Sir,' said we, 'command the gates to be opened that we may go to the Queen's enemies, we will break them open else; it is too much shame the gates should be thus shut for a few rebels; the Queen shall see us fell down her enemies this day before her face.' 'Masters,' said he, and put off his morion off his head, 'I shall desire you all, as you be gentlemen, to stay yourselves here that I may go up to the Queen to know her pleasure, and you shall have the gates opened; and, as I am a gentleman, I will make speed.' Upon this we stayed, and he made a speedy return, and brought us word the Queen was content we should have the gates opened. 'But her request is,' said he, 'that you will not go forth of her sight, for her only trust is in you for the defence of her person this day.' So the gate was opened, and we marched before the gallery window, where she spake unto us, requiring us, as we were gentlemen in whom she only trusted, that we would not go from that place. There we marched up and down the space of an hour, and then came a herald posting to bring news that Wyatt was taken. Immediately came Sir Maurice Berkeley and Wyatt behind him, unto whom he did yield at the Temple Gate, and Thomas Cobham behind and other gentlemen.

Anon after we were all brought unto the Queen's presence, and every one kissed her hand, of whom we had great thanks and large promises how good she would be unto us; but few or none of us got anything, although she was very liberal to many others that were enemies unto God's word, as few of us were.

1554

Elizabeth sent to the Tower

The most famous of all English propagandists for the Protestant cause was John Foxe, the 'martyrologist'. The accuracy of his stories is often questioned, but the best are written with verve: none more so than the celebrated narrative of Princess Elizabeth's obduracy when she was removed from Whitehall to the Tower of London and an uncertain fate early in her half-sister's reign. Foxe wrote this account when Elizabeth was securely on the throne.

Upon Saturday following, two lords of the council (the one was the Earl of Sussex, the other shall be nameless) came and certified her grace, that forthwith she must go unto the Tower, the barge being prepared for her, and the tide now ready, which tarrieth for nobody. In heavy mood her grace requested the lords that she might tarry another tide, trusting that the next would be better and more comfortable. But one of the lords replied, that neither time nor tide was to be delayed. And when her grace requested him that she might be suffered to write to the queen's majesty, he answered, that he durst not permit that; adding, that in his judgment it would rather hurt, than profit her grace, in so doing. But the other lord, more courteous and favourable (who was the Earl of Sussex), kneeling down, told her grace that she should have liberty to write, and, as he was a true man, he would deliver it to the queen's highness, and bring an answer of the same, whatsoever came thereof. Whereupon she wrote, albeit she could in no case be suffered to speak with the queen, to her great discomfort, being no offender against the queen's majesty.

And thus the time and tide passed away for that season, they privily appointing all things ready that she should go the next tide, which fell about midnight; but for fear she should be taken by the way, they durst not. So they staid till the next day, being Palm-Sunday, when, about nine of the clock, these two returned again, declaring that it was time for her grace to depart. She answered, 'If there be no remedy, I must be contented'; willing the lords to go on before. Being come forth into the garden, she did cast her eyes

The Princess Elizabeth consigned to the Tower, 1554. From a nineteenth-century painting.

towards the window, thinking to have seen the queen, which she could not; whereat she said, she marvelled much what the nobility of the realm meant, which in that sort would suffer her to be led into captivity, the Lord knew whither, for she did not. In the mean time, commandment was given in all London, that every one should keep the church, and carry their palms, while in the mean season she might be conveyed without all recourse of people into the Tower.

After all this, she took her barge with the two foresaid lords, three of the queen's gentlewomen, and three of her own, her gentleman-usher, and two of her grooms, lying and hovering upon the water a certain space, for that they could not shoot the bridge, the bargemen being very unwilling to shoot the same so soon as they did, because of the danger thereof: for the stern of the boat struck upon the ground, the fall was so big, and the water so shallow, that the boat being under the bridge, there staid again awhile. At landing she first stayed, and denied to land at those stairs where all traitors and offenders customably used to land, neither well could she, unless she should go over her shoes. The lords were gone out of the boat before, and asked why she came not. One of the lords went back again to her,

and brought word she would not come. Then said one of the lords, which shall be nameless, that she should not choose: and because it did then rain, he offered to her his cloak, which she, putting it back with her hand with a good dash, refused. So she coming out, having one foot upon the stair, said, 'Here landeth as true a subject, being prisoner, as ever landed at these stairs; and before thee, O God! I speak it, having no other friends but thee alone.' To whom the same lord answered again, that if it were so, it was the better for her...

After this, passing a little further, she sat down upon a cold stone, and there rested herself. To whom the lieutenant then being said, 'Madam, you were best to come out of the rain; for you sit unwholesomely.' She then replying, answered again, 'It is better sitting here, than in a worse place; for God knoweth, I know not whither you will bring me.' With that her gentleman-usher wept: she demanding of him what he meant so uncomfortably to use her, seeing she took him to be her comforter, and not to dismay her; especially for that she knew her truth to be such, that no man should have cause to weep for her. But forth she went into the prison.

65

1588–1625

ELIZABETHAN

and

JACOBEAN

LONDON

During Elizabeth I's reign the English language matured, as England became sure of itself as a nation-state. As a result, the whole manner of describing places, events and institutions grew suppler. Just when the first proper maps and panoramas of the city appear around 1550, so too descriptions of London start to assume life and individuality. This process took time to develop. Giordano Bruno's ludicrous account of what it was like trying to get from the Strand to Whitehall by boat in the 1580s, for instance, conveys the feeling of a particular experience which actually happened to an individual. At that time, it was hardly yet possible to describe London in such a way in English: which was one reason why Elizabethan intellectuals admired Italian writers. Twenty years later, when Thomas Dekker wrote the first of his London plague pamphlets, many of these barriers had been broken. The extravagance and range of Dekker's language are equal to Bruno's. It is not about personal experience, but it is personal in style –

rich, independent, yet with an edge of rawness still. Here is the authentic, unmistakable voice of London journalism.

Much of this change is due to the proliferation of cheap printing and pamphleteering. By the time of Elizabeth's accession, the technology of Gutenberg, as transmitted to London via Caxton, has become rapid and flexible. The steeple of St Paul's has hardly burnt down in 1561 before a news sheet is on sale narrating the event. Religious, literary and political controversies are being hotly disputed in print by the 1580s. Rival chronicles of English history begin to be published. One of the chroniclers, John Stow, devoted himself to the laborious study of his native city, coming out with his invaluable *Survey of London* in 1598. Stow and his continuators are responsible for a new sense of historical consciousness about London. All good European cities had a far-fetched version of their own pedigree, London's being that it was founded as 'Troynovant' by Brutus, a lineal descendant of Aeneas, then greatly renovated by the eponymous

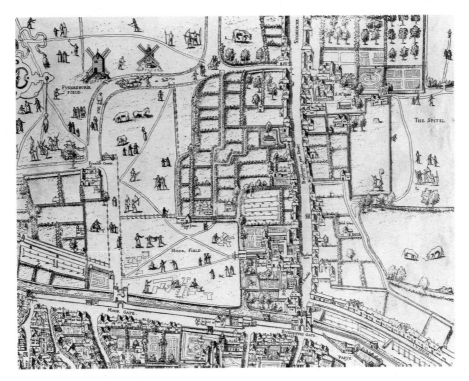

ABOVE *The City wall, Moorfields and Bishopsgate Without. From the 'copperplate map' of London, c.1559.*

OPPOSITE *London, with the bridge and Southwark. From a painting of 1575.*

OVERLEAF *View of London, c.1560.*

A VIEW of LONDO[N]

THE RIVER

The Remarkable Places in this Antient View of LONDON that are not distinguished by N[?]

A. St Margarets Ch. Westminst.
B. Fountain
C. Clock Tower
D. Parliament House
E. Palace Gates
F. Gates
G. Cock Pitt
H. Queens Gardens
I. St Mary Rouncival
K. Spring Garden

L. St Martins Church
M. St Giles's Church
N. Strand Bridge
O. Milford Lane
P. St Clement Dane's
Q. St Dunstans in the West
R. Temple Gate
S. Holborn Bars
T. Ely Place
V. St Andrews Holborn

W. Fleet Bridge
X. Bridewell Palace
Y. Walls along the River
Z. Fleet Hill
a. Lud Gate
b. Giltspur Street
c. Snow Hill
d. Hosier Lane
e. Pye Corner
f. Charter House

g. St Bartholomews Church
h. City Walls
i. Grey Fryers
k. Christ's Hospital
l. Ivy Lane
m. St Pauls Cathedral
n. Sermon Lane
o. St Mary Somerset
p. Old Change
q. Staining Lane

r. Silver Street
s. Mugwell Street
t. St Giles's Cripplegate
u. Barbican Cross
w. Cripple Gate
x. Oat Lane
y. Addle Street
z. St Alban Wood Street
1. Huggin Lane
2. Garlick Hill

Reduced to this Size from a Large Print in the Collection of St Ha[?]

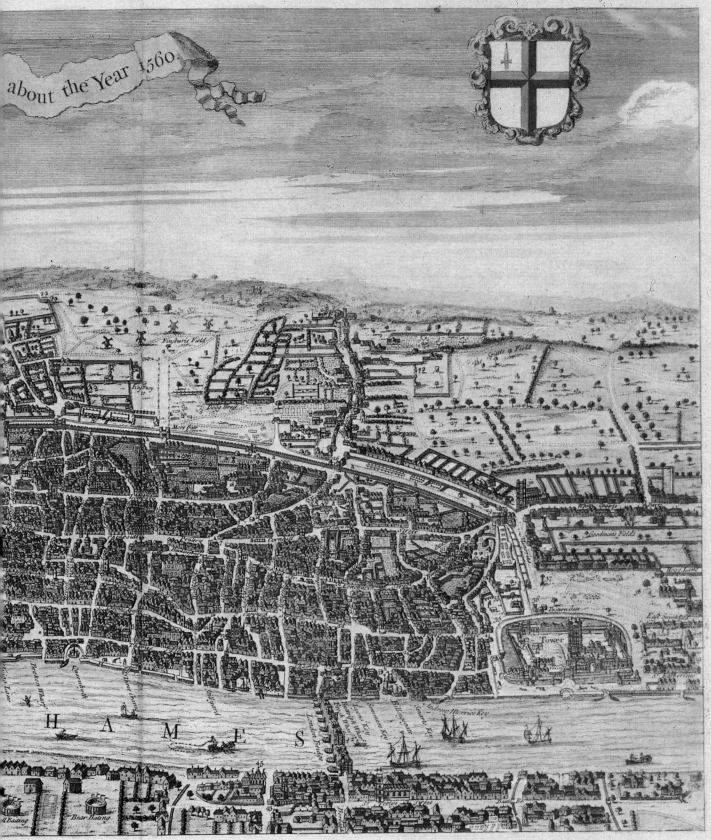

about the Year 1560.

H A M E S

...ts in the Body thereof, are referr'd to by Letters and Figures, as hereunder specified.

...itington's College	13. Bush Lane	23. Love Lane	33. Woodroof Lane	43. St Mary Overys Church	
...Tythes Lane	14. Eastcheap	24. St Dunstan's E.Ch. & Hill	34. Seething Lane	44. St Tooleys Church	
...ysing Hall	15. Burchin Lane	25. St Andrew Undershaft	35. Tower Hill	45. Winchester Place	
...ld Hall	16. St Anthonys Church	26. Bishops Gate	36. Tower hill Postern	46. Paris Garden	
...cks Market	17. Allhallons in the Wall	27. Spittle Fields	37. Minories Cross	47. Lambeth House	
...llbrooke Church	18. St Augustines Ch.	28. Cree Church	38. Abby of Grace		
...artholemew Lane	19. St Helens Church	29. Ald Gate	39. St Katherines Tower		
...ondon Stone	20. St Denniss Church	30. St Botolphs Aldgate	40. Tower Bridge		
...arbinder Lane	21. Fen Church	31. St Katherine Coleman	41. Barkin Church		
...Mary Botolph Lane	22. St Margaret's Church	32. Hart Street	42. Nonsuch House		

...ane Bar: anno 1738

King Lud. Stow by no means abandoned this. But his widely available *Survey* put modern flesh on antique bones.

The London of Stow's *Survey* differed from pre-Reformation London in crucial ways. It was a decidedly Protestant city. Calvinists occupied many of its pulpits and even, for a time, its bishop's palace. Sunday observance was fiercely insisted upon by the magistrates. The merchants clung firmly to the reformed religion, and the puritan party in the City was on the way to its formidable zenith. The least inkling of Catholic conspiracy produced uproar. Pageant and entertainments had not vanished; they had simply gone secular. The origins of the Elizabethan theatre are various. But it clearly answered a popular psychological need left unfulfilled when church ceremonial was abolished. That was partly why the authorities were disturbed by the playhouses and their older cousins, the amphitheatres for sports and baitings. They were rival attractions to the church, and better ones at that. In a city where public institutions were few, playhouses and bear gardens provoked an excitement we can hardly imagine today.

The second great difference between London as it was in 1558 and in 1625 was one of size. We cannot quantify the change accurately, but it was very great. The centralization of the court and monarchy under the early Tudors had stimulated London and the various palace suburbs. The closing of monasteries altered the rural economy and added to the lure of towns, London above all. But the chief cause was the sharp take-off of the capital's trading economy in late Elizabethan and Jacobean times, as new markets to the Indies and the Americas opened up. It is typical of London's and England's way of doing these things that government itself – the Crown and the City – stood back a little from this new field of enterprise. The running was made instead by individual courtiers and merchant-adventurers, who had to negotiate their way through a thicket of monopolies, privileges and dues before they could form new companies (distinct from the old livery companies), equip ships and sail. Yet such were the

trading prizes to be gained that some of the new enterprises – the East India Company, above all – were fabulously successful. Others like the Virginia Company were less important for what they did than what they portended; others again, like the attempt to colonize Ulster, were flops.

It took time before London's rulers grasped how fast the city was both spreading and condensing. By about 1580 the truth was clear, as old monastery gardens were built over, the burning of filthy sea-coal made London less and less amenable, and frequent bouts of plague made their vicious, seasonal inroads. The authorities then took a surprising line: that further building must stop and as many people as possible go back to the countryside. On the Crown's part, this policy reflects an old suspicion of municipal power, of public rioting, and of the dangers of leaving courtiers too much together in London for too long. The fate of Charles I proved these anxieties to be well founded. The City feared with equal justice that an enlarged London beyond the ancient boundaries meant a London outside the mayor and aldermen's control. So the injunctions against new building in London were taken gravely, especially under James I. But the forces for growth were too great for either Crown or City to contain. Efforts to export poor Londoners to the new colonies, for instance, were a failure.

There was a positive side to this action. Since the Reformation, expressions of civic pride had been lacking in London, apart from Sir Thomas Gresham's shrewd and spectacular donation of the Royal Exchange in 1566–70. From about 1610, men around the Court such as Sir George Buck began to speculate about ways in which London could be improved. Fresh building regulations outlawing timber construction were issued, probably under the influence of Inigo Jones, and James I took what seems to have been a personal interest in promoting open spaces. Much was promised at this time, but little achieved. The first fruit of the new royal approach to planning came only in Charles I's reign, with Covent Garden Piazza; while higher general standards of architecture had to await London's purgation by fire in 1666.

Dr King preaching at Paul's Cross in the presence of James I.

1561

Lightning strikes St Paul's

In 1561 lightning struck the spire of Old St Paul's and fire caught hold. The stone vaults saved the cathedral from complete destruction, but the spire fell, leaving the church stunted until the unquenchable conflagration of 1666. The disaster elicited an early piece of London journalism, written before regular newspapers existed: the news-sheet excerpted below came out just a week after the event.

On Wednesday being the fourth day of June in the year of our Lord 1561 . . . between one and two of the clock at afternoon was seen a marvellous great fiery lightning, and immediately ensued a most terrible hideous crack of thunder such as seldom hath been heard, and that by estimation of sense, directly over the City of London . . . Divers persons in time of the said tempest being on the river of Thames, and others being in the fields near adjoining to the City affirmed that they saw a long and a spear-pointed flame of fire (as it were) run through the top of the broach or shaft of Paul's steeple, from the east westward. And some of the parish of St Martin's being then in the street did feel a marvellous strong air or whirlwind with a smell like brimstone coming from Paul's Church … Between four and five of the clock a smoke was espied by divers to break out under the bowl of the said shaft of Paul's, and namely by Peter Johnson, principal registrar to the Bishop of London, who immediately brought word to the Bishop's house. But suddenly after, as it were in a moment, the flame brake forth in a circle like a garland round about the broach, about two yards to the estimation of sight under the bowl of the said shaft, and increased in such wise that within a quarter of an hour or little more, the cross and the eagle on the top fell down upon the south cross aisle…

Some there were, pretending experience in wars, that counselled the remnant of the steeple to be shot down with cannons, which counsel was not liked, as most perilous both for the dispersing the fire and destruction of houses and people. Others perceiving the steeple to be past all recovery, considering the hugeness of the fire and the dropping of the lead, thought best to get ladders and scale the church, and with axes to hew down a space of the roof of the church to stay the fire, at the least to save some part of the church: which was concluded. But before the ladders and buckets could be brought and things put in any order, and especially because the church was of such height that they could not scale it and no sufficient number of axes could be had, the labourers also being troubled with the multitude of idle gazers, the most part of the highest roof of the church was on fire.

First the fall of the cross and eagle fired the south cross aisle, which aisle was first consumed; the beams and brands of the steeple fell down on every side and fired the other three parts, that is to say, the chancel or choir, the north aisle and the body of the church … The state of the steeple and church seeming both desperate, my Lord Mayor was advised by one Master Winter of the Admiralty to convert the most part of his care and provision to preserve the Bishop's Palace adjoining to the north-west end of the church, lest from that house being large, the fire might spread to the streets adjoining. Whereupon the ladders, buckets and labourers were commanded thither, and by great labour and diligence a piece of the roof of the north aisle was cut down and the fire so stayed, and by much water that quenched and the said Bishop's house preserved. It pleased God at the same time both to turn and calm the wind, which afore was vehement, and continued still high and great in other parts without the city. There were about 500 persons that laboured in carrying and filling water etc. Divers substantial citizens took pains as if they had been labourers, so did also divers and sundry gentlemen … About ten of the clock the fierceness of the fire was past, the timber being fallen and lying burning upon the vaults of stone, the vaults yet (God be thanked) standing unperished, so as only the timber of the whole church was consumed and the lead molten, saving the most part of the two low aisles of the choir and a piece of the north aisle and another small piece of the south aisle in the body of the church … In divers parts and streets and within the houses both adjoining and of a good distance, as in Fleet Street and Newgate Market, by the violence of the fire burning coals of great bigness fell down almost as thick as hailstones, and flaws of lead were blown abroad into the gardens without the City like flaws of snow in breadth, without hurt, God be thanked, to any house or person.

1562–3
The fate of the Minories

The dissolved religious houses of London passed, via the Crown, through all sorts of owners and found all sorts of uses. Few were razed to the ground utterly, though the churches were much curtailed and any spare land was built upon. The secular parts of the monasteries were too solidly constructed to be wasted. Some became houses of grandees; others were refounded as hospitals or schools or almshouses.

An unusual case is that of the Minories or Minor Sisters of St Clare, near the Tower of London. Most of this abbey was acquired by the powerful Grey family during Edward VI's reign. Implicated in rebellion against Mary, they lost the property, were then restored to it by Elizabeth I, and sold it in 1562–3 for a handsome profit to the Marquess of Winchester, the Queen's Lord Treasurer. His motive was to supplement the ordnance arrangements at the Tower, as he tells Sir William Cecil in the following letter. So grudging was Elizabeth of public expenditure that Winchester had to risk buying the Minories himself and get his money back later. His tactic was successful: by the time of Stow's *Survey of London*, the Minories boasted 'divers fair and large storehouses for armour and habiliments of war, with divers workhouses serving to the same purposes'. The district remained famous for its armourers even after fire destroyed the surviving monastic buildings in 1797.

Three of the summers [beams] in the great loft of the ordnance house within the Tower be broken and stayed

Last vestiges of the Minories, at the end of the eighteenth century.

by posts and cannot be repaired till all the weight that lieth upon the same be taken away, which is too much for the floor by one half and can never be all placed there again and continue the floor ... And there is no housing in the Tower to place it in. And if the housing where it lieth was able to keep it, yet would it there be lost for lack of room. And what charge armour, weapons and powder hath been this year to the Queen I need not write to you, for it is to you well known, and therefore it requireth good keeping or else it will in short time not be worth half the money [and] were a great loss to her Grace.

The said considerations made me buy the Minories; I go through withal for myself because you wrote to me the Queen would none of it, and without the Queen's Majesty hath help at my hand in that house I know not where it is to be had. And there all things may be well placed, a smith's and carpenter's, timber wheels, lathes, axle-trees, cullem [?], cleaves and bowyer's without carriage of any of these things into the Tower, which shall be a great commodity to the Tower and a great

safeguard to the stone bridges; and withdrawn from the Tower the common repairs, which is one of the best things. Therefore I think it best her Grace take succour of that house by paying rent or giving money for it as I pay. More I will not ask, for I meant the house for her Grace at the beginning for the considerations aforesaid.

1570s/80s

The Royal Exchange and Somerset House

The symbolic commercial event of Elizabeth I's reign was the opening of the Royal Exchange in 1570. This was the brainchild of London's greatest merchant banker, Sir Thomas Gresham. For fifteen years Gresham plied back and forth between London and Antwerp, where the Exchange, or Bourse, contributed so much to the latter city's prosperity. In 1560 he received a letter (probably solicited) from his Antwerp factor, bidding him consider 'what a City London is and that in so many years they have not found the means to make a Bourse, but must walk in the rain when it raineth, more like pedlars than merchants'. In due course Gresham offered to build such a building, if the City would pay for the land – and to this the City agreed in 1566. There was an enclosed upper storey, or 'pawn', with retail shops, while merchants conferred in the court or arcade beneath. John Stow gives the following notices in his *Survey* of the opening of London's first purpose-built commercial institution; and in his *Annals* of the success that the upper-storey shops enjoyed after a slow start – showing that the concept of the 'loss-leader' is nothing new.

In the year 1570, on the 23rd of January, the Queen's Majesty attended with her nobility came from her house at the Strand called Somerset House, and entered the City by Temple Bar, through Fleet Street, Cheap, and so by the north side of the Bourse through Threadneedle Street to Sir Thomas Gresham's in Bishopsgate Street, where she dined. After dinner Her Majesty, returning through Cornhill, entered the Bourse on the south side; and after that she had viewed every part thereof above the ground, especially the Pawn, which was richly furnished with all sorts of the finest wares in the City, she caused the same Bourse by an herald and a trumpet to be proclaimed the Royal Exchange, and so to be called from thenceforth and not otherwise.

After the Royal Exchange, which is now called the eye of London, had been builded two or three years, it stood in a manner empty, and a little before her Majesty

The first Royal Exchange, showing shops along the outside and Gresham's grasshopper symbol on the roofs. From a Dutch engraving, c.*1569.*

was to come thither to view the beauty thereof and to give it a name, Sir Thomas Gresham in his own person went twice in one day round about the Upper Pawn and besought those few shopkeepers then present that they would furnish and adorn with wares and waxlights as many shops as they either could or would, and they should have all those shops so furnished rent-free the year, which otherwise at that time was 40s a shop by the year. And within two years after, he raised that rent unto four marks a year; and within a while after that, he raised the rent of every shop unto £4 10s a year, and then all shops were well furnished according to that time; for then the milliners or haberdashers in that place sold mousetraps, bird cages, shoeing horns, lanthorns and Jews' trumps etc. There was also at that time that kept shops in the Upper Pawn of the Royal Exchange that sold both old and new armour, apothecaries, booksellers, goldsmiths and glass-sellers, although now it is as plenteously stored with all kind of rich wares and commodities as any particular place in Europe: unto which place many foreign princes daily send, to be served of the best sort.

The first Somerset House on the Strand was built for Protector Somerset during his heyday, while he ruled the realm on behalf of Edward VI. Confiscated upon his downfall, it was much frequented as a kind of working central-London palace first by Mary and then by her half-sister, Elizabeth I. Because of its location midway between the City and Westminster, it was favoured for Councils of State. Godfrey Goodman, later Bishop of Gloucester, remembered as a boy being called in the Armada Year to watch Queen Elizabeth emerge from Council there.

In the year '88 I did then live at the upper end of the Strand, near St Clement's Church, when suddenly there was a report (it was then December, about five, and very dark) that the Queen was gone to Council; and I was told, 'If you will see the Queen, you must come quickly'. Then we all ran, when the Court gates were set open, and no man hindered us from coming in. There we stayed an hour and a half, and the yard was full, there being a great number of torches, when the Queen came out in great state. Then we cried 'God save your Majesty!' and the Queen turned to us and said, 'God bless you all, my good people!' Then we cried again, 'God save your Majesty! And the Queen said again to us, 'Ye may well have a greater prince, but ye shall never have a more loving prince.' And so the Queen and the crowd there looking upon one another awhile, her Majesty departed. This wrought an impression upon us, for shows and pageants are best seen by torchlight, that all the way long we did nothing but talk of what an admirable Queen she was, and how we would adventure all in her service. Now this was in the year when she had most enemies, and how easily they might have gotten into the crowd and multitude to do her mischief.

1580s

Along the Strand

A different vignette of the Elizabethan Strand is proffered by that strange and slippery Renaissance character, Giordano Bruno. The heretical friar and philosopher took refuge in England for a period in the 1580s, consorting with young intellectuals but dabbling also in intrigue and espionage. In London he lodged at the French Embassy, located off the Strand. A dialogue entitled *La Cena delle Ceneri* – The Ash Wednesday Dinner Party – is the main literary fruit of his stay. It commemorates what was no doubt a real dinner given at Sir Fulke Greville's house in Whitehall. Three of the guests (including Bruno, here called 'the Nolan') encounter some difficulties getting there. Once at the dinner table, they hold forth at learned and conceited length about the barbarity of manners in London. Here is

the gist of their long-winded tale, up to the point where they opt for walking along the Strand, only to be buffeted by passers-by.

Now although we were on the right road, we thought to do better and shorten the way. We turned toward the Thames to find a boat to take us towards the Palace. We reached Lord Buckhurst's private pier, and from there we called out 'oars!' (that is, 'boatmen'). But we waited so long that we could in the same space of time have made the entire journey on foot and performed some errands along the way. At last two boatmen answered from afar. With infinite slowness, as if they were going to their own hanging, they reached the bank. Then after many questions and answers about whence, where and why, and how and how much, they brought the prow of the boat up to the last step of the pier. One of the two men, who looked like the ancient ferryman from the kingdom of Tartarus, offered his hand to the Nolan; the other one, who I think was the son of the first although he seemed to be about 65, took care of us who followed . . .

The river front from Whitehall Palace to the Strand. From an Elizabethan map.

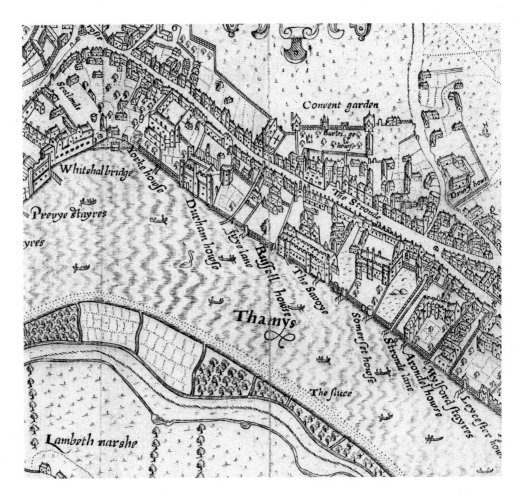

The South Bank theatres, from Wenzel Hollar's Long View of London, *1647. The names of the Globe and the Hope (used for bear-baiting) have been transposed in error.*

We went on little by little as much as the boat allowed, which (since worms and time had reduced it to such a condition that it could have been used as a cork) seemed with its *festina lente* to be as heavy as lead, while the arms of the two old men seemed broken. They stretched their bodies to their entire lengths while rowing, but succeeded only in making very slow progress ... In this way, proceeding through much time but little space and not having covered even a third of our journey, we reached a point just beyond the place called the Temple, when suddenly our *ciceroni*, instead of hurrying, turned the prow toward the bank. The Nolan asked, 'What are they doing? Do they perhaps want to catch their breath?' And his friend interpreted the answer, that they would go no further, as they had reached their house. We begged them again and again to no avail, as they were of that type of peasant in whose heart are blunted all the darts of the god of love worshipped by country folk ... To sum up, they dropped us there and, having paid and thanked them (since in this place you cannot do anything else when such canaille wrongs you), we were shown the quickest way to the road ...

There was a street which began as a mudhole around which, either by design or by chance, there was no detour. The Nolan ... suddenly fell so deeply into the mud that he could not pull his legs out: and thus, helping each other, we passed through that stretch of road hoping that that purgatory would not last long ... We only hoped that each step would bring the end, ever sinking knee-deep into the liquid mire ...

We thought we were in the Elysian Fields when we reached the main public road: when, from the appearance of the place and recalling whence the accursed detour had taken us, behold, we found ourselves twenty-two steps, more or less, from the spot which we had left in search of the boatmen and near the abode of the Nolan.

1584–94

Elizabethan entertainments

The form of the Elizabethan stage grew from amalgamating two traditions in London entertainment: the performing of early secular plays or 'interludes' in City inn yards, and the baiting of bears and bulls in amphitheatre-like rings, notably in Paris Garden, on the scruffy western edge of suburban Southwark. The baitings had been going on since time immemorial. They had reached a high state of the art by the time that Lupold von Wedel, one of several German travellers who have left us precious accounts of Elizabethan theatre and pastimes, visited Southwark in 1584.

There is a round building three stories high, in which are kept about a hundred large English dogs, with separate wooden kennels for each of them. These dogs were made to fight singly with three bears, the second bear being larger than the first and the third larger than the second. After this a horse was brought in and chased by the dogs, and at last a bull, who defended himself bravely. The next was that a number of men and women came forward from a separate compartment, dancing, conversing and fighting with each other: also a man who threw some white bread among the crowd, that scrambled for it. Right over the middle of the place a rose was fixed, this rose being set on fire by a rocket: suddenly lots of apples and pears fell out of it down upon the people standing below. Whilst the people were scrambling for the apples, some rockets were

made to fall down upon them out of the rose, which caused a great fright but amused the spectators. After this, rockets and other fireworks came flying out of all corners, and that was the end of the play.

During his visit to London in 1599 Thomas Platter from Basle caught an afternoon performance of Shakespeare's *Julius Caesar* at the first Globe Theatre on Bankside, then brand new. He followed this up with a 'comedy' at the Curtain in Shoreditch. *Julius Caesar* earns the shorter comment; no doubt the German-speaking Platter found it hard to follow compared with the simple, chauvinist entertainment at the Curtain.

After dinner on the 21st of September, at about two o'clock, I went with my companions over the water, and in the strewn roof-house saw the tragedy of the first Emperor Julius with at least fifteen characters very well acted. At the end of the comedy they danced according to their custom with extreme elegance. Two in men's clothes and two in women's gave this performance, in wonderful combination with each other.

On another occasion I also saw after dinner a comedy, not far from our inn, in the suburb; if I remember right, in Bishopsgate. Here they represented various nations, with whom on each occasion an Englishman fought for his daughter, and overcame them all except the German, who won the daughter in fight. He then sat down with him, and gave him and his servant strong drink, so that they both got drunk, and the servant threw his shoe at his master's head and they both fell asleep. Meanwhile the Englishman went into the tent, robbed the German of his gains, and thus he outwitted the German also. At the end they danced very elegantly both in English and in Irish fashion.

And thus every day at two o'clock in the afternoon in the city of London two and sometimes three comedies are performed at separate places, wherewith folk make merry together, and whichever does best gets the greatest audience. The places are so built that they play on a raised platform, and everyone can well see it all. There are however separate galleries, and there one stands more comfortably and moreover can sit, but one pays more for it. Thus anyone who remains on the level standing pays only one English penny; but if he wants to sit, he is let in at a further door and there he gives another penny. If he desires to sit on a cushion in the most comfortable place of all, where he not only sees everything well but can also be seen, then he gives yet another English penny at another door. And in the pauses of the comedy, food and drink are carried round amongst the people, and one can thus refresh himself at his own cost.

All through Elizabeth's reign there was controversy over the location and control of the London theatres. Courtiers (some of whom sponsored companies of players) and the common people liked them, but the Privy Council, the City magistrates and puritans accused them of causing public disorder, immorality and the spread of infection in time of plague. The constraints on theatres within the City led to an absolute ban on them in 1596, and the development of the famous South Bank playhouses. But because of an administrative anomaly, the Blackfriars survived inside the City, while the Theatre, the Curtain and the Fortune stood north of the river. The theatre promoters fenced the whole time with the authorities. Though under constant threat of restriction or total closure, they contributed much to London's prosperity. The watermen, for instance, were very dependent on the South Bank playhouses and felt the pinch whenever they shut down.

The Swan Theatre in about 1596. From a sketch found in the University Library of Utrecht.

Bishop Grindal of London to Sir William Cecil, 23 February 1564

Mr Calfhill this morning showed me your letter to him, wherein ye wish some politic orders to be devised against infection. I think it very necessary ... By search I do perceive that there is no one thing of late is more like to have renewed this contagion than the practice of an idle sort of people which have been infamous in all commonweals: I mean these *histriones*, common players, who now daily, but specially on holidays, set up bills, whereunto the youth resorteth excessively and there taketh infection: besides that God's word by their impure mouths is profaned and turned into scoffs. For remedy whereof in my judgement, ye should do very well to be a mean, that proclamation were set forth to inhibit all plays for one whole year (and if it were for ever, it were not amiss) within the City or three miles' compass, upon pains as well to the players as to the owners of the houses where they play their lewd interludes.

William Harrison's Chronology, 1572

Plays are banished for a time out of London, lest the resort unto them should engender a plague or rather disperse it, being already begun. Would to God these common plays were exiled for altogether, as seminaries of impiety, and their theatres pulled down as no better than houses of bawdry. It is an evident token of wicked times when players wax so rich that they can build such houses. As much I wish also to our common bear baitings used on the Sabbath day.

Lord Mayor Blank to Lord Burghley, 14 January 1583

It may please your Lordship to be further advertised (which I think you have already heard) of a great mishap at Paris Garden, where by ruin of all the scaffolds at once yesterday, a great number of people are some presently slain and some maimed and grievously hurt. It giveth great occasion to acknowledge the hand of God for such abuse of the Sabbath day, and moveth me in conscience to beseech your lordship to give order for redress of such contempt of God's service.

Petition of the watermen to Lord Admiral Howard when the Rose Theatre on Bankside was closed because of plague, c. *1592–3*

Whereas your good Lordship had directed your warrant unto her Majesty's Justices for the restraint of a playhouse belonging unto the said Philip Henslowe, one of the grooms of her Majesty's Chamber, so it is, if it please your good Lordship, that we your said poor watermen have had much help and relief for us our poor wives and children by means of the resort of such people as come unto the said playhouse. It may therefore please your good Lordship for God's sake and in the way of charity to respect us your poor watermen, and to give leave unto the said Philip Henslowe to have playing in his said house during such time as others have, according as it hath been accustomed.

Lord Hunsdon (Lord Chamberlain) to Lord Mayor Martin, 8 October 1594

Where my now company of players have been accustomed for the better exercise of their quality and for the service of her Majesty if need so require, to play this winter time within the City at the Cross Keys in Gracechurch Street, these are to require and pray your Lordship (the time being such as, thanks be to God, there is now no danger of the sickness) to permit and suffer them so to do. The which I pray you rather to do for that they have undertaken to me that, where heretofore they begin not their plays till towards four o'clock, they will now begin at two and have done between four and five, and will not use any drums or trumpets at all for the calling of people together, and shall be contributories to the poor of the parish where they play, according to their abilities.

1593

Marlowe murdered in Deptford

Male exuberance was a strong ingredient of the Elizabethan stage. Close beneath the surface of this exuberance lay violence. Ben Jonson killed a man in a duel; Christopher Marlowe was knifed in a Deptford tavern brawl of 1593, the first famous casualty of London literary life. We know that Marlowe lived a shady and racy life, but scholars do not quite agree on why he came to be killed, or whether indeed there was a reason over and above the bill – *le recknynge*, as it is called below. Here is a translation from the Latin of what the jury at the inquest was persuaded to believe took place. Marlowe throughout is referred to as 'Morley'.

Inquisition indented taken at Deptford Strand in the aforesaid county of Kent within the verge on the first day of June in the year of the reign of Elizabeth by the grace of God of England France and Ireland Queen defender of the faith etc. the thirty-fifth, in the presence of William Danby, gentleman, coroner of the household of our said lady the Queen, upon view of the body of Christopher Morley, there lying dead and slain . . .

A supposed portrait of Christopher Marlowe, knifed to death in a Deptford tavern, 1593.

A certain Ingram Ffrysar, late of London, gentleman, and the aforesaid Christopher Morley and one Nicholas Skeres, late of London, gentleman, and Robert Poley of London aforesaid, gentleman, on the thirtieth day of May in the thirty-fifth year above named, at Deptford Strand . . . met together in a room

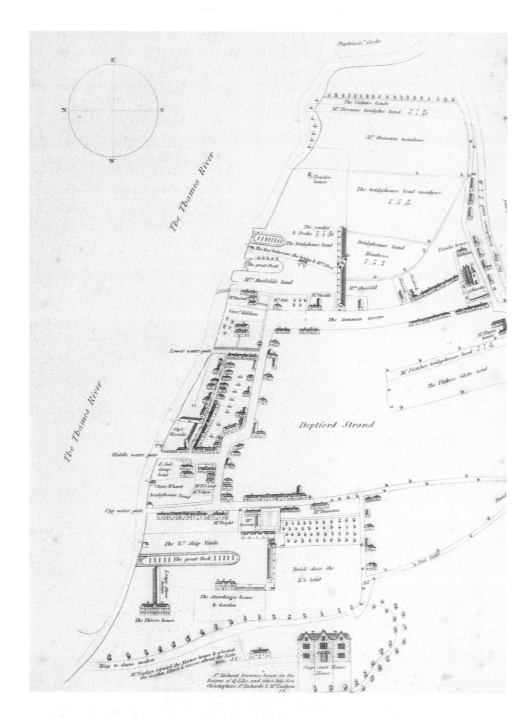

'Deptford Strand'. A map of 1623 showing the little Thames-side village beginning to develop into a port.

in the house of a certain Eleanor Bull, widow; and there passed the time together and dined, and after dinner were in quiet sort together there and walked in the garden belonging to the said house until the sixth hour after noon of the same day and then returned from the said garden to the room aforesaid and there together and in company supped . . .

And after supper the said Ingram and Christopher Morley were in speech and uttered one to the other divers malicious words for the reason that they could not be at one nor agree about the payment of the sum of pence, that is, *le recknynge*, there; and the said Christopher Morley then lying upon a bed in the room where they supped, and moved with anger against the said Ingram Ffrysar upon the words as aforesaid spoken between them, and the said Ingram then and there sitting in the room aforesaid with his back towards the bed where the said Christopher Morley was then lying, sitting near the bed and with the front part of his body towards the table, and the aforesaid Nicholas Skeres and Robert Poley sitting on either side of the said Ingram in such a manner that the same Ingram Ffrysar could in no wise take flight: it so befell that the said Christopher Morley on a sudden and of his malice towards the said Ingram aforethought, then and there maliciously drew the dagger of the said Ingram which was at his back, and with the same dagger the said Christopher Morley then and there maliciously gave the aforesaid Ingram two wounds on his head of the length of two inches and of the depth of a quarter of an inch. Whereupon the said Ingram, in fear of being slain and sitting in the manner aforesaid between the said Nicholas Skeres and Robert Poley so that he could not in any wise get away, in his own defence and for the saving of his life then and there struggled with the said Christopher Morley to get back from him his dagger aforesaid; in which affray the same Ingram could not get away from the said Christopher Morley. And so it befell in that affray that the said Ingram in defence of his life with the dagger aforesaid of the value of 12d. gave the said Christopher Morley then and there a mortal wound

and weight, and a nation in the process of forging a culture of its own. John Manningham, a gentleman diarist of the Inner Temple, tells us in the following extract how the long-expected news was received in London: soberly, sadly, but with relief that James I's succession had been calmly managed and that Scotland was now to be joined to England without conflict.

This morning about three at clock her Majesty departed this life, mildly like a lamb, easily like a ripe apple from the tree, *cum leve quadam febre, absque gemitu.* Dr Parry told me that he was present, and sent his prayers before her soul; and I doubt not but she is amongst the royal saints in heaven in eternal joy.

About ten at clock the Council and divers noblemen having been a while in consultation, proclaimed James the Sixth, King of Scots, the King of England, France and Ireland, beginning at Whitehall gates; where Sir Robert Cecil read the proclamation which he carried in his hand, and after read again in Cheapside. Many noblemen, lords spiritual and temporal, knights, five

The tomb of Elizabeth I, Westminster Abbey.

over his right eye of the depth of two inches and of the width of one inch; of which mortal wound the aforesaid Christopher Morley then and there instantly died.

1603

Death of Elizabeth I

A reign that had commenced in doubt ended illustriously in March 1603. Elizabeth's death left England securely Protestant, a power of growing international consciousness

trumpets, many heralds. The gates at Ludgate and portcullis were shut and down by the Lord Mayor's command, who was there present with the aldermen etc., and until he had a token ... that they would proclaim the King of Scots the King of England, he would not open.

Upon the death of a king or queen in England, the Lord Mayor is the greatest magistrate in England. All corporations and their governors continue; most of the other officers' authority is expired with the prince's breath. There was a diligent watch and ward kept at every gate and street, day and night, by householders, to prevent garboils: which, God be thanked, were more feared than perceived.

The proclamation was heard with great expectation and silent joy, no great shouting. I think the sorrow for her Majesty's departure was so deep in many hearts they could not so suddenly show any great joy, though it could not be less than exceeding great for the succession of so worthy a king. And at night they showed it by bonfires and ringing. No tumult, no contradiction, no disorder in the city; every man went about his business as readily, as peaceably, as securely as though there had been no change, nor any news ever heard of competitors. God be thanked, our king hath his right.

1603

Outbreak of plague

Plague in London was a familiar visitor well before the calamity of 1665. It was a common scourge of the summer and autumn months, playing unpredictable cat and mouse with the lives of citizens. Were Elizabethan and Jacobean outbreaks worse than medieval ones, or just better reported? We do not know. But London was growing more fetid, as immigrants poured in and the old monastic open spaces succumbed to piecemeal property development. Plague was commonly put down not to poor sanitation but to wickedness and became the topic of countless sermons. This type of commentary was turned to advantage by the satirical poet, playwright and journalist Thomas Dekker. His ghoulish plague pamphlets on the epidemics of 1603, 1625 and 1630 are the forerunners of Defoe's famous *Journal of the Plague Year*. Here is Dekker's baroque evocation of the 'sack' of the City by plague in 1603.

The Plague took sore pains for a breach, he laid about him cruelly ere he could get it, but at length he and his tyrannous band entered. His purple colours were presently (with the sound of Bow Bell) advanced and joined to the standard of the City. He marched even through Cheapside and the capital streets of Troynovant [London], the only blot of dishonour that stuck on this invader being this, that he played the tyrant, not the conqueror, making havoc of all, when he had all lying at the foot of his mercy. Men, women and children dropped down before him: houses were rifled, streets ransacked, beautiful maidens thrown on their beds and ravished by sickness, rich men's coffers broken open and shared amongst prodigal heirs and unthrifty

Death by plague wreaks havoc upon London and its environs. Engraving from a pamphlet by Thomas Dekker.

servants, poor men used poorly but not pitifully: he did very much hurt, yet some say he did very much good. Howsoever he behaved himself, this intelligence runs current, that every house looked like St Bartholomew's Hospital ... Lazarus lay groaning at every man's door; marry, no Dives was within to send him a crumb (for all your goldfinches were fled to the woods) nor a dog left to lick up his sores, for they (like curs) were knocked down like oxen, and fell thicker than acorns.

I am amazed to remember what dead marches were made of three thousand trooping together: husbands, wives and children being led as ordinarily to one grave as if they had gone to one bed. And those that could shift for a time and shrink their heads out of the collar (as many did), yet went they (most bitterly) miching and muffled up and down with rue and wormwood stuffed into their ears and nostrils, looking like so many boars' heads stuck with branches of rosemary, to be served in for brawn at Christmas.

This was a rare world for the Church, who had wont to complain for want of living, and now had more living thrust upon her than she knew how to bestow: to have been clerk now to a parish clerk was better than to serve some foolish justice of the peace, or the year before to have had a benefice. Sextons gave out, if they might (as they hoped) continue these doings but a twelvemonth longer, they and their posterity would all ride upon footclothes to the end of the world. Amongst which worm-eaten generation, the three bald sextons of limping St Giles, St Sepulchre's and St Olave's ruled the roost more hotly then ever did the triumviri of

Rome. Jehochanan, Simeon and Eleazar never kept such a plaguy coil in Jerusalem among the half-starved Jews as these three sharkers did in their parishes among naked Christians. Cursed they were, I am sure, by some to the pit of hell for tearing money out of their throats that had not a cross in their purses. But alas! they must have it, it is their fee, and therefore give the devil his due. Only herb-wives and gardeners (that never prayed before, unless it were for rain or fair weather) were now day and night upon their marybones that God would bless the labours of these mole-catchers, because they suck sweetness by this; for the price of flowers, herbs and garlands rose wonderfully. In so much that rosemary, which had wont to be sold for twelvepence an armful, went now for six shillings a handful.

1605

The Gunpowder Plot

The first great drama of James I's reign was the Gunpowder Plot or 'Powder Treason', as it was then dubbed: a murky affair and still something of a riddle, though most modern scholars believe it was an authentic conspiracy, not something trumped up by the Cecils. Guy Fawkes, alias Johnson, was only a minor actor in the business. The ringleaders were Robert Catesby, Thomas Percy and Everard Digby, Catholic gentlemen who had been disappointed in their hopes for toleration when James I

came to the throne. The plot was uncovered through a leak several days before. The famous search of the Parliament cellar was in fact the second, and took place on 4 (not 5) November 1605. Fawkes was not inside the cellar, as schoolchildren are taught, but standing sentinel at the door. In his deposition for the trial (made after torture and so perhaps not wholly reliable), he explains that the original plan had been to mine under the House of Lords from an adjacent house before setting off the charge. But after mining halfway through the Parliament House's foundations, the conspirators had been able to lease a coal cellar beneath the building instead. The trial proceedings narrate the moment of discovery.

To this purpose [a full search of royal premises] was Sir Thomas Knyvet (a gentleman of His Majesty's Privy Chamber) employed, being a Justice of Peace in Westminster, and one of whose ancient fidelity both the late Queen and our now Sovereign have had large proof; who, according to the trust committed unto him, went about the midnight next after to the Parliament House, accompanied with such a small number as was fit for that errand. But before his entry in the house, finding Thomas Percy's alleged man standing without

The conspirators of the Gunpowder Plot. This Dutch engraving describes the principals as 'seven English noblemen', with whom the hatless serving man Bates (left) is associated.

the doors, his clothes and boots on, at so dead a time of night, he resolved to apprehend him, as he did, and thereafter went forward to the searching of the house where, after he had caused to be overturned some of the billets and coals, he first found one of the small barrels of powder and afterwards all the rest, to the number of 36 barrels, great and small; and thereafter, searching the fellow whom he had taken, found three matches and all other instruments fit for blowing up the powder ready upon him, which made him readily confess his own guiltiness, declaring also unto him that if he had happened to be within the house when he took him, as he was immediately before (at the ending of his work) he would not have failed to have blown him up, house and all.

1613–14

The New River

The greatest improvement carried through in London between the Reformation and the Great Fire was the New River, whereby Hugh Myddleton, goldsmith and banker, channelled springs from Amwell in Hertfordshire and elsewhere and brought them by a cut of thirty-eight miles' length down to a reservoir head at Clerkenwell, hence to feed the City by gravity. The quality of London's water had been declining for several centuries; Myddleton's initiative,

completed in 1613, marks the start of the modern history of supply. It was a complex transaction, carried out with amazing speed due to the support of the Crown (James I bargained for half the profits), the City and Myddleton's entrepreneurial skills. The first idea was not his, but he made it his own and the remaining sections of the New River are Myddleton's lasting memorial. Below are two of the compensation receipts issued to those whose land was compulsorily purchased for the New River.

Received by me, William Hollyday of London, merchant, of the Mayor and Communality of the City of London by the hands of Hugh Myddleton, citizen and goldsmith of London, five pounds and five shillings of lawful money of England in full satisfaction of all my damages sustained in my meadows and lands in the parish of Islington in the county of Middlesex by reason of the cut and banks or otherwise for a trench cut through my land containing one and twenty poles for the passage of a stream of running water to the north parts of the City of London. In witness whereof I have put my hand and seal, the 22nd of April 1613.

Received by me, Samuel Backhouse of Swallowfield in the county of Berkshire, esquire, of the mayor and communality of the City of London by the hands of Hugh Myddleton, citizen and goldsmith of the same,

Detail from a portrait of Sir John Backhouse, a director of the New River Company, showing New River Head, Clerkenwell, with London behind, 1637.

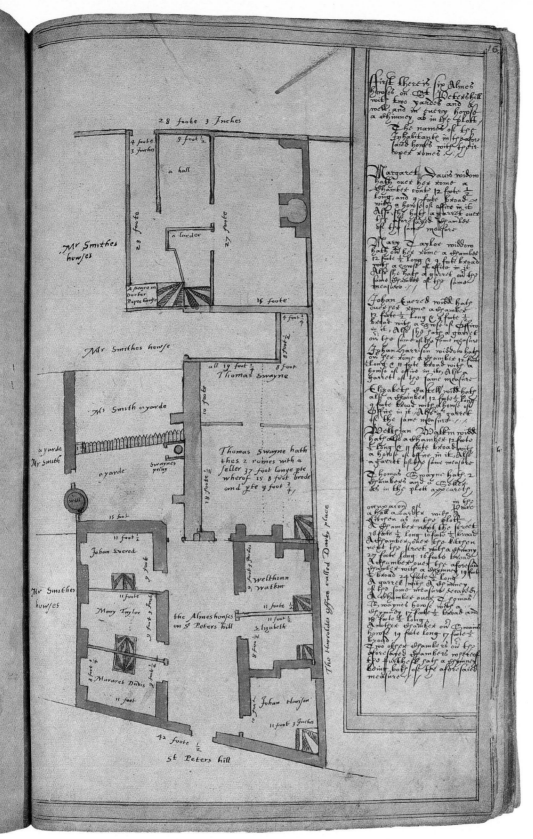

Almshouses on St Peter's Hill, surveyed by Robert Treswell 1611. Treswell's early and exact plans and descriptions of City property provide us with precious knowledge of how Londoners lived before the Great Fire. Margaret Davis, widow, the first of the residents listed on this survey, 'hath over her room a chamber 12 foot long and ½ long and 9 foot broad, with a house of office in it. Also, she hath a garret over the aforesaid chamber of the same measure'.

threescore and five pounds of lawful money of England in full satisfaction of all my damages and trespasses whatsoever as well by reason of the cut and banks or otherwise for a trench cut through my lands called the Mantles lying and being within the parish of Clerkenwell in the county of Middlesex for the passage of a stream of running water to the north parts of the said city, containing 18 poles and three foot or thereabouts, as also in consideration of all my damages and trespasses whatsoever sustained by reason of a brick wall and cistern house built in and upon the said lands called the Mantles for the conveying of the aforesaid stream into the City of London. In witness whereof I have put my hand and seal, the 3rd day of May Anno 1614.

85

1607–9

James I dines with the Merchant Taylors

The Merchant Taylors were among the City livery companies based upon commerce rather than craft, so they were well placed to engage in the lucrative business of adventuring, as it developed in Elizabethan and Jacobean times. This was not a straightforward process. If there was money to be made, the Crown and courtiers were interested. It became the habit of James I to grant monopolies, which rode roughshod over the companies' own charters and perceived rights. There was also a tendency for projects to be passed on from the Crown via the Mayor and Aldermen with a heavy hint that the companies ought to contribute towards them, irrespective of their commercial potential. When the Merchant Taylors spent £1000 on feasting James I in July 1607, they knew what they were doing.

Excerpts from records of preparation for banquet given to James I, 1607

The Company are informed that the King's most excellent Majesty with our gracious Queen and the noble Prince and divers honourable Lords and other determine to dine at our Hall on the day of the election of the Master and Wardens; therefore this meeting was appointed to advise and consult how everything may be performed for the reputation and credit of the Company and to give his Majesty best liking and contentment.

Mr Warden Wright is entreated from time to time to attend at Court to understand from my Lord Chamberlain and my Lord Salisbury what compliments are fit to be performed by the Company, and to know if his Majesty hold his resolution to come.

Sir John Swynnerton is entreated to confer with Mr Benjamin Jonson the poet about a speech to be made to welcome his Majesty, and for music and other inventions which may give liking and delight to his Majesty, by reason that the Company doubt that their schoolmaster and scholars be not acquainted with such kind of entertainments.

It is ordered that the mason shall presently cut a hole through the main wall at the upper end of the Hall and make a window out of the little room for the King to look into the hall.

Our Master and Wardens are entreated to cause discreet men to make special search in and about all the houses and rooms adjoining to the Hall to prevent all villainy and danger from all which we do most humbly beseech Almighty God to bless and defend his Majesty.

It is considered and agreed that the brick wall in the garden which adjoineth to the tavern shall presently be raised up to take away the prospect of such as use to walk upon the leads of the tavern and thereby would overlook the garden, and the King's chamber and the garden walls and the gate and the houses about the same to be beautified as much as time will admit.

Excerpts from the accounts for the banquet

For 19 lbs of rope at 3d the pound, and 31 lbs of rope at 3d more, for three pullies for to hoist up the ship, 6d the piece, 13s 6d.

To Mr Springham for 19 ells ½ of taffeta to make clothes for the three singers in the ship, and for him that made the speech to his Majesty at 13s 4d the ell, the sum of £13 0s 0d.

To John Allen the chief singer in the ship, £4 0s 0d.

To Thomas Lupo the second singer in the ship being his Majesty's musician, £3 0s 0d.

To John Richards the third singer in the ship, £3 0s 0d.

To Mr Hemmyngs for his direction of his boy that made the speech to his Majesty 40s., and 5s given to John Rise the speaker, £2 5s 0d.

For setting of the songs that were sung to his Majesty by Mr Copiarario, £12 0s 0d.

To Mr Benjamin Jonson, the poet, for inventing the speech to his Majesty and for making the songs, and his directions to others in that business, £20 0s 0d.

Given his Majesty in a purse, £100 in 20s pieces, £100. Memorandum, that it was agreed that £50 should have been given to the Queen, but by reason that she came not, £50 was saved.

To Mr John Bull, Doctor of Music, to pay to him that set up the wind instrument in the King's chamber where the King dined and for tuning it, with the carriage of it from and to Ruccolds, £2 18s 0d.

To Mr Edney, Mr Lancere and four others of his Majesty's musicians, players of wind instruments, being placed over the screen, £10 0s 0d.

1609

The deporting of vagrants

Shortly before this feast, Captain Christopher Newport had sailed with the first contingent of settlers from Blackwall to Virginia. In 1609 the Virginia Company was in difficulties and sent a letter to the mayor and aldermen, both soliciting investors and asking the City – at the Crown's request – to carry the expense of getting rid of some of London's excess population by sending them to America. The Merchant

Taylors took up the investment opportunity but ignored the invitation to sponsor emigration. In the event, some 200 vagrant children were sent from the Bridewell Hospital to Virginia in 1619–22; that was all.

Letter from the Virginia Company to the Lord Mayor and Aldermen

Whereas the Lords of his Majesty's Council..., desirous to ease the City and suburbs of a swarm of unnecessary inmates, as a continual cause of dearth and famine, and the very original cause of all the plagues that happen in this kingdom, have advised your Lordship and your brethren in a case of state, to make some voluntary contribution for their remove into this Plantation of Virginia, which we understand you all seemeth to like as an action pleasing to God and happy for this commonwealth; we, the Council and Company of this honourable Plantation ... have entered into consultation with ourselves what may be the charge of every private man and what of every private family which we send herewith at large, not as a thing which we seek to exact from you, but that you may see as in a true glass the precise charge which we wholly commend to your grave wisdoms both for the sum and manner of levy ...

And if your Lordship and Brethren shall be pleased to put in any private adventures for yourselves in particular, you shall be sure to receive according to the proportion of the adventure equal part with us adventurers from the beginning both of the commodities returned and lands to be divided. And because you shall see, being aldermen of so famous a City, we give you due respect, we are contented, having one badge of grace and favour from his Majesty, to participate with you therein and to make as many of you as shall adventure fifty pounds or more, fellow councillors from the first day with us who have spent double and treble as much as is required, abiding the hazard of three several discoveries with much care and diligence and many days' attendance.

1615

City improvements

Sir George Buc or Buck (1563–1623) was one of many Jacobeans who took a lively interest and pride in London's development. Over and above his duties as Master of the Revels, Buck found time to write a treatise of 1615 called *The Third University of England*. He argues that so much is going on in London in the way of learning – he gives a brief history of the inns of court and colleges then existing – that all that is wanting is for James I to appoint a chancellor. He then gets carried away and lists all the capital projects which benefactors might undertake for the city's improvement. London had to wait over two centuries for its university, and a hundred years before new suburban churches were systematically built. But Buck's suggestion for a piazza found fruit in Covent Garden.

I have here provided for the help of their good inclination an inventory or note of divers necessary, charitable and honourable works fit to be done for and in this city of London, as namely:

To build a theatre for the more safe and certain and wholesome hearing of the sermons in Paul's Churchyard.

Item, to repair and beautify Paul's steeple and to refurnish the belfry thereof.

Item, to make a fair piazza or market place within London, such as is or ought to be in every good city, and to be placed as the manner is near to the town hall, viz. between the Guildhall and Bow Church.

Item, to pave Smithfield.

Item, to erect fair arched gates at the bounds of the Liberties, where now beast fences or wooden bars and rails stand.

Item, to enlarge the cumbersome and dangerous straits of the royal and more public ways of this city, as for examples those of Ludgate Hill, of St Martins-le-Grand, of New Fish Street Hill and Wood Street, and the most vulnerable car stocks of Thames Street, and especially and last of all that of the Old Change, that the hallowed ground of St Paul's Churchyard may no more be trampled and profaned with beasts and carts and coaches, to the end that through that street those coaches, carts and beasts may continually pass to their old and proper way of Carter Lane.

Item, to deliver the walls of the City and the town ditch from the pester and encumbrances of tenements and gardens and other private uses, and to open that ditch and to bring a river or fresh current into it.

And lastly (and which is a matter of great conscience and of necessity), to supply the suburbs with new parish churches, wherein by reason of the exceeding increase of new houses and tenements, the people and inhabitants are so extremely multiplied, as the old churches (whereunto these new houses and places and streets belong) are not able to contain the fourth part of the people, no, nor the tenth part of them in some of the suburbs.

1617

Building regulations

The ungovernable growth of London spurred Tudor and Stuart monarchs to issue a series of draconian edicts from 1580 onwards, inhibiting or forbidding new building. James I in particular was warm on the subject. The idea was that noblemen and gentlemen should dwell on their estates for as much of the year as possible, not hang around Westminster; the common people also would be easier to control if London were kept within bounds. The City authorities went along with this reasoning, if only because they had no jurisdiction over the erupting suburbs. Why then did London continue to grow? One reason was poor or intermittent policing. In addition, James I and Charles I could not resist granting exemptions from control in exchange for a fine; Covent Garden Piazza was built in this way. So the system was more flexible than it at first appears.

There was a blitz of royal initiatives on London's amenities in the years 1617–19, just after Inigo Jones had become surveyor to James I. Building regulations were passed specifying for the first time that new construction must be in brick with ample storey heights. The need for open space was pressed upon the City, and unauthorized new buildings were pulled down. The autocratic language in which the Privy Council couched its demands helps to explain why the Stuarts and their agents began to be unpopular among Londoners.

The Privy Council to the City of London and others, May 1617

Whereas divers gentlemen of the Inns of Court and Chancery and of four adjoining parishes . . . have of late been humble suitors to his Majesty that the fields commonly called Lincoln's Inn Fields, being parcel of his Majesty's inheritance, might for their general commodity and health be converted into walks after the same manner as Moorfields are now made, to the great pleasure and benefit of that city, which petition of theirs his Majesty did take in very gracious and acceptable part and did highly commend and allow of the same as a matter both of special benefit and ornament to that part of the city, and hath commanded us . . . to pray and entreat you to further the same, as well by your example as persuasion and mediation to the citizens and inhabitants of that city, for some such free and liberal contribution towards the charge thereof as may express their readiness and good affection to so worthy and commendable a work. And the rather in regard it will be a means to frustrate the covetous and greedy endeavours of such persons as daily seek to fill up that small remainder of air in those parts with unnecessary and unprofitable buildings, which have been found the greatest means of breeding and harbouring scarcity and infection, to the general inconvenience of the whole kingdom. And that the good affection of that city to a work of this consequence and public benefit may the better appear, we pray you to set down particularly what shall be so contributed by the City, and deliver the same to the bearer or bearers hereof, together with such sums of money as shall be gathered in that behalf.

The Privy Council to the High Sheriff of Middlesex, November 1617

Whereas there are certain tenements of timber erected in Milford Lane upon part of an old brewhouse standing near the waterside, and that contrary to his Majesty's proclamations, as well in respect of the manner of building, being of timber, not of brick, as also for that they are of one part only of an old house, become now several divided tenements, and the rest of the said house remaining still a brewhouse as it was before. Forasmuch as the contempt deserveth exemplary punishment, the rather because the builders as it appeareth by their confession had warning given to them to take heed of erecting that building contrary to the proclamation before the same was raised, and yet proceeded to the finishing thereof, these shall in his Majesty's name to will and command you according to

his own express pleasure signified and declared *viva voce* in the Star Chamber touching the proceeding against such insolent offenders, that you immediately repair unto the tenements aforementioned, and cause them to be demolished and pulled down unto the ground, that by this example others may learn to beware how they presumptuously offend his Majesty's laws and disobey his commandments.

1621

Merchant shipping on the Thames

The other view of London, dimly emerging in the early seventeenth century, was that it must be allowed every freedom to develop without inhibitions, for the good of the country's economy. Such was the thinking of Thomas Mun, the theorist of 'mercantilism'. Mun came from a mercer's family, traded prosperously with Italy and the Levant, and in 1615 became a director of the East India Company, founded fifteen years before. His *Discourse of Trade* (1621) is concerned with the benefits that England derived from foreign trade. It contains also the following snapshot of early East India shipping upon the Thames at Blackwall, downstream.

In trade of merchandise our ships must go and come, they are not made to stay at home. Yet nevertheless, the East India Company are well prepared at all times to serve his Majesty and his kingdoms with many warlike provisions, which they always keep in store, such as timber, planks, ironworks, masts, cordage, anchors, cask, ordnance, powder, victuals ready packed, cider and a world of other things, fitting the present building, repairing and dispatch of ships to sea: as may be plentifully seen in their yards and storehouses at Deptford, and more especially in those at Blackwall, which are grown so famous that they are daily visited and viewed by strangers, as well ambassadors as others, to their great admiration of his Majesty's strength and glory in one only company of his merchants, able at short warning to set forth a fleet of ships of great force and power.

For it is well known to all men who please truly to be informed, that the East India Company ... are continually building, repairing, rigging, victualling and furnishing to sea, with all provision needful for such a long voyage, some seven or eight ships yearly; which are to be seen at an anchor in the river of Thames in a great forwardness some five or six months together before they commonly depart for the Indies, which is about the month of March. And they are no sooner got off from the coast of England, but shortly after is the season of our ships to return from the Indies, who come not home so weak as some would have them, for how often hath experience been made of our ships which have performed two or three several voyages to the East Indies? Yet at their return they have been endocked, new trimmed and launched out again, fitted for the like voyages, in less than two months.

1625–1660

LONDON

between KING

and

PARLIAMENT

When Charles I succeeded his father in 1625, the wildest soothsayer would not have foretold that within the span of the next thirty-five years, England would have ejected the Stuarts and killed its king, flirted for ten years with modern republicanism and all but disestablished the state church, then changed its mind and gone back to the old ways. This national saga, sometimes tragic, sometimes muddled but always gripping, dominates London's history in the middle years of the seventeenth century.

What was London's role in the story? In physical terms London suffered extraordinarily little, given the bitterness of the Civil War and the strategic and political importance of the capital. After the king won his early victory at Edgehill in 1642, it looked as though London might be taken, but the royalists were too uncertain about what they wanted to press their luck. The elaborate earth fortifications rushed up afterwards were never tested. About the only action London saw was in the later clash between Army and Parliament in 1647, when Colonel Rainsborough secured the City via Southwark one night without loss of life. That is not to say that there were not riots, deaths, all the difficulties associated with the continual presence of soldiers, and a great deal of urban tension, notably in 1642–3 and 1647–9. But very little damage was done, and there is no doubt that London benefited from the war economy after a bad trade depression around 1641.

It is harder to say simply whose side London was on. At the start of the conflict there was a strong bond of anti-royalist anger between Parliament and the City, which more or less survived the war. Charles would never have left London in 1642 had not London been intensely against him. On the other hand, plenty of royalists remained behind, and many more people, perhaps the majority, hoped for a compromise. The City puritans were strong, articulate and well organized, as 'Mercurius Civicus' explains in his pamphlet of 1643, putting the main blame for the war upon London. But they were also divided; as time went on, the same differences emerged between them as those that emerged between factions in Parliament and in the Army. In 1650 there was indeed an argument over election rights and representation on the Common Council of the City that was very much like the celebrated debate that took place in Putney

ABOVE *Westminster Hall, Parliament and the Abbey behind. Engraving by Hollar.*

OPPOSITE *Charles I and Henrietta Maria dine in public at Whitehall Palace. Painting by Gerrit Houckgeest.*

LEFT *The new Covent Garden Piazza with St Paul's Church. Engraving by Hollar, c.1640.*

OPPOSITE *Charles I and Henrietta Maria hold court at St James's Palace. Note the fleurs-de-lys on the walls. From a French engraving.*

Church three years earlier between the Army regiments and commanders. In the period of the Second Civil War, the magistrates on the whole sided with Parliament. But the merchant classes kept a weather eye out for the Army and were quick to submit when trouble loomed over issues like soldiers' pay. One thing is certain: very few Londoners were happy to see Charles I executed. The memory of that dark event paved the psychological way to the Restoration.

Before the eruption of the war, there had been a growing tinge of glamour to court life and significant changes to the fabric of London. Charles I maintained his father's tight control over urban expansion. Inigo Jones was retained as court architect and was probably imposed upon the Earl of Bedford (no friend to the Crown) when the latter obtained a royal licence in the 1630s to lay out Covent Garden as London's first square. The new model of the brick town house that grew out of that development was in due course to become standard. More important for contemporaries was Jones's recasing of St Paul's, with a gigantic new portico in front. This was the symbolic climax of the policy, initiated by William Laud when he became Bishop of London in 1628, to do something about the filthy and neglected state of London's churches. Laud's intentions were often admirable and far-sighted, but his lack of tact and his autocratic temper led to great anger against him

and contributed to London's alienation from the king.

It is too easy to think of London under the Commonwealth as a drab place compared to London under the patronage of the early Stuart court. It may have felt like that at Westminster, but was hardly perceived so in the City, where – religious observance apart – the 1650s were a lively time that saw all sorts of innovations in technology and commerce and closer relations between merchants and the new breed of 'scientists', especially over navigation. The Port of London flourished, the colonizing spirit that had been awoken under James I was vigorous as ever, and there was a growing sense of rivalry with the sister seagoing republic of the Dutch. Nevertheless, something was wrong at heart. It hardly showed itself until Cromwell died. Then, with strange suddenness the whole polity frayed and puritan London found itself cheering itself hoarse, as Charles II rode back to triumph in 1660.

1625–6

A Catholic queen in a Protestant court

The teenage Henrietta Maria's arrival from France in 1625 as Charles I's consort, complete with an entourage of priests, sparked a fresh bout of anti-Catholic feeling. Such too was the early friction between the king and queen that some of her household was expelled, and a French delegation had to be sent over to patch things up. It was headed by the Chevalier de Bassompierre, a swashbuckling Alsatian who had enjoyed the favour of Henri IV. Bassompierre kept a mordant diary of the visit, complete with the usual French carelessness about foreign names. Among the allegations he had to deal with was that Henrietta Maria and her followers had paid a special visit to pray at Tyburn gallows, where many Catholics had been hanged. This the Queen vehemently denied.

Bassompierre's journal

October 7th 1626 I embarked on the Thames, and came by the warehouses for shipbuilding of the East Indies, then by *Grenwich*, a house of the King's, near which the Earl of *Dorchit*, Knight of the Garter, of the family of *Hacfil*, came to speak to me from the King, and having made me get into the King's barge, brought me close to the Tower of London where the King's carriages were waiting for me, which carried me to my lodgings where the said Earl of Dorchit left me. I was neither lodged nor entertained at the King's expense, and they were scarcely able to send this Earl of Dorchit, according to the usual custom, to receive me. However this did not prevent my being well lodged, furnished and accommodated.

November 9th, which is the election of the Mayor, I came in the morning to Sommerset [House] to meet the Queen, who had come there to see him go on the Thames on his way to Westminster to be sworn in, with a magnificent display of boats. Then the Queen dined, and afterwards got into her coach and placed me at the same door with her. The Duke of *Boukinkam* also by her commands got into her coach, and we went into the street called *Shipside* to see the ceremony, which is the greatest that is made at the reception of any officer in the world. While waiting for it to pass, the Queen played at primero with the Duke, the Earl of Dorchit and me; and afterwards the Duke took me to dine with the Lord Mayor, who that day gave a dinner to more than 800 persons.

Extract from allegations of English Commissioners to Bassompierre about the conduct of Henrietta Maria's retinue

They abused the influence which they had acquired over the tender and religious mind of Her Majesty so far as to lead her a long way on foot through a park, the gates of which had been expressly ordered by the Count de Tilliers to be kept open, to go in devotion to a place [Tyburn] where it has been the custom to execute the

most infamous malefactors and criminals of all sorts, exposed on the entrance of a high road: an act not only of shame and mockery towards the Queen, but of reproach and calumny of the King's predecessors of glorious memory, as accusing them of tyranny in having put to death innocent persons, whom these people look upon as martyrs; although, on the contrary, not one of them had been executed on account of religion, but of high treason. And it was this last act above all which provoked the royal resentment and anger beyond the bounds of his patience, which until then had enabled him to support all the rest.

Answer of Bassompierre

The Queen of Great Britain with the permission of the King her husband attended service at the Chapel of the Oratorian Fathers at St *Gemmes* with the devotion fit for a great princess, well-born and zealous in her religious observance as she is; which devotions ended at vespers. And a little time after, the heat of the sun having passed, she betook herself for a walk in the park of St Gemmes and from there to *Hipparc* adjacent, as she has at other times been wont to do, and often in the company of the King her husband. But that she was in procession, that anyone said public or private prayers, loudly or softly, that anyone came within fifty feet of the gallows, that they were on their knees with garlands or rosaries in their hands, not even slander has up to now dared to maintain . . . I am indeed sure, sirs, that finding nothing to blame in their actions or their words, you lay accusations against their most secret thoughts; and for ridding yourselves of the Queen's household, contrary to your promises, you grasp at this remarkable idea, that they may have thought of God on seeing a gallows. Miscreants and malefactors were hung there, you say; so much I accept, but that they prayed to God on their behalf I deny; had they done so, they should have done well.

1628

A Jesuit cell in Clerkenwell

From various episodes in the life of London in the 1620s and 30s, one can sense the coming religious and constitutional crisis. Puritanism, always at its most active and outspoken among the London merchant classes, was on the march again. Charles I, never so shrewd as his father, unwisely chose to meet it head on by appointing William Laud as Bishop of London in 1628. In the same year, the paranoia against Catholic conspiracy that had been so marked a feature of the Guy Fawkes story, found a new outlet when a Jesuit cell or 'college' in Clerkenwell was uncovered by government agents. Here is the account of its discovery given by Sir Robert Heath, the Attorney General.

About Christmas last Humphrey Cross, one of the messengers in ordinary, gave me notice that the neighbours in St John's saw provisions carried into the corner house upon the broadway above Clerkenwell, but knew none that dwelt there. In March following, about the beginning of Parliament, Cross brought word that divers lights were observed in the house, and that some company were gathered thither. The time considered, I thought fit to make no further delay, and therefore gave warrant to the said Cross with Mr Longe and the constables next adjoining to enter the house and to search what persons resorted thither, and to what end they concealed their being there. At their entry they found one that called himself Thomas Latham, who pretended to be keeper of the house for the Earl of Shrewsbury. They found another named George Kemp, said to be the gardener, and a woman called Margaret Isham. But when they desired to go further into the upper rooms, which (whilst they had made way

into the hall) were all shut up and made fast, Latham told them plainly that if they offered to go further they would find resistance and should do it at their perils. They thereupon repaired to my house and desired more help, and a more ample warrant for their proceedings . . . But by this protraction they within the upper rooms got advantage to retire themselves by secret passages into their vaults or lurking-places, which themselves called securities, so as when the officers came up they found no man above stairs save only a sick man in his bed, with one servant attending him. The sick man called himself by the name of Weeden, who is since discovered to be truly called Plowden. And the servant called himself John Penington, as in the examinations may appear. More they found not, till going down again into the cellars, Cross espied a brick wall newly made, which he caused to be pierced, and there within the vault they found Daniel Stanhope, whom I take to be Father Bankes, the Rector of their college, George Holland alias Guy Holt, Joseph Underhill alias Thomas Poulton, Robert Beaumond, and Edward Moore the priest. And the next day, in the like lurking-place, they found Edward Parre. All these Mr Longe examined, but could draw nothing from them saving formal denials that they were priests, or had taken any orders from the see of Rome, or that they knew one another, or that they came thither otherwise than casually upon acquaintance with Latham, who pretendeth that the house is the Earl his master's, and that the household stuff, Latin books and most of the pictures are his lordship's; but that the massing stuff, Jesuits' pictures, English books and manuscripts are all his own, given him by his dead master and by a friend beyond the seas. Yet upon their examinations they confessed themselves to be recusants and contradicted one another, and ministered matter sufficient for their legal conviction and for confiscation of the goods to His Majesty at the assizes at Newgate, when they were indicted and proceeded against.

1634

Collections of curiosities

London had no museums in the seventeenth century, but it did have a medley of sights and collections of curiosities that well-connected travellers and savants could arrange to see. One of the most remarkable was the Lambeth physic garden of the two John Tradescants, father and son. A place of great importance in the development of English horticulture, it was eked out also with the miscellany of art works, dubious relics and exotic specimens so much then loved. Peter Mundy, an indefatigable sea voyager, found leisure in 1634 while fleetingly in London to visit the Tradescant collection. He went on to admire an early camera obscura at Sir Henry Moody's in the Strand and take in the Tower of London – long the most popular of metropolitan sights. Mundy was then rapidly off on his travels again.

In the meantime I was invited by Mr Thomas Barlow (who went into India with my Lord of Denbigh and returned with us on the *Mary*) to view some rarities at John Tradescant's, so went with him and one friend more, where we spent that whole day in perusing, and that superficially, such as he had gathered together, as beasts, fowl, fishes, serpents, worms (real, although dead and dried), precious stones and other arms, coins, shells, feathers etc. of sundry nations, countries, form, colours; also divers curiosities in carving, painting etc., as 80 faces carved on a cherry stone, pictures to be seen by a cylinder which otherwise appear to be confused blots, medals of sundry sorts, etc. Moreover a little garden with divers outlandish herbs and flowers, whereof some that I had not seen elsewhere but in India, being supplied by noblemen, gentlemen, sea commanders etc., with such toys as they could bring or procure from other parts. So that I am almost persuaded a man might in one day behold and collect into one place more curiosities than he should see if he spent all his life in travel …

Also at Sir Henry Moody's, lying in the Strand, one of his gentlemen showed me divers conceits of his master's. Among the rest, the room being made quite dark, only one little hole in it with a glass through which a light struck to the opposite side where was placed white paper, and thereon was represented as in a glass all that was without, as boats rowing on the Thames, men riding on the other side, trees etc., but all reversed or upside down, in their true colours.

Not long after I went to the Tower of London, where I saw a unicorn's horn, about 1½ yards in length and 2 or 2½ inches diameter at the bigger end, going taperwise and wreathed, although somewhat smooth (I think by often handling). It was white, resembling the substance of an elephant's tooth, estimated at 18 or 20,000 pounds sterling. This, as all the rest are, is conceived to be rather the horn of some fish than of a beast, because such a beast nowadays is not to be found, although discoveries at present are in far greater perfection than they were then.

1634

Early traffic disputes

One consequence of Elizabethan and Jacobean London's growth and greater wealth was the onset of serious traffic problems. Before about 1580 there were carts but very few coaches; people on ordinary business either walked or rode. Yet by 1631 coaches were common enough for householders in Blackfriars to petition the Privy Council about the nuisance fashionable people caused when they came by coach to the theatre there. Hackney carriages, ancestors of the modern taxicab, proliferated until Cromwell brought them under control with a licence system. And in 1634, complicating street life still further, French-style sedans came in. This novelty inspired Henry Peacham, under the pseudonym 'Mis-Amaxias', to write a comic dialogue entitled *Coach and Sedan*. Among the cast of characters are 'coach and sedan pleasantly disputing for place and precedence, the brewer's cart being the moderator', and a surveyor who gripes about traffic jams.

It was just about the time when the cuckoo (not daring to come nearer the City than Islington) warned the milkmaids it was high time to be gone with their pails into Finsbury … when myself with an English tailor

Title page of Coach and Sedan, *1636, by Henry Peacham.*

and a Frenchman ... coming down Jackanapes Lane, we perceived two lusty fellows to jostle for the wall, and almost ready to fall together by the ears.

The one (the lesser of the two) was in a suit of green after a strange manner, windowed before and behind with isinglass, having two handsome fellows in green coats attending him. The one went ever before, the other came behind. Their coats were laced down the back with a greenlace suitable, so were their half-sleeves, which persuaded me at first they were some cast suits of their masters. Their backs were harnessed with leather cingles cut out of a hide, as broad as Dutch collars of bacon, whereat I wondered not a little, being but newly come out of the country and not having seen the like before.

The other was a thick, burly square-set fellow in a doublet of black leather, brass-buttoned down the breast, back, sleeves and wings, with monstrous wide boots, fringed at the top with a net fringe and a round breech (after the old fashion) gilded, and on his backside an achievement of sundry coats in their proper colours, quartered with crest, helm and mantle, besides here and there on the sides a single escutcheon or crest, with some emblematical word or other. I supposed they were made of some pendant or banners that had been stolen from some monument where they had been long hung in a church. He had only one man before him, wrapped in a red cloak with wide sleeves turned up at the hands and cudgelled thick on the back and shoulders with broad shining lace (not much unlike that which mummers make of straw hats) and of each side of him went a lackey. The one, a French boy (as I learnt afterward), when his master was in the country, taught his lady and her daughter French, ushered them abroad to public meetings and assemblies, all saving the church, whither she never came. The other went on errands, helped the maid to beat bucks, fetch in water, carried up meat and waited at the table ...

Surveyor: ... it is most fit and requisite that princes, nobility, the more eminent and abler among the gentry should be allowed their coaches and caroches, and all others who hold any place of dignity, either in church or commonwealth, as our bishops, the reverend judges, doctors of divinity, law, physic, with the chief magistrates of eminent and honourable cities, with other of like and equal rank. But what, I pray you, are the coaches of these few to the multitude at this day in England, when in London, the suburbs and within four miles' compass without are reckoned to the number of 6,000 and odd?

I easily (quoth I) believe it, when in certain places of the City, as I have often observed, I have never come but I have there the way barricadoed up with a coach, two, or three, that what haste or business so ever a man hath, he must wait my lady's (I know not whose) leisure (who is in the next shop, buying pendants for her ears or a collar for her dog) ere he can find any passage.

The most eminent places for stoppage are Paul's-gate into Cheapside, Ludgate and Ludgate Hill, especially when the play is done at the Friars, then Holborn Conduit and Holborn Bridge is villainously pestered with them, Hosier Lane, Smithfield and Cow Lane sending all about their new or old mended coaches, then about the Stocks and Poultry, Temple Bar, Fetter Lane and Shoe Lane next to Fleet Street. But to see their multitude either when there is a masque at Whitehall, a Lord Mayor's feast, a new play at some of the playhouses, you would admire to see them, how close they stand together (like mutton pies in a cook's oven), that hardly you can thrust a pole between them.

1628–44

The rise and fall of William Laud

As Bishop of London between 1628 and 1633, William Laud was dynamic but inflexible. He was shocked by the state of St Paul's and procured the court architect, Inigo Jones, to remodel it. He also insisted, with Charles I's support, on the reinstatement of proper chancels in churches throughout his diocese. Many documents attest the haughty resolution with which Laud pursued his goals and the resistance that he met. First, the text of a notice posted in St Paul's in about 1632.

His Majesty's special command is, that these articles following be observed by all, upon pain of his displeasure, and such danger as shall follow.

I. His Majesty's pleasure is, that no man of what quality so ever shall presume to walk in the aisles of the choir, or in the body or aisles of the church, during the time of divine service or the celebration of the blessed sacrament or sermons, or any part of them, neither do anything that may disturb the service of the church or diminish the honour due to so holy a place.

II. His Majesty's pleasure is, that no man presume to profane the church by the carriage of burdens or baskets, or any portage whatsoever.

III. That all parents and masters of families do strictly forbid their children and servants to play at any time in

Inigo Jones's design for the colossal west portico for St Paul's.

the church, or any way misdemean themselves in that place, in time of divine service or otherwise. And if any children or servants shall be found so doing, besides the punishment of delinquents, their parents and masters shall be subject to such censures and punishments as is thought fit to be inflicted.

These articles, by command of His Majesty, are now published to the intent that no man may hereafter pretend ignorance for his excuse in any of them.

Laud was soon promoted by Charles I to be Archbishop of Canterbury and for a while seemed to enjoy unassailable power. But the London puritans, encouraged by their leader

William Prynne, made common cause with Parliament, gathered strength and began to strike back. By 1640 the king, absent in Scotland, could not support Laud and he became the object of open hatred. His diary entries convey the shock of his sharp descent from royal support and from the pomp of Lambeth Palace to vilification, charges of treason, and long confinement in the Tower once the Civil War had begun. They stop abruptly in 1643, when Laud's diary was confiscated.

May 11 [1640] At midnight my house at Lambeth was beset with 500 of these rascal routers. I had notice, and strengthened the house as well as I could, and God be thanked, I had no harm; they continued there full two hours. Since, I have fortified my house as well as I can, and hope all may be made safe. But yet libels are continually set up in all places of note in the city.

August 22 A vile libel brought me, found in Covent Garden, animating the apprentices and soldiers to fall upon me in the King's absence.

May 1 [1643] My chapel windows at Lambeth defaced, and the steps torn up.

May 2 The Cross in Cheapside taken down.

May 9 All my goods seized upon, books and all.

Palatium Archiepiscopi Cantuariensis propè Londinum vulgè Lambeth House.

LEFT *Lambeth Palace not long after Archbishop Laud's execution. Engraving by Hollar, 1647.*

BELOW *A godly Puritan contrasted with the worldly or devilish Laud.*

December 18 I was accused by the House of Commons for high treason, without any particular charge laid against me ... Soon after, the charge was brought into the Upper House by the Scottish Commissioners, tending to prove me an incendiary. I was presently committed to the Gentleman Usher, but was permitted to go in his company to my house at Lambeth for a book or two to read in, and such papers as pertained to my defence against the Scots. I stayed at Lambeth till the evening to avoid the gazing of the people ... As I went to my barge, hundreds of my poor neighbours stood there and prayed for my safety and return to my house, for which I bless God and them.

March 1 [1641] I went in Mr Maxwell's coach to the Tower. No noise, till I came into Cheapside. But from thence to the Tower, I was followed and railed at by the apprentices and rabble in great numbers to the very Tower gates, where I left them.

March 13 Divers Lords dined with the Lord Herbert at his new house by Vauxhall in Lambeth. Three of these Lords in the boat together, when one of them saying he was sorry for my commitment because the building of St Paul's went on slow therewhile, the Lord Brooke replied, 'I hope some of us shall live to see no one stone left upon another of that building.'

May 12 The Earl of Strafford beheaded upon Tower Hill.

Of God, Of Man, Of the Divell.

The penultimate act of the story of Archbishop Laud was his trial in 1644, to be followed by his execution the next year. Some of the lesser accusations made at the trial show that Londoners had neither forgotten nor forgiven his former peremptoriness. Among them were parishioners from the puritan stronghold of St Gregory's, where many houses were pulled down and their church had to be repaired because of the works on the cathedral next to it. Riverside brewers from Westminster and Lambeth, whom Laud had hounded in his excessive zeal to check pollution from sea coal, were also bitter for revenge.

CONCERNING THE PULLING DOWN OF HOUSES
BY THE ARCHBISHOP'S MEANS

John Bentley deponed that above sixty houses near St Gregory's Church were pulled down ten to twenty years distant, but he knows not by what order. Gerard Gore deponed that 60 houses were pulled down. The church of St Gregory's cost £1,700 repairing. That the Archbishop said that there was never a house there above sixty years' standing. He said it was by virtue of an order of the Council table subscribed by the Archbishop. Captain Walter Bigg deponed that he heard the archbishop say that 'I was opposed in the pulling down the houses near Paul's Church'.

LAUD'S ANSWER

The recompense made was for more than sixty houses were worth and they were pulled down by virtue of the Great Seal. In III Elizabeth 3 [Act of Parliament] no houses were suffered to be within the churchyard within the wall which was beyond the drapers' shops. In former times, one made a chimney in one of the houses near Paul's church and it was complained of in Westminster Hall. It was not his fault that they had no service in so long a time. He was against the pulling it down at the Council table, but Inigo Jones would have it pulled down. He acknowledged he set on the repair of Paul's, and therefore might say he was opposed in it.

CONCERNING THE BREWERS' BUSINESS

Edward Bond deponed that about six years [ago] he was called to the Council table because the smoke of two brewhouses did offend the King's houses and they must be pulled down, or else he must enter into a bond of £1,000 never to brew with sea coals; he refusing, he was ordered to be committed close prisoner until he did seal the bond. His Majesty told him he should brew peaceably again and passed by his offence, but the Archbishop told him he would take another course with him. An information was in the Star [Chamber] against him by Sir John Bankes. At last he was forced to agree to give £1,000 to the repair of Paul's, to save his house from pulling down.

LAUD'S ANSWER

It might be he told Bond of entering into a bond of £1,000 for not brewing with sea coal but it was but the saying of the board... If he offered it willingly, where is the forcing and oppression? He believes he did not pay a groat.

MICHAEL ARNOLD

Michael Arnold deponed that the Archbishop told him he must enter into bond £2,000 not to burn sea coals in his brewhouse. That Secretary Windebank said that the Archbishop told him he did burn sea coal. That in the frost Mr Attorney came to Lambeth to his house, and told him that the Archbishop told him he did burn sea coal 'and it did annoy him'. He came to the Archbishop and offered him £10 per annum to Paul's that he might burn sea coals, and the Archbishop told him that he 'might give £20 now the other brewers are put down'.

LAUD'S ANSWER

Mr Attorney and he walking in his garden at Lambeth, they were sufficiently smoked by the brewhouse. This [the offering of money by Arnold] is a sign that there [is] stronger proof against him, than anything the Archbishop could say.

1642–9

London in the Civil War

The protracted quarrel between King and Parliament finally erupted into war when Charles I raised his standard at Nottingham in 1642. London, as the chief centre of opposition, drew in anti-royalists from all over the country, and regiments were formed in haste. It was correctly anticipated that the King would advance smartly to reclaim his capital. After his tactical victory at Edgehill in October, Charles moved slowly south. Many then thought that there would be a rapprochement rather than a drawn-out conflict, but the trained bands and new regiments were put on sharp alert. In the event a sharp skirmish when the royalists took Brentford ended negotiations before they had really begun and steeled the hearts of Parliament and the City. As Clarendon explains, a strong force was sent out from London to Turnham Green, where an inconclusive stand-off took place between the two sides.

The alarum [of the taking of Brentford] came to London with the same dire yell as if the army were entered their gates, and the King was accused of treachery, perfidy and blood, and that he had given the spoil and wealth of the City as pillage to his army, which advanced with no other purpose. They who believed nothing of those calumnies were not yet willing the King should enter the City with an army, which they knew would not be governable in so rich quarters. Therefore, with unspeakable expedition, the army under the Earl of Essex was not only drawn together but all the train-bands of London were led out in their brightest equipage upon the heath next Brentford. There they had indeed a full army of horse and foot, fit to have decided the title of a crown with an equal adversary. The view and prospect of this strength, which nothing but that sudden emergency could have brought together, so that the army was really raised by King and Parliament, extremely puffed them up, not only as it was an ample security against the present danger, but as it looked a safe power to encounter any emergency. They had then before their eyes the King's little handful of men, and then began to wonder and blush at their own fears, and all this might be without excess of courage, for their numbers then, without the advantage of equipage (which to soldiers is a great addition of mettle) were five times greater than the King's harassed, weatherbeaten and half-starved troops.

I have heard many knowing men, and some who were then in the City regiments, say that if the King had advanced and charged that massy body, it had presently given ground, and that the King had so great a party in every regiment that it would have made no resistance. But it would have been madness, which no success could have vindicated, to have made that attempt; and the King easily discerned that he had brought himself into straits and difficulties which would be hardly mastered, and exposed his victorious army to a view at too near a distance of his two enemies, the Parliament and the City. Yet he stood all that day in battalia to receive them, who only played upon him with their cannon, to the loss only of four or five horses and not one man. The constitution of their forces (where there were very many not at all affected to the company they were in) was a good argument to them not to charge the King; and, for the same reason, it would have been an ill plan for the King to charge them.

When the evening drew on, and it appeared that great body stood only for the defence of the City, the King appointed his army to draw off to Kingston, which the rebels had kindly quitted ... After a day's stay at Hampton Court, the King removed himself to his house at Oatlands, leaving the greater part of his army still at Kingston and thereabouts. But being then informed of the high imputations they had laid upon him of breach of faith by his march to Brentford, and that the City was really inflamed with an opinion that he meant to have surprised them and to have sacked the town ... he gave direction for all his forces to retire to Reading.

Though the king drew off after Turnham Green, never to return to his capital except as a prisoner, the parliamentary side still felt weak and vulnerable. London had no defences beyond the obsolete City wall. To meet the need, the authorities commandeered a mixture of voluntary, military and pressganged labour to build an impromptu ring of earthworks from Wapping to Westminster on the north and from Lambeth to Rotherhithe on the south. The ring was finished by June 1643, when William Lithgow, a Scottish traveller, looked over all the fortifications and marvelled at their completeness and at the energy London had displayed.

The City hath many Courts du Guard with new barricadoed posts and they strongly girded with great chains of iron, and all the opening passages at street ends for the fields and roadways are in like manner strictly watched. The sides of the river as at Billingsgate and other places have also Courts du Guard and they nightly guarded with companies of the trained band ... Beyond the river in the borough of Southwark is the selfsame discipline observed and all under the command of the City. So is Westminster, the Strand and all the liberties there now taken in under the custody of London ... I found the street-enravelled court before Whitehall Gate guarded with a Court du Guard, a novelty beyond novelties, and what was more rarer, I found the grass growing deep in the royal courts of the King's house ... The daily musters and shows of all sorts of Londoners here were wondrous and commendable in marching to the fields and outworks (as merchants, silkmen, mercers, shopkeepers etc.) with great activity carrying on their shoulders iron mattocks and wooden shovels, with roaring drums, flying colours and girded swords; most companies being interlarded with ladies, women and girls, two and two carrying baskets to advance the labour, where divers wrought till they fell sick of their pains ...

Marching along the circulary line, I grieved to see so many rich grounds of grass utterly spoiled with the erection of these works, in so much that horse and cattle certain else will come short of their food there for seven years and the owners thereof must fall pitifully short of their yearly profits, for where trouble is there cometh misery. Having left the aforesaid fort [near Tottenham Court Road] I saluted the Banqueting House fortress, composed of two forts upon Tyburn Way and Marylebone Fields. Here I found both the forts answerable to other, the way only dividing them and they both pallisaded, double-ditched and barricaded with iron pikes, the one clad with eight demi-culverins and the other fenced with four demi-culverins of iron, both wondrous defensible.

As the war drew on, and it looked less likely that Charles

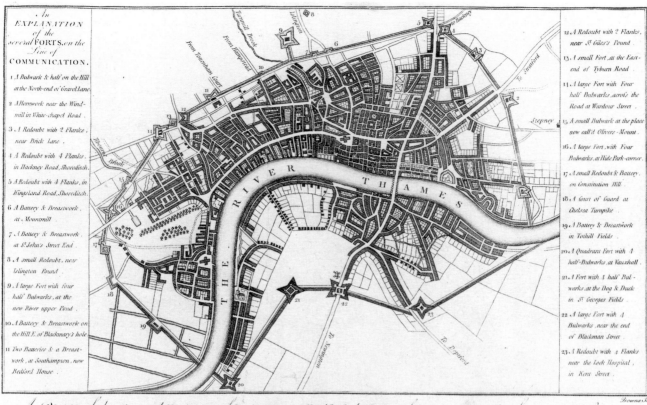

An
EXPLANATION
of the
several FORTS *on the*
Line of
COMMUNICATION.

1 *A Bulwark & half on the Hill*
at the North-end of Gravel Lane.

2 *A Hornwork near the Wind-*
mill in White-chapel Road.

3 *A Redoubt with 2 Flanks,*
near Brick Lane.

4 *A Redoubt with 4 Flanks,*
in Hackney Road, Shoreditch.

5 *A Redoubt with 4 Flanks, in*
Kingsland Road, Shoreditch.

6 *A Battery & Breastwork,*
at Mountmill.

7 *A Battery & Breastwork*
at St. John's Street End.

8 *A small Redoubt, near*
Islington Pound.

9 *A large Fort with four*
half Bulwarks, at the
new River upper Pond.

10 *A Battery & Breastwork on*
the Hill E. of Blacknary's hole.

11 *Two Batteries & a Breast-*
work, at Southampton, now
Bedford House.

12 *A Redoubt with 2 Flanks,*
near St. Giles's Pound.

13 *A small Fort, at the East-*
end of Tyburn Road.

14 *A large Fort with Four*
half Bulwarks, across the
Road at Wardour Street.

15 *A small Bulwark at the place*
now call'd Olivers-Mount.

16 *A large Fort, with Four*
Bulwarks, at Hide-Park-corner.

17 *A small Redoubt & Battery*
on Constitution Hill.

18 *A Court of Guard at*
Chelsea Turnpike.

19 *A Battery & Breastwork*
in Tothill Fields.

20 *A Quadrant Fort with 4*
half-Bulwarks, at Vauxhall.

21 *A Fort with 4 half Bul-*
warks, at the Dog & Duck
in St. Georges Fields.

22 *A large Fort with 4*
Bulwarks, near the end
of Blackman Street.

23 *A Redoubt with 4 Flanks*
near the Lock Hospital,
in Kent Street.

A PLAN *of the* City *and* Environs *of* LONDON, *as* Fortified *by Order of* PARLIAMENT, *in the* Years *1642 & 1643.*

would be able to resume his throne, unhappy royalists in London – of whom there were many – fell to analysing what had gone wrong and who was to blame. One such went by the pen name of Mercurius Civicus. In a pamphlet of 1643 that poses as a letter to his friend Mercurius Rusticus, he attempted to assess why 'the beginning and the obstinate pursuance of this horrid rebellion is principally to be ascribed to that rebellious City'.

If we shall without partiality consider the several helps which this City hath contributed to this rebellion, we must confess that both the beginning and continuance of this unnatural war may be ascribed to us; so that in all England there is but one rebel, and that is London . . .

For first you may well remember when the Puritans here did as much abominate the Military Yard or Artillery Garden, as Paris Garden itself; they would not mingle with the profane. But at last when it was instilled into them, that the blessed reformation intended could not be effected but by the sword, these places were instantly filled with few or none but of that faction. We were wont, you know, to make very merry at their training; some of them in two years' practice could not be brought to discharge a musket without winking. We

George Vertue's map of the fortifications of London ordered by Parliament after Edgehill, 1642–3.

did little imagine then, that they were ever likely to grow formidable to the state . . .

Secondly, that they might fill all places of authority with such as should advance the design, all care is taken to fill the bench of the Common Council with men disaffected to the government, both ecclesiastical and civil . . . Nay, some will tell you, and I am much of their opinion, that the faction have had so great care in this, that they have chosen some men to places of the best esteem in the City, whose estates were not able to defray the charges, but have been supported by a common purse . . .

Thirdly, because all this could not compass the end they aimed at, unless the clergy did conspire with them and contribute their help (except Dr Gough, Mr Jackson, Votier, Simons, Walker and a very few more compliant with their endeavours), they laboured by all means possible to introduce that *gibbus* or excrescency of the clergy called lecturers over their parochial ministers' heads, whose maintenance being dependent . . . must preach such doctrine as may foment disloyalty,

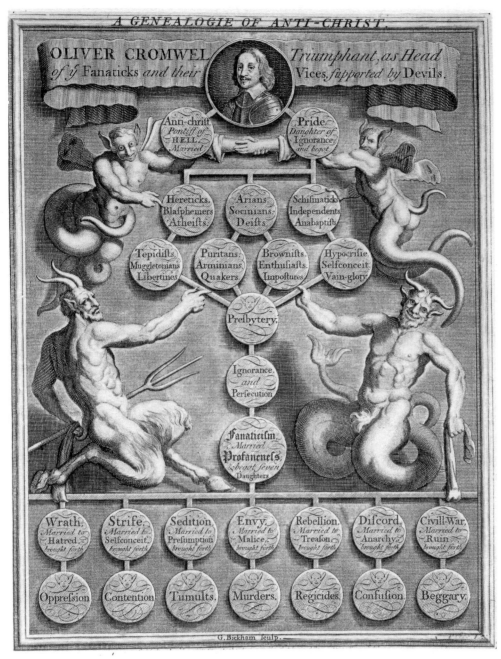

A GENEALOGIE OF ANTI-CHRIST

OLIVER CROMWEL, *of ÿ* Fanaticks *and their* Triumphant, *as* Head *Vices, supported by* Devils.

Oliver Cromwell as retrospectively depicted by royalist propagandists.

and instill such principles into their auditors as may first dispose them to, and after engage them in, rebellion when things were ripe, or else they shall want bread to put into their heads. The truth is, Brother Rusticus, these military preparations had effected little, had not the fire been given from the pulpit . . .

If therefore posterity shall ask, who broke down the bounds to those streams of blood that have stained this earth, if they ask who made liberty captive, truth criminal, rapine just, tyranny and oppression lawful . . . if they ask, who would have pulled the crown from the King's head, taken the government off the hinges,

dissolved the monarchy, enslaved the laws, and ruined their country: say, 'twas the proud, unthankful, schismatical, rebellious, bloody City of London, so that what they wanted of devouring this kingdom by cheating and cozening, they mean to finish by the sword.

For London, the tensest time of the entire Civil War came in the summer and autumn of 1647. Charles I had been beaten and captured, but his opponents were divided and in danger of rending one another. In the victorious Army, religious and political radicals were increasingly vocal but not strong enough to shake off the discipline of Cromwell, Ironside and Fairfax. Parliament, under Presbyterian influence, tried to assert its independence but lacked the power of force. Meanwhile, the City teetered between the two. When Parliament refused to address its grievances, the Army started to move ominously from Saffron Walden towards London in June, whence friends sent the following newsletter.

Our chief news here is of your Army, and I can assure you we have twenty stories in a day and scarce ever a true one; but your coming near London I promise you put the Parliament and City into a shrewd fright. The Parliament sat hard at it Friday and Saturday, and so did the Militia and Common Council; it was much urged to raise forces against you, and they would have done it if they could have found any way how. Many officers Friday and Saturday listed themselves at the Committee at Derby House, and the Militia were consulting how to put the City into a posture, and to arm all, and have also listed some, but they find so much difficulty in the manner, they have laid all aside again, and now intend to come to you with good words and are sending an answer to your letter by four aldermen and eight councilmen ... On Saturday morning things wrought after another manner, for upon the report of your being near, all the trained bands of London were commanded to rise up on pain of death and all the shops to be shut up ... but this design came to nothing, for the trained bands would not budge, not ten men of some companies appeared, and many companies none at all but the officers; nay, the very boys in the streets jeered the drums as they went about with their charge upon pain of death. The Westminster Regiment made a great appearance, and the Lord Mayor was in person very active to compel the shopkeepers to shut up shop, by which means most about the Exchange and Cornhill were shut, but few in other places; and those that did shut up were of the right stamp, and these many of them, understanding upon what slight ground that command was and being laughed at by others, opened their shops again in the afternoon, when also the trained bands were discharged, but stronger guards kept than formerly.

The Army now cautiously advanced to the west of London, just as the royalists had done in 1642. Charles I was once again at Hampton Court, but now confined there under a delicate kind of house arrest. Cromwell and Fairfax took their time. Then, early in August they sent Colonel Thomas Rainsborough, a Wapping man who was a rising star in the Army on account of his bravery and radicalism, to secure London by an indirect route, from the south. The task was performed with dispatch, as Clarendon relates.

They quartered their Army about Brentford and Hounslow, Twickenham and the adjacent villages, without restraining any provisions – which every day, according to custom, were carried to London – or doing the least action that might disoblige or displease the City. The Army was in truth under so excellent discipline that nobody could complain of any damage sustained by them, or any provocation by word or deed. However, in this calm they sent over Colonel Rainsborough with a brigade of horse and foot and cannon at Hampton Court to possess Southwark and those works which secured that end of London Bridge. This he did with so little noise that in one night's march he found himself master, without any opposition, not only of the borough of Southwark but of all the works and forts which were to defend it, the soldiers within shaking hands with those without, and refusing to obey their officers which were to command them. The City, without knowing that any such thing was in agitation, found in the morning that all that avenue to the town was possessed by the enemy that they were providing to resist on the other side, being as confident of this that they had lost as of any gate to the City.

1648

The purging of Parliament

The year 1648 saw the Army tighten its hold on London. The unpredictability of Parliament and the rash of little royalist uprisings that followed Charles's secret and futile negotiations with the Scots, caused outbreaks of urban violence and determined Cromwell to quarter regular troops in Westminster. In December of that year came the purging of Parliament and the extension of Army control to the City, preparatory to the final showdown of the royal trial and execution. This is how an anonymous correspondent of the pro-Army party saw the events of that month:

Mr Prynne, the firebrand of England, Major-General Massey, Mr Gewen, Sir John Clotworthy and in all about 40 members were seized upon by the Army going to the House; and others desired to forbear to come thither who were men who were of the same stamp or the same faction. Upon Thursday the House sat, and

ABOVE *Cromwell dissolves the Long Parliament, 1652. From a Dutch engraving.*

RIGHT *The beheading of Charles I before the Banqueting House in Whitehall. A Stuart icon.*

though it was an undoubted breach of their privilege to have the Members thus seized, yet the Members had so abused the privilege by their perpetuity there, taking advantage thereby not only to wrong the subject but to vent malice and passion in particular without control, as it was frequent with these time-serving Members; whereupon the House resolved to proceed with the business of the Army's Remonstrance and the settlement of the kingdom, and to let their Members alone till another opportunity.

On Friday the House kept a fast and adjourned till Tuesday, the army being passive all this while, charging the suburbs with provisions and lying upon bare boards in Whitehall, St James' etc., hoping the City would not fail to send moneys for the paying of the Army (considering the City was £100,000 in arrears) and beds, that so the soldiers might be accommodated as not to be necessitated to come into London; which the Army to avoid by all means possible had patience from Saturday to Friday last, and the City of London in all that time not being able (or rather not willing) to advance one 10-days pay out of all their arrears, necessitating the Army to resolve to march into the City and there to quarter, which accordingly they did on Friday last in Paul's, Blackfriars and in parts thereabouts. When the City saw the Army was in good earnest and that their own folly by not advancing that which they owed unto the Army

had wrought this upon them, then they began to vote to raise £10,000 and to provide bedding for the soldiers, hoping the Army would retire out of the City. But the Army being hitherto deceived with their dilatoriness, understood where £27,000 was in bank at Weavers Hall, went and seized upon the same, that the City might see that though they could not raise £10,000 (10 days' pay) for the Army, yet the Army could tell how to find a month's pay ready in cash. This terrified the malignant merchants and goldsmiths, fearing their estates should be seized upon, though there was no real cause to suspect them, said in so humble a manner that they all professed themselves to be servants of the Army. Hereupon the General sent some colonels unto the City to assure them never a goldsmith should lose the value of a thimble or merchant 2d in his goods, who did not obstinately refuse to pay the just arrears that were behind from the City to the Army.

1649

Execution of Charles I

Of the several accounts of Charles 1's execution in January 1649 on the scaffold outside the Banqueting House, none is simpler or more moving than that of Philip Henry. Henry was just seventeen at the time and a student at Oxford. His father had held a minor post at Whitehall Palace and lived in a small house there; on occasions Philip had played with the royal children. Though not a sympathizer with the royalist cause – he was to become a dissenting divine – he, like everyone present, was moved by the tragic spectacle of the event and dismayed by the ruthlessness with which the Army dispersed the onlookers.

At the latter end of the year 1648 I had leave given me to go to London to see my father, and during my stay there at that time at Whitehall it was that I saw the beheading of King Charles I. He went by our door on foot each day that he was carried by water to Westminster, for he took barge at Garden Stairs where we lived, and once spake to my father and said 'Art thou alive yet?'. On the day of his execution, which was Tuesday, Jan. 30, I stood amongst the crowd in the street before Whitehall Gate where the scaffold was erected, and saw what was done but was not so near as to hear anything. The blow I saw given, and can truly say with a sad heart; at the instant whereof, I remember well, there was such a groan given by the thousands then present as I never heard before and desire I may never hear again. There was according to order one troop immediately marching fromwards Charing Cross to Westminster and another fromwards Westminster to Charing Cross purposely to master the people and disperse and scatter them, so that I had much ado amongst the rest to escape home without hurt.

1650

An employment agency

Despite the suppression of London's religious and royal entertainments during the interregnum, there was intense economic vigour, prosperity and innovation in the merchant community, so much so that glimpses of the modern financial City of London now appear. In 1650, for instance, an ingenious radical merchant called Henry Robinson floated the first known information and job centre in Threadneedle Street. We do not know how long it lasted, but this is how he advertised it.

The Office of

ADDRESSES

and

ENCOUNTERS

where all people of each rank and quality may receive direction and advice for the most cheap and speedy way of attaining whatsoever they can lawfully desire

OR

The only course for poor people to get speedy employment and to keep others from approaching poverty, for want of EMPLOYMENT

To the multiplying of trade, the advancement of navigation, and the establishing this famous City of LONDON in a more plentiful and flourishing condition than ever, as is earnestly desired and shall be diligently endeavoured by a well-willer of hers

HENRY ROBINSON.

The optimistic inventor believed the uses of his office could 'extend as far as human necessity, which is little less than infinite'. Below are a few of the specific services he offered.

* To entertain, or to be entertained, professors of the liberal sciences and languages, chaplains, tutors, schoolmasters, gentleman ushers, stewards, butlers, cooks, barbers, serving men, or as factors, agents or as journeymen of any manner of occupations.
* To entertain, or to be entertained, waiting gentlewomen, schoolmistresses, nurse-keepers, nurses, chambermaids, dairymaids, cookmaids or for any other kind of lawful services.
* To employ or be employed as captains, masters of ships, masters' mates, factors, pursers, boatswains, surgeons, gunners, cooks, pilots or common mariners.
* To be sent, or send others abroad, into any of our plantations.
* Here, whosoever desires to travel or make a journey, may give in his name beforehand and have notice what other company there is for any of the principal roads or towns of England or any foreign parts.
* Here may resort such poor people as desire relief, and to know what means and legacies are given to pious uses; and such as would willingly meet fit objects of their charity and bounty.
* Such as desire to dispose of themselves or friends in marriage may here likewise be informed what encounters there are to be had, both of persons and portions.

1657

Wren's astronomical view

Several great Londoners whom we think of as quintessential Restoration figures were already active in the last years of the Commonwealth. One such was Christopher Wren. As yet, the future architect's thoughts had not turned to building. It was as a brilliant young astronomer that he first made his mark, and as Professor of Astronomy at Gresham College – in many ways the precursor of the Royal Society – that he came in 1657 to live and work in London. The closing sentences of his inaugural address are more than a learned panegyric. They uphold the connection between commerce, mathematical skill, technological ability and invention that Wren and other enlightened spirits of the age admired and wanted to see promoted in London.

And now, since the professorship I am honoured with is a benefit I enjoy from this City, I cannot conclude without a good omen to it. I must needs celebrate it as a City particularly favoured by the celestial influences, a Pandora on which each planet hath contributed something. Saturn hath given it diuturnity, and to reckon an earlier era *ab urbe condita* than Rome itself. Jupiter hath made it the perpetual seat of kings and of courts of justice, and filled it with inexhaustible wealth. Mars has armed it with power. The Sun looks benignly on it, for what city in the world so vastly populous doth enjoy so healthy an air, so fertile a soil? Venus hath given it a pleasant situation, watered by the most amene river of Europe and beautified with the external splendour of myriads of fine buildings. Mercury hath nourished it in mechanical arts and trade to be equal with any city in the world, nor hath forgotten to furnish it abundantly with liberal sciences, amongst which I must congratulate this City that I find in it so general a relish of mathematics and the *libera philosophia* in such a measure as is hardly to be found in the academies themselves.

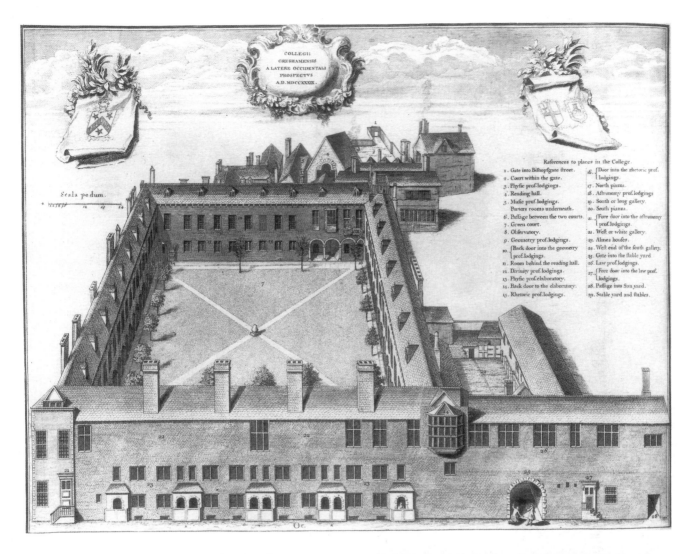

References to places in the College.

1. Gate into Bishopsgate street.
2. Court within the gate.
3. Physic prof. lodgings.
4. Reading hall.
5. Music prof. lodgings. Porters rooms underneath.
6. Passage between the two courts.
7. Green court.
8. Observatory.
9. Geometry prof. lodgings.
10. Back door into the geometry prof. lodgings.
11. Room behind the reading hall.
12. Divinity prof. lodgings.
13. Physic prof. elaboratory.
14. Back door to the elaboratory.
15. Rhetoric prof. lodgings.
16. Door into the rhetoric prof. lodgings.
17. North piazza.
18. Astronomy prof. lodgings.
19. South or long gallery.
20. South piazza.
21. Fore door into the astronomy prof. lodgings.
22. West or white gallery.
23. Almes houses.
24. West end of the south gallery.
25. Gate into the stable yard.
26. Law prof. lodgings.
27. Fore door into the law prof. lodgings.
28. Passage into Sun yard.
29. Stable yard and stables.

ABOVE *Gresham College, Bishopsgate.* BELOW *Sir Christopher Wren, Professor of Astronomy at the college.*

Lastly, the Moon, the lady of the waters, seems amorously to court this place ... For to what city doth she invite the ocean so far within land as here, communicating by the Thames whatever the banks of Maragnon or Indus can produce, and at the reflux warming the frigid zones with our cloth, and sometimes carrying and returning safe those carines that have encompassed the whole globe? And now, since navigation brings with it both wealth, splendour, politeness and learning, what greater happiness can I wish to the Londoners than that they may continually deserve to be deemed as formerly the great navigators of the world, that they always may be what the Tyrians first and then the Rhodians were called, 'the masters of the sea', and that London may be an Alexandria, the established residence of mathematical arts?

1660–1714

LONDON

under the

LATER
STUARTS

Restoration London enjoys two incomparable chroniclers, Pepys and Evelyn. Their intertwining diaries bring the city to life during a momentous epoch of transition, calamity and recovery. Their records of plague in 1665 and fire in 1666, successive and savage blows to the heart of London, are the original classics of disaster reportage in English. They make us eye-witnesses of how Londoners from every class behaved under the stress of exceptional events. No other period in London's history boasts testimony of such gripping force and candour.

Charles II was genuinely welcomed in 1660 by Londoners. The gaiety and irresponsibility of his followers began as a spontaneous reaction against the drabness of life under the Commonwealth. But zealotry was by no means extinguished. Puritanism and anti-Catholicism were still powerful among City merchants, tradesmen and craftsmen. The Crown could not crush them, because it sorely needed their growing financial revenues and expertise. In response to the Government's need for money, particularly for waging war, the City began from about 1675 to develop and diversify its skills into insurance, stock-jobbing and joint-stock banking. The Bank of England, founded in 1694, set the coping stone on what we now think of as the basic structure of the City's activities. The City

that sober enquiry had established the cause as 'the hand of God, a great wind and a very dry season'. When James II was challenged by the Duke of Monmouth in 1685, the City's position was crucial to Monmouth's failure. Its change of attitude in 1688 did much to tip the balance in William III's favour.

Even by London's energetic standards, the period was one of robustness and vigour. 'Restoration' has both a literal and a dynastic meaning. Even before the Fire, the first enclosed London theatres had been built, at Drury Lane and Lincoln's Inn Fields. These were the originals of the West End's theatreland and the forum for the court-patronized novelties of Italian opera and Restoration drama. Christopher Wren, soon to preside over the City's reconstruction, had already been distracted from astronomy and was testing the idea of a dome for the crossing of Old St Paul's. The catastrophes of 1665–6 once past, London put itself together again with urgency. The ideal urban plans presented by Wren, Hooke, Evelyn and others were rapidly jettisoned as impracticable. Such was the haste that even a scheme to improve the Port of London by reconstructing the waterfront was only half undertaken, at the mouth of the Fleet River. Instead, experts from the Crown and the City put their heads together to draft new

Loſt in *St. Jameſes Park* Novemb 15 1671, about eight of the Clock at night, a little Spaniel Dog of his Royal Highneſſes; he will anſwer to the name *Towſer*, he is Liver Colour'd and white ſpotted, his Legs ſpeckled with Liver Colour and White, with long Hair, growing upon his hind Leggs, Long Ears, and his under Lip a little hanging; if any can give notice of him, they ſhall have five pounds for their pains.

ABOVE *Royalty advertises in the* London Gazette, *1671.*

OPPOSITE *Caius Gabriel Cibber's allegorical relief panel on the west side of the Monument.*

Corporation was still a political force, too, which had to be conciliated. The poor baker at whose house the Great Fire of London had started was eventually hanged as a French agent. And the inscription on the Monument, the official memorial to London's revival, was amended in 1681 to blame the fire on a Popish plot: this despite the fact

building regulations covering street and house construction. The main elements of these ordinances were still in force 250 years later; to them, London owes much of its character and looks today. At a more measured pace, Wren and his colleagues laboured to replace the burnt churches and public buildings, above all St Paul's.

Part of Ogilby and Morgan's map of London, 1681–2, with Morgan presenting his completed map to the King and Queen.

The renaissance of court life at St James's and Whitehall and the disasters of the 1660s shifted London's population northwards and westwards. There was a displacement of suburbs away from the old City-to-Westminster axis. Smart developments appeared in St James's, Holborn and Soho, and a string of noblemen's houses along Piccadilly is visible on Ogilby and Morgan's fine map of 1682. New squares sprang up after the early precedent of Covent Garden, while the economist and speculator Nicholas Barbon systematized methods of building leasehold houses.

To the east of London, on the river at Greenwich, Charles II hoped to leave his mark by rebuilding the old palace. The naval docks nearby at Deptford and Woolwich were in full operation (and a constant concern of Pepys and Evelyn) throughout these years. Up above the palace on Greenwich Hill, the King authorized the building of the Royal Observatory, whose first priority was to establish longitude at sea: such was the dependency, in peace and war, of Restoration London and England upon maritime technique. In London's long and complex duel with Amsterdam and Paris, the welfare of its merchant and naval shipping held the key. Yet Charles, lacking money, was never to complete his palace at Greenwich. It was left to William III to finish and convert it into a naval hospital. William, the asthmatic soldier-king, preferred Kensington and Hampton Court to the damp of Whitehall and Greenwich; no more would English monarchs live right by the Thames.

Another great feature of Restoration London was the growth of a scientific community, symbolized by the founding of the Royal Society in 1660. 'Science' in the modern sense was not a term which the early luminaries of the Royal Society – Newton, Wren, Boyle, Hooke, Petty, Evelyn and others – would have understood. Their outlook was as often international as national, and several of the key members did not live in London. Yet the capital was their natural meeting place, because of its breadth of resources and skills – above all, those of the horologists and instrument-makers. It was out of empirically minded Gresham College in the City that the Royal Society chiefly derived. In the growth of scientific enquiry and exchange in Britain, the urgencies of London life had a role to play every bit as vital as the calm of Oxford or Cambridge.

After the fresh uncertainties about religion under James II, William and Mary's reign and that of Queen Anne were good times for London. The City looked strong again, financially if not politically. Money was needed for the long French wars; this, while things went well, the merchants were happy to supply through new means like the Million Lottery and the Bank of England. There was fair freedom of speech, and the press began to flourish. The periodical essay is more or less an invention of these years. In the pages of early journalists like Defoe or the scurrilous Ned Ward, publisher of *The London Spy*, we get a first flavour of London's low life. That is not because the places and events they describe were all new, but because money was now to be made out of writing and reading about them. Soon a politer, up-market version of the descriptive periodical essay about London established itself in the *Tatler* and *Spectator* from the pens of Addison and Steele. Their reflective style of writing was to become one model for prose in the Georgian era to come.

1660

London welcomes the restored King

When Charles II was restored in 1660, John Evelyn was forty. After years abroad, where he had become known to the king and queen, he returned to London in the 1650s. One of many royalist gentlemen who had established an uneasy *modus vivendi* with the Commonwealth authorities, he lived a sober life on his suburban estate at Deptford, busying himself with literary and horticultural projects and keeping his diary. Evelyn seems to have been genuinely surprised by the speed with which the republican regime collapsed during the early months of 1660. His account of the King's reception into London catches a note of authentic gladness.

29 May 1660 This day came in His Majesty Charles II to London after a sad and long exile, and calamitous suffering both of the King and Church, being seventeen years. This was also his birthday, and with a triumph of about 20,000 horse and foot, brandishing their swords and shouting with unexpressible joy, the ways strewed with flowers, the bells ringing, the streets hung with tapisserie, fountains running with wine; the Mayor, aldermen, all the companies in their liveries, chains of gold, banners; lords and nobles, cloth of silver, gold and velvet everybody clad in, the windows and balconies all set with ladies, trumpets, music, and myriads of people flocking the streets and was as far as Rochester, so as they were seven hours in passing the City, even from two in the afternoon till nine at night. I stood in the Strand and beheld it and blessed God, and all this without one drop of blood, and by that very army which rebelled against him. But it was the Lord's doing, *et mirabile in oculis nostris*, for such a restoration

was never seen in the mention of any history, ancient or modern, since the return of the Babylonian Captivity, nor so joyful a day and so bright ever seen in this nation, this happening when to expect or effect it was past all human policy.

4 June 1660 I received letters of Sir R Browne's landing at Dover, and also letters from the Queen, which I was to deliver at Whitehall, not as yet presenting myself to His Majesty by reason of the infinite concourse of people. It was indeed intolerable, as well as unexpressible, the greediness of all sorts, men, women and children to see His Majesty and kiss his hands, in so much as he had scarce leisure to eat for some days, coming as they did from all parts of the nation. And the King on the other side as willing to give them that satisfaction, would have none kept out, but gave free access to all sorts of people.

1665

The plague year

The scale of the 1665 plague epidemic was unique, at least since the Black Death. The Bills of Mortality – the returns of births and deaths which the London parishes were obliged to make from Elizabethan times – give the number of deaths by plague in this year at 97,306, a certain underestimate. Perhaps people were more susceptible because there had been something of a lull in the incidence of plague over the previous thirty years. At all events, 1665 was also the last really violent outbreak of plague suffered by London. The higher standards of housing ushered in after the Great Fire had much to do with this, just as Victorian sanitary reform was the key to bringing down London's death rates after 1880.

Defoe's famous *Journal of the Plague Year* is omitted here. Clever and painstaking though it is, it is a work of 'faction' written fifty-seven years after the events it describes. For authentic eye-witness accounts, there are three better sources: the diary entries of Pepys and of Evelyn; and the lesser-known letters of John Allin, an ejected nonconforming parson writing home to his friends in Rye. Pieced together, they catch the terror with which the shadow of this unseen assailant gripped every Londoner daily, all through the late summer and autumn of 1665.

August 2nd was the solemn fast through England to

LEFT *The triumphant restoration of Charles II.*

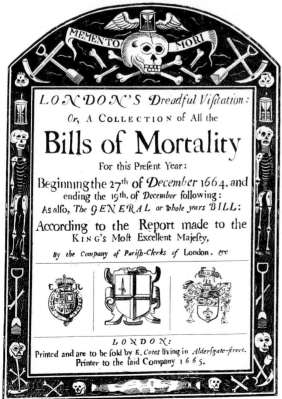

BELOW LEFT *Frontispiece from a cheap edition of the collected* Bills of Mortality in London *for 1665.*

deprecate God's displeasure against the land by pestilence and war. Our Doctor preaching on 26 Leviticus 41, 42. *8th* ... there dying this week in London 4,000. *13th* was so tempestuous that we could not go to church. There perished this week 5,000.   EVELYN

August 15th ... it was dark before I could get home, and so land at churchyard stairs, where to my great trouble I met a dead corpse of the plague in the narrow alley ... *16th*. To the Exchange, where I have not been a great while. But Lord! how sad a sight it is to see the streets empty of people, and very few people upon the Change. Jealous of every door that one sees shut up, lest it should be the plague; and about us two shops in three, if not more, generally shut up.   PEPYS

August 24th I am, through mercy, yet well in the midst of death, and that too approaching nearer and nearer; not many doors off, and the pit open daily within view of my chamber window. The Lord fit me and all of us for our last end ... Here are many who wear amulets made of the poison of the toad which, if there be no infection, works nothing, but upon any infection invading from time to time, raises a blister, which a plaster heals, and so they are well ...   ALLIN

113

August 25th This day I am told that Dr Burnett, my physician, is this morning dead of the plague; which is strange, his man dying so long ago, and his house this month open again. Now himself dead. Poor unfortunate man! *26th* . . . by water home, in my way seeing a man taken up dead, out of the hold of a small ketch that lay at Deptford. I doubt it might be the plague, which, with the thought of Dr Burnett, did something disturb me. So home, sooner than ordinary, and, after supper, to read melancholy alone, and then to bed.   PEPYS

September 2nd It hath pleased God to take from me the best friend I have in the world, and one wherein my children stood as much concerned as in myself with reference to what they should have expected from the relations of my wife: it is my brother, Peter Smith, who was abroad on Lord's day last in the morning; towards evening a little ill, then took something to sweat, which that night brought forth a stiffness under his ear, where he had a swelling that could not be brought to rise and break, but choked him; he died last Thursday night. I bless God I am well; was not with my brother after we see what it would be, as little else upon any distemper here can be expected.   ALLIN

September 3rd Up, and put on my coloured silk suit, very fine, and my new periwig, bought a good while since, but durst not wear, because the plague was in Westminster when I bought it; and it is a wonder what will be the fashion after the plague is done as to periwigs, for nobody will dare to buy any hair for fear of the infection, that it had been cut off the heads of people dead of the plague . . . After dinner by water to Greenwich, where much ado to be suffered to come into town because of the sickness, for fear I should come from London, till I told them who I was. Church being done, my Lord Brouncker, Sir J. Minnes and I up to the Vestry at the desire of the Justices of the Peace in order to the doing something for the keeping the plague from growing; but Lord! to consider the madness of people of the town, who will, because they are forbid, come in crowds along with the dead corpses to see them buried; but we agreed on some orders for the prevention thereof. Among other stories one was very passionate, methought, of a complaint brought against a man in the town for taking a child from London from an infected house. Alderman Hooker told us it was the child of a very able citizen in Gracious Street, a saddler, who had buried all the rest of his children of the plague, and himself and wife now being shut up in despair of escaping, did desire only to save the life of this little

View of the Great Fire of London, in a half-imaginary landscape. Painting by Thomas Wyck.

child; and so prevailed to have it received stark naked into the arms of a friend, who brought it, having put it into new fresh clothes, to Greenwich; where, upon hearing the story, we did agree it should be permitted to be received and kept in the town.   PEPYS

September 7th The increasing sickness hath now drawn very nigh me, and God knoweth whether I may write any more or no: it is at the next door on both hands of me, and under the same roof . . . but I have no place of retiring, neither in the city nor country . . . These three days hath been sea coal fires made in the streets about every twelfth door, but that will not do the work of stopping God's hand: nothing but repentance will do that, of which no sign yet, but oppressions etc yet increasing.   ALLIN

September 17th By the way calling in to see my other brother at Woodcote, as I was at dinner, I was surprised with a fainting fit, which much alarmed the family, as well it might, I coming lately from infected places, but I bless God it went off, so as I got home that night.

EVELYN

December 3rd Our Doctor preached at Deptford (nor had that good man stirred from his charge) on 2

Habbakuk 1; I received the blessed Communion. The contagion now abated also in this parish. *30th*. Now blessed be God, for his extraordinary mercies and preservations of me this year when thousands and ten thousands perished and were swept away on each side of me, there dying in this parish this year 406 of the pestilence.　　　　　　　　　　　　　　　　EVELYN

1666

The Great Fire

No event – not even the Blitz – had such an impact on London as the Great Fire of September 1666. The changes wrought by the clearance of no less than two-thirds of the City were more than physical. Since rebuilding took place more or less to the old street pattern, an opportunity was in a sense missed, as planners have never tired of complaining. On the other hand, the Fire forced merchants, tradesmen and their families to restructure their lives and habits of work. Those that could do so began to think of living in the healthier and safer West End, while commerce flourished in the older quarters as never before. Much of all this was due to London's growing financial strength; but it would not have occurred with such vigour and urgency had it not been

for the *tabula rasa* created by the conflagration.

That is to take the long-term view. For those who lost their substance, it was, simply, a catastrophe, especially in the wake of the previous summer's plague and recent reverses in the Dutch wars. It could only be explained as a visitation by the Almighty. Once again, Pepys and Evelyn offer equally precious human testimony to how people feel and act in the throes of civic and personal tragedy. Pepys shows more interest in the particulars of the events: Evelyn, with an eye to literary posterity, takes a larger view.

September 2nd Some of our maids sitting up late last night to get things ready against our feast today, Jane called us up about three in the morning, to tell us of a great fire they saw in the City. So I rose, and slipped on my night-gown and went to her window, and thought it to be on the back side of Mark Lane at the farthest; but, being unused to such fires as followed, I thought it far enough off, and so went to bed again, and to sleep . . . By and by Jane comes and tells me that she hears that above 300 houses have been burned down tonight by the fire we saw, and that is now burning down all Fish Street, by London Bridge. So I made myself ready presently, and walked to the Tower; and there got up upon one of the high places, Sir J. Robinson's little son going up with me; and there I did see the houses at that end of the bridge all on fire, and an infinite great fire on this and the other side the end of the bridge; which, among other people, did trouble me for poor little Michell and our Sarah on the bridge.

So down, with my heart full of trouble, to the Lieutenant of the Tower, who tells me that it began this morning in the King's baker's house in Pudding Lane, and that it hath burned St Magnus's Church and most part of Fish Street already. So I rode down to the water-side, and there got a boat, and through bridge, and there saw a lamentable fire ... Everybody endeavouring to remove their goods, and flinging into the river or bringing them into lighters that lay off; poor people staying in their houses as long as till the very fire touched them, and then running into boats, or clambering from one pair of stairs by the waterside to another. And among other things, the poor pigeons, I perceive, were loth to leave their houses, but hovered about the windows and balconies, till they some of them burned their wings and fell down.

Having stayed, and in an hour's time seen the fire rage every way, and nobody to my sight endeavouring to quench it ... I to Whitehall (with a gentleman with me, who desired to go off from the Tower to see the fire in my boat); and there up to the King's closet in the Chapel, where people came about me, and I did give them an account dismayed them all, and the word was carried in to the King. So I was called for, and did tell the King and Duke of York what I saw; and that, unless His Majesty did command houses to be pulled down, nothing could stop the fire. They seemed much troubled, and the King commanded me to go to my Lord Mayor from him, and command him to spare no houses, but to pull down before the fire every way ...

Meeting with Captain Cocke, I in his coach, which he lent me, and Creed with me, to Paul's; and there walked along Watling Street, as well as I could, every creature coming away laden with goods to save and, here and there, sick people carried away in beds. Extraordinary goods carried in carts and on backs. At last met my Lord Mayor in Cannon Street, like a man spent, with a handkercher about his neck. To the King's message he cried, like a fainting woman, 'Lord, what can I do? I am spent: people will not obey me. I have been pulling down houses, but the fire overtakes us faster than we can do it.' ... So he left me, and I him, and walked home; seeing people all distracted, and no manner of means used to quench the fire. The houses, too, so very thick thereabouts, and full of matter for burning, as pitch and tar, in Thames Street; and warehouses of oil and wines and brandy and other things.   PEPYS

September 3rd The fire having continued all this night (if I may call that night, which was as light as day for ten miles round about after a dreadful manner) when conspiring with a fierce eastern wind in a very dry season, I went on foot to the same place [Bankside], when I saw the whole south part of the City burning from Cheapside to the Thames, and all along Cornhill ... Tower Street, Fenchurch Street, Gracious Street, and so along to Baynard Castle, and was now taking hold of St Paul's Church, to which the scaffolds contributed exceedingly ... it burned both in breadth and length the churches, public halls, exchange, monuments and ornaments, leaping after a prodigious manner from house to house and street to street at great distance one from the other, for the heat (with a long set of fair and warm weather) had even ignited the air, and prepared the materials to conceive the fire, which devoured after an incredible manner houses, furniture and everything ... O the miserable and calamitous spectacle, such as happily the whole world had not seen the like since the foundation of it, nor to be outdone till the universal conflagration of it! All the sky were of a fiery aspect, like the top of a burning oven, and the light seen above forty miles round about for many nights. God grant mine eyes may never behold the like, who now saw above ten thousand houses all in one flame, the noise and crackling and thunder of the impetuous flames, the shrieking of women and children, the hurry of people, the fall of towers, houses and churches was like an hideous storm, and the air all about so hot and inflamed that at the last one was not able to approach it, so as they were forced to stand still, and let the flames consume on which they did for near two whole miles in length and one in breadth. The clouds also of smoke were dismal, and reached upon computation near fifty miles in length. Thus I left it this afternoon burning, a resemblance of Sodom or the last day. It called to mind that of 4 Hebrews, *non enim hic habemus stabilem civitatem*, the ruins resembling the picture of Troy; London was, but is no more.   EVELYN

September 4th Up by break of day, to get away the remainder of my things; which I did by a lighter at the Irongate; and my hands so few, that it was the afternoon before we could get them all away. Sir W. Penn and I to the Tower Street, and there met the fire burning three or four doors beyond Mr Howell's, whose goods, poor man, his trays and dishes, shovels etc were flung all along Tower Street in the kennels, and people working therewith from one end to the other; the fire coming on in that narrow street on both sides, with infinite fury. Sir W. Batten not knowing how to remove his wine, did dig a pit in the garden and laid it in there; and I took the opportunity of laying all the papers of my office that I could not otherwise dispose of. And in the evening Sir W. Penn and I did dig another and put our wine in it; and I my Parmesan cheese, as well as my wine and some other things . . .

Now begins the practice of blowing up of houses in Tower Street, those next the Tower, which at first did frighten people more than anything; but it stopped the fire where it was done, it bringing down the houses to the ground in the place where they stood, and then it was easy to quench what little fire was in it, though it kindled nothing almost. PEPYS

September 7th I went this morning on foot from Whitehall as far as London Bridge, through the late Fleet Street, Ludgate Hill, by St Paul's, Cheapside, Exchange, Bishopsgate, Aldersgate and out to Moorfields, thence through Cornhill: with extraordinary difficulty, clambering over mountains of yet smoking rubbish and frequently mistaking where I was, the ground under my feet so hot as made me not only sweat but even burnt the soles of my shoes . . .

I was infinitely concerned to find that goodly church St Paul's now a sad ruin, and that beautiful portico (for structure comparable to any in Europe, as not long before repaired by the late King) now rent in pieces, flakes of vast stone split in sunder, and nothing remaining entire but the inscription in the architrave which, showing by whom it was built, had not one letter of it defaced; which I could not but take notice of. It was astonishing to see what immense stones the heat had in a manner calcined, so as all the ornaments, columns, friezes, capitals and projectures of massy Portland stone flew off, even to the very roof, where a sheet of lead covering no less than six acres by measure, being totally melted, the ruins of the vaulted roof falling broke into St Faith's, which being filled with the magazines of books belonging to the Stationers and carried thither for safety, they were all consumed, burning for a week following. It is also observable, that the lead over the altar at the east end was untouched, and among the divers monuments, the body of one bishop remained entire. Thus lay in ashes that most venerable church, one of the ancientest pieces of early

piety in the Christian world, beside near a hundred more, the lead, ironwork, bells, plate etc. all melted.

The exquisitely wrought Mercer's Chapel, the sumptuous Exchange, the august fabric of Christ Church, all the rest of the companies' halls, sumptuous buildings, arches, entries, all in dust. The fountains dried up and ruined, whilst the very waters remained boiling; the voragoes of subterranean cellars, wells and dungeons, formerly warehouses, still burning in stench and dark clouds of smoke like hell, so as in five or six miles traversing about, I did not see one load of timber unconsumed, nor many stones but what were calcined white as snow, so as the people who now walked about the ruins appeared like men in some dismal desert, or rather in some great city laid waste by an impetuous and cruel enemy, to which was added the stench that came from some poor creatures' bodies, beds and other combustible goods. EVELYN

1666/1681

The Monument

There was never any doubt that the Great Fire would be formally commemorated. The first Act of Parliament of 1666 authorizing reconstruction called for a 'column or pillar of brass or stone' to be set up near the place where the fire started. Like all the great new buildings of the City, The Monument was designed by Sir Christopher Wren and his assistants – in this case, Wren's fellow scientist and architect, Robert Hooke. Wren and Hooke proposed a phoenix to top their massive column of stone, but Charles II opted for a strange golden ball bristling with flames. On the base are long Latin inscriptions composed by Thomas Gale, High Master of St Paul's School.

In 1666 the Fire was officially attributed to 'the hand of God, a great wind and a very dry season'. By the time The Monument was finished in 1677, with the City still (despite the propaganda claims of the inscription) far from fully rebuilt, a scapegoat was wanted for the long years of agony and effort. One arose in the real or imaginary Popish conspiracies of 1678–80, and in 1681 extra words were inscribed on the north side alleging that the Fire had been set by Catholic agents. This disreputable text was erased when James II came to the throne, later restored and 'very deeply chiselled in' following the Glorious Revolution of 1688, to be excised in 1831, after Catholic Emancipation.

North Side

In the year of Christ 1666, the 2nd day of September, eastward from hence at a distance of 202 feet (the height of this column), about midnight a most terrible fire broke out which, driven on by a high wind, not only wasted the adjacent quarters but also places very remote with incredible noise and fury. It consumed 89 churches, the city gates, the Guildhall, many public structures, hospitals, schools, libraries, a vast number of stately edifices, 13,200 dwelling houses and 400 streets; of 26 wards it utterly destroyed fifteen, and left eight shattered and half burnt. The ruins were 436 acres, from the Tower by the Thames side to the Temple Church, and from the north-east gate along the city wall to Holborn Bridge. To the estates and fortunes

the petitions of the magistrates and inhabitants to the Parliament, who immediately passed an Act, that public works should be restored to greater beauty with public money to be raised by an imposition on coal; that churches and the cathedral of St Paul's should be rebuilt from their foundations with all magnificence; that bridges, gates and prisons should be new made, the sewers cleansed, the streets made straight and regular, such as were steep levelled and those too narrow widened, markets and shambles removed to separate places. They also enacted that every house should be built with party walls and all in front raised of equal

LEFT *The Monument in its original setting. A Georgian engraving.*

OPPOSITE *Under the great dome in Wren's St Paul's.*

of the citizens it was merciless, but to their lives very favourable, that it might in all things resemble the last conflagration of the world. The destruction was sudden; for in a small space of time the same city was seen most flourishing, and reduced to nothing. Three days after, when this fatal fire had baffled all human counsels and endeavours in the opinion of all, as it were by the will of heaven it stopped and on every side was extinguished. [Added in 1681] But popish frenzy which perpetrated such malice is not yet extinguished.

South Side

Charles II, son of Charles the Martyr, King of Great Britain, France and Ireland, defender of the faith, a most gracious prince, commiserating the deplorable state of things, whilst the ruins were yet smoking provided for the comfort of his citizens and the ornament of his city; remitted their taxes, and referred

height, and those walls all of square stone or brick, and that no man should delay to build beyond the space of seven years. Moreover, care was taken by law to prevent all suits about their bounds. Also anniversary prayers were enjoined; and, to perpetuate the memory hereof to posterity, they caused this column to be erected. The work was carried on with diligence, and London is restored, whether with greater speed or beauty cannot be said. The space of a mere three years saw the completion of a work which was imagined to be the business of an age.

Added all round the base in 1681

This pillar was set up in perpetual remembrance of the most dreadful burning of this protestant city, begun and carried out by the treachery and malice of the popish faction in the beginning of September in the year of Our Lord 1666, in order to the carrying on their horrid plot for extirpating the protestant religion and Old English liberty, and the introducing popery and slavery.

1670s/80s

Reconstructing St Paul's

Wren was a man of formidable intellectual range, industry and meticulousness. At first sight he seems to have been everywhere and done everything connected with rebuilding the City. In reality he commanded a whole team of surveyors and artisans, whose creative contributions to the

1670s; the second explains what Wren considered most important about his great dome when it was finished thirty years later.

The pulling down the walls, being about 80 feet high and five feet thick, was a great and troublesome work. The men stood above and worked them down with their pickaxes, whilst labourers below moved away the materials that fell and dispersed them into heaps. The want of room made this way slow and dangerous, and some men lost their lives. The heaps grew steep and large, and yet this was to be done before the masons

new City churches and other buildings were often as great as his own. For the reconstruction of St Paul's, however, where Wren had already been engaged before the Great Fire, he summoned up his utmost powers as artist, mathematician and technologist. It is the cathedral that takes pride of place in the semi-autobiographical account of Wren's architecture that appeared after his death in *Parentalia*. The two extracts below both convey the technical slant of Wren's interest in building. The first concerns the ticklish work of demolishing Old St Paul's, which was a perilous ruin when rebuilding began in the

could begin to lay the foundations. The City, having streets to pave anew, bought from the rubbish most of the stone called Kentish rag, which gave some room to dig and to lay foundations, which yet was not easy to perform with any exactness but by this method. The Surveyor [Wren] placed scaffolds high enough to extend his lines over the heaps that lay in the way, and then by perpendiculars set out the places below, from the lines drawn with care upon the level plan of the scaffold.

Thus he proceeded, gaining every day more room,

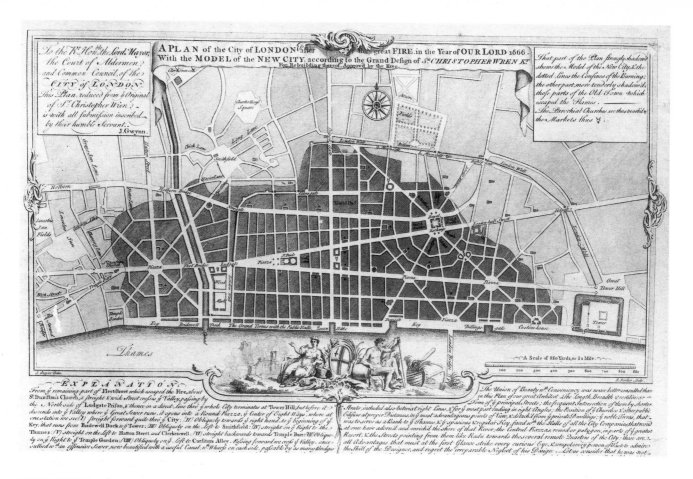

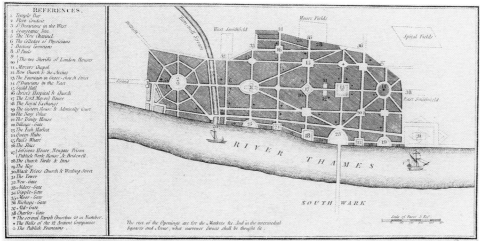

Ideal plans submitted by Wren (ABOVE) and Evelyn (LEFT) for rebuilding London after the Great Fire.

till he came to the middle tower that bore the steeple. The remains of the tower being near 200 feet high, the labourers were afraid to work above; thereupon he concluded to facilitate this work by the use of gunpowder. He dug a hole of about four feet wide down by the side of the north-west pillar of the tower, the four pillars of which were about fourteen feet diameter. When he had dug to the foundation, he then with crows and tools made on purpose wrought a hole two feet square level into the centre of the pillar. There he placed a little deal box containing eighteen pounds of powder

and no more. A cane was fixed to the box with a quick-match (as gunners call it) within the cane, which reached to the box from the ground above, and along the ground was laid a train of powder with a match. After the mine was carefully closed up again with stone and mortar to the top of the ground, he then observed the effect of the blow.

This little quantity of powder not only lifted up the whole angle of the tower with two great arches that rested upon it, but also two adjoining arches of the aisles and all above them; and this it seemed to do somewhat leisurely, cracking the walls to the top, lifting visibly the whole weight about nine inches, which suddenly jumping down made a great heap of ruin in the place without scattering; it was half a minute before the heap already fallen opened in two or three places, and emitted some smoke. By this description may be observed the incredible force of powder; eighteen pounds only of which lifted above 3,000 ton, and saved the work of 1,000 labourers.

Among all the composures of the ancients, we find no cupolas raised above the necessary loading of the hemisphere, as is seen particularly in the Pantheon. In after ages the dome of Florence and of the great church of Venice was raised higher. The Saracens mightily affected it, in imitation of the first most eminent pattern given by Justinian, in his Temple of Sancta Sophia at Constantinople. Bramante would not fall short of those examples; nor could the Surveyor do otherwise than gratify the general taste of the age, which had been so used to steeples that these round designs were hardly digested, unless raised to a remarkable height. Thus St Paul's is lofty enough to be discerned at sea eastward, and at Windsor westward. But our air, being frequently hazy, prevents those distant views except when the sun shines out, after a shower of rain has washed down the clouds of sea-coal smoke that hang over the city from so many thousand fires kindled every morning, besides glasshouses, brewhouses and foundries, every one of which emits a blacker smoke than twenty houses.

In the beginning of the new works of St Paul's, an incident was taken notice of by some people as a memorable omen. When the Surveyor in person had set out upon the place the dimensions of the great dome, and fixed upon the centre, a common labourer was ordered to bring a flat stone from the heaps of rubbish (such as should first come to hand) to be laid for a mark and direction to the masons. The stone which was immediately brought and laid down for that purpose happened to be a piece of gravestone, with nothing remaining of the inscription but this single word in large capitals, RESURGAM.

The first stone of this basilica was laid in the year 1675, and the works carried on with such care and industry that by the year 1685 the walls of the choir and side aisles were finished, with the circular north and south porticoes, and the great pillars of the dome brought to the same height; and it pleased God in his mercy to bless the Surveyor with health and length of days, and to enable him to complete the whole structure

in the year 1710 to the glory of his most holy name, and promotion of his divine worship, the principal ornament of the imperial seat of this realm.

1684

The Thames freezes over

Gone now are the famous London fogs, though credulous foreigners nurtured on Dickens and Henry James still come looking for them. Longer gone, though their memory is prettily preserved in painting, are the occasional winters when the Thames froze over and frost fairs took place on the ice. Until the mid-eighteenth century they could be relied upon once or twice in a long lifetime. Changes to the river, not the climate, caused their disappearance. When the Thames was broader, unembanked and undredged, its current was naturally more sluggish; and the broad, close piers of Old London Bridge formed an effective dam. Once the openings of the bridge had been enlarged in the 1750s, frost fairs like the one recorded by John Evelyn in 1684 were doomed. For Evelyn, author of a tract against the pollution of London by coal-smoke, weather like this meant less for the diversions it afforded than for the pain it caused his lungs and for the general stoppage of trade.

23 December 1683 It was exceedingly mortal at this time, and the season was unsufferably cold. The Thames frozen, etc.

1 January 1684 The weather continuing intolerably severe, so as streets of booths were set up upon the Thames etc., and the air so very cold and thick, as of many years there had not been the like.

24 January 1684 The frost still continuing more and more severe, the Thames before London was planted with booths in formal streets as in a city, or continual fair, all sorts of trades and shops furnished and full of commodities even to a printing press, where the people and ladies took a fancy to have their names printed, and the day and the years set down when printed on the Thames. This humour took so universally, that 'twas estimated the printer gained five pound a day for printing a line only, at sixpence a name, besides what he got by ballads etc. Coaches now plied from Westminster to the Temple, and from several other stairs to and fro, as in the streets; also on sleds, sliding with skates. There was likewise bull-baiting, horse and coach races, puppet plays and interludes, cooks and tippling, and lewder places, so as it seemed to be a bacchanalia, triumph or carnival on the water . . . London, by reason

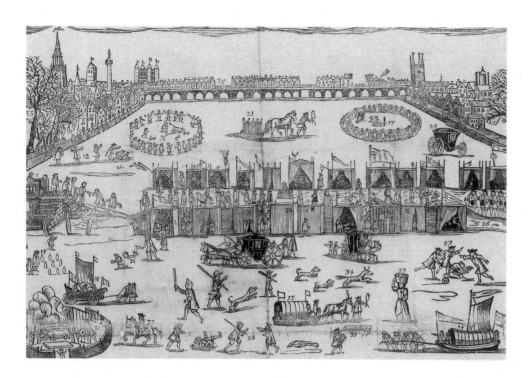

of the excessive coldness of the air hindering the ascent of the smoke, was so filled with the fuliginous steam of the sea-coal that hardly could one see cross the street, and this filling the lungs with its gross particles exceedingly obstructed the breast, so as one could scarce breathe. There was no water to be had from the pipes and engines, nor could the brewers and divers other tradesmen work, and every moment was full of disastrous accidents.

1680s

A building boom

London has always had sharp building booms followed by years of stagnation or slump. A bonanza of special intensity occurred in the early 1680s, when the methods of house-building sanctioned and tested in the reconstruction of the City were applied on a bold scale to new squares and terraces in Holborn and the West End. The financing of London leasehold property development became a high art in the hands of the monetary theorist and speculator, Dr Nicholas Barbon. Barbon was the frequent object of hostility and even violence like that shown at the inception of his Red Lion Square project. But he generally got his way.

Very different from Barbon's attitude was that of Evelyn, who was asked to advise on cutting up the gardens of one of the ample new aristocratic houses of Piccadilly for speculative development. After less than twenty years of

existence, Lord Clarendon's mansion there was demolished in favour of terrace housing, and his neighbour Lady Berkeley of Stratton was offered an inducement to follow suit. From then on, modest terrace houses rather than big, French-style *hôtels* were to be the typical London dwelling for all except the grandest members of the peerage.

10 June 1684 Dr Barbon, the great builder, having some time since bought the Red Lion fields near Gray's Inn walks to build on, and having for that purpose employed several workmen to go on with the same, the gentlemen of Gray's Inn took notice of it and, thinking it an injury to them, went with a considerable body of a hundred persons; upon which the workmen assaulted the gentlemen and flung bricks at them, and the gentlemen at them again. So a sharp engagement ensued, but the gentlemen routed them at last and brought away one or two of the workmen to Gray's Inn. In this skirmish one or two of the gentlemen and servants of the house were hurt, and several of the workmen. NARCISSUS LUTTRELL

12 June 1684 I went to advise and give direction about the building of two streets in Berkeley Gardens, reserving the house and as much of the garden as the breadth of the house. In the meantime I could not but deplore that sweet place (by far the most pleasant and noble gardens, courts and accommodations, stately porticoes etc. anywhere about the town) should so much of it be straightened and turned into tenements. But that magnificent pile and gardens contiguous to it (built by the late Lord Chancellor Hyde with so vast cost) being all demolished and designed for piazzas and buildings, was some excuse for my Lady Berkeley's resolution of letting out her ground also for so excessive a price as was offered, advancing her revenue near a thousand pounds per annum in mere ground rents. To such a mad intemperance the age was come of building about a city, by far too disproportionate already to the nation, I having in my time seen it almost as large more than it was within my memory.

JOHN EVELYN

1688–1702
The Glorious Revolution

The ejection of James II in favour of William and Mary in November 1688 caused little fuss in London, where popular sentiment backed the Prince of Orange. There was brief confusion, however, and the mob took the opportunity for a few token anti-Catholic rampages and bayed for Judge Jeffreys' blood, as William Longueville, the first Viscount Hatton's London man of business, and Sir Edmund King, Hatton's physician, nervously recount to his lordship.

Hatton's correspondents keep him abreast of other metropolitan incidents during the joint reign that ensued. In 1697 fashionable London gathers in the new St James's Square to celebrate the military edge gained by William III over Louis XIV and acknowledged in the Treaty of Ryswick. Soon afterwards most of Whitehall Palace burns down, the Banqueting House apart. Disliked by William, Whitehall is abandoned as a royal residence in favour of St James's and Kensington, and becomes henceforward an enclave of government.

William Longueville to Viscount Hatton, 13 November 1688

The Prince of Orange, being at Exeter, hath made much marching hence for Salisbury Plain, whither our King is hastening, and by Monday will be setting hence, they say. The mobile has been very turbulent hereabouts and, after sundry appearances against the Popish chapels of Budge Row and Lime Street, they have been last Sunday furiously bent for the destroying that in the late house of Earl Berkeley, and with much ado were beaten off when they had showed their discontent. But yesternight, as part of the goods were removing from thence, the said mobile took the cart and goods and burnt all in Holborn or in some other place. Some were hurt and, as 'tis said, killed on that commotion.

Lieutenant-General Worden is to be here with some 5 or 6,000 men, to keep all quiet if he can.

Sir Edmund King to Viscount Hatton, 13 December 1688

Every day brings new alarms and wonders ... The mobile have been extremely insolent and ungovernable, and yet are not suppressed. This day about one o'clock, we had news that the King was stopped by fisher boats, and that he is now at Faversham in Kent. I went to Whitehall and met my Lord Preston's lady, who said it was true, and so said Lady Peterborough and Lady Cleveland and many more; and this night the Duke of Grafton is come to town. I went to greet him, but he was with the Lords in council tonight; and I find this news has choked their measures for the present, but I believe they must proceed now. The Prince of Orange is not yet come ... We hear 24 priests taken in one vessel, and all wish it true. I was in Cheapside when the Chancellor [Judge Jeffreys] was brought to my Lord Mayor. There never was such joy; not a man sorry that we could see. They longed to have him out of the coach, had he not had a good guard. Dr Oates, I am told, is dressed in all his doctor's robes again, and expects liberty quickly.

We had a terrible alarm last night. At 12 o'clock in the night cried 'Arm! arm! arm!', 7,000 Irish was come from the army, disbanded but in a body and killing all they met. We was all up in arms till five in the morning. It arose from some disorder amongst them in Brentford, and was allayed by telling the Prince's vanguard of horse pursued them and cut them to pieces. It's a strange thing we have not the truth out yet. We do not think we are safe till the Prince comes; all the Protestants long for him. Ho! you are happy in your quiet place.

Charles Hatton to Viscount Hatton, 4 December 1697

My wife, my Lord, did last Thursday return her most humble thanks to your Lordship and my Lady Hatton for your obliging present of excellent venison, and gave an account how she had disposed of it. To hers I now, my Lord, add mine, being prevented writing then by going to see the fireworks, for which there had been so long and costly preparations ... The day they were to be I had three or four tickets sent me, and by my wife's earnest persuasion I went, but my curiosity was as little satisfied as any person's there. It is generally reported the expense of them was amounted to £12,000. There was in St James's Square a sort of triumphal arch built, but very ill-designed, on the top of which were four figures made of wood and painted, one in each corner, and had there not been the names of what they were designed for, no person could have guessed what they were meant for. Peace out of a cornucopia flung out rockets of wild fire. Conduct had a death's head in one of her hands. Concord held in a dish a flaming heart; and Valour had by it a ravenous lion. The whole was an emblem. There was a great unnecessary expense of treasure, several killed, a vast number of crackers, and all ended in smoke and stink. Sir Martin Beckman [army engineer and gunner] hath got the curses of a great many, the praises of nobody. There was only a vast number of chambers shot off, and a prodigious number of serpents and large rockets, the cases and sticks of which were so large that when they fell down, killed three or four persons, hurted many more. One falling upon the Lord Halifax's house broke quite through the roof, but hurt nobody.

Charles Hatton to Viscount Hatton, 6 January 1698

Last Tuesday I acquainted you that Whitehall was then in flames, which burnt till six of the clock next morning, and by that time had consumed all the buildings except the Banqueting House ... The fire broke out betwixt three or four of the clock in a garret in the lodgings, as some say, of Colonel Stanley, next to the Lord Portland, occasioned by a Dutch serving maid laying a sack of charcoal so near the fire it all took fire, and the servants hoping to quench it without any help from others, but it increased so violently it occasioned the ruin of the whole palace. All persons were intent to save their goods, and all the gates locked up to prevent the mob coming in; and, when the houses were blown up, most of which were blown up very high, the timber and the rafters lay bare and there wanted hands to remove them, so that instead of stopping the fire it helped to increase it. All the buildings westward joining to the Banqueting House by being blown up about six of the clock on Wednesday morning saved that which remains as monument where the Blessed Martyr, King Charles the First, was murdered by his rebellious subjects. God divert his just judgments!

1694

Investing in the Bank of England

Samuel Jeake, a small-time merchant and diarist from Rye with nonconforming politics and a superstitious cast of mind, is the only known individual who records in any detail investing in the newly founded Bank of England. The

Bank, a private venture, came into being in 1694 as a more reliable way of funding William III's war-loans. It epitomized the many steps that the City of London was taking in the last quarter of the century towards better-capitalized banking and insurance. From Jeake's provincial point of view, the Bank represented one of a limited number of options, all centred upon London, for the safe investment of his money. Others, like the Million Lottery of the same year, sound less sophisticated now, but Jeake was even more interested in that. He made special trips up from Sussex for such purposes when necessary, but usually relied on a general trading agent in town, Thomas Miller.

13 April 1694 Last night at my coming to London, I was acquainted by Mr Miller at whose house I lodged that the Act for the Million Adventure filled apace, and that

Transactions at the infant Bank of England. From a pamphlet of 1694. The Bank did not have purpose-built premises until the 1730s, making do in its early years with a primitive counting house.

he intended to put in £400 and would have wrote to me to have known whether I would have put in any; but that knowing of my coming to London, he deferred the acquainting me by writing. Upon which, having considered this day, I resolved to put in £100 if I could get money in London upon return to do it, looking upon it as providential that I should come at this time, for had I stayed at Rye I believe I should have put none in, for want of being animated by the example of the Londoners ... And this being not a luxury but a civil lot, and the putting the Act in execution (when once made) being now become necessary for the support of the Government in the war against France, I was the better satisfied to be concerned in it.

20 April About 10 a.m. I received the £25 which Mr James lent me to make up my money for ten tickets in the Million Adventure. And then I went to R. Smith's at the Grasshopper in Lombard Street, one of the receivers appointed by the Act. Came thither about 11 a.m. About 11.30 a.m. I paid £93 16s 7d for ten tickets and just at noon I received the tickets ... The numbers of my tickets were 44M461 to 44M470 inclusive.

25 June About 9.30 or 10 a.m. advice from Mr Miller by letter dated the 23rd instant that unless I got a bill to be paid at sight or came up myself for greater certainty, I should come too late for the Bank, there having been £733,000 subscribed to it since Thursday last, viz. in three days' time ...

26 June At 6 a.m. I went from Lamberhurst and arrived at London by 4 p.m. having, thanks be to God, good weather and good success in my journey. I met with Mr Miller in Fenchurch Street, who told me he had subscribed £200 for me yesterday and paid down £50, the quarter part of said subscription, out of moneys he had lately received by bill I had remitted him before. And now understanding that one who subscribed less than £500 could have a vote by the Charter, I resolved to subscribe £300 more to make mine up to £500. And accordingly about 6 p.m. I went with Mr Miller to Grocers' Hall and at 6.30 p.m. or thereabouts and paid down £75 and subscribed for £300 more.

29 October About 10 a.m. news per post per Mr Miller's letter of the 27th instant that that day I had a benefitted ticket risen to me of £10 per annum by the Million Adventure, No. 44M465 ...

5 November Advice from Mr Miller dated 3rd instant that at a General Court of the Bank of England held the 2nd instant, the Governor had acquainted them that with the payment of a tenth more of the several subscriptions into the Bank ... they should be able to pay the whole into the Exchequer by the first of January, they having a great stock of money by them.

1690s

Hummums Bagnio

Edward – or Ned – Ward, publican and writer (1667–1731), was a key figure in the growth of London journalism. Ward was a knockabout character who wrote satirical poems in the manner of Samuel Butler and ran a pub near Gray's Inn. A visit to the West Indies first suggested to him the genre that he made famous – the 'trip about town', issued in monthly instalments and describing high and low life with equal insolence. *A Trip to Jamaica* was followed by *The London Spy*, which ran between 1698 and 1700 and enjoyed

many editions in book form. Ward's regard for truth was not strict, but the picture he draws of Hummums Bagnio and other places of pleasure is accurate in feeling. It anticipates the tastes and subject matter of Hogarth's generation. The Hummums was an establishment on the east side of Covent Garden Piazza, where according to an

Hummums Bagnio, Covent Garden, as advertised in the early nineteenth century. Private bathing establishments like the Hummums straddled the border between decency and seediness; they declined in the Victorian period.

advertisement of 1701 'persons may sweat and bath in the cleanliest and be cupped after the newest manner ... The price, as was always, for sweating and bathing is 5s 6d. For two in a room, 8s; but who lodges there all night, 10s'.

'Now,' says my friend, 'we are so near, I'll carry you to see the Hummums, where I have an honest old acquaintance that is a cupper, and if you will pay your club towards eight shillings, we'll go in and sweat, and you shall feel the effects of this noble invention' ... Accordingly he conducted me to the house, through which we passed into a long gallery, where my friend's acquaintance received him with much gladness.

I had not walked above once the length of the gallery, but I began to find myself as warm as a cricket at an oven's mouth. My friend telling him we designed to sweat, he from thence introduced us into a warmer climate ...

We now began to unstrip and put ourselves in a condition of enduring an hour's baking, and when we had reduced ourselves into the original state of mankind, having nothing before us to cover ourselves but a clout no bigger than a figleaf, our guide led us to the end of our journey, the next apartment, which I am sure was as hot as a pastry cook's oven for to bake a white-pot; that I began immediately to melt like a piece of butter in a basting ladle and was afraid I should have run all to oil by the time I had been in six minutes.

The bottom of the room was paved with free-stone, to defend our feet from the excessive heat of which we had got on a pair of new-fashioned brogues with wooden soles after the French mode, cut out of an inch deal board; or else like the fellow in the fair, we might as well have walked cross a hot iron bar, as ventured here to have trod barefoot. As soon as the fire had tapped us all over, and we began to run like a conduit pipe at every pore, our rubber arms his right hand with a gauntlet of coarse hair camlet, and began to curry us with as much labour as a Yorkshire groom does his master's best stone horse, till he made us as smooth as a fair lady's cheeks just washed with lemon posset and greased over with pomatum.

At last I grew so very faint with the expense of much spirits, that I begged as hard for a mouthful of fresh air as Dives did for a drop of water, which our attendant let in a sash window no broader than a Deptford cheesecake, but however it let in at a comfortable breeze that was very reviving. When I had fouled about as many calico napkins as a child does double clouts in a week, our rubber draws a cistern full of hot water, that we might go and boil out those gross humours that could not be emitted by a mere gentle perspiration. Thus almost baked to a crust, we went into the hot bath to moisten our clay, where we lay soddening ourselves till we were almost parboiled.

I talking by accident of a pain that sometimes affected my shoulder occasioned by a fall from my horse, my friend by all means advised me to be cupped for it, telling me 'twas the best operation in the world for the removal of all such grievances ... Upon this the operator fetched in his instruments, and fixes three glasses at my back which, by drawing out the air, stuck to me as close as a Cantharides plaster to the head of a lunatic, and sucked as hard as so many leeches at a wench's fundament troubled with the Hemorhoides,

till I thought they would have crept into me and have come out on t'other side.

When by virtue of his hocus-pocus stratagem, he had conjured all the ill blood out of my body under his glass juggling cups, he plucks out an ill-favoured instrument, at which I was as much frightened as an absconding debtor is at the sight of a bill of Middlesex, takes off his glasses, which had my shoulder as weary as a porter's back under a heavy burden, and begins to scarify my skin, as a cook does a loin of pork to be roasted, but with such ease and dexterity that I could have suffered him to have pinked me all over as full of eyelet holes, as the tailor did the shoemaker's cloak, had my malady

Edward Hatton

Edward Hatton's New View of London, *a boosterish guidebook of 1708.*

required it, without flinching. When he had drawn away as much blood as he thought necessary for the removal of my pain, he covered the places he had carbonaded with a new skin provided for that purpose, and healed the scarifications he had made in an instant; then taking me up like a scalded swine out of my greasy broth, after he had wiped o'er my wet buttocks with a dry clout and telling us we had sweat enough, he relieved us of our purgatory and carried us into the dressing room, which gave us such refreshment after

we had been stewing in our own gravy, that we thought ourselves as happy as a couple of English travellers transported in an instant by a miracle from the torrid zone into their own country.

Our expense of spirits had weakened nature and made us drowsy, so having the conveniency of a bed, we lay down and were rubbed like a couple of racehorses after a course, till we were become as cool as the affections of a passionate lover after a night's enjoyment.

1708

A guidebook to London

More meticulous than Ward was Edward Hatton, one of London's first proper guidebook and directory writers. From Stow onwards there had been London surveys or guidebooks of a kind and since the 1670s intermittent directories. Hatton's remarkable *New View of London,* published in 1708, is on a more ambitious scale and businesslike footing. It describes all London's principal institutions and monuments, often in puffing and garrulous detail, and lists the major enterprises. Hatton is especially good on such new commercial enterprises as banking and underwriting.

MERCHANTS' HOUSES

Those especially about half a mile in compass round the Royal Exchange, particularly eastward therefrom, are so numerous and magnificent with courts, offices and all other necessary apartments enclosed to themselves, and noble gates and frontispieces of some towards the street, but chiefly so ornamental, commodious and richly furnished within, that it would require too much room to give the names and situations, much less can their descriptions, as magnitude, beauty and usefulness be expected particularly to be accounted for in this book. They are for conveniencies aforesaid, and because of the great quantity of ground they are built on, generally situate backward, and by that means the City appears not to strangers who walk the street near so stately and beautiful as it really is and would show itself were these ornaments exposed to public view. And the same in many respects many be said for *Taverns* (abating the richness of finishing and furniture in the merchants' houses, which outdoes these), many of which go at £200 or £300 per annum and upward, and wherein is at least one very capacious room proper for public entertainments on most occasions, as the master, wardens and commonalty of a company, clubs, weddings and other solemnities; but whose magnitude and ornament are seldom visible to the street, no more than those of the magnificent and beautiful halls of several companies, though like so many palaces of princes.

GREENWICH HOSPITAL

Because out of the Bills of Mortality I am not to account for it, and shall only tell the stranger, that at Greenwich about five miles eastward of London Bridge there is now building one of the most sumptuous hospitals in the world, much liker the palace of a prince than a harbour for the indigent. It is called THE ROYAL HOSPITAL AT GREENWICH, partly built in the reign of King Charles II, carried on by King William's commission, and 'tis hoped will be finished in the reign of Queen Anne, who to forward the same granted one commission in July 1703 and another in April 1704 to the Lord High Admiral and others, for promoting the work and finishing the building, and to take gifts, bequests, lands, money etc. for the use of the hospital, which is for the maintaining superannuated and disabled seamen and the widows of such as were killed in the Queen's service by sea.

THE INSURANCE OFFICES BY FIRE ARE

1. The Phoenix Office at the Rainbow Coffee House, Fleet Street, established about the year 1682, whose undertakers for 30s paid them in hand insure £100 for seven years, and in proportion for other sums, for the payment of which losses they have settled a fund. They employ several men (with liveries and badges) to extinguish fires on occasion. The first undertaker was Dr Nicholas Barbon, and now there are several gentlemen concerned. Their number is about 10,000.

2. The Friendly Society Office, in Redgrave Court without Temple Bar, is the next office, but the first that insured from fire by mutual contribution (Anno 1684), the sole project of the late ingenious Henry Spelman, Esq., deceased … They employ several men (with liveries and badges) to extinguish fire. Their number is about 18,000.

3. Amicable Contributors, whose office is kept in St Martin's Lane, was set up about the year 1695. Insurances being made as in the project of the said Mr Spelman, only here they propose profit to their members of what interest they can make of the sum paid in; but then such members do bear their proportion of all the incident charges of the office, which those of the Friendly Society do not. This office have several watermen who they employ to extinguish fires, and give liveries and badges to them, but have no land security as the other two have; their number is upward

Coffee houses were a new development in London's social life after the Restoration. From a painting c. 1668.

of 13,000. This office is chiefly carried on and supported by workmen and those concerned in building, who sign the policies.

Offices that insure ships or their cargo are many about the Royal Exchange, as Mr Hall's, Mr Bevis's etc., who for a premium paid down procure those that will subscribe policies for insuring ships (with their cargo) bound to or from any part of the world, the premium being proportioned to the distance, danger of seas, enemies etc. But in these offices 'tis customary upon paying the money at a loss, to discount 16 per cent.

to turn his coffee house into a museum of curiosities, described mordantly by Steele in *The Tatler* for 1709. There was a catalogue to the Saltero collection, which according to Richard Altick included 'a nuns' penitential whip, four evangelists' heads carved on a cherry stone, "the Pope's infallible candle" (whatever that may have been), a starved cat found many years earlier between the walls of Westminster Abbey, William the Conqueror's flaming sword, Queen Elizabeth's strawberry dish, a cockatrice, petrified rain, barnacles, a rose from Jericho . . . a necklace made of Job's tears, "a whale's pizzle", "a wooden clock, with a man mowing the grass from the top", manna from Canaan, a petrified oyster, a pair of garter snakes from South Carolina, an Indian ladies' back scratcher, a fifteen-inch-long frog, and the horns of a "shamway" (chamois)'.

When I came into the coffee-house, I had not time to salute the company before my eye was diverted by ten thousand gimcracks round the room and on the ceiling. When my first astonishment was over, comes to me a sage of thin and meagre countenance; which aspect made me doubt whether reading or fretting had made it so philosophic. But I very soon perceived him to be of that sect which the ancients call Gingivistae, in our language, tooth-drawers. I immediately had a respect for the man; for these practical philosophers go upon a very rational hypothesis, not to cure but to take away the part affected. My love of mankind made me very benevolent to Mr Salter, for such is the name of this eminent barber and antiquary . . . The barber in 'Don Quixote' is one of the principal characters in the history, which gave me satisfaction in the doubt why Don Saltero writ his name with a Spanish termination; for he is descended in a right line not from John Tradescant, as he himself asserts, but from that memorable companion of the Knight of Mancha . . . Though I go thus far in favour of Don Saltero's great merit, I cannot allow the liberty he takes of imposing several names (without my licence) on the collections he has made, to the abuse of the good people of England; one of which is particularly calculated to deceive religious persons, to the great scandal of the well disposed, and may introduce heterodox opinions. He shows you a straw hat, which I know to be made by Madge Peskad, within three miles of Bedford; and tells you, it is Pontius Pilate's wife's chambermaid's sister's hat. To my knowledge of this very hat, it may be added that the covering of straw was never used among the Jews, since it was demanded of them to make bricks without it.

1709

Don Saltero's coffee house

Richard Steele was a more topographically minded writer than his more famous and contemplative fellow essayist, Joseph Addison. Having an eye for quirkiness, Steele was attracted by Don Saltero's coffee house on Cheyne Walk in suburban Chelsea. Coffee houses could function as information exchanges, commercial centres for insurance and other business dealings, but were equally in vogue for sheer dalliance and chat. James Salter, as Don Saltero was really called, had been a servant of the great collector and naturalist Sir Hans Sloane. He also practised the trades of tooth-puller and harmless fraud. Acquiring duplicates and cast-offs from Sloane, he took it into his head

1714–1789

HANOVERIAN
LONDON

With the House of Hanover securely, sometimes sleepily, on the throne, London ceased to take its tone from the doings and directives of kings. Certainly the Court, most often during the reigns of the first two Georges at St James's, was still a vital factor in metropolitan life and commerce. The runaway success of Georgian Mayfair as a smart place to live, of the clubs of St James's, and of Bond Street and Oxford Street as a venue for luxury trades and shops, was premised on their proximity to the Court and the lustre of the social season. The destiny of princes, courtesans and favourites had yet to become just a matter of idle metropolitan gossip.

But the centres of London life had shifted subtly. Whitehall and Westminster were turning into what we think of them as now – the respective centres of administrative and executive action. There was still equipoise of a kind between the two Houses of Parliament, meeting in the ramshackle old Palace of Westminster. But under the long leadership of Robert Walpole (1721–42) the Com-

mons found a new rhythm and confidence, which the Hanoverian kings could not rival. After acceding to the throne in 1760, George III was persuaded by Lord Bute to flex his political muscles; but he aroused such prompt hostility that he was glad to retreat into domesticity, choosing to live in Buckingham House – not a palace, with all that it implied, but a home. Further east, the City found itself richer than ever, but with no fixed place in the Georgian political firmament. It responded by retreating in its own way too, and building the Mansion House – a place for guzzling in rather than ruling from. The puritan tradition of City politics gave way to intermittent radicalism, best exemplified by the career of the rakish, effervescent John Wilkes, Lord Mayor in 1774, diligent defender of press liberties, occasional rabble-rouser, yet suppressor of the Gordon Riots. It is significant that the stage on which Wilkes played out his programme was not the Court of Common Council but the hustings of successive parliamentary elections.

ABOVE *The Thames and the entrance to the Fleet River before the Fleet was covered over and Blackfriars Bridge built in the 1760s. Painting by Samuel Scott.*

OPPOSITE *The Mansion House in the 1780s.*

What catches our imagination today about Georgian London is the social and cultural energy of a great merchant city at peace. Peace may seem an odd term for the perpetual turbulence, filth, drunkenness and criminality that every writer or visitor to London seems half to admire and half to deplore. But compared to the conditions of the previous hundred years, London was indeed peaceful in the eighteenth century. It was hardly touched by the '15 and the '45 rebellions; it escaped repetition of the great natural calamities of plague and fire; and the muted religious tolerance that developed was only underscored by the universally condemned viciousness of the Gordon Riots in 1780, with its sacking of Catholic chapels. Window-breaking mobs, hitherto so frequent in London streets, had by then become rarer.

It is peace, too, that permits the beginnings of a definite bourgeois social reform movement in the London of the 1730s and '40s. Artists like William Hogarth, writers like Henry Fielding, actors like David Garrick, seamen like Thomas Coram, merchants like Jonas Hanway and doctors like William Heberden all play a part in this. However grim the human degradation they reveal, we are able to see it precisely because they are the first commentators to depict in detail the conditions in which so many Londoners lived – and may well have done for centuries – and to propose secular remedies. Many hospitals, including Guy's, St George's, the Westminster, the London and the celebrated Foundling, are products of the period. The Metropolitan Police and the London police courts go back to the reforms of an eccentric blind entrepreneur and magistrate, Sir John Fielding. A little later come the sober enquiries of John Howard into the state of Britain's prisons, and the beginnings of a milder urban philanthropy.

It was to be a hundred and fifty years before these efforts made permanent inroads on the condition of an under-regulated, industrializing and ever more crowded city. So the creative talent of Georgian London stands out against a dark backdrop that served for some as a stimulus, for others as something from which to take refuge. Boswell, Johnson, Goldsmith and their set mostly enjoyed the density and opportunity of the city. They needed to be there because the printers, publishers, journals and readers were there. Likewise, dramatists, musicians and actors depended upon London audiences.

In the visual arts there was a division. Hogarth, the London painter *par excellence*, had an urban vision of the arts and the crafts that was missing from the aristocratic internationalism of Reynolds. In the architecture of the period and the lively criticism that it generates, there is a struggle almost against the nature of London, to impose order on the unorderable, refinement upon rawness. The interior of the grand London house, not its exterior, is preferred to its outside as the place for display; it is where the great London craftsmen – furniture makers, upholsterers, and society dressmakers – shine. But it is in the great suburban retreats, such as Osterley, Chiswick, Kenwood, Wanstead and Wricklemarsh, that patrons, architects and their new-fangled gardeners seem to breathe most freely. Aristocratic taste, in other words, is in danger of deserting the chaos of bourgeois London – to the city's grievous cost.

1720

Defoe on the suburbs

By George I's accession in 1714, London was what we now call a world city – even, *the* world city. The dispute between London and Paris about which was the bigger was soon to be settled in London's favour. Under a weakened Hanoverian monarchy, attempts to limit metropolitan growth were dropped. It took time to grasp all the hostages to fortune given by this gargantuan expansion. The veteran Daniel Defoe, describing London in his *Tour of Great Britain* of the mid-1720s, still surveys the spread of his native city in boosterish terms. His journalist's eye for striking novelty is at its best on the new suburbs, which grew up principally along the main roads leading to and from the capital.

WOOLWICH
Through this town [Greenwich] lies the road to Woolwich, a town on the bank of the same river wholly taken up by, and in a manner raised from, the yards and public works erected there for the public service. Here, when the business of the Royal Navy increased and Queen Elizabeth built larger and greater ships of war

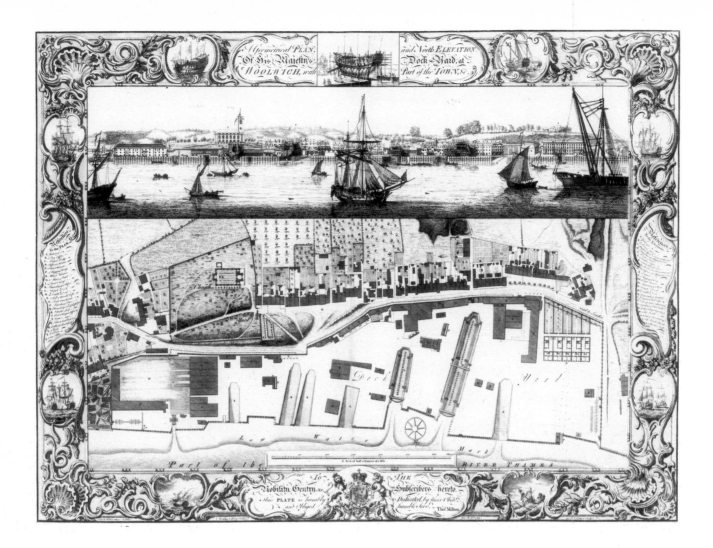

The Royal dockyard and the Thames bank at Woolwich, 1733.

than were usually employed before, new docks and launches were erected and places prepared for the building and repairing ships of the largest size; because, as here was a greater depth of water and a freer channel than at Deptford (where the chief yard in the River of Thames was before), so there was less hazard in the great ships going up and down, the crowd of merchant ships at Deptford being always such as that it could not be so safe to come up thither as to put in at Woolwich.

At this dock the *Royal Sovereign* was built, once the largest ship in the Royal Navy, and in particular esteemed for so large a ship the best sailor in the world. Here also was rebuilt the *Royal Prince*, now called the *Queen*, a first rate carrying a hundred guns, and several others. Close under the south shore from the west end of Woolwich, the Thames is very deep, and the men of war lie there moored and, as we call it, laid up, their topmasts and all their small rigging taken down and laid in warehouses. This reaches as high as the point over against Bow River and is called Bugsby's Hole.

The docks, yards and all the buildings belonging to it are encompassed with a high wall, and are exceeding spacious and convenient; and are also prodigious full of all manner of stores of timber, plank, masts, pitch, tar and all manner of naval provisions, to such a degree as is scarce to be calculated.

UP RIVER

It is not easy to describe the beauty with which the banks of the Thames shine on either side of the river from hence to London, much more than our ancestors even of but one age ago knew anything of ... From Richmond to London, the river sides are full of villages so full of beautiful buildings, charming gardens and rich habitations of gentlemen of quality that nothing in the world can imitate it, no, not the country for twenty miles round Paris, though that indeed is a kind of prodigy ...

That these houses and gardens are admirably beautiful in their kind and in their separate and distinct beauties such as their situation, decoration, architect, furniture and the like, must be granted; and many descriptions have been accurately given of them, as of Ham House, Kew Green, the Prince's House, Sir William Temple's, Sir Charles Hedges, Syon House, Osterley, Lord Ranelagh's at Chelsea Hospital, the

many noble seats in Isleworth, Twickenham, Hammersmith, Fulham, Putney, Chelsea, Battersea and the like. But I find none has spoken of what I call the distant glory of all these buildings. There is a beauty in these things at a distance, taking them *en passant* and in perspective, which few people value and fewer understand; and yet here they are more truly great than in all their private beauties whatsoever. Here they reflect beauty and magnificence upon the whole country and give a kind of character to the island of Great Britain in general.

SPITALFIELDS

Within the memory of the writer hereof, all those numberless ranges of buildings called Spitalfields, reaching from Spital Yard at Norton Folgate and from Artillery Lane in Bishopsgate Street, with all the new streets beginning at Hoxton and the back of Shoreditch Church, north; and reaching to Brick Lane and to the end of Hare Street on the way to Bethnal Green, east; then sloping away quite to Whitechapel Road, southeast; containing, as some people say who pretend to know by good observation, above 320 acres of ground which are all now close built and well inhabited with an

infinite number of people – I say, all these have been built new from the ground since the year 1666.

The lanes were deep, dirty and unfrequented; that part now called Spitalfields Market was a field of grass with cows feeding on it since the year 1670. The old Artillery Ground (where the Parliament listed their first soldiers against the King) took up all those long streets leading out of Artillery Lane to Spital Yard Back Gate, and so on to the end of Wheeler Street. Brick Lane, which is now a long well-paved street, was a deep dirty road frequented chiefly by carts fetching bricks that way into Whitechapel from brick kilns in those fields, and had its name on that account. In a word, it is computed that above 200,000 inhabitants dwell now in that part of London, where within about fifty years past there was not a house standing.

1730s/40s

Actors and artists

John Rich was the outstanding impresario of the early Georgian theatre. There was nothing of the purist about him. An actor-manager and much admired Harlequin, he all but invented English pantomime; yet he was also a great

ABOVE *John Rich arrives for the opening of the first Covent Garden Theatre, 1732. By William Hogarth.*

LEFT *Chiswick* c. *1675–80 with Old Corney House. Painting by Jacob Knyff.*

patron of Handel's. The runaway success of *The Beggar's Opera*, staged at Rich's theatre in Lincoln's Inn Fields, provided him with the capital to build a small new one in 1731–2 at Covent Garden. This was to be the ancestor of the present Royal Opera House. Rich premiered Handel's new operas at the Covent Garden Theatre in 1735–7. Despite their fame today, they proved too highbrow and were a financial flop. In 1738 we find Rich writing to his landlord, the Duke of Bedford, to ask for a deferment of his rent. The letter is a reminder of the eternal precariousness of theatrical enterprise in London, as well as of the burdens of the leasehold tenure that was then the norm.

My Lord Duke

I was in hopes ere this of having moneys come into my hands to have discharged the rent due to Your Grace, which has been occasioned by severe losses by the operas etc. carried on by Mr Handel and myself at Covent Garden Theatre for these three years last past, in so much that I must entreat Your Grace's patience for a time ... I'll assure Your Grace it concerns me much that I should trouble Your Lordship on this subject having been a tenant to your noble family these forty years and never in arrear till now.

I must likewise beg to lay before Your Grace the other affair depending, concerning the houses in the playhouse passage leading to Drury Lane Theatre which lease expired Christmas last. When my father took the same, the houses were in a very mean and bad condition and the rents but small and the fine demanded was but £50. He laid out a pretty large sum that improved and made them tenantable, but considering the time the repairs took up, the tenements unlet and the moneys expended on 'em, they did not nearly bring in the moneys laid out before such leases expired. At which time my father died and then my brother and myself renewed the same, paying then a fine of £200, since which we in wainscotting, new flooring, sashing, building upon part of the waste and thoroughly fitting up, laid out upwards of £1,000 ... On application made to Mr Holt to renew, the fine demanded is £400. Now if Your Grace would be so good as to take it into consideration and lessen some part of the fine, which is wholly owing to the improvements made, it would at all times be an encouragement for a tenant to enrich an estate rather than let it decay and wear out with the lease, which I'm afraid is too often the case. These particulars I submit to Your Grace's determination, first begging pardon for this long epistle, and next leave to subscribe myself

Your Grace's most obedient humble servant
John Rich

Great advances were made in the status of the visual arts in London during the reign of George II. Starting from a base of low self-esteem, painters, sculptors and designers began to band together in order to share ideas and promote styles.

135

The movement culminated in the founding of the Royal Academy in 1768. But it had begun much earlier, through the energies of Sir James Thornhill and his son-in-law, William Hogarth. It was Hogarth who had most to do with setting up the liveliest of these informal groups, the St Martin's Lane Academy, in 1735. Late in life that most chauvinist, puritanical, truculent and urban of great British

the form of the French plan but with less fuss and solemnity. Little as it was, it was soon ridiculed; jealousies arose, parties were formed and [the] president with all adherents found themselves comically represented in procession round the walls of the room. The first proprietors soon put a padlock upon the door, the rest as subscribers did the same, and thus ended this

Could new dumb Fauſtus, to reform the Age,
Conjure up Shakeſpear's or Ben Johnſon's Ghoſt,
They'd bluſh for ſhame, to ſee the Engliſh Stage
Debauch'd by fool'ries, at ſo great a coſt.
Price 1 Shilling 1724

What would their Manes ſay? ſhould they behold
Monſters and Maſquerades, where uſefull Plays
Adorn'd the fruitfull Theatre of old.
And Rival Wits contended for the Bays.

LEFT *Hogarth mocks the state of the arts in London, 1724. At the back, the gate to Burlington House, the seat of Lord Burlington's private 'accademy of art'.*

OPPOSITE *The Foundling Hospital, established by Captain Coram and built to the plans of Theodore Jacobsen in 1742–52.*

painters set down his version of the event. Unpublished in his lifetime, his account is hardly well written, but has all the spirit of his pictures.

We hear much of the academies of painting abroad, rooms where naked men stand in certain posture to be drawn after ... Lewis the 14th got more honour by establishing a pompous parading one at Paris than the academician[s] advantage by their admission into it ... We have had in St Martin's Lane, supported by a trifling subscription of young, near these thirty years one to all intent and purposes as useful ... The first place of this sort was in Queen Street about sixty years ago begun by some gentlemen painters of the first rank who imitated

academy. Sir James Thornhill at the head of one party then set up an academy in [a] place he built at the back of his own house in the piazza now next the playhouse and furnished gratis to all that required admission, but so few would [come] under that obligation that it soon [ended]. Mr Vanderbank headed the rebellious party and converted an old presbyterian meeting house into an academy upon a footing with the addition of a woman figure to make it the more inviting to subscribers. This lasted a few years, but the treasurer sinking the subscription money, the lamp, stove etc. were seized for rent and the whole affair put a stop to. Sir James Thornhill dying, I became [possessed] of his neglected apparatus and began by subscription that in the same place in St Martin's Lane, as it was founded upon a still more free footing, each subscriber having equal power, which regulation has [been] preserve[d] to this day, as perfect an academy as any in Europe.

Hogarth is famous for depicting the seedier sides of London life. But he also believed that painting should have a public

about 170 persons. Great benefactions given then towards the hospital. At the same time was seen the four paintings newly put up, done gratis by four eminent painters, by Hayman, Hogarth, Highmore and Wills, and by most people generally approved and commended as works in history painting in a higher degree of merit than has heretofore been done by English

function. He wanted it to ornament not just the apartments of kings and queens but the great charitable institutions, funded by independent, benevolent citizens, that were such a novelty in Georgian London. Hogarth painted the staircase at the rebuilt St Bartholomew's Hospital. He was also a proud supporter of Captain Thomas Coram's Foundling Hospital, the outstanding social venture of the age, which opened its doors to unwanted children in 1745. The engraver and proto-art historian George Vertue records an early fund-raising event for the foundation.

Wednesday the first of April 1747 at the Foundling Hospital was an entertainment or public dinner of the governors and other gentlemen that had inclination –

painters. Some other portraits are done and doing by Ramsay, Hudson, and landscapes etc. It's generally said and allowed that Hogarth's piece gives most striking satisfaction and approbation.

1734/56

Exteriors and interiors

A long building boom in the 1720s and '30s underlined London's stability and prosperity. Out of it emerged the first clear voice of urban criticism in London. Up until then, individual buildings had been praised or condemned according to taste, with little thought for how London was or might be developing. With James Ralph's *Critical Review* of the *Publick Buildings, Statues and Ornaments in and about London and Westminster*, published in 1734, a more consistent note is struck. Ralph's judgements are often splenetic. Few people would now be as brutal as he is on Hawksmoor's church of St George's, Bloomsbury. But his no-nonsense approach led to a tone of robust architectural polemic still practised in London.

ST GEORGE'S, BLOOMSBURY

'Twill be impossible to pass by the new church of St. George, Bloomsbury, without giving it a very particular survey. 'Tis built all of stone, is adorned with a pompous portico, can boast many other decorations, has been stinted in no expense; and yet, upon the whole, is ridiculous and absurd even to a proverb. The reason is this, the builder mistook whim for genius, and ornament for taste. He has even erred so much, that the very portico does not seem to be in the middle of the church, and as to the steeple, it is stuck on like a wen to the rest of the building; then the execrable conceit of setting up the King on the top of it, excites nothing but laughter in the ignorant and contempt in the judge. In short, 'tis a lasting reflection on the fame of the architect and the understanding of those who employed him.

SOHO SQUARE

The square commonly called Soho is the next place which claims any regard, and that too, like most of the other things of the like nature in this city, only because it is a square. The buildings round it are not scandalous, 'tis true, but they have not the least pretentions to taste or order. It has, beside, a little contemptible garden in the middle of the area, and a worse statue if it be possible in the middle of that. The place indeed is not so entirely neglected as many others of the same sort about town, and therefore deserves the less censure if it is not entitled to praise. My Lord Bateman's house on the south side is built at a good deal of expense, and was meant for something grand and magnificent. But I am afraid the architect had a very slender notion of what either of them meant...

Visiting foreigners in the eighteen century regularly pronounced London houses to be dull outside, rich and comfortable within. The top London cabinet-makers, upholsterers and seamstresses depended for their livelihood on costly reception rooms commissioned by the aristocracy for the London season, which in their turn furnished a backdrop to the even more perishable commodities of dress and beauty, as shown off at 'levées' and 'routs'. In a sparkling family letter of 1756, William Farington recounts

St George's, Bloomsbury, by Nicholas Hawksmoor, with the steeple topped by George I and derided by James Ralph.

the reopening of the state apartments at Norfolk House in St James's Square, after an extravagant reconstruction by Signor Borra from Turin. The 'great room' of this minipalazzo, now otherwise destroyed, is preserved in the Victoria and Albert Museum.

Dear Isabella and Mary,

... I promised in my last letter to my mother you should have an account of Norfolk House, the Duchess having been so kind to send me a ticket on opening the grand apartment, which as was expected proved the finest assembly ever known in this kingdom. There were in all eleven rooms open ...

On the left hand you enter a large room hung and furnished with a green damask let in with a handsome gilt moulding and several very fine paintings on the hangings. Through this into a wainscotted room, with pictures but not very elegant. Then to the stairs, which are very large and the lights beautifully placed; 'twas entirely covered with a French carpet, and in the angles stood large china jars with perfumes. The ante-chamber was much like the last-mentioned room, though something superior. The next room is large, wainscotted in a whimsical taste, the panels filled with extreme fine carvings, the arts and sciences all gilt as well as the ceiling, which was the same design. Here the Duchess sat the whole night that she might speak to everyone as they came in.

Lady Granby's were I think the finest; Lady Rockingham had none at all on, which was not civil, as everyone endeavoured to make themselves fine. A Miss Vineyard [Wynyard] was thought the prettiest woman there. As to fashions, there was not two ladies' heads dressed alike, the more whimsical and absurd the better. The clothes on them were all vastly rich. I heard one

LEFT *Soho Square in the early nineteenth century.*

BELOW *Fireplace and overmantel from the Norfolk House music room, now in the Victoria and Albert Museum.*

Having paid your regards, you then walk forwards. The next room was hung and furnished with blue damask covered with very fine paintings – the girandoles fixed in the frames of the pictures, which had an odd effect and I can't think will be so good for the paint. The next room a crimson damask, no paintings except over the chimney, where there is a round landscape let into the looking glass which rises from the chimney to the top of the room, as do most of the glasses. The girandoles here are monstrous large but the carvings in a beautiful taste and being gilt have a good effect upon the damask.

You now enter the great room, which is not to be described. The tapestry is the finest picture I ever saw, chiefly with beasts. It cost in France nine pounds a yard, the hangings just cost nine hundred pounds, the glasses a thousand, being the largest plates I fancy that ever were brought over. But throughout the whole house the glass is thought the most remarkable furniture . . .

Everyone paid their compliments to the Duke in the great room, and Miss Clifford, the Duchess's niece, stood there to fix those to cards who chose to play. There was a vast crowd and a great blaze of diamonds.

single shop sold above a hundred suits, so you judge what numbers were bought. Mine was a figured velvet of a Pompadour colour which is the taste, an entire silver cling-clong [clinquant] waistcoat with a loose net trimming waved over the skirts and my hair dressed French. Don't you think your brother is growing very youthful? There was several richer clothes, but none I think prettier than my own ... If I could have sold my ticket, it would have brought a very large sum, for many fine folks were just undone about them, but the Duchess would not suffer any but those who visited her to have them.

1746

Beheadings at Tower Hill

London was unaffected by the Jacobite uprisings of 1715 and 1745. But until the reign of George III, the Tower of London remained the great prison of state. There it was that major political prisoners were still held and, if necessary, killed. Between 1722 and 1747 the Deputy Lieutenant or resident governor at the Tower was Adam Williamson, veteran of Marlborough's campaigns, staunch Hanoverian – and diarist. It fell to Williamson to superintend some of the last executions at the Tower. In 1746 he had the charge of guarding four Scottish peers captured after the Battle of Culloden and held in the Tower: Lords Lovat, Balmerino, Kilmarnock and Traquair. Balmerino and Kilmarnock were promptly handed over to the sheriffs and beheaded on Tower Hill.

August 18th 1746 The Lords beheaded. The stage, rooms of the house and the stairs being covered with black, all prepared at the expense of the sheriffs, they came at 10 o'clock precisely and knocked at the Outward Gate, which with all the others were kept close shut, and demanded the prisoners ... We immediately set out from their apartments, and I had the doors locked after them and the keys given to me, that if any valuable thing was left in them I might secure it as my perquisite.

When we came into the street, we went on foot in the following manner. First went their four warders, two and two, then I followed singly. After me followed Lord Kilmarnock, the prisoner, with the major, then followed the chaplains and two friends, then Lord Balmerino attended by the gentleman gaoler, after him two friends but no chaplain (his non-juring chaplain having taken leave of him the night before), then followed an officer and fifteen men, after them the two hearses with the coffins for the two Lords, then a

The beheading of the Jacobite lords, Kilmarnock and Balmerino, at Tower Hill, 1746.

sergeant with fifteen men more, all with their bayonets fixed. Thus we marched to the gate, which being opened we delivered the Lord there to the sheriffs, who conducted them in the same order on foot to the house of the scaffold ...

By the Lords' direction, the block was desired to be two feet high and a piece of red baize to be had in which to catch their heads and not to let them fall into the sawdust and filth of the stage, which was done; and the Earl of Kilmarnock had his head severed from the body at one stroke, all but a little skin which with a little chop was soon separated. He had ordered one of his warders to attend him as his valet du chambre and to keep down the body from struggling or violent convulsive motion, but it only flounced backward on the separation of his head and lay on its back, with very little motion. Lord Balmerino's fate was otherwise, for though he was a resolute Jacobite and seemed to have more than ordinary courage and indifference for death, yet when he laid his head on the block, it is said by those on the

scaffold that when he made his own signal for decoll-ation he withdrew his body, so that he had three cuts with the axe before his head was severed, and that the bystanders were forced to hold his body and head to the block while the separation was making.

After all was over and I had dined, I sent my servants with the keys to open their prisons and bring all their effects to me as of right I ought, they belonging to my office as commanding officer on the spot. But being little worth and no plate or things of dignity, I gave them all to the warders that attended them, and they took them as my gift with thanks.

1748/65

Two foreign observers

A visit to London was becoming *de rigueur* for the educated man or woman by 1750. The liveliest visitors had their own particular agenda. In 1748 Peter Kalm, the Swedish botanist, enjoyed grubbing around the outskirts.

The land around Chelsea is almost entirely devoted to nursery and vegetable gardens. The same is true of the land on all sides round about London, that it is mostly used as pleasure gardens, nurseries and market gardens; because the vastness of London and the fearful number of people which crawl there in the streets pay the gardeners manyfold for their labour and outlay. These nurseries and market gardens are surrounded either with earth-banks or walls or wooden fences, or living hedges of trees, or with walls of oxhorn . . . Plank fences made of boards were also used here in many places, but the boards which were used for this purpose were no other than those they had bought from old, broken-up ships and boats which were still quite full of nails . . . Hawthorn was the tree of which most hedges were consisted, but besides this I also saw hedges of elm, especially a small kind of it, also of yew, maple, sloe etc. In gardens, no tree was so much used for hedges as yew, which admitted of being clipped and managed in various ways . . . Besides ordinary vegetables, there were planted in the market gardens all sorts of flowers, which the passers-by bought and carried with them. I saw also the whole of this season both men, old women and girls walk or sit in the streets of London with baskets full of all kinds of flowers bound in small bunches which they offered to the passers-by, who bought them in great numbers. The vegetables which were most numerous in the market gardens at this season [late spring] were beans, peas, cabbages of different sorts, chives, radishes, lettuce, asparagus and spinach. The greater part of these were sown in rows, so that they could more easily clear away the weeds between them with English hoes and keep the earth loose ... The mould was moved on to the stalks of the plants more and more as they grew, so that they stood as it were banked up ... Between the plants which were sown thicker the earth was cleared of weeds and hoed up with quite small hoes of about two inches broad and with a handle two feet long; but it cost enough to the hoer, who was thus obliged to go very crook-backed and stooping the whole day.

Pierre-Jean Grosley from Troyes was among the most meticulous of eighteenth-century commentators upon London. During his stay in 1765 he noted everything useful and progressive that he saw, in the enquiring, Anglophilic spirit of the French Enlightenment. But a pall was cast on his visit by the damp and smuts of London, to which he constantly refers.

CLEANLINESS

The humid and dark air which enwraps London requires the greatest cleanliness imaginable, and in this respect the citizens seem to vie with the Hollanders. The plate, hearthstones, moveables, apartments, doors, stairs, the very street-doors, their locks and the large brass knockers are every day washed, scoured or rubbed. Even in lodging houses the middle of the stairs is often covered with carpeting, to prevent them from being soiled. All the apartments in the house have mats or carpets; and the use of them has been adopted some years since by the French ... The houses in London are all wainscotted with deal; the stairs and the floors are composed of the same materials, and cannot bear the continual rubbing of feet without being cracked and worn. This renders carpets and coverings necessary. Add to this, that these floors (which are of excellent deal and are washed and rubbed almost daily) have a whiteish appearance and an air of freshness and cleanliness which the finest inlaid floor has not always.

'Tis purely to defend themselves against humidity that the English make so constant a practice of washing their apartments – a custom which renders a fire absolutely necessary when it might be most easy to do without one. But even in those seasons it would, as they affirm, be still more necessary, if the water did not absorb the humidity which the air leaves behind it wherever it pervades. Hence London would be uninhabitable, if to supply it with constant fuel it had not a resource in sea-coal, which immense forests would be insufficient to furnish.

SERVANTS

The care of servants is here equal to the punctuality of masters who, generally speaking, follow one invariable order in the whole progress of their lives. All the domestics of the citizens are dressed in plain but good clothes; and insolence is not the characteristic of any in that station in life. Coachmen as a mark of distinction wear an upper coat adorned with a long cape of two or three rows, each of which has a fringe ... With regard to outward appearance and demeanour, the coachman of a minister or of the first nobleman or of the most eminent merchant in London has nothing to distinguish him from his comrades, who do not seem to consider even the meanest hackney coachmen as their inferiors.

The servant maids of citizens' wives, the waiting women of ladies of the first quality and of the middling gentry, attend their ladies in the streets and in the public walks in such a dress that if the mistress be not known, it is no easy matter to distinguish her from her maid.

The assiduity, the care, the cleanliness and the industry which the English require in their servants fix the value of their wages: that is to say, their wages are very considerable. The reader may form a judgement of them from those given by my landlord to a fat Welsh girl who was just come out of the country, scarce understood a word of English, was capable of nothing but washing, scouring and sweeping the rooms, and had no inclination to learn anything more. The wages of this girl were six guineas a year, besides a guinea a year for her tea, which all servant maids either take in money or have it found for them twice a day.

LODGINGS

Lodging is exorbitantly dear at London ... The house in which I occupied an apartment, built upon an irregular ground in the shape of a harpsichord only sixty feet high and fourteen broad, and which had but three stories comprising the kitchen, a pantry and other places below stairs, was rented at thirty-eight guineas a

A drawing room in St Martin's Lane, c.1796. The family of John Middleton, artist's colourman, is shown, with their housekeeper seated to the left.

year. The landlord was moveover obliged to pay a guinea a year for water, with which the houses of London are supplied at the yearly taxation, besides two towards the poors' tax, and three for window-lights, scavengers and the watch. This water, with which all the houses in London are supplied, is regularly distributed to them three times a week in proportion to the quantity made use of in each house. It comes through subterraneous pipes of a diameter suited to the quantity to be distributed, from whence it is received and preserved in great leaden cisterns.

1760s

Vice after dark

From the Georgian era we start to get a sharper picture of low life in the capital – of drinking, gaming, wenching, criminality and sport. There was nothing new in these pursuits; but they begin to be written about with a fuller, more objective, more troubled, and sometimes – as with James Boswell and William Hickey – confessionary tone. London's hordes of prostitutes, for instance, always provided journalists with good copy. They invade even Oliver Goldsmith's satirical *The Citizen of the World*, which he contributed to the *Public Ledger* in 1760–1. Its instalments purport to be the letters of a naive Chinese visitor.

The manners of the ladies in this city are so very open and so vastly engaging that I am inclined to pass over the more glaring defects of their persons ... What though they want black teeth or are deprived of the allurements of feet no bigger than thumbs, yet still they have souls, my friend, such souls, so free, so pressing, so hospitable and so engaging. I have received more invitations in the streets of London from the sex in one night than I have met with at Pekin in twelve revolutions of the moon.

Every evening as I return home from my usual solitary excursions, I am met by several of those well-disposed daughters of hospitality at different times and in different streets, richly dressed and with minds no less noble than their appearance. You know that nature has indulged me with a person by no means agreeable, yet are they too generous to object to my homely appearance. They feel no repugnance at my broad face and flat nose; they perceive me to be a stranger, and that alone is sufficient recommendation. They even seem to think it their duty to do the honours of the country by every act of complaisance in their power. One takes me under the arm and in a manner forces me along; another catches me round the neck and desires to partake in this office of hospitality; while a third, kinder still, invites me to refresh my spirit with wine. Wine is in England

Vice for sale on Ludgate Hill, 1749. The main London thoroughfares and the London parks were the favourite venues for cheap prostitution. The authorities interfered little with the trade.

only reserved for the rich, yet here even wine is given away to the stranger.

A few nights ago one of those generous creatures, dressed all in white and flaunting like a meteor by my side, forcibly attended me home to my own apartment. She seemed charmed with the elegance of the furniture and the convenience of my situation. And well indeed she might, for I have hired an apartment for not less than two shillings of their money every week. But her civility did not rest here; for at parting, being desirous to know the hour and perceiving my watch out of order, she kindly took it to be repaired by a relation of her own, which you may imagine will save some expense, and she assures me that it will cost her nothing. I shall have it back in a few days when mended, and am preparing a proper speech expressive of my gratitude on the occasion.

The candour of the London journal that the young James Boswell kept in 1762–3 still has the capacity to startle. Boswell was not then long down from Scotland and full of undirected energy. His moods shifted constantly, from

literary ambition to raw animal spirits and hence to languorous fits of remorse. For a time he kept a semi-permanent mistress. The arrangement was agreed between the two with businesslike coolness, though Boswell was certainly keen on her. But this did not hold him back from outdoor encounters with cheap whores. St James's Park and the Strand were among their traditional venues after dark.

4 June 1763 It was the King's birthnight, and I resolved to be a blackguard and to see all that was to be seen. I dressed myself in my second-morning suit, in which I had been powdered many months, dirty buckskin breeches and black stockings, a shirt of Lord Eglinton's which I had worn two days, and little round hat with tarnished silver lace belonging to a disbanded officer of the Royal Volunteers. I had in my hand an old oaken stick battered against the pavement. And was I not a complete blackguard? I went to the Park, picked up a low brimstone, called myself a barber and agreed with her for sixpence, went to the bottom of the Park arm in arm, dipped my machine in the canal and performed most manfully. I then went as far as St Paul's Church-yard, roaring along, and then came to Ashley's Punch-house and drank three threepenny bowls. In the Strand I picked up a little profligate wretch and gave her sixpence. She allowed me entrance. But the miscreant refused me performance. I was much stronger than her, and *volens nolens* pushed her up against the wall. She however gave a sudden spring from me; and screaming out, a parcel of more whores and soldiers came to her relief. 'Brother soldiers,' I said, 'should not a half-pay officer r*g*r for sixpence? And here she used me so and so.' I got them on my side and I abused her in blackguard style, and then left them. At Whitehall I picked up another girl to whom I called myself a highwayman and told her I had no money and begged she would trust me. But she would not. My vanity was somewhat gratified tonight that, notwithstanding of my dress, I was always taken for a gentleman in disguise. I came home about two o'clock, much fatigued.

William Hickey was an observant young man with money who was easily led astray. According to his memoirs, written in retrospect, Hickey's propensity for getting dragged by friends into London low-life caused his respectable parents much anxiety and heart-searching. After a period of good behaviour, his friends lured him off one night to a Hogarthian den.

At the customary hour, being brim full of wine, we sallied forth, went the old Bow Street rounds, from whence I was led into an absolute hell upon earth. The first impression on my mind upon entering these diabolical regions never will be effaced from my memory. This den was distinguished by the name of Wetherby's, situate in the narrowest part of Little Russell Street, Drury Lane. Upon ringing at a door, strongly secured with knobs of iron, a cut-throat-looking rascal opened a small wicket which was also secured with iron bars, who in a hoarse and ferocious voice asked, 'Who's there?' Being answered 'Friends', we were cautiously admitted one at a time and, when the last had entered, the door was instantly closed and secured, not only by an immense lock and key but a massy iron bolt and chain ... My companions conducted me into a room where such a scene was exhibiting that I involuntarily shrunk back with disgust and dismay, and would have retreated from the apartment, but that I found my surprise and alarm were so visible in my countenance as to have attracted the attention of several persons who came up, and good-naturedly enough encouraged me, observing that I was a young hand but should soon be familiarized and enjoy the fun.

At this time the whole room was in an uproar, men and women promiscuously mounted upon chairs, tables and benches, in order to see a sort of general conflict carried on upon the floor. Two she-devils, for they scarce had a human appearance, were engaged in a scratching and boxing match, their faces entirely covered with blood, bosoms bare and the clothes nearly torn from their bodies. For several minutes not a creature interfered between them or seemed to care a straw what mischief they might do each other, and the contest went on with unabated fury.

In another corner of the room, an uncommonly athletic young man of about twenty-five seemed to be the object of universal attack. No less than three Amazonian tigresses were pummelling him with all their might, and it appeared to me that some of the males at times dealt him blows with their sticks. He however made a capital defence, not sparing the women a bit more than the men but knocking each down as opportunity occurred. As fresh hands continued pouring in upon him, he must at last have been miserably beaten, had not two of the gentlemen who went with me (both very stout fellows) offended at the shameful odds used against a single person, interfered and after a few knock-me-down arguments succeeded in putting an end to the unequal conflict.

1780

The Gordon Riots

The climax of renewed mob violence in London, and the nastiest moment in the city's eighteenth-century history, came in June 1780, when the unstable Lord George Gordon whipped up an anti-Catholic frenzy. The situation got out of all control as the riot shifted over several days into generalized violence against authority. Not only houses and chapels but prisons were sacked before the dithering authorities could calm things down. The hero of the hour was John Wilkes, the radical rabble-rouser of the 1760s. The events were recounted in their different but equally Tory styles by Horace Walpole writing to Sir Horace Mann, and by Doctor Johnson to Mrs Thrale. This was the last great aimless London riot. Later agitations were more disciplined and on the whole had more articulate political aims and ends.

Walpole to Mann, 5 June 1780

Lord George Gordon gave notice to the House of Commons last week that he would on Friday bring the petition of the Protestant Association; and he openly declared to his disciples that he would not carry it unless a noble army of martyrs, not fewer than forty thousand, would accompany him. Forty thousand led by such a lamb were more likely to prove butchers than victims, and so in good truth they were very near being . . .

Early on Friday morning the conservators of the Church of England assembled in St George's Fields to encounter the dragon, the old serpent, and marched in lines of six and six (13,000 only, as they were computed) with a petition as long as the procession, which the apostle himself presented. But though he had given out most Christian injunctions for peaceable behaviour, he did everything in his power to promote a massacre. He demanded immediate repeal of toleration, told Lord North he could have him torn to pieces, and running every minute to the door or windows bawled to the populace that Lord North would give them no redress and that now this member, now that, was speaking against them.

In the meantime the peers, going to their own chamber and as yet not concerned in the petition, were assaulted. Many of their glasses were broken and many of their persons torn out of the carriages . . . Lord North and that House behaved with great firmness, and would not submit to give any other satisfaction to the rioters than to take the Popish laws into consideration on the following Tuesday; and calling the Justices of the Peace, empowered them to call out the whole force of the county to quell the riot.

The magistrates soon brought the horse and foot guards and the pious ragamuffins fled, so little enthusiasm fortunately had inspired them. At least, all their religion consisted in outrage and plunder, for the Duke of Northumberland, General Grant, Mr Mackinsy and others had their pockets picked of their watches and snuff boxes. Happily, not a single life was lost.

This tumult, which was over between nine and ten at night, had scarce ceased before it broke out in two other quarters. Old Haslang's chapel was broken open and plundered; and as he is a prince of smugglers as well as Bavarian minister, great quantities of rum, tea and contraband goods were found in his house . . . Monsieur Cordon, the Sardinian minister, suffered still more. The mob forced his chapel, stole two silver lamps, demolished everything else, threw the benches in the street, set them on fire, and when the engines came would not suffer them to play till the Guards arrived and saved the house and probably all that part of the town.

Johnson to Mrs Thrale, 5–8 June 1780

On Tuesday night they pulled down Fielding's house, and burnt his goods in the street. They had gutted on Monday Sir George Savile's house, but the building was saved. On Tuesday evening, leaving Fielding's ruins, they went to Newgate to demand their companions who had been seized demolishing the chapel. The keeper could not release them but by the Mayor's permission, which he went to ask; at his return he found all the prisoners released and Newgate in a blaze . . . On Wednesday I walked with Dr Scott to look at Newgate and found it in ruins, with the fire yet glowing. As I

went by, the Protestants were plundering the Sessions House at the Old Bailey. There were not, I believe, a hundred, but they did their work at leisure in full security, without sentinels, without trepidation, as men lawfully employed, in full day. Such is the cowardice of a commercial place. On Wednesday they broke open the Fleet and King's Bench and the Marshalsea and Wood Street Compter and Clerkenwell Bridewell and released all the prisoners . . . they set fire to the Fleet and to the King's Bench and I know not how many other places, and one might see the glare of conflagration fill the sky from many parts. The sight was dreadful . . .

Several chapels have been destroyed and several inoffensive Papists have been plundered, but the high sport was to burn the gaols. This was a good rabble trick. The debtors and the criminals were all set at liberty; but of the criminals, as has always happened, many are already retaken . . .

The public has escaped a very heavy calamity. The rioters attempted the Bank on Wednesday night but in no great numbers – and like other thieves, with no great resolution. Jack Wilkes headed the party that drove them away. It is agreed that if they had seized the Bank on Tuesday at the height of the panic, when no resistance had been prepared, they might have carried irrecoverably away whatever they had found. Jack, who was always zealous for order and decency, declares that if he be trusted with power, he will not leave a rioter alive.

RIGHT *Conference at Wesley's Chapel, City Road, with John Wesley preaching, probably in 1779.*

OPPOSITE *The sack and burning of Newgate Gaol during the Gordon Riots, 1780.*

1739–83

The seeds of social reform

Efforts to combat the viciousness and violence of London life had a long history by the time of the Gordon Riots. Where the start of 'social reform' in London's history should best be placed is debatable; but it is connected with the transformation of the puritan religious tradition during the Georgian period. We tend to think of Georgian London as a secularized city. Yet it was always susceptible to serious religious influence, as the numbers of those who responded to John Wesley remind us. His estimates may be exaggerated, but the Wesleys, George Whitefield, and the great London dissenting ministers who succeeded them had an incalculable effect in making sober people, particularly of the merchant class, face up to the great issues of conscience.

14 June 1739 I went with Mr Whitefield to Blackheath, where were, I believe, twelve or fourteen thousand people ... I was greatly moved with compassion for the

rich that were there, to whom I made a particular application. Some of them seemed to attend, while others drove away their coaches from so uncouth a preacher.

15 June In the evening I went to a society at Wapping, weary in body and faint in spirit ... While I was earnestly inviting all sinners to 'enter into the holiest' by this 'new and living way', many of those that heard began to call upon God with strong cries and tears. Some sunk down, and there remained no strength in them; others exceedingly trembled and quaked; some were torn with a kind of convulsive motion in every part of their bodies, and that so violently that often four or five persons could not hold one of them.

17 June I preached at seven at Upper Moorfields to (I believe) six or seven thousand people. At five I preached on Kennington Common to about fifteen thousand people on those words, 'Look unto me and be ye saved, all the ends of the earth'.

9 September I declared to about ten thousand in Moorfields what they must do to be saved. My mother went with us, about five, to Kennington, where were supposed to be twenty thousand people ... From Kennington I went to a society at Lambeth. The house being filled, the rest stood in the garden.

Many efforts at secular reform can be traced back to the extraordinary Fielding brothers – Henry, the novelist and barrister, and his longer-lived brother John, the 'Blind Beak' of Bow Street. Magistrates, entrepreneurs and self-publicists, the energetic Fieldings laid down the rudiments of London's modern police and police court system. All sorts of curious schemes for London were promoted through the pages of the *Public Advertiser*, which Sir John Fielding owned. But they also had a disinterested commitment to civic welfare and safety in an age when the

George, Bloomsbury, one woman alone occupies seven of these houses, all properly accommodated with miserable beds from the cellar to the garret for such twopenny lodgers. That in these beds, several of which are in the same room, men and women, often strangers to each other, lie promiscuously, the price of a double bed being no more than threepence, as an encouragement to them to lie together. That as these places are

LEFT *Gin Lane: Hogarth's celebrated indictment of metropolitan poverty and depravity. Note St George's, Bloomsbury in the background.*

OPPOSITE *The first Bow Street magistrates' court, with blind Sir John Fielding presiding.*

politics of self-interest were taken for granted. The Fieldings' movement goes back to an enquiry published by Henry Fielding in 1750, four years before his early death, into the increase of robberies in London. By rooting crime in poverty, it is an early classic of social investigation.

The following account I have had from Mr Welch, the High Constable of Holborn; and none who know that gentleman will want any confirmation of the truth of it. That in the parish of St Giles's there are great numbers of houses set apart for the reception of idle persons and vagabonds, who have their lodgings there for twopence a night. That in the above parish and in St

thus adapted to whoredom, so are they no less provided for drunkenness, gin being sold in them all at a penny a quartern, so that the smallest sum serves for intoxication. That in the execution of search warrants, Mr Welch rarely finds less than twenty of these houses open for the receipt of all comers at the latest hours. That in one of these houses, and that not a large one, he hath numbered 58 persons of both sexes, the stench of whom was so intolerable that it compelled him in a very short time to quit the place ... Among other mischiefs attending this wretched nuisance, the greater increase of thieves must necessarily be one. The wonder in fact is that we have not a thousand more robbers than we have; indeed, that all these wretches are not thieves must give us either a very high idea of their honesty or a very mean one of their capacity and courage.

Fielding's blind brother John succeeded to Henry's magistracy, which he ran from his house in Bow Street, Covent Garden. It was soon turned also to a police office, by means of notices like the following in the *Public Advertiser*.

Whereas many thieves and robbers daily escape justice for want of immediate pursuit, it is therefore recommended to all persons who shall henceforth be robbed on the highway or in the streets, or whose shops are broken into, that they give immediate notice thereof with as accurate description of the offenders as possible to JOHN FIELDING, Esq, at his house in Bow Street, Covent Garden; by which means, joined to an advertisement containing an account of the things lost (which is also taken in there) thieves and robbers will seldom escape, as most of the principal pawnbrokers take in this paper, and by the intelligence they get from it assist daily in discovering and apprehending rogues.

And if they would send a special messenger on these occasions, Mr Fielding would not only pay that messenger for his trouble but would immediately dispatch a set of brave fellows in pursuit who have been long engaged for such purposes, and are always ready to set out to any part of this town or kingdom on a quarter of an hour's notice.

John Fielding's 'set of brave fellows' was an attempt to improve on the corrupt amateur system of thief-taking previously used in London. In due course they were supplemented by a mobile 'horse patrol' to combat highway robbery. Its extended beat is thus reported in the *Public Advertiser* for 1764.

We hear that the present Horse Patrol passes by Pimlico and Chelsea and along the King's Road to Fulham, and through the turnpikes at Hyde Park and Hammersmith to Brentford, round Acton, Ealing, Tyburn, Paddington, Tottenham Court, Hendon, Highgate, through Holloway to Islington, Stamford Hill, Shoreditch, the New City Road, Whitechapel, and on the Surrey side over Westminster Bridge to Greenwich, Clapham, Newington, Kennington Lane and towards Wandsworth; and that in case of notice of any robbery left at any of those turnpikes committed farther on, they have directions to collect their force and pursue to any distance; and as this patrol is constantly in motion, every part of these roads is constantly guarded. We hear that most of the commissioners of the several turnpike roads round London have politely offered to Sir John Fielding that the Horse Patrol ... shall be permitted to pass and repass toll free.

The lengths to which Sir John Fielding went in trying to reduce the incidence of theft led him into close touch with the Jewish community of the inner East End, where many of London's receivers – the ancestors of Dickens's Fagin – were based. The following carefully worded exchange took place in 1766 between the 'Blind Beak' and the Presidents of the Great Synagogue in Duke's Place.

Sir John Fielding presents his respectful compliments to Mr Napthaly Franks and Mr Napthaly Myers; thinks himself much obliged to them, as is the public, for the assistance they have already given to the civil power to detect the receivers of stolen goods in Duke's Place and Houndsditch, and also for their laudable declarations to continue their assistance till the evil itself is suppressed. And Sir John Fielding is persuaded that as this practice has been carried on by a few persons only, that the countenance and protection of the respectable part of their body to the magistrates in their endeavours to cause such offenders to be apprehended will discourage this atrocious practice, benefit the public and reflect honour on themselves.

Answer

Sir,

We are honoured with your letter of yesterday, and are very happy in receiving your approbation of our endeavours to detect those Jew infamous receivers of stolen goods about Duke's Place and Houndsditch: wretches, who are a pest to every community . . .

We are firmly convinced that in pursuance of this our fixed resolution, we shall receive the applause of every Jew who is not totally ignorant of the laws of God, the duty of his own religion, the true regard for public justice and the obedience due to the laws of this kingdom . . .

> N. Franks
> N. H. Myers
> Presidents of the Great Synagogue

A more enlightened attitude towards punishment and better detection was needed if the roots of urban crime were to be tackled. No Georgian reformer did more in making this possible than John Howard, who spent the 1770s and 1780s methodically visiting Britain's prisons and exposing their fearful defects. His plain-speaking and beautifully produced books mostly just lay out the facts; but these are eloquent enough. Here is Howard's account of the Marshalsea, far from the worst of London's prisons, which he visited eight times between 1774 and 1783.

To this prison of the Court of the Marshalsea and of the King's Palace Court of Westminster are brought debtors arrested for the lowest sums anywhere within twelve miles of the palace, except in the City of London: and also persons committed for piracy.

This prison is held under several leases by the widow of the late deputy marshal at the yearly rent of £101. It is an old irregular building (rather several buildings) in a spacious court. There are in the whole near sixty rooms; and yet only six of them left for common-side debtors. Of the other rooms – five were let to a man who was not a prisoner; in one of them he kept a chandler's shop, in two he lived with his family; the other two he let to prisoners. Four rooms, the Oaks, were for women. They were too few for the number; and the more modest women complained of the bad company in which they were confined. There were above 44 rooms for men on the master's side in which were about 60 beds. Yet at my first visits many prisoners had no beds nor any places to sleep in but the chapel and the tap room. The chamber rent wants regulation, for in several rooms where four lie in two beds, and in some dark rooms where two lie in one bed, each pays 3s 6d for his lodgings.

The prison is greatly out of repair. No infirmary. The court is well supplied with water. In it the prisoners play at rackets etc., and in a little back court, the Park, at skittles.

The tap was let to a prisoner in the rules of the King's Bench Prison, this prison being just within those rules. I was credibly informed that one Sunday in the year 1775 about 600 pots of beer were brought in from a public house in the neighbourhood (Ashmore's), the prisoners not then liking the tapster's beer.

In March 1775 when the number of prisoners was 175, there were with them in this incommodious prison wives and children 46.

Since the Act of the 19th of George III Chap LXX, there are not so many debtors in this prison as formerly. Yet they are increasing, for I find here and in other prisons many debtors whose original debts are much under £10, but for the purpose of imprisoning such debtors they are prosecuted either in the court of the exchequer or in other inferior courts until the expense of such prosecutions when added to the original amount to £10. A fresh action is then taken out in the superior courts for the small original debt and the accumulated costs of prosecution. Thus the salutary purposes of the said act are defeated.

Mr Henry Allnott, who was many years hence a prisoner here, had during his confinement a large estate bequeathed to him. He learnt sympathy by his sufferings, and left £100 a year for discharging poor debtors from hence whose debts do not exceed £4. As he bound his manor of Goring in Oxfordshire for charitable uses, this is called the Oxford charity. Many are cleared by it every year.

1775

Shopping in Oxford Street

Shopping is what foreign visitors to London most want to do today; and it was the same two hundred years ago. The French, having Paris, were not quite so impressed with the glitter and richness of London's shops as the Germans.

Even so sober a figure as the pastor and scientist Lichtenberg could not get over the glamour of Cheapside and Fleet Street in 1775. All the more smitten, then, eleven years later was the bourgeois socialite Sophie von la Roche, as she window-shopped along the well-paved length of Oxford Street, admiring goods lit up by the brilliance of the newly invented Argand oil lamps.

We strolled up and down lovely Oxford Street this evening, for some goods look more attractive by artificial light. Just imagine, dear children, a street taking half an hour to cover from end to end, with double rows of brightly shining lamps, in the middle of which stands an equally long row of beautifully lacquered coaches, and on each side of these there is room for two coaches to pass one another; and the pavement, inlaid with flagstones, can stand six people deep and allows one to gaze at the splendidly lit shop fronts in comfort. First one passes a watchmaker's, then a silk or fan store, now a silversmith's, a china or glass shop. The spirit booths are particularly tempting, for the English are in any case fond of strong drink. Here crystal flasks of every shape and form are exhibited: each one has a light behind it which makes all the different coloured spirits sparkle. Just as alluring are the confectioners and fruiterers where, behind the handsome glass windows, pyramids of pineapples, figs, grapes, oranges and all manner of fruits are on show ... Up to eleven o'clock at night there are as many people along this street as at Frankfurt during the fair, not to mention the eternal stream of coaches. The arrangement of the shops in good perspective, with their adjoining living rooms, makes a very pleasant sight. For right through the excellently illuminated shop one can see many a charming family scene enacted: some are still at work, others drinking tea, a third party is entertaining a friendly visitor; in a fourth parents are joking and playing with children. Such a series of tableaux of domestic and busy life is hardly to be met within an hour as I witnessed here.

1788

The trial of Warren Hastings

In 1788 commenced in Westminster Hall the intermittent inquisition of Warren Hastings, impeached for impropriety during his time as Governor General in India. Edmund Burke led the politically motivated prosecution of this great fallen star, and all London society was agog to see what would happen. A certain Mary Frampton, then fifteen, later

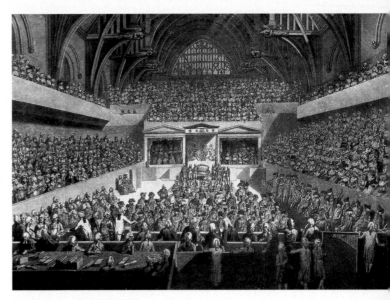

Early days at the trial of Warren Hastings, Westminster Hall, 1788.

recollected the festive atmosphere of those opening days. But people, as she explains, soon got bored with the Hastings trial. When Hastings was acquitted in 1795, Burke's star too had faded. London, its high society, and the world seemed a quite different place; for the French Revolution and its consequences were beginning to overshadow everything.

In 1788 the impeachment and trial of Warren Hastings were the subjects of frequent conversation, and the attendance at his trial for the first few years was the object of everyone's desire. I was fortunate, and had a ticket for the Duke of Newcastle's gallery where, besides the advantage of getting to your seat in Westminster Hall quite quietly through a fine house, in the passage which communicated with that gallery there was for the first year or two a handsome cold collation regularly set out for those admitted by the Duke's ticket. My aunt, Elizabeth Fanquier, attended with me constantly one year, and I heard Mr Burke make his opening speech and several of the other managers declaim against Mr Hastings and, being very young, was of course carried away by their eloquence to believe all the charges ... The *coup d'œil* was magnificent: that fine building, Westminster Hall, full in every part, with gentlemen and ladies full dressed and the peers in their robes. The Prince of Wales's bow to the throne on entering and before taking his seat was universally admired ... The length of the trial put an end by degrees not only to the Duke of Newcastle's collations, which were omitted entirely after the second year, but to all interest respecting the parties concerned on either side, and empty benches and woolsacks as well as empty galleries succeeded to the crowding and pressure for places and tickets of admission.

1789–1837

LONDON

in the

ERA *of*

REVOLUTION

In these years, London achieved its own eccentric, terrible greatness. The star of France waned, waxed and waned again, leaving Britain the unrivalled arbiter of nations. Compared to the turbulence of Paris, London relished growth, peace and prosperity. But it was far from unalloyed. Terror of revolution in the early 1790s and again in 1816–19; economic ups and downs of a magnitude not known since the South Sea Bubble; a creeping ruthlessness in the organization of manufacturing and commercial life: such was the tarnish upon Regency London. Above all, London had swollen to a size that frightened people. Not for nothing did William Cobbett christen it the 'great wen', and advocate dispersing its population to the countryside. Slumps there might be, but nothing could stem the constant drip of skilled and unskilled labour into London from the country. Though London meant dirt and danger, it also meant variety, glamour, wages and matchless opportunity.

Hitherto, the metropolis had been just a forest of streets, yards, stables, wharves and houses, little or large, punctuated by the occasional church spire and, in the West End, a sprinkling of smart squares. The number of public buildings was tiny; trade and craft struggled along as best they might in adapted houses. Now, all this changed. The first new buildings on the larger scale were the bonded warehouses, grim brick hulks pioneered in the heart of the City by the East India Company during the 1790s to guard their precious spices from the thievery plethoric in the Pool of London. These were taken up and aggrandized in the series of enclosed docks, undertakings of Roman ambition, engineered down-river from the Tower after 1800: the West India Dock, the London Dock, the East India Dock, the Surrey Docks, and – added in the 1820s – the St Katharine's Dock. Along with the new docks and the reform of the port came a network of man-made waterways, chiefly the Regent's Canal, linking the Thames with the coal, iron and pottery of the Midlands via the Grand Junction Canal; fresh bridges at Vauxhall, Waterloo, Southwark and a rebuilt London Bridge; and the world's first joint-stock railroad, the horse-

ABOVE *The opening of the West India Docks. By P.W. Tomkins, 1802.*

OPPOSITE *Section through the approaches to the Thames Tunnel.
By Benjamin Schlick, 1826.*

drawn Surrey Iron Railway (1801–3), bearing freight from Croydon to a basin and wharf at Wandsworth. Industry too took up the challenge of scale. Large factories were unknown in London before the short-lived Albion Mill of 1783–6, a corn-grinding plant next to Blackfriars Bridge. Over the next half-century brewers, printers, cabinet-makers and even silk-weavers all raised heavy brick warehouse-style buildings for the purposes of technological efficiency and control. London was too industrially various ever to be dominated by the factory system. But the age of the large London employer and his needful watchdog, the trades union for skilled workers, began between 1800 and 1830.

Typically for London, this revolution of metropolitan scale proceeds out of private commercial ambition rather than public pride. Its rightful heroes are engineers like John Rennie and William Jessop, not architects like Soane or Nash. Great public buildings of course now arose in London; Britain's wealth, responsibilities and new-found consciousness of power demanded them. After 1815 there was a half-formulated urge to emulate Paris. Public projects of the era include a lavish British Museum, a stinted National Gallery, and the rebuilding of Buckingham Palace for that most free-spending of British sovereigns, George IV. Acts of Parliament in 1818–19 decreed subsidies for Anglican church-building throughout the land in the hope of shoring up social mores, and gave birth to a bevy of cheap Greek and Gothic churches in London suburbs. Nevertheless, foreigners were amazed that schemes they assumed to have been promoted by government were in fact the fruit of unaided private enterprise. Waterloo Bridge, the greatest of Rennie's bridges, was the work of a joint-stock company; it got its name only after fine words about an official monument to victory over Napoleon had come to nothing. The Prince Regent condescended to open it in 1817, but the bridge never received a penny of public money. Even the proud layout of Regent Street and Regent's Park was not strictly a public project but a grand speculation on Crown land. So it is unsurprising that there were meretricious and opportunistic sides to the skills of the greatest London architect of the age, John Nash. But the abounding

Opened in 1800, London Dock was the first of the great enclosed docks along the Thames. Aquatint by Daniel and Robert Havell.

brick and stucco squares and crescents that sprang up in all quarters of London in the 1820s owe everything to Nash's scenic inventiveness.

The self-consciousness of London in this era is marked by a new kind of writing about it. Journalists, diarists and travellers hitherto had revelled in the quaintness, horror and spice of metropolitan life. What we now get in Wordsworth, Lamb, De Quincey, Leigh Hunt – and, in small measure, even in Blake – is a new kind of urban word-painting, less remarked upon than the contemporary romantic approach to scenery. The changing impressions of London, above all its street scenes, roll indiscriminately over these authors. They may not approve of what they see, but it touches their heart and that is what they record.

Only the faintest touches of this impressionism are found in contemporary painting of London. The greatest strength of the visual arts as regards London at this time lies in caricature. As yet there is no powerful depiction of the gulf between wealth and poverty which, in the opulent but nerve-racking Tory years after Waterloo, is beginning to exercise thoughtful people. Peers and clubs may rebuild their homes on a palatial scale in emulation of George IV; salons may relish high sophistication of manners and intellect. But the Spitalfields silk industry is starting to collapse, and the inner East End is on the point of sinking with it into irredeemable, crowded slummery. Radicalized artisans, frustrated by wages and prices, meet at Spa Fields, talk revolution, half-riot and are dispersed; a few swing in consequence. The nearest that revolution comes to fruition is the pathetic Cato Street Conspiracy to assassinate the Cabinet: in reality, the power of the London mob is in decline.

From this time onwards, the concept of urban reform catches fire. Many, both radicals and conservatives, see the answer to London's problems as lying in a renewal of religion. That is why so many churches and chapels are opened in the 1820s. But the Church of England has lost the loyalty of so many merchants and artisans that the old link between Church and State is beginning to fray; by the time of Queen Victoria's accession, the secular and religious functions of London's parishes have been sundered. More important for the future welfare of the city than its new churches are the voluntary schools for the poor started after 1810: National Schools by the Anglicans, British and Foreign Schools by Nonconformists. From this seed grows the great educational movement that did so much to civilize London and Londoners in the nineteenth century.

1791–2

Haydn in London

Joseph Haydn made his first visit to London in 1791–2. He was lionized wherever he went and on the whole thoroughly enjoyed himself. He jotted down oddments and impressions of all kinds and in all sorts of languages. They convey the great composer's pert, incisive but very human reaction to the vast metropolis. He is at his warmest and harshest on his beloved subject – music.

On 5th November I was guest at a lunch given in honour of the Lord Mayor. The new Lord Mayor and his wife ate at the first table, No. 1, then the Lord Chancellor and both the sheriffs, Duke of Leeds, Minister Pitt and the other judges of the first rank. At No. 2, I ate with Mr Silvester, the greatest lawyer and first alderman of London. In this room, which is called the Guildhall, there were sixteen tables besides others in the adjoining rooms; in all, nearly 1,200 persons dined, all with the greatest pomp. The food was very nice and well-cooked; many kinds of wine in abundance . . . At 9 o'clock No. 1 rose and went to a small room, at which point the ball began; in this room there is, *a parte*, an elevated place for the high noblesse where the Lord Mayor is seated on a throne together with his wife . . . In this small room there are four tiers of raised benches on each side, where the fair sex mostly has the upper hand. Nothing but minuets are danced in this room. I couldn't stand it longer than a quarter of an hour, first because the heat caused by so many people in such a small room was so great; and secondly, because of the wretched dance band, the entire orchestra consisting only of two violins and a violoncello. The minuets were more Polish than in our or the Italian manner. From there I went to another room which was more like a subterraneous cavern, and where the dance was English; the music was a little better, because there was a

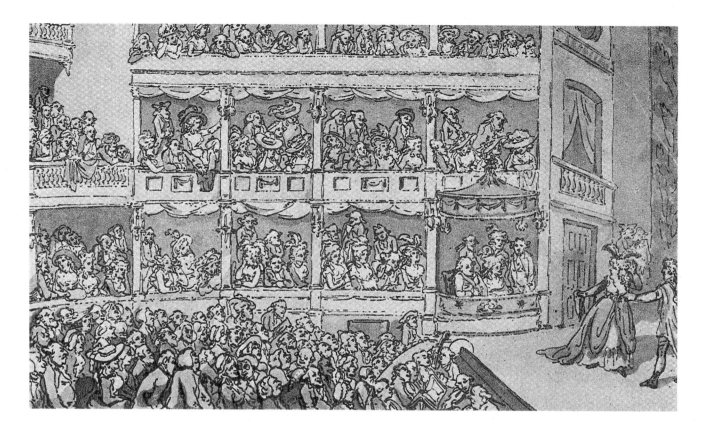

drum in the band which drowned the misery of the violins. I went on to the great hall where we had eaten, and there the band was larger and more bearable. The dance was English, but only on the raised platform where the Lord Mayor and the first four numbers had dined. The other tables, however, were all occupied again by men who, as usual, drank enormously the whole night. The most curious thing, though, is that a part of the company went on dancing without hearing a single note of the music, for first at one table, then at another, some were yelling songs and some swilling it down and drinking toasts amid terrific roars of 'Hooray, Hooray, Hooray' and waving of glasses. The hall and all the other rooms are illuminated with lamps which give out an unpleasant odour.

The City of London consumes eight times one hundred thousand cartloads of coal each year; each cart holds thirteen sacks, each sack holds two dry measures: most of the coal comes from Newcastle. Often 200 loaded ships arrive at once. A cartload costs £2½. [Added later:] In the year 1795, the coal measure or dry measure £7. Within the last thirty years, 38,000 houses were built.

Today, 4 June 1792, I was in Vauxhall where the King's birthday is celebrated. Over 30,000 lamps were burning, but because of the severe cold very few people were

Covent Garden Theatre in 1786. The lights remained up in theatres during the eighteenth century; audiences were as interested in one another as in the action on stage. Aquatint by Rowlandson.

present. The grounds and its variety are perhaps unique in the world. There are 155 little dining booths in various places, most charmingly situated, each comfortably seating six persons. There are very large alleys of trees which form a wonderful roof above, and are magnificently illuminated. Tea, coffee and milk with almonds all cost nothing. The entrance fee is half a crown per person. The music is fairly good. A stone statue of Handel has been erected. On the 2nd inst. there was a masked ball, and on this evening they took in 3,000 guineas.

Covent Garden is the national theatre. I was there on 10 December and saw an opera called *The Woodman* [by William Shield]. It was the very day on which the life story of Madam Billington, both from the good as well as from the bad sides, was announced; such impertinent enterprises are generally undertaken for interests. She sang rather timidly this evening, but very well all the same ... The Theatre is very dark and dirty, and is almost as large as the Vienna Court Theatre. The common people in the galleries of all the theatres are very impertinent; they set the fashion with all their unrestrained impetuosity, and whether something is repeated or not is determined by their yells. The parterre and all the boxes sometimes have to applaud a great deal to have something good repeated. That was just what happened this evening, with the Duet in the Third Act, which was very beautiful; and the pros and contras went on for nearly a quarter of an hour, till finally the parterre and the boxes won, and they repeated the Duet. Both the performers stood on the stage quite terrified, first retiring, then coming forward. THE ORCHESTRA IS SLEEPY.

The City of London keeps 4,000 carts for cleaning the streets, and 2,000 of these work every day.

1791

Two literary views

William Wordsworth lived in London for some months in 1791, just when Haydn was there, and celebrated the city in Book VII of *The Prelude*. His language and tone could not be more different from that of the Viennese composer, but he conveys the same passionate curiosity over metropolitan bustle, chaos and diversity.

– And first the look and aspect of the place
The broad high-way appearance, as it strikes
On strangers of all ages, the quick dance
Of colours, lights and forms, the Babel din
The endless stream of men, and moving things,
From hour to hour the illimitable walk
Still among streets with clouds and sky above,
The wealth, the bustle and the eagerness,
The glittering chariots with their pampered steeds,
Stalls, barrows, porters; midway in the street
The scavenger, who begs with hat in hand,
The labouring hackney coaches, the rash speed
Of coaches travelling far, whirled on with horn
Loud blowing, and the sturdy drayman's team,
Ascending from some alley of the Thames
And striking right across the crowded Strand
Till the fore horse veer round with punctual skill:
Here there and everywhere a weary throng
The comers and the goers face to face,
Face after face; the string of dazzling wares,
Shop after shop, with symbols, blazoned names,
And all the tradesman's honours overhead;
Here, fronts of houses, like a title-page
With letters huge inscribed from top to toe;
Stationed above the door, like guardian saints,
There, allegoric shapes, female or male;

Or physiognomies of real men,
Land-warriors, kings, or admirals of the sea,
Boyle, Shakespeare, Newton, or the attractive head
Of some Scotch doctor, famous in his day.

Meanwhile the roar continues, till at length,
Escaped as from an enemy, we turn
Abruptly into some sequestered nook
Still as a sheltered place when winds blow loud:
At leisure thence, through tracts of thin resort,
And sights and sounds that come at intervals,
We take our way: a raree-show is here
With children gathered round, another street
Presents a company of dancing dogs,
Or dromedary, with an antic pair
Of monkies on his back, a minstrel band
Of Savoyards, or, single and alone
An English ballad-singer. Private courts,
Gloomy as coffins, and unsightly lanes
Thrilled by some female vendor's scream, belike
The very shrillest of all London cries,
May then entangle us awhile,
Conducted through those labyrinths unawares
To privileged regions and inviolate,
Where from their airy lodges studious lawyers
Look out on waters, walks and gardens green.

Thence back into the throng, until we reach,
Following the tide that slackens by degrees,
Some half-frequented scene where wider streets
Bring straggling breezes of suburban air;
Here files of ballads dangle from dead walls,
Advertisements of giant size, from high
Press forward in all colours on the sight;
These, bold in conscious merit; lower down
That, fronted with a most imposing word,
Is, peradventure, one in masquerade.
As on the broadening causeway we advance,
Behold a face turned up towards us, strong
In lineaments, and red with over-toil;
'Tis one perhaps, already met elsewhere,
A travelling cripple, by the trunk cut short,
And stumping with his arms: in sailor's garb
Another lies at length beside a range
Of written characters, with chalk inscribed
Upon the smooth flat stones: the nurse is here,
The bachelor that loves to sun himself,
The military idler, and the dame,
That field-ward takes her walk in decency.

Now, homeward through the thickening hubbub, where

See, among less distinguishable shapes,
The Italian, with his frame of images
Upon his head; with basket at his waist
The Jew; the stately and slow-moving Turk
With freight of slippers piled beneath his arm.
Briefly, we find, if tired of random sights
And haply to that search our thoughts should turn,
Among the crowd, conspicuous less or more,
As we proceed, all specimens of man
Through all the colours which the sun bestows,
And every character of form and face,
The Swede, the Russian; from the genial south,
The Frenchman and the Spaniard; from remote
America, the hunter-Indian; Moors,
Malays, Lascars, the Tartar and Chinese,
And negro ladies in white muslin gowns.

No greater London patriot ever lived than Charles Lamb.
He much preferred the hurly-burly of the city to the
countryside's charms. Lamb was far from being rough,
tough and virile. His nerves were frail, he liked solitude and
he was easily wounded. Yet he looked upon London street
life as a dish more savoury and subtle than the rural
sublimity that his friend Wordsworth and all his romantic
fellow travellers were constantly trumpeting. More than any
other writer Lamb expresses why London attracts and
entrances lonely people.

Lamb to William Wordsworth, 30 January 1801

Separate from the pleasure of your company, I don't
much care if I never see a mountain in my life. I have
passed all my days in London, until I have formed as
many and intense local attachments as any of you
mountaineers can have done with dead Nature. The
lighted shops of Strand and Fleet Street; the innumerable trades, tradesmen and customers, coaches, waggons, playhouses; all the bustle and wickedness round
about Covent Garden; the very women of the town; the
watchmen, drunken scenes, rattles; life awake, if you
awake, at all hours of the night; the impossibility of
being dull in Fleet Street; the crowds, the very dirt and
mud, the sun shining upon houses and pavements, the
print-shops, the old bookstalls, parsons cheapening
books, coffee houses, steams of soups from kitchens,
the pantomime – London itself a pantomime and
masquerade – all these things work themselves into my
mind and feed me, without a power of satiating me. The
wonder of these sights impels me into night-walks
about her crowded streets, and I often shed tears in the
motley Strand from fullness of joy at so much life. All

these emotions must be strange to you; so are your rural
emotions to me.

1794

The London Corresponding Society

London political life was shaken to its roots by the French
Revolution. At first the best of the English governing class
felt a fatherly pride in the new constitutional tendency
abroad in France. But as in 1792–3 the Girondins gave way
to the Jacobins, exiles began to flood over, and Louis XVI
and his queen were taken by tumbril to be executed, a mood
of anger and suspicion, not to say panic, set in. Democratic
idealists like Tom Paine were proscribed, dissenting liberals
like Joseph Priestley and Richard Price persecuted. William
Pitt now set spies to keep tabs on the movement of radical
but generally respectable artisans which had sprung up
seeking self-improvement and reform in the wake of the
Revolution. The outstanding fruit of this movement was
the London Corresponding Society. It managed to survive
severe harassment from 1792 to 1799 but was nearly crushed
in the spring of 1794, when the government arrested its
leaders, Thomas Hardy, John Thelwall and others, after an
innocuous meeting at Chalk Farm. In the event, they were
acquitted of treason.

Report of Chalk Farm meeting, 14 April 1794, from John Groves, a spy

I was in Store Street about one o'clock; there were then
but seven or eight citizens before the door. They were
in deep discourse, and Mr Reeves' relation standing
close by, who left them as soon as he saw me. He walked
up and down the street and placed himself at the corner
of Tottenham Court Road. In a few minutes Thelwall
appeared and stuck up the paper giving notice of the
adjournment to Chalk Farm . . .

The crowds that packed there were inconceivable
and beyond all my ideas. Every person delivered his
ticket at the garden gate, which was torn and one part
returned to be placed in the hat in order to prevent any
person getting in or remaining there without a ticket.
The example was set by Thelwall. By 3 o'clock I am
sure there were upwards of 2,000 persons . . .

Before the business began there was some bread and
beer called for. Pearce and two or three others pulled
out large knives with white ivory or bone handles and
long blades (pointed) evidently made at one manufactory, and they said all the citizens had them. I enquired
of Pearce where I could get one, he replied Green sold
them and laughed, saying 'they will not fly back when

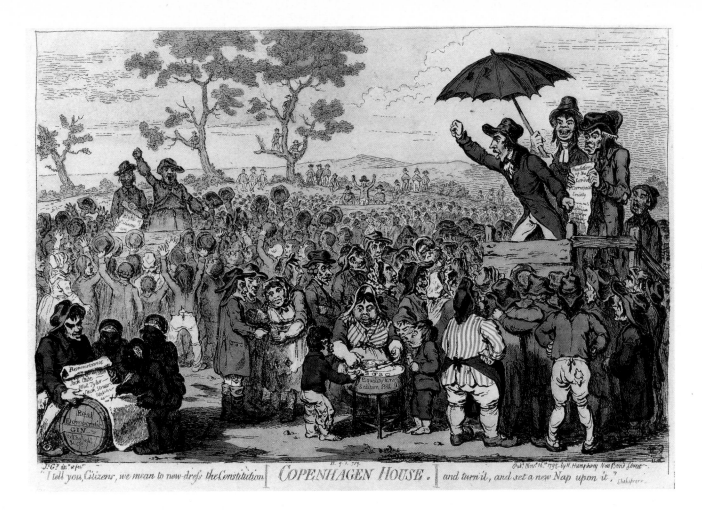

J.^s G^y del^t et fec^t

"I tell you, Citizens, we mean to new-dress the Constitution | COPENHAGEN HOUSE. | and turn it, and set a new Nap upon it." Shakspeare.

Pub^d. Novr 16.th 1795. by H. Humphrey New Bond Street.

you strike'. They are what the French call *couteau secret* – you cannot shut them without being acquainted with the secret spring.

Every division had a supper in the evening. I went to Compton Street; Thelwall was chairman. Except a great number of jokes about sansculottes and swinish multitude, there was nothing worth notice but the two following circumstances. First, Mr Thelwall took a pot of porter and blowing off the head, said, 'This is the way I would serve kings'. Second, he gave a toast as follows: 'The lamp iron at the end of Parliament Street' . . .

Thomas Hardy the shoemaker's recollection of his arrest

Agreeably to your request, I have endeavoured to give you as near as I can recollect at this distance of time some of the particulars respecting that infamous seizure of my person and property which was effected on the 12th of May 1794 at 6 o'clock in the morning at my house, No. 9 Piccadilly. At that early hour there was an uncommon loud knocking at the street door which awakened me, and I instantly got up hastily, put on my breeches and slippers only, and went to see what it could mean. When I opened the door, in a moment E. Lawzun rushed in. At that time he was an assistant King's Messenger, a new hand but very active in his new situation. He was followed by John Gurnel, a

Mass meeting called by the London Corresponding Society, Copenhagen Fields, 1795.

King's Messenger, P. Macmanus and John Townshend, constables of Bow Street Office (more generally known as thief takers), John King, Esq., now Sir John, one of the undersecretaries of state, and I think two or three more. They all followed me into the parlour. Lawzun then took a paper out of his pocket and said it was warrant from the secretary of state to apprehend me on a charge of high treason, and to search my house . . . He then asked my for my keys, which I refused. He then took the poker from the fireplace and said 'I shall soon open them'. Mr King said, 'No, no, send for the smith', who was waiting at the street door ready to be called in with a large basket of tools fit to open all sorts of locks, which he effected in a few minutes. Then the plunder began. They ransacked trunks, boxes, drawers and desk. Hundreds of letters and manuscript papers belonging to the London Corresponding Society were seized, which they carried away in four silk handkerchiefs; and many old and valuable private letters from kind friends in America and other places. They were not satisfied with letters and papers only, but they took books and pamphlets which nearly filled a corn sack . . . When they had ransacked every place in our bedroom that they thought fit, they then went into the shop, expecting no doubt to find treason hatching among the boots and shoes. Before the plunderers had left the parlour, I was sent off in charge of Mr Gurnel, the King's Messenger, in a hackney coach with the silk handkerchiefs full of the letters and papers, with Townshend to assist him to take care of his prisoner. I was taken to Mr Gurnel's house, where I remained and

the parishes round London were convened in January 1795 to investigate the matter.

The Meeting were made acquainted with the particulars of the lately discovered depredation in Lambeth Burial Ground ... Whereby it appeared, that the robberies of the said burial ground were discovered by three men being disturbed as they were conveying from thence

'Resurrectionists' at work. From an engraving by Robert Seymour, 1829.

FOR THE GOOD OF POSTERITY.
I say Bill, have you heard of this march of Intellect? they say every Body will sell themselves.

was civilly treated by him and his family until the 29th of May, the anniversary of the Restoration, which ought now to be blotted out as a day of rejoicing. The park and Tower guns were firing when I was on my way to the Tower in a hackney coach. Mr Gurnel sat beside me, and a sergeant of the Guards on the seat before me with his drawn sword, and a pair of pistols lay beside him. When Mr Gurnel arrived at the Tower he delivered me over to the Governor of the Tower, and then went home, very happy no doubt when he was relieved from his unpleasant charge.

1795

The body snatchers

In the midst of the nerve-racking 1790s London was plagued with an outbreak of the sordid crime of tomb robbing. Such was the concern that the churchwardens of

five human bodies in three sacks, in the night of the 18th of February last; that in consequence of such discovery, people of all descriptions whose relations had been interred in that ground resorted thereto, and demanded to dig for them; which being refused, they in great numbers forced their way in, and in spite of every effort the parish officers could use, began like mad people to tear up the ground, at the same time charging the officers and everyone that offered them any opposition with being privy to the robberies, and in general terms threatening them. Thus circumstanced, the parish officers finding nothing but downright force (and that of more strength than the civil power) could prevent the populace, and fearing to bring on a riot ... were necessitated to give way and let the people go on in their searches; by which a great number of empty coffins were discovered, the corpses having been stolen from them. Great distress and agitation of mind was manifest in everyone, and some in a kind of frenzy ran away with the coffins of their deceased relations; and the generality of the populace were so ripe for mischief, that they attacked a house with stones and brickbats upon the bare suspicion that the occupier had been concerned in or privy to the robbery of the ground, and it was with difficulty they were prevented from demolishing it.

To restore order and discover the offenders if possible, a large reward was offered and the committee aforesaid appointed; by whose enquiries it was found the gravedigger and three other persons were the robbers, and that the bodies had been conveyed away in a coach to different people for various purposes, as was made appear to them by informations upon oath: the material points of one of which informations being now read, showed that within the knowledge of the informant, eight surgeons of public repute and a man who calls himself an articulator (and by handbills openly avows the trade), exclusive of others of less note, are in the habit of buying stolen dead bodies during the winter half-year; in whose service the following fifteen persons are generally employed, namely Daniel Arnot alias Harding, John Gilmore, Thomas Gilmore, Thomas Pain, Peter McIntire alias McIntosh, James Profit, Jeremiah Keefe, Morris Hogarty, – White, a man called Long John the Coachman, John Butler, John Howison, Samuel Hatton, John Parker and Henry Wheeler, whose depredations had extended to thirty burial grounds that the informant knows of; and that gravediggers and those entrusted with the care of burial grounds are frequently accessory in the robberies and receive five shillings per corpse for every one that with their privity is carried off, by which means many hundred are taken from their graves annually. That with the surgeons and the men above alluded to, there is a set price for dead bodies, viz. for an adult two guineas and a crown, and for every one under age, six shillings for the first foot and ninepence per inch for all it measures more in length; that bodies thus procured are used here in various ways, and the flesh by some burnt, by others buried, and by others the informant did not know how it was disposed of; that some bodies are prepared or made into skeletons and sent to America and the West Indies; and many, with the flesh on or made into skeletons, are sent into different parts of this kingdom. By another information upon oath, the whole of which was also now read, it appeared that the aforesaid articulator makes the most wanton use of some that fell into his hands, substituting human skulls

for nail boxes, and having the skeleton of a child instead of a doll for his own child to play with.

The Chairman also acquainted the meeting that from other evidence (which though not upon oath is yet such as may be relied on) information is given that experiments have been tried and perfected whereby human flesh has been converted into a substance like spermaceti and candles made of it, and that soap has also been made of the same material.

The Chairman further informed the meeting that the parishioners of Lambeth, anxious to punish the unnatural depredators who by their practices had so much disturbed the parish and endangered the public peace, were much concerned to find this kind of offence was not punishable by law, and that the punishments generally inflicted upon delinquents when convicted were not likely even to check the evil; in proof of which, the copies of two sentences passed on convicts of this description were produced and read.

1790s

The night plunderers

The great concern of London merchants in the 1790s, especially after war with Revolutionary France had begun, was improving the port. London then handled two-thirds of Britain's exports and over half the value of its imports. Most of all this was loaded or unloaded along the small strip of river frontage between the Tower and London Bridge. When ships came into the Thames in convoy, as they did in wartime, the traffic was chaotic; and the lack of secure docking or storage made corruption and theft endemic. The magistrate Patrick Colquhoun was one of many authors to deplore the situation and suggest reforms. Below is his account of just one class of criminals who preyed on London's shipping, the 'night plunderers, denominated light horsemen'. The solution was close at hand when Colquhoun wrote. Enclosed docks on a heroic scale began rapidly to spring up after 1800 along the river eastward from Wapping to Blackwall. They were to save the Port of London from the danger of choking and collapse, and to revitalize the metropolitan economy.

Among the various classes of depredators on the West India trade in the Port of London, those denominated *Light Horsemen* seem to have been by far the most pernicious ... The receivers who resided in the vicinity of the river on both sides were the chief leaders in those peculiar system of plunder; and it was always carried on by the connivance of the mate and revenue officers, in consequence of a preconcerted plan, and agreement to pay them a certain sum of money for the liberty of opening and removing from such casks and packages as were accessible as much sugar, coffee and other articles as could be conveyed away in four or five hours during the dead of night. For such a licence to plunder, from 20 to 30 guineas per night were usually paid to the mate and revenue officers, who generally went to bed while the mischief was going forward, that they might not see it.

These infamous proceedings were carried on according to a regular system. The gangs, denominated *Light Horsemen*, were generally composed of one or more receivers, together with coopers, watermen and lumpers, who were all necessary in their different occupations to the accomplishment of these iniquitous designs. They went on board completely prepared with iron crows, adzes and other utensils, to open and again head-up the casks – with shovels to take out the sugar and a number of bags made to contain 100 lbs each. These bags were denominated 'black strap', having been previously dyed black to prevent their being seen in the night when stowed in the bottom of a wherry.

The different members of the gang had each a peculiar province assigned. The receivers generally furnished the money necessary to bribe the officers and mate in the first instance, and also provided the 'black strap'. The watermen procured as many boats as were wanted. The lumpers unstowed the casks in the hold. The coopers took out the heads, and all hands assisted afterwards in filling the bags, dispatching one boat after another to an appointed place, and making the best use of the infamous licence they had purchased in removing as large a quantity of property as could be carried off by the utmost exertions of excessive labour, which seldom amounted to less than the value of from £150 to £200 a night...

This dreadful system of nightly robbery was not confined to sugar alone. Wherever coffee made a part of the cargo, the plunder of that article, from its being more accessible, was always enormous. Rum was also pillaged in considerable quantities. This was obtained by means of a regular system immediately applicable to the nature of the article. Skins and large bladders with wooden nozzles were secretly conveyed on board. A bribe was given, as in the case of sugar and coffee, to the mate and revenue officers for a licence to draw off a certain quantity from each cask, for which purpose a pump, usually denominated a 'jigger', was previously provided, and also tin tubes calculated to render the booty accessible in every situation. By such devices the skins and bladders were filled, and large quantities removed to the houses of the receivers during the night. All the ships thus circumstanced were denominated 'game ships'. It is not possible to ascertain what proportion in a fleet of 370 to 400 sail might be in this unfortunate predicament. The information of persons who had access to know much of what was going forward state it at one-fourth; while others do not suppose that this systematic depredation could extend to more than one-fifth. Certain however it is, that the plunder through this medium was excessive, and went to an extent in sugar, coffee, rum, pimento, ginger and other articles which exceeds all credibility.

1800

French exiles

Around the year 1800 London was thronged with noble but all too often impoverished French exiles from the Revolution. They congregated especially in the outer western suburbs, places like Kensington, Twickenham and Richmond. Though they did their best to keep their spirits up, they could hardly conceal their dislike of the land in which they found themselves. Many slipped back to France after the Treaty of Amiens in 1802, but others stayed right up to Waterloo. Richard Lalor Sheil, an Irish playwright and politician, was sent as a young Catholic in London to a Jesuit school in Kensington run mainly for little French boys. This was his first impression:

It was a large, old fashioned house, with many remains of decayed splendour. In a beautiful walk of trees, which ran down from the rear of the building through the playground, I saw several French boys playing at swing-swang; and the moment I entered, my ears were filled with the shrill vociferation of some hundreds of little emigrants, who were engaged in their little amusements and babbled, screamed, laughed and shouted in all the velocity of their rapid and joyous language. I did not hear a word of English, and at once perceived that I was as much amongst Frenchmen as if I had been suddenly transferred to a Parisian college. Having got this peep at the gaiety of the school into which I was to be introduced, I was led with my companion to a chamber covered with faded gilding and which had once been richly tapestried; where I found the head of the establishment in the person of a French nobleman, Monsieur le Prince de Broglie...

The school was full of the children of the French

Kensington House, the school for French emigrés where Robert Lalor Sheil was a pupil in 1802–4.

planters, who had been sent over to learn English among the refugees from the Revolution ... In general, the children of the French exiles amalgamated readily with these Creoles: there were, to be sure, some points of substantial difference, the French West Indians being all rich *roturiers*, and the little emigrants having their veins full of the best blood of France, without a groat in their pockets. But there was one point of reconciliation between them – they all concurred in hating England and its government ... Whenever news arrived of a victory won by Bonaparte, the whole school was thrown into a ferment; and I cannot, even at this distance of time, forget the exultation with which the sons of the decapitated or the exiled hailed the triumph of the French arms, the humiliation of England and the glory of the nation whose greatness they had learned to lisp ...

I recollect upon one occasion having been witness to a very remarkable scene. Monsieur, as he was then called, the present King of France, waited one day with a large retinue of French nobility upon the Prince de Broglie. The whole body of the schoolboys was assembled to receive him. We were gathered in a circle at the bottom of a flight of stone stairs that led from the principal room into the playground. The future King of France appeared with his *cortège* of illustrious exiles at the glass folding-doors which were at the top of the stairs, and the moment he was seen we all exclaimed, with a shrill shout of beardless loyalty, 'Vive le Roi!' Monsieur seemed greatly gratified by this spectacle, and

in a very gracious and condescending manner went down amongst the little boys, who were at first awed a good deal by his presence but were afterwards speedily familiarized with the natural benignity of Charles the Tenth. He asked the names of those who were about him, and when he heard them and saw in the boys by whom he was encompassed the descendants of some of the noblest families of France, he seemed to be sensibly affected. One or two names which were associated with peculiarly melancholy recollections made him thrill. 'Hélas! mon enfant!' he used to say, as some orphan was brought up to him; and he would then lean down to caress the child of a friend who had perished on the scaffolds of the Revolution.

1806

Nelson's funeral

Pickled in rum, the greatest of Britain's admirals, Lord Nelson, was borne home slowly by sea after his demise in the moment of victory at Trafalgar. He was to be buried in St Paul's, the national pantheon for military heroes. The body arrived at Greenwich early in 1806 and after lying in state, was transported with pomp up-river on 13 January. The British are believed to be good at ceremonial. But that was not how Nelson's funeral procession struck Miss Mary Berry, the former confidante of Horace Walpole.

It is much easier to set down upon paper the regulations of a ceremony, such as that the boats of the river

fencibles are to line each side of the procession etc., than to give the effect of a procession so lined on the water in the foggy atmosphere of the Thames. The distance of time between the minute guns fired by these river fencibles was too long to command continued attention, and therefore, I think, failed in effect. The music, too, was not sufficiently loud to have any effect at all; the barge which contained his honoured remains was neither sufficiently large nor sufficiently distinguished to command the eye and the attention of every spectator, which by some means or other it ought to have done. I was looking over the wall of Lord Fife's garden, which forms one side of Whitehall Stairs, so that I saw the coffin in the very act of being landed; saw it placed on the bier on which it was borne to the Admiralty. The only really impressive moment was when the coffin first touched the ground. At that instant the sky, which but a few minutes before had been clear, poured down at once a torrent of rain and hail, and a

sudden gust of wind arose the violence of which was not less remarkable than the moment at which it took place . . .

On shore the whole ceremony was still less calculated to gratify the feelings it naturally inspired . . . Instead of presenting to their eager eyes the surviving heroes of Trafalgar following the corpse of their illustrious leader, the naval officers were all put into mourning coaches, which immediately became equally uninteresting to the spectators, whether they contained a vice-admiral or a herald; indeed the heralds, from their dress, were the only conspicuous persons. The sailors, too, of the *Victory*, the immediate witnesses of their Nelson's glory . . . instead of being allowed to surround the coffin from which they had proved themselves so unwilling to separate, were marshalled by themselves in another part of the procession, without music, without officers, without any naval accompaniments whatsoever . . . I will not talk of the disproportions and perfect bad taste of the funeral car, because good taste in forms I never expect here; but I *did* expect sufficient good taste in moral feeling not to have entrusted the conduct of such a ceremony, the tribute of such a nation to such a chief, as a job to the Heralds' Office and their hireling undertakers! The only moment in which the mind the most disposed to enthusiasm could for a moment indulge it (I speak not of the ceremony in St Paul's, which I did not see), was that in which the funeral car passed Charing Cross. Here nothing could be seen on

OPPOSITE *Nelson's funeral car arrives at St Paul's, 1806. Aquatint by Merigot and Pugin.*

applied science by Silliman's compatriot, the dynamic Count Rumford. By 1805 the young chemist Humphry Davy (whom Silliman met on a return visit) was starting to move the Royal Institution in a purer direction.

Mr Accum, to whom I have been indebted for many instances of kindness since I came to London, this morning conducted me to see the Royal Institution. This institution was set on foot a few years ago for the purpose of encouraging useful knowledge in general,

RIGHT *Stinks at the Royal Institution: Thomas Young experiments on Sir John Hippisley and Humphry Davy blows the bellows, while Count Rumford watches from the sidelines. Cartoon by James Gillray, 1802.*

every side but pyramids of heads, and every head uncovered, from respect to the object on which every eye was entirely bent. One general feeling pervading a great multitude must ever tend to the sublime.

1805

The Royal Institution

In the years after 1800 London was the unrivalled centre of the technological world. Visitors came from afar to marvel at the new docks, bridges, and canals, gape at the rapid spread of gas lighting or buy from the city's instrument makers and machine craftsmen. One such purchaser was Benjamin Silliman of Connecticut, who came to London in 1805 to acquire chemistry apparatus and books for Yale College, then first venturing into the sciences. He had good introductions and called upon many of London's leading scientists. One place that intrigued him was the Royal Institution, founded in 1799 to popularize and diffuse

and for facilitating the introduction of useful mechanical improvements. Now, public lectures are delivered in the institution on different branches of science, and particularly on natural philosophy and chemistry. The establishment was munificently endowed, and Count Rumford was placed at its head, where he had opportunity to give full scope to his culinary and other experiments . . .

A number of contiguous houses in Albemarle Street have been so connected as to form one building, and this contains the numerous apartments of the Royal Institution. There are rooms for reading the journals and newspapers; others devoted to the library, which is already considerably extensive; others to the philosophical apparatus, the lectures, the minerals, the professors, the cookery, servants etc. In the lowest apartment they pointed out a great number of culinary utensils, consisting of stew pans, boilers, roasters and other similar things which Count Rumford has at various times invented for reducing the humble process of the kitchen to philosophical principles. The experiments were carried quite through, for one of the objects of the institution was to give experimental dinners, at which the Count presided and the patrons of his experiments attended, to judge of the merits of any newly invented mode of cooking or of any new dish. It was probably not very difficult to recruit a sufficient number of men for this service in a country where good living is so much in fashion . . .

They showed me also the system of boilers and pipes by means of which the Count has contrived to carry steam through his extensive edifice, and effectually to warm the theatre by diffusing through it the air which has become heated by contact with the pipes containing the steam. The theatre is the room where the lectures are given. It is a superb apartment, and fitted up with great convenience. It is semicircular and contains a pit and gallery in which the seats rise row behind row. It is lighted above through a circular orifice which, whenever the lecturer wishes to darken the room, can be shut at pleasure by a horizontal screen connected with a cord. This theatre has often contained a thousand persons. It is so fashionable a resort that the ladies of Westminster are in the habit of coming to the Royal Institution to derive instruction from the rational pursuits of philosophy. Surely everyone would commend this preference, when the competition lies between routs and masquerades and the delightful recreations of experimental science. But, as one object of the institution has been to attract an audience, of course everything has worn a popular air, and the amusing and the brilliant have been as studiously pursued as well as the useful. The apparatus is by no means so extensive as I expected to find it.

1814

Fireworks in St James's Park

The supposedly final victory over France in 1814 delivered international mastery to Britain. The Prince Regent decreed lavish celebrations. The biggest firework display London had ever seen was staged in St James's Park on 1 August, under the management of the rocketeer Sir William Congreve, with supporting architectural trumpery by John Nash. Events of this kind were always dangerous. At the height of proceedings, Nash's great pagoda burst into flames and two workmen were killed. This was missed by the painter Joseph Farington, who (wisely perhaps) preferred a further vantage point.

Bob called . . . Having a ticket for St James's Park purchased some time since, I walked with him to St James's Park which we entered through Storey's Gate, and there found H. Hammond and Wm Offley, with whom we walked. The day was delightfully fine and the company numerous but not the least crowded. Many booths and tents were erected and in one of the booths we dined, and there saw J. Aytoun and Carlisle. Everybody seemed gratified with the scene. We then continued to walk till tea-time, when owing to some difficulty in obtaining it, we were accidentally separated and I had tea in one of the tents with a young man, a stranger. About 9 o'clock some fireworks were set off, and I endeavoured to find a good situation for seeing the grand display. This I could not do in that part of the park to which the tickets admitted us; I therefore passed through Storey's Gate and went round by the Horse Guards along the Parade and to the Mall, and took a station in the line open to the public opposite to the Temple of Concord, and saw the display in all its effect. The fireworks were beautiful and the people appeared to be highly gratified. They commenced about 10

A VIEW OF THE TEMPLE OF CONCORD,

o'clock, and the Temple of Concord after having been first exhibited as the Castle of Discord with all its horrors of fire and destruction, was presented forming a beautiful structure, the lines composed of lighted lamps and large transparent paintings representing subjects exhibiting the devastations of war and the evils of despotism and tyranny. At half-past 12 o'clock I left the park and walked home among numbers who like myself had their curiosity gratified. Upon this occasion the public curiosity appeared to be indulged to the utmost

RIGHT *Chelsea Pensioners reading the news of the Battle of Waterloo, 1822. Painting by Sir David Wilkie.*

OPPOSITE *The Temple of Concord, from the victory fireworks in St James's Park, 1814.*

degree, and I saw or heard nothing but what showed general satisfaction, but the last display was too long protracted.

1815

Dispatches from Waterloo

During Napoleon's hundred days in 1815, London was convulsed with conflicting rumours from France and Belgium, which reached their pitch as smatterings of news about the final clash at Waterloo filtered through. Legend has it that Nathan Meyer Rothschild the banker was the earliest to hear the definitive outcome of the battle, and made much money from it. The prosaic truth is that Lord Castlereagh, the Foreign Secretary, knew first. Meanwhile, old soldiers like Sir Robert Wilson sat around in clubs and drawing rooms dispensing wisdom and inducing panic among the ladies, as Thomas Raikes relates.

On the day of that evening when we received the news of the great victory at Waterloo, I dined with the present Lord and Lady Willoughby de Eresby in Piccadilly: there was a large party, among whom I remember Miss Mercer (now Madame de Flahault), Sir H. Cooke and Sir R. W[ilson], who entered the room with a grave portentous countenance, as if he knew more than he was willing to communicate. Every one at

the time was in breathless impatience for the result, and as we proceeded to the dining room Miss Mercer enquired of me in a whisper whether I had heard any news, adding that she feared from Sir R.W.'s manner that some misfortune had occurred. I felt little alarm at his prognostics, as I had heard that Rothschild was purchasing stock largely, and that the funds had risen two per cent.

When the ladies had retired and the wine had opened Sir R.W.'s heart, he condescended to inform the company that he had received a private dispatch from Brussels announcing the total defeat of the Anglo-Prussian army by the French, with the additional circumstance that Napoleon after his decided victory had supped with the Prince d'Aremberg at his palace in that city. On doubts being expressed as to the correctness of his information, he offered readily to bet any sum on the strength of his dispatches. We took him at his word; betted with him £400 or £500, and others did the same to the amount of above £1,000.

There was a ball that night at Sir George Talbot's; and when I arrived there about eleven o'clock, I found the whole house in confusion and dismay; ladies calling for their carriages, and others fainting in the ante-room, particularly the Ladies Paget who seemed in the utmost distress. The mystery however was soon cleared up. Lady Castlereagh had just made her appearance in the ballroom with the official account of the battle and a partial list of the killed and wounded, which had caused so much distress among the various relatives of the sufferers. She had been at a grand dinner given by Mrs Boehm in St James's Square to the Prince Regent, during which Colonel Percy, having first driven to Carlton House, had arrived in a chaise and four at the house and presented to his royal highness at table the official dispatches from the Duke of Wellington (recounting his victory) as well as the French eagles, which he had brought as trophies with him in the carriage.

1821

Queen Caroline barred from coronation

George IV's coronation in July 1821 was exceptional on two accounts. It was the first modern coronation, in the sense that the pageantry was orchestrated with a new historical self-consciousness. In this the King himself, the greatest dresser-up and shower-off ever to grace the British throne, had a major hand. The other notable feature of the occasion was that the estranged Queen Caroline was not invited. True to her naive and brassy nature and believing she had popular support, Caroline sensationally turned up for the coronation. She was refused entry, to everyone's chagrin. This was partly the fault of her partisan, Henry Brougham, who had brilliantly defended the Queen before the House of Lords when George tried to divorce her the previous autumn but who now made the mistake of thinking they could together undermine the king in his moment of glory. Brougham related the week's events to his friend Thomas Creevey.

Today the Q's being allowed to enter the Abbey is doubted ... but I still think it possible the Big Man may have gout and not be up to it.

The paroxysm rather increases than diminishes, and literally extends to all classes ... The Ministers are still sitting and squabbling; nor have they to this hour (5) made up their minds whether to stop her or not. My belief is that they will let her pass, and also admit her at the Abbey if she persists. She is quite resolved to do so, and comes to sleep at Cambridge House for the purpose. But she is sure to blunder about the hour, and to give them excuses for turning her back by being late.

Thursday [Coronation Day]. The Queen (as I found on going to her house at 20 minutes before six this morning) started at a quarter past five, and drove down Constitution Hill in the mulberry – Lady Anne Hamil-

RIGHT *The coronation of George IV, July 1821. Aquatint by F.C. Lewis.*

OPPOSITE BELOW *Rennie's Waterloo Bridge and warehouses along the Thames. From a photograph, c.1854, taken before the Victoria Embankment was built.*

ton and Lady Hood sitting opposite, Hesse (in uniform) and Lord Hood in another carriage went before. I followed on foot and found she had swept the crowd after her; it was very great, even at that hour. She passed through Storeys Gate and then round Dean's Yard, where she was separated from the crowd by the gates being closed. The refusal was peremptory at all the doors of the Abbey when she tried, and one was banged in her face ... She was saluted by all the soldiery, and even the people in the seats who had paid ten and five guineas down and might be expected to hiss most at the untimely interruption, hissed very little and applauded loudly in most places. In some they were silent, but the applause and waving handkerchiefs prevailed ...

About ½ past six she had finished her walks and calls at the doors, and got into the carriage to return. She came by Whitehall, Pall Mall and Piccadilly. The crowd in the Broad Street off Whitehall was immense (the barriers being across Parliament Street and King Street). All or nearly all followed her and risked losing their places. They crammed Cockspur Street and Pall Mall, etc., hooting and cursing the King and his friends and huzzaing her. A vast multitude followed her home, and then broke windows. But they soon (in two or three hours) dispersed or went back.

I had just got home and she sent for me, so I went and

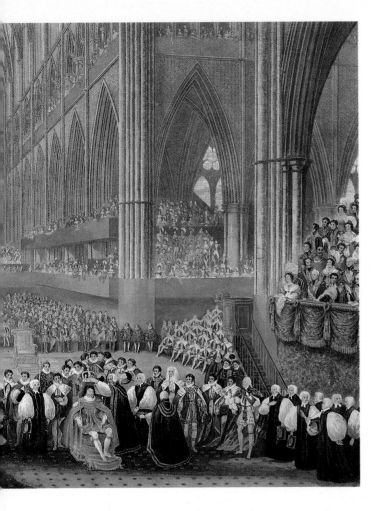

following letter the Anglophile 'Marquis' remarks admiringly on how the various improvements to London, in particular the Regent Street and Regent's Park development, have been financed.

I am induced to conclude that the progress made since the signature of the last treaty of peace in extending and beautifying London is almost miraculous. Most extraordinary does it indeed appear to strangers, that after having maintained almost exclusively at your own expense the burden of one of the longest and most expensive wars which Europe ever witnessed, you should at its termination find the means of erecting such numerous and costly piles of elegant architecture; nor can we in beholding them fail to reflect how incalculable are the resources of a free, enlightened and united people.

One of the first objects which drew my attention was Waterloo Bridge, 'in seeing which', observed Canova (no contemptible authority on such a subject), 'the traveller is amply rewarded for the trouble of a journey from Rome to the English capital.' After admiring the lightness and symmetry of this far-famed structure, I

breakfasted with her, and am now going to dine, which makes me break off; but I must add that the King was *not* well received at all – silence in many places, and a mixture of hisses and groans in others. However there were some bounds kept with him … The general feeling of her own partisans was very much against her going, but far more against their behaviour to her … I think her very lucky in being excluded. They put it on not being at liberty to recognise her or anyone except as ticket-bearers. Lord Hood showed me one which they said of course would pass any one of the party, but she refused to go in except as Queen and without a ticket.

1820s

Paying for improvements

Despite the long previous history of mistrust and war, Anglo-French relations were never perhaps as close as during the 1820s. What the British saw in Paris was a capital of unrivalled artistic taste. What the French found in London was a place where things got done in a seeming climate of stability, and despite rather than because of the influence of government. One of the sharper of the decade's many books describing London consists of a fictitious exchange between two travellers, the Marquis de Vermont in London and Sir Charles Darnley in Paris. In the

lamented, on hearing that a million of your money had been expended in raising it, that so heavy a burden should be thrown on the shoulders of the people; when I learned to my surprise that this stupendous work, as well as that of the London and West India Docks (besides the various canals, by which manufactures and commerce circulate from one end of the kingdom to the other) were all the unprotected efforts of private speculators.

In France we are so accustomed to see similar enterprises executed by the Government only, that it is

with difficulty we are brought to understand how such wonders can be affected by the exertion and at the hazard of voluntary associations.

When I extended my researches and visited the fine theatres of Drury Lane, Covent Garden and the Opera House and found that they also were private property; and when in pursuing my enquiries I heard that the splendid new street, or rather the succession of splendid streets by which Pall Mall communicates with Portland Place, those which are now erecting on the spot lately occupied by the royal stables, and several terraces of large and beautiful houses decorated with pillars and pilasters which front the Regent's Park, not to speak of the many elegant villas dispersed about that fine piece of ground (equally useful as a place of exercise and as a source of health to the inhabitants of this colossal town); I say, when I heard that these buildings, though standing on land belonging to the Crown and laid out agreeably to a plan sketched by the royal architect, were all raised at the expense of *individuals*, who had also undertaken to pay an annual quit-rent amply sufficient to remunerate the Government for the sums advanced in making the preparations which preceded these improvements, a new train of ideas was presented to my mind; and I contemplated with equal pleasure and surprise the scene before me, exemplifying so beautifully the mighty powers of accumulated capital, of capital created by industry and trade under the guardian banners of law and liberty.

1820s

A cabinet-maker's story

In the early nineteenth century we begin to hear the authentic voice of the respectable London working man. Literacy, though still restricted, is starting to spread. There are extant autobiographies of London life by articulate footmen, schoolboys and artisans alike. One such was William Lovett, who, like so many of the best London workmen, was a chapel-bred immigrant from the country. He arrived in London as a penniless Cornish ropemaker but rose to be president of the Cabinet Makers' Society.

I left home on the 23rd of June 1821, and in the course of a few days, I forget how many, for we were becalmed a portion of the time, I arrived in the great city with the clear sum of thirty shillings in my pocket, knowing no one nor being known to any. Having heard a great many stories in the country about London crimping-houses and London thieves, I thought it best to lodge near the wharf at first, till I had become a little acquainted with the place. I was therefore induced to put up at a public house near the wharf where the Cornish vessels generally land; and early the next morning I set out with my recommendatory letters. In passing the Borough end of the old London Bridge I recollect being forcibly struck with the number of blackened eyes and scratched and battered faces that I met with among the labourers going to their employments: the result, I afterwards learnt, of their Saturday evening and Sunday sprees. Owing however to the general slackness of the ropemaking business at that period, my recommendatory letters failed of procuring me employment ... I began to think myself very unfortunate. However I fared very hard and sought about for work in every direction, as I had made up my mind to accept of any kind of honest employment rather than go home again without any.

By dint of persistence Lovett got a carpenting job and learnt the trade as he went on. In time he graduated to the cabinet-making business by making small items of furniture in lieu

Cumberland Terrace, longest of the Nash frontispieces bordering Regent's Park.

of rent during a period without work, and by hawking others among furniture brokers.

After walking about some days I got employment in a small shop in Castle Street, Oxford Market, a place where repairs of buhl-work, marquetry and antique furniture were principally executed. Here I was fortunate enough to meet with a journeyman of the name of David Todd, a native of Peebles, one of the most intelligent, kind-hearted and best disposed men I ever met with. He, finding that I had not served an apprenticeship to the business, not only gave me every assistance and information I required in my work, but advised me as to my best mode of proceeding with all the benevolence and anxiety of a father. By his advice I was induced to offer myself as a member of the Cabinet-Makers' Society, he having kindly pointed out to me the extreme difficulty I should have of ever obtaining employment in any respectable shop unless I belong to them. But as I had not 'worked or served five years to the business' (as their rules required), and as a jealous countryman of mine had informed them that I had served my time to a ropemaker and not a cabinet-maker, they refused to admit me. Failing in this object, my kind friend got me a situation at Messrs — cabinet manufactory, where I entered into an agreement to work for them for twelve months for a guinea a week. They were at that time cabinet-makers to the King, and consequently executed a great variety of work. At the time I am speaking of, this was not a Society shop, and a number of persons were employed there of very drunken and dissipated habits. When I first went among them they talked of 'setting Mother Shorney at me'; this is a cant term in the trade, and meant the putting away of your tools, the injuring of your work and annoying you in such a way as to drive you out of

the shop. This feeling against me was occasioned by my coming to work there without having served an apprenticeship to the business. As soon therefore as I was made acquainted with their feelings and intentions towards me, I though it best to call a shop-meeting and lay my case before them. To call a meeting of this description the first requisite was to send for a quantity of drink (generally a gallon of ale) and then to strike your hammer and holdfast together, which making a bell-like sound is a summons causing all the shop to assemble around your bench. A chairman is then appointed, and you are called upon to state your business. In my case, I briefly told them that the reason of my calling them together was on account of the feeling they manifested towards me, which I hoped would be removed when they had heard my story. I then went on to describe how I had wasted the prime of my life in learning a trade which I found comparatively useless; and appealed to their sense of justice to determine whether it was right to prevent me from learning another. By thus appealing to them, in time the majority of them took my part, and others were eventually won over and induced to be friendly. But the demands made upon me for drink by individuals among them for being shown the manner of doing any particular kind of work, together with fines and shop scores, often amounted to seven or eight shillings a week out of my guinea. However, by taking particular notice of every description of work I saw done in the shop, I became tolerably well acquainted with the general run of work by the expiration of my time.

1826

The lure of technology

Schinkel, the greatest of German architects, came with the Prussian civil servant Peter Beuth on an official fact-finding tour of Britain in 1826. In London, what they wanted to see and what Schinkel noted down was not so much the high-class architecture by the leading designers of the day, as the details of the magical new British technology: gas lighting, iron construction, machine-tool manufacturing shops, the docks, the Thames Tunnel works and so on.

Friday 2 June Holtzappfel and Deyerlein [lathe manufacturers in Charing Cross Road], turning of a fluted wooden hemisphere . . . Beuth ordered a large lathe.
   Maudsley's workshop [celebrated machine-tool factory in Lambeth], a stout friendly man, his iron roof had collapsed, much damage. He took us round. A steam-

engine, his own invention, with one cylinder takes up little room. Magnificent lathes, iron roofs. Iron vaulting. Iron staircases. The slender iron columns supporting the roof of one of the rooms also function as outlets for waste water. The foundry is installed on an iron-and-brick vault; roller which makes holes, slits and incisions, for nail holes in the steam boiler. A hammer simultaneously punching profiles, with a clamped head. A cut-off worm acts as a brake on the fall of the hammer.

From Maudsley's to the Office of Gaslight. Enormous plant, 17 sheet-iron gasometers, 40ft in diameter, 18ft high, set up in great sheds. The gas passes through all the retorts into a common horizontal pipe and is then redistributed . . .

Saturday 3 June London Docks, Mr Isaak Solly as guide, new construction of wine cellars. Dock basin for 250 ships, storerooms, stone steps and double iron doors, iron rails, iron cranes; wine cellar with 22,000 barrels, above these storerooms for tobacco, around 400ft wide, 800ft long. New basin, construction of locks, erection of a weir beam. Swing bridge. Surrounding walls. Boat

trip on the river between the Thames ships, across the stretch where the tunnel is being built. To the West India Docks. New construction, good planning: sheds of iron and wood right round the basins, well-constructed roof, covered with corrugated iron sheets. On one side there are flaps for protection against the weather. Intercolumniation 12ft.

Monday 5 June Count Lottum breakfasted with us at 7 o'clock in the morning, we went to the Custom House, got in a boat and set off for Woolwich . . . We inspected first the model collection in the pavilion constructed specially for it. Ropes tied fast to a central post, with metal sheets in between. Among the models Gibraltar, Rio de Janeiro and Quebec were of interest. A copperplate engraving machine which automatically does the printing and removal. A rain machine from Drury Lane Theatre. In one of the rooms Napoleon's field-kitchen, wagon and hearse can be seen. The soldiers' quarters, eight men were eating mutton chops and potatoes, food looked well prepared. Stables, riding arena. Stores. The Royal Arsenal, thousands of cannon in neat rows on the floor. The prison ship, tack stores, here we heard complaints about moths. Iron rails. Very fine sawmill with steam engine. There are extra gadgets for cutting cross-section by circular saw; a cogwheel is attached for decoration ... The dockyards. Huge sheds, usually two standing next to each other. Awesome anchoring equipment. Excellent smiths' workshop, big iron construction, steam-engine, bellows, enormous great hammers. Smiths' workshop in Woolwich dockyards.

Tuesday 6 June Walk to Mr Brunel's office ... We walked through a poor part of the city, and took a boat to the tunnel. A steam-engine with two horizontal cylinders pumps the water out in the 20ft wide bricked well. The boiler is outside it, the steam is channelled into the building. Work has progressed as far as the edge of the river ... The connections between the two tunnels will be dug later, they were in the process of digging the first of these; the vault is three bricks thick. The sections are bricked together without any bonding, with Roman cement $\frac{3}{4}$in thick. They progress 2ft per day; 10 inches are always left clear of the roof for bricking the vault. Light for the work is provided by transportable gas ... Giant screws move forward the ramming machine, which is made entirely of iron.

1820s

Schools and a schoolboy

George Pocock (1778–1829) was a middling kind of builder-developer typical in the London of George IV. He did well out of a new street in Hoxton, then moved his family to outlying Kilburn and the expectation of prosperity. There he began to build villas, but was crushed by the slump of 1825–6. Like so many others he failed, spent a spell in debtors' prison and had to sell off his property, his health meanwhile declining under the shame and strain. Pocock's was an all-too-common story. We would know nothing of it, had not his son John started a diary in 1826, in which he records the daily events and tribulations of a London schoolboy's life, the variety of employments to which he was prematurely put to help his family out, and the slow downward spiral of events which led to his father's death and his own emigration in 1830.

11 November 1826 My father arrested this morning ...

12 November Papa at Banco Regis [King's Bench Prison. Pocock senior was allowed day-leave to redeem his debts, but had to sleep at the prison.]

23 April 1827 Our house advertised to be sold by public auction, sale to take place in a fortnight. Papa intends selling off all his property on the Priory, with the exception of the little cottage on Greville Hill, into which we are to remove, our house being much too large for us.

5 May 1827 Old Mr Monk who had been so long away from our school came back today. Mr Garrett turned him away for being drunk. This man once had the largest school in the metropolis before he took to drinking. He is a perfect master of seven languages and affords a lamentable instance of the misery produced by this degrading vice, for he has now scarcely a coat to his back.

7 August Monk kicked up a fine hullabulleroo at my Latin as my Exempla Minima exercises were imperfect, who cares for old Monkey?

8 August Got to school pretty early and went through the ugly Latin a little better, what crackjaws the Romans must have had.

23 August Mr Garrett invited me to a gipsy hunting party as he called it. He hired the Lords Cricket Ground for the day upon which we played at that healthy game. I got only 8 runs, coming in the last innings. Our side lost the day.

24 August Removed some of the drawing-room furniture to Suffolk St, Southwark, Papa having parted with it ...

19 January 1828 ... Saw one of Gurney's new steam carriages running up Edgware Road in style.

29 February Papa went to Town this morning and arranged with Mr Cocker for me to attend in his office as a junior clerk ...

3 March My dear mother's birthday. Walked with Josiah [Wright] ... as far as the Stingo, and then went on to the office with Papa in Nassau Street, Soho. I felt very timid at first and was given a long letter to copy for a Mr Evan Evans in Wales. There are two clerks, Messrs Stevens and Whittaker, besides Mr Barker who is almost a partner, and Mr Cocker ...

22 March ... Mr Barker gave me a copy of a writ to serve on a man residing in Bury Street, Fulham Road, but it would not do. 'Not at home – quite uncertain when he will be in' – which proved a dead hit.

2 April Had my hair cut most shamefully by a rascally Paddington barber ...

19 June My father obtained me a situation with Mr

Francis, a house agent, at 28/- per mensem to commence with and I am to go on Monday.

21 June This day I leave Alfred Richard Cocker Esqre solicitor of No. 11 Nassau Street Soho having been four months with the said Alfred Richard Cocker of No. 11 Nassau Street Soho aforesaid for which said service of four months I do not receive the value of four pence. I cannot say that I like the profession much, it is exceedingly dry...

26 June My father gave me some abstracts to copy, on my complaining I had not enough to do. The house agency business I clearly see is to be perfectly understood in a week.

21 August Mr Bilney has left Garrett's and commenced a school under the cognomen of 'Mentor Lodge' at Kensal Green, Harrow Road.

27 August To Mr Bilney in the morning who taught me in cyphering etc. ...

10 September My father has decided I shall go to Bilney's as a border for six months on Saturday next; this is to finish my education and at the expiration of that time it is thought my uncle will take me in his office. I am not to learn any more Latin but to attend particularly to book-keeping. I am also to learn drawing and dancing.

20 February 1829 A beautiful stag, hunted by His Majesty's hounds and about 60 riders of distinction, passed our schoolroom windows. He made off for Kilburn and was turned close by our house; the whole neighbourhood presented a very lively appearance from the number of huntsmen in their scarlet coats. The stag set off in the direction of Paddington and, coming to the Grand Junction Canal, swam across towards the church. It so happened the door was open and he bounded in and was caught inside the Church! ...

16 April ... Called on Mr Price who wishes me to superintend his timberyard.

19 May To Hubert's, Lambeth and Parliament Street for Mr P in the morning. Mr Price is a 'rum' one, he has been many years abroad and spent some considerable time at Sierra Leone where all the people were dying about him 'like sticks a-breaking!' but he, being a little piece of uncommon 'stubborn stuff', weathered the storm and is a buxom, sprightly old beau of 70 – his wife's age multiplied by $3\frac{1}{4}$ just makes his own. He brought a large cargo of mahogany home on his last trip – much of which, with subsequent additions, is in the yard still. He wishes to enlarge his business with the

St Mary's infant school at Walthamstow, conducted according to the principles of Samuel Wilderspin, c.1825, with uplifting sentiments on the walls and the children leading one another in play and song.

aid of my father, but I think the old gent is rather too fond of rum to be an able master for me.

31 October I awoke at 7 o'clock and found my dear father in his last moments ...

12 November ... The beloved remains of my dear father were interred [at St John's Wood Chapel] in the grave, No. 4b, letter T, and very near the resting place of Joanna Southcott, the noted imposter.

17 November To St Bride's with my uncle in the chaise, then walked to Mr Holmes to enquire concerning the new Swan River [a settlement in Australia], as my uncle thinks of me going out there with a Mr Carter, surgeon and a friend of his ... With my uncle to Mr Carter, where he left me and I went with him to St Katharine's Dock, where the vessel is loading in which he had taken his passage – the 'Medina' of 600 tons, Walter Pace, commander. We went over his cabin which is spacious and well fitted up and has a pianoforte etc. ...

1 January 1830 Took Breakfast with Betsy, Martha and Lewis – wished the ladies farewell and then came to take my final leave of my mother and the dear children. I kissed them severally and ran into the front garden. My cousin Lewis was waiting in the gig for me. However I ran back again to give my poor mother an extra kiss; she was crying bitterly but I consoled her by the prospects of a happy meeting hereafter. I then tore myself away from them and ran to the gate. Just as the house was closing from my views, little Maria ran out and cried, 'Goodbye, John'. These were the last words I heard – another minute we were driving at a fine rate to the metropolis. I looked back upon Kilburn as long as I could catch a glimpse of the place and I never knew Kilburn look so lovely before.

The years after 1800 saw great strides made in educating the poor. Joseph Lancaster, a Quaker, began a famous free school in Southwark which used the 'monitorial system' as a way of teaching large numbers of children together. Hence derived the model for the so-called British Schools, run by nonconformists. The Church of England soon responded with its own network of National Schools. Infant education also took on an identity of its own, thanks greatly to the efforts of Samuel Wilderspin. Wilderspin, a Swedenborgian idealist of humble background, was inspired by the example of London's pioneering infant school, founded in Westminster by a disciple of Robert Owen's. His own first mark was made in Spitalfields, where a charitable silkweaver asked the as yet untried Wilderspin to take on a school for the infant poor in 1821.

One day a gentleman called on me in the City where I was employed ... and asked me if I thought I could undertake such a school as that at Brewer's Green. I at once accepted the offer, and a place was promised to be provided for me at the East End of the town, the gentleman engaging to find all the money that was necessary. I went home to my wife, who was at dinner, with the news, and that we should have to take care of two hundred children! 'How many?' said she, laying down her knife and fork. 'Two hundred, my dear!' It spoilt her dinner completely. She always thought I had some strange visionary notions ...

We entered upon our new duties, and I found myself surrounded by one hundred and sixty-five infants from two to seven years of age who were left at the school by their mothers or guardians, who received injunctions to call for them at twelve o'clock. Of course they thought their children were going to be taught to read that very morning! For I had a number of ABC's of all colours round the room. The children were all huddled together not knowing what to make of it, and when the door closed on the last mother, now thought I to begin! But there soon began from one a faint cry of 'Mammy', then another 'Ma', and in a few seconds it became epidemic, and such a universal chorus of grief I think I never before heard. My wife soon exclaimed, 'Oh, my head, I can stand it no longer', and was obliged to go out. I began to waver, and at length I was forced to go out too! I thought it was a just judgement for my presumptuous folly. I would gladly have let them all out, but I had promised to keep them till twelve. At this moment of despair, I cast my eyes on a cap of my wife's which lay on her table, and immediately seizing hold of it and placing it to the end of a prop which lay in the yard, thrust it through the window in sight of the children. This simple expedient soon changed the scene; the grief was succeeded in a moment by surprise, and on giving the pole a shake to move the cap about, it was instantly changed into a shout of laughter, and each shake of the prop failed not to extract a new peal. The sight of one hundred and sixty-five little creatures who, almost dead with grief, were thus suddenly changed to mirth, produced important reflections, and I no longer despaired of making them entirely at ease and gaining their confidence and affection. I said, 'Now we will all play at "Duck", and I will be the great duck!' They could not resist, and thereon began an universal chorus of 'Quack, quack, quack?'. I said, 'Now we will play at "Hen and Chickens", and I will be the old hen, and when I cry cup-biddy, cup-biddy, you must all come.' It succeeded to a miracle; their fear was entirely dissipated, and twelve o'clock came before we knew where we were. Of course the question put by the mothers was, 'Well, Tommy, what book have you been reading?' 'Oh, Ma, we have not been reading any book at all, we've been playing at "Duck" and "Hen and Chickens"!' A very queer school they thought! A committee of mothers very shortly waited on me, and I saw a storm brewing. 'My boy says, Sir, he has been playing at "Duck" here, but I sent him to learn his book and not to play at such nonsense.'

It was in vain to explain to them the difficulty and necessity of resorting to any expedient to make them feel at ease, and gaining their confidence at finding themselves suddenly left by their parents and with a perfect stranger, and fearful you would not come to fetch them. I said it would take a week yet properly to do it. The school was soon reduced to eighty, then to fifty, and with these I worked away. It was soon found that the children who had been with me had rapid progress in their training, and I gradually got all my pupils back again.

1825

Crisis at a City bank

The great slump of 1825 dragged down London bankers as well as builders. One bank that went under was the firm of Pole, Thornton, Free, Down and Scott of Birchin Lane. This was the source of the wealth of the Thornton family, respectable evangelicals and intellectuals closely involved with William Wilberforce and the so-called 'Clapham Sect'. The collapse was not total; the younger Henry Thornton escaped and was able to team up with old friends to form the long-lived Williams and Deacon's Bank. But the moment-to-moment tension and panic that attended an anticipated insolvency is graphically conveyed in letters from Henry Thornton's sister, Marianne.

That dreadful Saturday I shall never forget – the run increased to a frightful degree, everybody came in to take *out* their balance, no one brought any in. One old steady customer who had usually £30,000 there drew it out without, as is usual, giving any warning, and in order to pay it the House was left literally empty. Henry went out to endeavour to borrow but people made shuffling excuses – some said they would go and fetch some and never returned – in short, both he and Mr Free were unsuccessful. Such a moment of peril completely turned Mr Free's head; he insisted on proclaiming themselves bankrupts at once, and raved and self-accused himself, and in short quite lost his powers of action.

Old Scott cried like a child of five years old but could suggest nothing, Pole and Down were both out of town. Henry saw it all lay upon him. Had he believed the House was really insolvent he said he would have stopped instantly sooner than have involved a human being any farther, but he was sure the money was theirs, only they could not get at it, and he resolved to fight it out to the last minute, though what he endured knowing that if any *large* bill was presented they *must* stop, he says he never shall forget.

There had always been such a jealousy between their House and Smith's (the Carrington Smiths I mean) that Free had often observed that morning how pleased they would be to hear they had broken, but John Smith had been an early friend of the Sykes and particularly kind

to Henry, and to him he resolved to go – but not according to bankers' etiquette, as if he did not care whether he gave it him or not – but he told him honestly he believed they must break, and he could hardly expect him to lend it, but yet if he could get him on till five, it would be an inexpressible relief. John Smith asked if he could give his word of honour that all was safe, that is, that the House was solvent, Henry said he could. Well! then he said they should have everything they could spare, which was not quite enough though, for they had been hard-pressed themselves that day, but he went back with Henry to watch the event.

Two people had chanced to pay *in* some money whilst Henry had been absent; this with what he had borrowed exactly met the demand upon them. But never, he says, shall he forget watching the clock to see when five would strike and end their immediate terror, or whether anyone would come in for any more payments. The clock did strike at last, and they were safe for the moment, but as Henry heard the door locked and the shutters put up, he felt they would not open again at that dear House, which every association led him to love so dearly.

1820s/30s

Zoos and menageries

Chunee the elephant was one of Regency London's favourite attractions. He lived in the famous menagerie at Exeter Change off the Strand – cramped predecessor to the Regent's Park Zoo. Chunee had made his name in Covent Garden pantomimes and was popular with schoolchildren. In 1825, however, the poor caged animal began to behave dangerously and killed a keeper. The menagerie's owner, Cross, gave him purgatives to calm him, without effect. The following February it was decided to put Chunee down. Poison failing, guns were called for. The grisly scene that ensued was much described and illustrated. One marksman recalled it thus.

I was at the gunmaker's, Stevens of Holborn, when Mr Hering of the New Road came in to borrow rifles and beg Mr Stevens to return with him to the 'Change to shoot the elephant. Mr Stevens was a man in years and full of gout, and I knew directly what would happen. He pointed to me as one for his substitute, and in a very few minutes I had selected the rifles, cast balls etc and we were on our way to the Exeter 'Change. We arrived and found the greatest confusion; beasts and birds most uproarious, set on by witnessing the struggle to keep in

The slaughter of Chunee the elephant at Exeter Change menagerie, 1825.

order the ungovernable elephant ... Mr Cross was much vexed with his coming loss, and Mrs Cross in tears.

I was supposed in that day a steady rifle shot, and with Mr Hering in my conceit and ignorance intended to kill the poor brute with our first fire. Dr Brooks had tried the poisons, and by his directions we fired into a crease rather below the bladebone. I expected to see him fall; instead of which he made a sharp hissing noise and struck heavily at us with his trunk and tried to make after us, and would but for the formidable double-edged spears of the keepers. These spears were ten feet long at least, wielded from a spiked end below, and the trunk wounded itself in endeavours to seize the double-edged blades. It was most fortunate the poor beast stood our fires so long afterwards, for, had he fallen suddenly and struggled in death, his struggles would have brought him from out of his cage or den, and if he had fallen from the strong flooring built under for the support of his great weight, my belief is through the whole flooring we should have all gone together, lions and men, tigers and birds. He struggled much to come after us, and we were compelled to reload in the passage, and after firing about six shots more the soldiers came from Somerset House; they had but three cartridges each man ... He bore the presence of the soldiers much better than ours, and I for a time was compelled to load the muskets for the men; they had

not the least notion of a flask: they ran the powder into the musket-barrels in most uncertain quantities, and I was compelled to unload and reload for them, or we should have had some much worse accident. The murderous assault was at length closing, and I entered with a loaded gun, taking the last shot as the noble brute seated himself on his haunches; he then folded his forelegs under him, adjusted his trunk, and ceased to live, the only peaceful one among us cruel wretches; and the only excuse I can now find for the cruel slaughter is that it was commenced and must be finished. Poor brute! It was a necessary though cruel act; he was ungovernable in a frail tenement.

Najaf Koolee Meerza, a princely Persian visitor to London in the 1830s, saw just the same sights as everyone else, but his descriptions have a subtly different flavour. One day he takes in the zoo in Regent's Park (opened in 1828), the new National Gallery and an unnamed emporium for performing fleas. He seems to like the fleas best.

This morning we were invited by some beautiful houris to accompany them to the Zoological Gardens; and as it was of importance to accept the invitation of the possessors of such charming eyes, we joined their party. In these gardens we saw a very large rhinoceros, which broke his cage of iron and made a dreadful noise; many of the attendants followed him till he became tired, when they seized him and restored him to his cage. We also beheld many wonderful and strange beasts and birds, which are indescribable . . .

Afterwards we went to a huge and lofty edifice which was built by the Government for the public. This place is adorned with many splendid pictures. Every person is allowed to enter gratis. The innumerable and beautiful pictures that we saw here are beyond description. There is also in this place a picture of Jesus, the son of Mary (peace be upon him!) with his disciples healing some diseased and dying persons. By the powerful influence of his spirit, he granted to them restoration to health and life. These pictures cost 8,000 or 10,000 tomans. It was indeed a very interesting visit.

From this place we went to the house of a person whose business is to take care of fleas and tame them. The relation of what we saw of these fleas at this place, how they are tamed and taught to act most wonderfully, will undoubtedly be taken for a lie. No one would ever believe that these little insects could be instructed in such a manner . . . These fleas are kept in a damp place, where they grow. They are placed in a glass case, which magnifies them exceedingly. There are some apartments in this box where they are quartered. They are broken to draw carriages, just as our horses are taught to draw carriages of cannon . . . Four of these fleas drew a carriage of ten drachms in weight, in harness, and turned exactly like horses. Two others stood for coachmen, with a whip of hair to drive the rest. On one side of their box there is a vessel full of water, on which there is a little thing in the form of a ship with sails, and an anchor on the water, just like a vessel in harbour. About ten or twelve fleas drew the anchor up, others went up the masts and spread the sails, their chief or captain taking the helm; and thus this ship of fleas actually sailed on the water. In another place we observed a wheel and a rope in perfect order. In the box there was a little musical instrument on which the fleas played; other fleas played on the rope, and some danced. We observed also a large flea which was a soothsayer, telling fortunes and future events. This was done as follows: a plate is figured in lines of different colours like an astrolabe. Some of these indicate good and others bad fortunes. There is fixed to it a kind of pointer, attached by a chain to the neck of the flea. The person who wishes to have his fortune told puts his question. The flea will then walk about, and the pointer move. Whenever it stops, it will inform him whether he has a good or bad fortune. These fleas are fed on human blood twice a day, once early in the morning and again in the evening. Those that are educated, that is, such as become tame, are well fed, and those that are not tamed are allowed but little till they become learned; and then they are sold and purchased. The master of these fleas has one which he has kept for two years; he would not take a horse for it. In fine, we think we had better stop, as what we saw of the curious and most wonderful acts performed by these fleas would require much time to describe.

1831/4

The last days of the old Parliament

Flora Tristan, visiting from France, was one of the very few women ever to see Parliament in action under the old dispensation, before the Reform Bill of 1832 generated the first spark of professionalism among politicians. Technically women were not allowed into the visitors' galleries until 1835, but the indomitable and radical Flora sneaked in wearing oriental disguise in 1831. She was not enamoured of what she saw – least of all by the House of Commons.

In appearance nothing could be meaner of more commonplace; it puts one in mind of a shop. It is rectangular in shape, small and very cramped; the ceiling is low, the galleries above overhang and partly hide the aisles beneath; the wooden benches are stained a walnut-brown colour. The chamber has no outstanding feature, nothing to show it has a lofty function to fulfil. It could just as well serve as a village chapel or house an assembly of grocers, what you will; its architecture and furnishings have no dignity whatsoever. The gas lighting however is absolutely magnificent, and this is the only thing I can find to praise.

The honourable members recline on the benches in bored and weary poses – several even stretch right out and go to sleep . . . The starchy English, who take offence at the least lapse or the slightest negligence, display an utter contempt for every convention of polite society when they are in the House. It is good parliamentary form to appear at a session in everyday clothes, covered in mud, an umbrella under one's arm; or to arrive at the House on horseback and enter in full hunting array, complete with spurs and riding crop . . . Only when a member addresses the House does he take off his hat; he leans upon his stick or umbrella, sticks his thumbs in his waistcoat or his trouser pockets. They all tend to speak at great length and do not expect anybody to pay any attention to what they say – indeed, they do not seem to be very interested in it themselves!

Certainly a far deeper silence reigns there than in our chamber of deputies, as most of the members are either asleep or reading their newspapers . . .

We proceeded to the House of Lords . . . Their chamber is hardly any better than the Commons, it is built on the same plan, with the same rough unfinished masonry devoid of any decoration. The noble lords conduct themselves no differently from their fellows in the lower chamber; they too keep their hats upon their heads, but this is from pride in their rank rather than lack of manners, and they require spectators in the public galleries and witnesses summoned to appear at their Bar to bare their heads, even if they are members of the Commons. When Lord Wellington had finished speaking, he sprawled across his bench with his legs on the back of the bench above and his head lower than his feet – a most grotesque posture, just like a horse with its legs in the air, as we French would say.

I left these two chambers hardly edified by what I had seen, and certainly more scandalized by the behaviour of the gentlemen of the House of Commons than they had been by my clothes!

In so far as the habits of British parliamentarians that shocked Miss Tristan have ever been purged, they were purged not by reform but by the great fire of October 1834 that burnt down most of the Palace of Westminster. This celebrated and not unhappy event – since a mess was replaced by a masterpiece – marked the symbolic close of

The Houses of Parliament smouldering in the late stages of the fire, 1834. The Palace at Westminster had become a rabbit warren, and its destruction was little lamented. Painting by David Roberts.

the whole Hanoverian era. J.M.W. Turner and many other artists depicted it. One who did not was the nervous, poverty-stricken history painter, Benjamin Haydon. He was to dream instead of great canvases in the new Houses of Parliament. But he killed himself before he had the chance to paint them.

October 16 Good God! I am just returned from the terrific burning of the Houses of Lords and Commons. Mary and I went in a cab and drove over the bridge. From the bridge it was sublime. We alighted and went into the room of a public house, which was full. To witness the feeling among the people was extraordinary – the jokes and radicalism were universal. If Ministers had heard the shrewd sense and intelligence of these drunken remarks! I hurried Mary away. Good God, and are that throne and tapestry gone – with all their associations?

The comfort is there is now a better prospect of painting a House of Lords. Lord Grey said there was no intention of taking the tapestry down – little did he think how soon it would be.

It is really awful and ominous – one does not like to think. 'There is no House of Lords,' said one of the half drunken fellows; 'they are extinguished, Sir.'

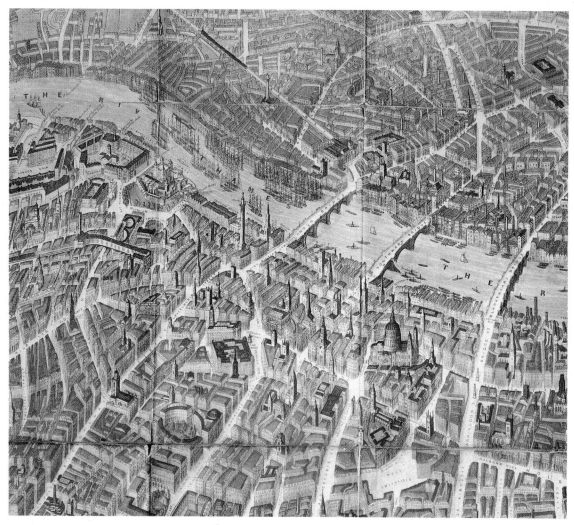

1837–1887

FIFTY

Years of

VICTORIAN

LONDON

Seen from overseas early Victorian London was a city like nowhere else on earth. People called it a wonder of the world; there seemed no other suitable phrase. London had more traffic on the streets, more goods in the shops, more railway lines (above and below ground), even the first under-river tunnel in the modern world. There was a uniformed but civil police and, in her palace at the end of the Mall, a remarkable queen – presiding over an empire covering much of the earth's surface.

Those who visited London and recorded their impressions ranged from the incurably critical to the insatiably enthusiastic. Expectations were high, and few escaped a real shock when they encountered, however fleetingly, the kind of poverty that might have seemed until then a product of the over-active imagination of Charles Dickens.

The texture of London was intricately interwoven. Shivers at the top of society affected the entire body. 'The falling off in the glass-cutting trade is to be ascribed, first to the terrible railway losses amongst the upper classes two years ago: followed up by the commercial panic, and tremendous losses occasioned by the excessive importation of foreign corn. Rich cut glass is an article of luxury, and when the means of the consumers of luxuries are crippled they must cease to purchase. They are obliged to suffer their houses to go unpainted another year, make no alterations or additions to their buildings, change no old furniture for new, buy no new jewellery, make their apparel last twice the usual time, and economize in their number of balls and entertainments' (*Weekly Dispatch*, 16 April 1848).

On closer examination the percipient traveller, and there were many, hailing from North America and Russia, continental Europe and even the first diplomatic mission from China, could see that all was not well. In Queen Victoria's reign the population grew at a staggering pace, almost doubling every twenty years. The city area grew from 22 to 120 square miles.

At the very outset of the queen's reign the

ABOVE *The royal opening of the Great Exhibition, May 1851. The Hyde Park trees were preserved inside Paxton's building. Painting by Henry Selous.*

OPPOSITE *Balloon view of London (detail) in 1851 showing clearly the density of riverside buildings, both warehouses and factories, especially on the south bank of the Thames.*

Registrar General's report found the death rate of the East End twice that in the West End. The extremes of human existance even then were remarkable. Already in 1837 James Fenimore Cooper could write, 'I frequently stop and look about me in wonder, distrusting my eyes, at the exhibition of wealth and luxury that is concentrated in such narrow limits.'

Run-down areas, often just a street away from a wealthy district, were absorbing the vastly increased population, much of it without any means of support. Cholera epidemics swept the slums, misunderstood in their causes, and returned over and over again – the infection set off by the continuing parlous state of public hygiene. Despite reforms that began in the 1830s there was no significant drop in the death rate until the 1880s. Even then, for the sick and the poor, hospital beds were few and far between.

At the beginning of Queen Victoria's reign London was a metropolis ringed by low hills, upon which existing villages – soon to be suburbs – looked down on the mass below. As the railways pushed out to the four corners of London, the builders followed them. Before long Kentish Town and Gospel Oak joined Hampstead to the West End, Dalston and Hackney linked Stoke Newington to the City, Shepherd's Bush and Fulham grew to the west beyond Bayswater and Kensington. By the time of Queen Victoria's Golden Jubilee the scene was of almost seamless development.

In some outer areas new housing consisted of salubrious villas set in ample grounds; in most districts boxy semi-detached houses alternated with terraces of varying scale. Periodically, builders overestimated demand and found themselves with a massive glut of unlet properties.

As the bricks and mortar spread, the need for green space to replace the open countryside, farmland and nursery ground that had been sold for development was acute. Primrose Hill and Victoria Park were opened respectively in 1842 and 1845. The contrast between the two was telling.

Primrose Hill was a royal gift, a pleasant spur

St Pancras Hotel and Station from Pentonville Road, 1884. George Gilbert Scott's Midland Hotel was completed in 1872 and became one of the great London hotels – closing in 1935. Painting by John O'Connor.

rising to a considerable height, beyond the Regent's Park in the comfortable north-western suburbs. Victoria Park was the result of an energetic campaign to give the East Enders somewhere to breathe, an essential open space bought by the Crown Estates with funds raised by the sale of York House, the property of the Crown. Crystal Palace and Battersea followed in 1856, parks for the poor of London south of the river. Peckham Rye and Finsbury Park opened in 1868 and 1869 respectively. The chronology mirrors the development of London nicely.

While London grew at the edges, what of the centre? The setting up of the Metropolitan Board of Works set in train the modernization of London's infrastructure. Sewers, water supply, embankments for the Thames and a major re-

modelling of thoroughfares and viaducts were all part of the gigantic building programme during the 1860s and 1870s. The construction of railway termini, bridges, hotels, office chambers and warehouses that congregated around each main-line station simply added to the confusion, preceded in every case by swathes of demolition – mostly of low-grade slum courts and thickly populated back streets.

The political and functional relationship of London to the provinces – quite different from its European neighbours – ensured that all roads led to and from London. Lines of communication originated there, starting with a postal and telegraph service and then, in 1879, the establishment of the first telephone exchange in the United Kingdom.

London absorbed and distributed produce from home and abroad, in markets scattered throughout the capital, ranging from the pungent Bermondsey Leather Market to Covent Garden. As Charles Dickens the younger put it in his guide book, 'Country visitors will go away from Covent Garden with the conviction that to see flowers and fruits in perfection it is necessary to come to London.'

Inevitably, as an unrivalled port, London was the focus of international trade and commerce, a point which the Great Exhibition of 1851 demonstrated definitively.

In the City of London the large residential population withered away to be replaced by a dense commercial world of financial houses, agencies, exchanges and commodity markets to which hundreds of thousands of people came to work. Initially on foot, then by rail and horse-drawn omnibus, they poured into the Square Mile. Historic buildings counted for little; the City had to have new kinds of buildings with large floor areas to service the business of the world. They might be in historic costume but were facing the future.

Before the Prince Consort's death Queen Victoria was a highly visible and industrious head of state. The visit of the King of Saxony and the Emperor of Russia, to which the observant Dr Carus was attached, was the first state visit in the modern sense. More followed.

Queen Victoria vanished indoors with the death of the Prince Consort in 1861, scarcely seen until the mid-1870s, yet life in London society did not grind to a halt. The Prince and Princess of Wales kept the party going with a new cast list – by then the financiers and the plutocrats were beginning to edge out the aristocracy.

Nor was life in the thin air around the very wealthy simply concerned with extravagance and fashionable aesthetics, crystal staircases and private picture galleries. Grosvenor House was redesigned in 1870, but the first Duke of Westminster's Italian Renaissance remodelling of his mansion was just a detail; he reserved his real enthusiasm for the introduction of electricity – in which race he beat all his noble peers.

Meanwhile, the literary and artistic worlds were finding their own corners in the capital. In the 1870s the new suburb of Bedford Park, Chelsea studios in Cheyne Walk and Tite Street, artists' villas in St John's Wood, Hampstead or Holland Park all attracted their own milieu, in some cases the arts and intellectual Establishment, in others high Bohemia. Lacking a café society, social contact tended to be in each other's houses.

London offered a safe haven – long term or short – to refugees from all kinds of trouble at home, Mazzini, Marx, Engels and Herzen among them. The view of London as a great whirlpool into which someone could disappear and find a quiet toe-hold was shared by many.

London managed to convey, at home and

abroad, a sense of institutional stability that sheltered and encouraged its dynamism in many areas of life. After all, the new Palace of Westminster, weighed down with its retrospective and allusive ornament, could still turn out the Reform Bill.

1838

From Euston by train

The railways would transform the relationship between the capital and the countryside. Louisa Twining's journey, described in her diary, was to Berkhamsted, taking the London and Birmingham Railway out of Euston, which had been open only a year. Travellers from Euston would have entered beneath Philip Hardwick's Doric portico, or Propylaeum, linking two lodges inscribed with names of destinations, before finding themselves in a rather humdrum shed behind. Still, at the age of eighteen, the future philanthropist Louisa Twining was impressed.

June 2 1838 Went up to the station at Euston Square at eleven. I had no idea of the extent of the arrangements here or of the building. Nothing can be more regularly or beautifully managed. There is a large covered-in space from which the trains start; so having chosen our places in a most comfortable, soft carriage, we heard the bell, and began gliding off. The novelty of the whole

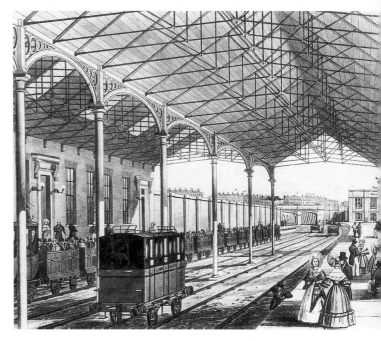

Euston station, seen in an Ackerman print published in 1837, the year in which the terminus for the London and Birmingham Railroad opened.

thing made it very entertaining; we went very quietly at first till the steam-engine was put on, then our speed gradually increased till it quite equalled my expectations. The motion, however, disappointed me; the shaking far exceeded any I ever felt in a coach ... The enjoyment is, I think, greatly lessened by the frequent stops we made at different stations; the three tunnels, too, are unpleasant; the longest a mile, and of course in total darkness; each carriage is provided with a lamp, but ours soon went out, and then we could discern nothing during the three minutes we were underground. It is certainly a strange sensation, rushing on at so tremendous a pace, and with so great a noise into the darkness, and appears to me to show the confidence people place in this wonderous power, more than anything; the coldness of the air as you rush through is disagreeable ... We reached the object of our journey, twenty-seven miles, in an hour and a quarter, and the time had seemed so short, I was quite sorry when it was over.

1840s

Theatre, concerts and the opera

Theatre in early Victorian London was still living on the memory, and reprises, of the great Regency actors. Louisa Twining could not manage to steal a glimpse of the newly married queen with the Prince Consort overhead but she did see Charles Kemble's return to the boards in a comedy at Covent Garden, and recorded the event in her diary.

March 1840 We were delighted to hear that Mr. Lane's plan for the reappearance of Charles Kemble on the stage has succeeded, and that he was to act in the *Wonder*. Mr. Lane procured us seats in the box next to the stage; the Queen and Prince were to be present, but of them we saw nothing, as we sat exactly underneath them. However, the whole theatre was a beautiful sight crowded in every part, and the effect most brilliant ... the Queen arrived, but ... did not appear till the end of the play. Then, again, what rapturous applause when Kemble appeared. Considering he is upwards of sixty, I was surprised to see the light, bounding step with which he met Violante, and the gracefulness of his figure, ease, elegance, variety of expression, and then his voice, how charming and musical! The tones rang in my ears long afterwards.

By coincidence, the young Felix Mendelssohn, being lionized in the musical circles of London, also found himself

Poster for a performance of Wonder *at the Theatre Royal, Covent Garden, the comedy which Louisa Twining enjoyed in the company of Queen Victoria and Prince Albert.*

in the company of both Queen Victoria and Charles Kemble. He also took a whistle-stop tour of the principal sites of London.

JUNE 21 1842

Dear Mother,

... we daily see the most beautiful and splendid things. But I am somewhat fatigued by the all-too-mad activities of the last week ... They have really asked a little too much of me. Recently when I played the organ in Christ Church, Newgate Street, I thought for a few moments that I would suffocate, so great was the crowd and pressure around my bench at the organ. Then, too, several days later I had to play in Exeter Hall before three thousand people, who shouted hurrahs and waved their handkerchiefs, and stamped their feet till the hall quaked ... Add to this the pretty and most charming Queen Victoria, who looks so youthful and is so shyly friendly and courteous, and who speaks such good German and who knows all my music so well . . . my A minor Symphony has had great success with the people here, who one and all receive us with a degree of amiability and kindness which exceeds everything I have ever known in the way of hospitality . . .

June 22nd – Today . . . I have slept away my weary mood and feel again well and fresh. Yesterday evening I played my concerto in D minor and directed my ''Hebrides'' in the Philharmonic where I was received like an old friend and where they played with a degree of enthusiasm which gave me more pleasure than I can say . . .

This evening at seven o'clock we dine with Bunsen, and as we do not know what to do with our evening afterwards, we shall probably drive to Charles Kemble's about eleven o'clock and be among his early guests; the late ones will not arrive till after midnight. And the persistently bright and beautiful weather besides all this! The other morning we first went to see the Tower, then the Katherine Docks, then the Tunnel, then ate fish at Blackwall, had tea at Greenwich, and came home by way of Peckham; we travelled on foot, in a carriage, on a railway, in a boat, and in a steamboat . . .

A few years later, having 'walked through a thunderstorm to the Station, got to Leeds and whirled up by a Night train to London', Charlotte Brontë and her sister Anne, at the end of an enormously wearying day spent introducing 'Currer Bell' to Smith and Elder, reluctantly found themselves whisked off to the opera by her kindly publishers, Mr Smith and Mr Williams. By then the Covent Garden Theatre had been reopened as the Royal Italian Opera House.

Charlotte Bronte to Mary Taylor. Haworth, 4 September 1848

Another recognition – a long, nervous shaking of hands – then followed talk-talk-talk – Mr Williams being silent – Mr Smith loquacious . . .

How long do you stay in London? You must make the most of the time – to-night you must go to the Italian opera . . .

He told us he should bring his sisters to call on us that evening – We returned to our Inn [Chapter Coffee House] – and I paid for the excitement of the interview by a thundering head-ache and harrassing [sic] sickness – towards evening as I got no better and expected the Smiths to call I took a strong dose of sal volatile – it roused me a little – still I was in grievous bodily case when they were announced – they came in two elegant, young ladies in full dress – prepared for the Opera –

Smith himself in evening costume white gloves etc a distinguished, handsome fellow enough – We had by no means understood that it was settled that we were to go to the Opera – and were not ready – Moreover we had no fine, elegant dresses either with us or in the world. However on brief rumination, I though[sic] it would be wise to make no objections – I put my headache in my pocket – we attired ourselves in the plain – high-made, country garments we possessed – and went with them to their carriage – where we found Williams likewise in full dress. They must have thought us queer, quizzical looking beings – especially me with my spectacles – I smiled inwardly at the contrast which must have been apparent between me and Mr Smith as I walked with him up the crimson carpeted staircase of the Opera House and stood amongst a brilliant throng at the box-door which was not yet open. Fine ladies and gentlemen glanced at us with a slight, graceful super-ciliousness quite warranted by the circumstances – Still I felt pleasurably excited – in spite of head-ache sickness and conscious clownishness, and I saw Anne was calm and gentle which she always is –

The Performance was Rosini's [sic] opera of the "Barber of Seville" – very brilliant though I fancy there are things I should like better – We got home after one o'clock – We had never been in bed the night before – had been in constant excitement for 24 hours – you may imagine we were tired.

1830s

The horrors of St Giles

Dickens's evocation of the institutions and varied corners of London are well known, but in *Sketches by Boz*, the earliest of his writings on the city, he caught day-to-day life, with its underlay of misery, with a pen both matter of fact and agonizingly acute. The St Giles district, including the old Monmouth Street, had become the epitome of a slum. In his account of it Dickens gives a fascinating description of the diverse activities found on the many floors of a single building and the vitality that this brought to the scene. The 1831 census figures for the district, known as 'little Dublin', gave a staggering population of 36,432 people.

The inhabitants of Monmouth Street are a distinct class; a peaceable and retiring race, who immerse themselves for the most part in deep cellars, or small back parlours, and who seldom come forth into the world, except in the dusk and coolness of evening, when they may be seen seated, in chairs on the pavement, smoking their

George Cruikshank's illustration in Sketches by Boz *by Charles Dickens, showing Monmouth Street, centre of the second-hand clothes trade and a notorious slum.*

pipes, or watching the gambols of their engaging children as they revel in the gutter, a happy troop of infantine scavengers ... 'A Monmouth-Street laced coat' was a by-word a century ago; and still we find Monmouth-Street the same ...

Wretched houses with broken windows patched with rags and paper, every room let out to a different family and in many instances to two or even three; fruit and 'sweet-stuff' manufacturers in the cellars, barbers and red-herring vendors in the front parlours, and cobblers in the back; a bird-fancier in the first floor, three families on the second, starvation in the attics, Irishmen in the passage; a 'musician' in the front kitchen, and a charwoman and five hungry children in the back one – filth everywhere – a gutter before the houses and a drain behind them – clothes drying and slops emptying from the windows; girls of fourteen or fifteen with matted hair walking about barefoot, and in white great-coats, almost their only covering; boys of all ages, in coats of all sizes and no coats at all; men and women, in every variety of scanty and dirty apparel, lounging, scolding, drinking, smoking, squabbling, fighting and swearing.

Flora Tristan, an ardent French feminist revolutionary, visited London at much the same time as Dickens was writing his account and corroborated his picture of the horrors of St Giles.

At its starting-point, the elegant, long thoroughfare of Oxford Street, with its throng of carriages, its wide pavements and splendid shops, it joined almost at right angles by Tottenham Court Road; just off this street ... there is a narrow alley ... the entrance to the Irish quarter.

It is not without fear that the visitor ventures into the dark, narrow alley known as Bainbridge Street. Hardly have you gone ten paces when you are almost suffocated by the poisonous smell. The alley, completely blocked by the huge coal-yard, is impassable. We turned off to the right into another unpaved muddy alley with evil-smelling soapy water and other household slops even more fetid lying everywhere in stagnant pools ... there is no fresh air to breathe nor daylight to guide your steps. The wretched inhabitants wash their tattered garments themselves and hang them on poles across the street, shutting out all pure air and sunshine. The slimy mud beneath your feet gives off all manner of noxious vapours, while the wretched rags above you drip their dirty rain upon your head ...

Picture, if you can, barefoot men, women and children picking their way through the foul morass ... unless you have seen it for yourself, it is impossible to imagine such extreme poverty, such total degradation. I saw children *without a stitch of clothing*, barefoot girls and women with babies at their breast, wearing nothing but a torn shirt that revealed almost the whole of their bodies; I saw old men cowering on dunghills, young men covered in rags ...

Inside and out, the tumbledown hovels are entirely in keeping with the ragged population who inhabit them ... doors and windows lack fastenings and the floor is unpaved; the only furniture is a rough old oak table, a wooden bench, a stool ... and a sort of *kennel* where father, mother, sons, daughters, and friends all sleep together regardless.

1840s

The Metropolitan Police

The Metropolitan Police was founded in 1829, an underpaid collection of 3,000 men covering most but not all of London. The Thames Police and the Bow Street runners came under the umbrella of the Metropolitan force, following the Metropolitan Police Act of 1839, which created a police district stretching fifteen miles around Charing Cross and the county of Middlesex. The force numbered 3,444 by 1839, and the Act also established the separate City of London police. One officer recalled his uniform, many years later.

The Metropolitan policeman of the 'forties was a strange-looking individual. I wore a swallow-tailed coat with bright buttons, and a tall hat. The hat was a fine protection for the head, and saved me from damage from many a Chartist's bludgeon. It had a rim of stout leather around the top, and a strip of covered steel on each side. Then I had a truncheon, a weapon that was capable of doing a lot of execution, and gave a good account of itself in those rough and dangerous times.

Other impressions of the police were offered by a German visitor, the King of Saxony's physician, Dr Carus, and William Cullen Bryant, the American essayist, poet, journalist and lawyer, who found Londoners surprisingly trusting but sensed (and experienced) the social tensions that would lead to a more active role for the Victorian police.

The London constabulary are not provided with arms of any description, but merely carry a short staff of office in the breast pocket, which, although short, is heavy, and may, when occasion requires, be used as a weapon both of offence and defence. In the police, however, the people recognise the preservers of peace, order, and law, and cases are very rare in which any opposition is offered, or resistance made to their authority.

———————

June 24 1845 I called the other day on a friend, an American, who told me that he had that morning spoken with his landlady about her carelessness in leaving the shutters of her lower rooms unclosed during the night. She answered that she never took the trouble to close them, that so secure was the city from ordinary burglaries, under the arrangements of the new police, that it was not worth the trouble ... All classes of the people appear to be satisfied with the new police. The officers are men of respectable appearance and respectable manners. If I lose my way, or stand in need of any local information, I apply to a person in the uniform of a police officer. They are sometimes more stupid in regard to these matters than there is any occasion for but it is one of their duties ... to assist strangers with local information.

Begging is repressed by the new police regulations, and want skulks in holes and corners, and prefers its petitions where it can not be overheard by men armed with the authority of the law ...

Walking in Hampstead Heath a day or two since, with an English friend, we were accosted by two labourers, who were sitting on a bank, and who said that they had come to that neighbourhood in search of employment in hay-making, and had not been able to get either work or food. My friend appeared to distrust their story. But in the evening ... we passed a company of some four or five labourers ... who asked us for something to eat ... 'we have come for work, and nobody will hire us; we have had nothing to eat all day.' Their tone was dissatisfied, almost menacing; and the Englishman ... referred to it several times afterward, with an expression of anxiety and alarm.

I hear it often remarked here, that the difference of condition between the poorer and the richer classes becomes greater every day, and what the end will be the wisest pretend not to foresee.

1839/48

Chartist unrest

The Chartist movement took its name from 'The People's Charter' of 1838 calling for reforms to parliamentary practice and universal male suffrage. Grounded in the newly industrialized areas of the country, Chartism originally had little following in London. Piece-workers and craftsmen comprised the city's complex, interconnected industrial base but formed a working class difficult to radicalize. Exhortations such as the 1838 handbill below were largely futile. However, eighteen months later Fergus O'Connor led a march on the House of Commons, which he described with characteristic hyperbole.

Men of London! assemble in Smithfield on Sunday, the 10th of November [1839], at 3 o'clock in the afternoon. Wales is in a state of insurrection; justice calls aloud that the people's grievances should be redressed! Ye lovers of life, property, and religion, attend this great and solemn meeting, to petition the Queen to dismiss from her councils her present weak and wicked ministers, and save our country from a civil war! – Parents keep your children at home, and may God preside at the councils of the people!

———————

Our procession took one hour and ten minutes to pass one spot. Procession did I say! we had no procession! it

The first known photograph of a political demonstration, the Chartist meeting on Kennington Common, 10 April 1848. Photograph by William Kilburn.

was a dense mass of streets full!! Procession means a number of persons marshalled four or five a-breast, but our numbers could not have been marshalled. The 'Times' allow us 50,000. Now you may safely multiply that by 10. It was acknowledged by all that it was the largest, the very largest gathering of people that ever was seen in London.

In 1848, the year of European revolution, London was living on its nerves. The February revolution in Paris led to such unlikely events as the playing of the Marseillaise at Sadler's Wells. The ferocious winter of 1847–8 had coincided with a desperate economic depression and a terrible outbreak of cholera. All these factors took their toll and radicalized the working classes. The atmosphere was apprehensive. The announcement of a Chartist demonstration for 10 April led to panic in government and among the wealthy and led to the setting up of a special constabulary, numbering some 85,000, to assist the Metropolitan Police. The Bank of England was given protection on war-time footing. These were busy weeks for the police, who found themselves the object of popular hatred, as two reports from April and May 1848 indicate.

A breastwork of sandbags, with loopholes for muskets and small guns, had been thrown up along the parapet wall of [the Bank of England] ... at each corner of the building, musket batteries, bullet-proof, were raised, having loopholes for small carronades. The line of road from the Strand to the new Houses of Parliament has all the appearance of a thoroughfare in a besieged capital ... Notices from the Police Commissioners, that no

carts, vans or omnibuses are to be allowed upon the road from Abingdon-street to Cockspur-street after eleven o'clock, and that no delay is to be permitted in the other streets, agitate the public, and the appearance of patrols of mounted police, and of single files of soldiers in the usually quiet street, is ominous and alarming.

_____

We, in the forties, used to brush the mobs off the streets, and out of the way. The chief thing was to get rid of them ... There was plenty of ammunition going, because the streets were not what they are now, and there were heaps of rubbish at hand ... A famous battle ground was Clerkenwell Green, and another place I remember well was Cowcross Street. There was plenty of open space on the Green for fighting, and many houses in which the Chartists could hide and throw things at us ... Day after day we came into collision with them.

1851

Omnibus drivers

Henry Mayhew's chronicle of the city, entitled *London Labour and the London Poor* and originally published in three volumes in 1851, gave the first thorough social survey of working life. A journalist and author with strong principles of social reform, he looked penetratingly at a wide range across the working class, as well as at those far down the social order who were living off their wits and surviving with difficulty. He frequently used verbatim accounts from the individuals he interviewed. Mayhew's survey was the first of many in the late nineteenth century, but it was also the direct inspiration for Charles Booth's survey (see p.229), as the title suggests.

Mayhew's accounts of 'street-folk', such as costermongers and mudlarks, depict without sentimentality the struggle to survive, but his description of a more solid livelihood, that of the omnibus driver, gives a picture of another stratum of London working-class life.

The omnibus drivers have been butchers, farmers, horsebreakers, cheesemongers, old stage-coachmen, broken-down gentlemen, turf-men, gentlemen's servants, grooms and a very small sprinkling of mechanics.

unmarried men, before they start; and dine at the inn ... at one or another of [the omnibus's] destinations ... From a driver I had the following statement:

... I was brought up as a builder, but had friends that was using horses ... I got to like that sort of work ... and first got employed as a time-keeper; but I've been a driver for fourteen years ... It's very hard work for the horses ... The starting after stopping is the hardest work for them; it's such a terrible strain. I've felt for the poor things on a wet night, with a 'bus full of big people ... there's a fine for the least delay. I can't say it's often levied; but still we are liable to it. If I've been blocked, I must make up for the block by galloping; and if I'm

LEFT *Peak hour omnibus traffic. From* The Illustrated London News, *1 May 1847.*

OPPOSITE *The scene in Pentonville prison chapel as described by Dr Carus, each convict enclosed in a separate box. From Mayhew and Minney's* Criminal Prisons of London.

Nearly all can read and write ... all must have produced good characters before their appointment. The majority of them are married men with families; their residences being in all parts, and on both sides of the Thames. I did not hear of any of the wives of coachmen in regular employ working for the slop-tailors. 'We can keep our wives too respectable for that' one of them said ... Their children, too, are generally sent to school; frequently to the national schools. Their work is exceedingly hard, their lives being almost literally spent on the coach-box. The most of them must enter 'the yard' at a quarter to eight in the morning, and must see that the horses and carriages are in a proper condition for work; and at half-past eight they start on their long day's labour. They perform (I speak of the most frequented lines), twelve journeys during the day, and are so engaged until a quarter-past eleven at night ... They generally breakfast at home, or at a coffee-shop, if

seen to gallop, and anybody tells our people, I'm hauled over the coals ... Some companies save twelve guineas a week by the doing away of toll-gates ... I'm an unmarried man. A 'bus driver never has time to look out for a wife. Every horse in our stables has one day's rest in every four; but it's no rest for the driver.

1848

An American in London

When Ralph Waldo Emerson, the American poet, essayist and thinker, visited London in 1848, he overlooked little. His telegraphic diary entries tell a great deal of the atmosphere, and changes, in the city.

Plural London Immeasureable London, evidently the capital of the world, where men have lived ever since there were men ... An aggregation of capitals.

There are several little nations here. A German quarter in Whitechapel, a French quarter where they still carry on a silk business in Spitalfields.

In London only could such a place as Kew Gardens be overlooked. Wealth of shops bursting into the streets; piles of plates breast-high on Ludgate Hill. In a London dock Mr Bates said he had seen nineteen miles of pipes of wine piled up to the ceiling.

Many of the characterizing features of London are new. Such as gas-light, the omnibuses, the steam ferries, the penny-post, and the building up the West End.

One goes from show to show, dines out, and lives in extremes. Electric sparks six feet long; light is polarized; Grisi sings; Rothschild is your banker; Owen and Faraday lecture; Macaulay talks; Soyer cooks. Is there not an economy in coming where thus all the dependence is on the first men of their kind?

April 15. Among the trades of despair is the searching the filth of the sewers for rings, shillings, teaspoons, etc., which have been washed out of the sinks. These sewers are so large that you can go underground great distances. Mr Colman saw a man coming out of the ground with a bunch of candles. 'Pray, sir, where did you come from?' 'Oh, I've been seven miles,' the man replied. They say that Chadwick rode all under London on a little brown pony.

1844

Pentonville prison

London's gaols were a notorious collection of institutions. Dr Carus, personal physician to the King of Saxony, who was on the first ever State visit to Britain, visited several, but he was most interested in the new Pentonville prison, which had opened in 1842. The model prison was based on the scheme of the Eastern Penitentiary in Philadelphia, in which all prisoners could be held in solitary confinement. Pentonville was for men between the ages of eighteen and thirty-five, condemned to transportation for no more than fifteen years. They would be held there eighteen months (later reduced considerably)– prior to transportation, and their conduct during that period determined their treatment on arrival in Van Diemen's Land. Dr Carus, a humane man, was disturbed by the effect prolonged solitary confinement might have on the mental state of the prisoners. The royal party was reassured but Carus remarked, 'Longer experience will tell us more'.

The day now approaches when we must leave London;

and the time is, therefore zealously used, in order to learn as much as possible of this peculiar world!

First, his majesty the king was to be shown the new Pentonville Model Prison, built as a model and ... a trial of the complete system of solitary confinement. We drove out early to this building, only eighteen months completed, situated towards the northern extremity of London, where the streets and buildings extend continually more and more into the fields, at an expense of 85,000L. (a pretty large sum for a trial). I was much interested in the arrangements ... The ground plan of this building is in so far like that of the Penitentiary, that the wings radiate like a star; but here only a half-

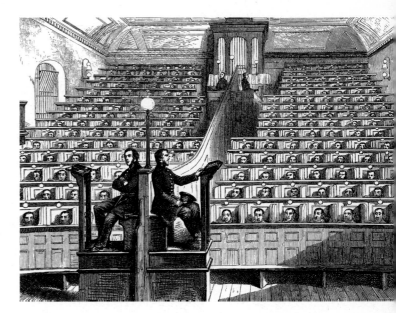

star is formed. Each of these four wings consists of a high and long hall, lighted from above, in which are an underground floor, and three stories of cells one above the another. Four galleries run round each floor, and form the means by which the overseers visit the cells; and iron spiral staircases lead from one floor to the other.

Each of the four wings can thus contain more than 100 cells, and 520 prisoners altogether can be placed here, each in his separate cell. Every thing is kept in the greatest order and cleanliness, the walls merely white-washed, and the iron painted black; and above, between the galleries, passes a sort of railway, upon which is placed the carriage which contains the food, as brought up from the underground story ... In a quarter of an hour a few overseers can distribute food to 500 prisoners. Each cell contains a hammock, a chest of drawers, a table and chair, a metal washing-basin, and a gas-holder; also every prisoner can give notice, by pressing on a spring, that he wishes to speak to the overseer. The cells are well provided with fresh air, by ventilation, and are heated with warm air in winter.

In every cell arrangements are made for some employment ... so that the unfortunate man is enabled to resist the fearful solitude by some occupation, and at the same time to make reflections on his former life ... Order is preserved ... with military strictness; and when the prisoners assemble, either in church or for instruction, or to walk ... within a walled court, or to any common labour ... absolute silence reigns. Besides this, they wear a peculiar sort of cap, the shade of which falls over the face, and being provided with two holes for the eyes, forms a sort of mask, rendering all mutual recognition impossible ... no names exist, but each prisoner is denoted and called for by the number of his cell ...

The chapel of the institution presents a singular spectacle! In semi-circular rows above one another, high wooden boxes are erected, which are so constructed, as to allow the prisoner in them a sight of the pulpit, but at the same time to render him perfectly invisible to any of the other prisoners ... the sight was particularly depressing, when ... suddenly a number of boxes were filled with masked prisoners. As soon as they sit down, they throw back their mask, and their faces are seen for the first time ...

Above the chapel is a platform, from which one has a view of the as yet free and open position of the prison, and the range of hills to the north of London. It was a dull morning – everything looked desolate round about – places for building were being prepared, and some smaller houses actually built, looking like newly settled colonies –whilst in the other direction every thing was lost in a mass of houses covered with mist and smoke – quite a November picture in the middle of June!

1848/55

The new Houses of Parliament

After the devastating fire at the Palace of Westminster an architectural competition was held, and Charles Barry's Gothic Revival design was chosen from the ninety-seven entrants. Work began in 1837, and Barry was assisted by A.W. Pugin, who detailed the scheme in authentic Gothic style. In 1848 Ralph Waldo Emerson disliked the repetitious nationalistic ornament, while in 1855 his compatriot Nathaniel Hawthorne feared that it expressed the last flowering of a fading empire.

London March [1848] In the new Parliament House, great poverty of ornament, the ball and crown repeated tediously all over the grand gate, near the Abbey, and *Vivat Regina* written incessantly all over the casements of the House of Lords. Houses of Parliament a magnificent document of English power and of their intention to make it last. The Irish harp and shamrock are carved with the rose and thistle all over the house. The houses cover some eight acres, and are built of Bolsover stone. Fault, that there is no single view commanding great lines; only, when, it is finished, the Speaker of the House of Commons will be able with a telescope to see the Lord Chancellor in the Lords.

———————————

September 30th, Sunday [1855] Yesterday ... we took a cab ... and went to the Two Houses of Parliament – the immensest building, methinks, that ever was built, and not yet finished, though it has now been occupied for years. Its exterior lies hugely along the ground, and its great unfinished tower is still climbing towards the sky; but the result (unless it be the river-front, which I have not yet seen) seems not very impressive. The interior is much more successful. Nothing can be more magnificent and gravely gorgeous than the Chamber of Peers ... everywhere, throughout the hall, there is embellishment of colour and carving ... a most noble and splendid hall ... the House of Commons ... is larger than the Chamber of Peers, and much less richly ornamented, though it would have appeared splendid had it come first in order ...

LEFT *The Houses of Parliament under construction, viewed over a still cluttered Thames waterfront, later Victoria Tower Gardens. Watercolour by James Carmichael.*

RIGHT *Lithograph showing visitors to the Thames Tunnel. The gas lamps were pierced and covered by tissue paper, so that the image would glow when placed against the light.*

I cannot help imagining that this rich and noble edifice has more to do with the past than with the future; that it is the glory of a declining empire; and that the perfect bloom of this great stone flower, growing out of the institutions of England, forebodes that they have nearly lived out their life. It sums up all. Its beauty and magnificence are made out of ideas that are gone by.

1844/55

The Thames Tunnel

'The Tunnel' between Rotherhithe and Wapping was one engineering achievement on the itinerary of every visitor to London, whether travelling in a grand retinue as did Dr Carus, or as a regular tourist, such as the 21-year-old Tchaikovsky, who wrote in a letter home that he 'nearly fainted for lack of air'. It was begun by Marc Isambard Brunel in 1825 and completed, despite a series of disasters, in 1834. Carus visited it the following year, met the great engineer, and recorded his impressions. Unfortunately, the steep gradients to either approach ruled it out for horse traffic, and it was only accessible to passengers on foot.

We now drove further and further towards the more remote districts of the city; the coachman, although undoubtedly well acquainted with the town, was several times at fault, sometimes the pavement ceased altogether, and instead of houses, we saw huts surrounded with gardens ... This was on our way to the most gigantic work of modern London, the Tunnel. At last we arrived at the entrance, leading from the left bank down under the bed of the river; as yet, however, no carriage can penetrate these depths, but foot passengers only are admitted, on payment of a small sum, and are allowed to pass through. In order to be able to lay down a carriage road, much more ground would have to be bought, and the present owners demand enormous prices; so that the matter is as yet to be left alone. It is easily seen, indeed, from the very gradual development of those parts of London which the Tunnel was intended to connect, that this enormous work is of little use, except to prove the determination of the English spirit in carrying out any idea once started. Should London ever become as populous in this part as it is more west, it will not only be necessary to make it passable for carriages, but a new tunnel must be built – perhaps even a railway tunnel.

It was particularly interesting to me that Mr Brunel himself was present, in order to show his majesty his plans of the work, and to explain by what means (vaulted shields, sacks covered with tar, and artificial layers of clay) he was enabled to protect this double arch of 1300 feet long, twenty feet high, and thirty-five broad (each arch being fourteen feet across) against the Thames, here broad and deep enough to carry merchant vessels. Brunel's physiognomy is characteristic; his figure is short and rough, the form of his head broad, with a large development in the forehead and back part of the skull.

Nathaniel Hawthorne, visiting in 1855, found that the tunnel had taken on the attributes of a cheap tourist attraction. In 1865 it was taken over by the East London Railway Company and reopened as an underground railway tunnel in 1869.

At London Bridge, we got aboard of a Woolwich steamer, and went farther down the river ... At the Thames Tunnel (two miles, I believe, below London Bridge) we left the steamer.

The entrance to the Thames Tunnel is beneath a large circular building, which is lighted from the top, so as to throw down the daylight into the great depth to which we descend, by a winding staircase, before reaching the level of the bore ... On reaching the bottom, we saw a closed door, which we opened, and passing through it, found ourselves in the Tunnel – an arched corridor, of apparently interminable length, gloomily lighted with jets of gas at regular intervals – plastered at the side, and stone beneath the feet. It would have made an admirable prison, or series of dungeons ... All along the extent of this corridor, in little alcoves, there are stalls or shops, kept principally by women, who, as you approach, are seen through the dusk, offering for sale views of the Tunnel, put up, with a little magnifying glass, in cases of Derbyshire spar; also, cheap jewelry and multifarious trumpery; also cakes, candy, ginger-beer, and such small refreshment. There was one shop that must, I think, have opened into the other corridor of the Tunnel, so capacious it seemed; and here were dioramic views of various cities and scenes of the daylight-world, all shown by gas, while the Thames rolled its tide and its shipping over our heads. So far as any present use is concerned, the Tunnel is an entire failure, and labour and immensity of money thrown away. I did not meet or pass above half a dozen passengers through its whole extent ... Perhaps, in coming ages, the approaches to the Tunnel will be obliterated, its corridors choked up with mud, its precise locality unknown, and nothing be left of it but an obscure tradition. Meantime, it is rather a pleasant idea, that I have actually passed under the bed of the Thames, and emerged into daylight on the other side.

1851/5

The Great Exhibition

The Great Exhibition opened in Hyde Park on 1 May 1851 and closed on 15 October. Joseph Paxton's great building contained prodigious quantities of glass (almost 300,000

panes) covering its massive iron-and-timber frame. Owen Jones's decorative scheme for the interior was in red, light blue, yellow and white, with scarlet banners announcing the country or category of display. Three mature elm trees remained inside the building, together with some smaller specimens. The Duke of Wellington, one of the six million visitors, chose to come on the busiest day of the entire exhibition and once spotted caused a near riot. Some French porcelain was broken, but nobody was injured. Queen Victoria's journal shows that she went three or four times a week, sometimes taking visitors, always seriously observing the displays.

February 18 After breakfast we drove with the 5 children to look at the Crystal Palace, which was not finished when we last went, and really now is one of the wonders of the world, which we English may indeed be proud of ... The galleries are finished, and from the top of them the effect is quite wonderful. The sun shining in through the Transept gave a fairy-like appearance. We were again cheered loudly by the 2000 workmen, as we came away. It made me feel proud and happy.

May 1 This day is one of the greatest and most glorious days of our lives ... The Green Park and Hyde Park were one mass of densely crowded human beings, in the highest good humour and most enthusiastic. I never saw Hyde Park look as it did, being filled with crowds as far as the eye could reach. A little rain fell, just as we started, but before we neared the Crystal Palace, the sun shone and gleamed upon the gigantic edifice, upon which the flags of every nation were flying ... The glimpse, through the iron gates of the Transept, the waving palms and flowers, the myriads of people filling the galleries and seats around, together with the flourish of trumpets as we entered the building, gave a sensation I shall never forget ... The tremendous cheering, the joy expressed in every face, the vastness of the building, with all its decorations and exhibits, the sound of the organ (with 200 instruments and 600 voices, which seemed nothing) and my beloved husband, the creator of this peace festival 'uniting the industry and art of all nations of the earth', all this was indeed moving, and a day to live for ever.

Nov. 11 ... went to the Crystal Palace. The flags have been removed and the English side is almost entirely empty ... everywhere there are numerous packing cases. The organ is left ... One cannot bear to think of its all coming down, and yet I fear it will be the best and wisest thing ... It is sad to think all is past now!

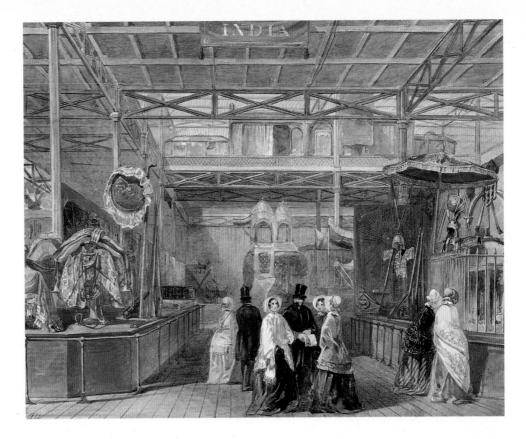

Indian court with elephant trappings at the Great Exhibition. Painting by Walter Goodhall.

The Queen's account is laudatory throughout, but others, such as Jane Carlyle, were less impressed, as she relatres in the first passage. Once the Crystal Palace had moved to Sydenham, it became a major visitor attraction. In the second extract Nathaniel Hawthorne, characteristically an observer of mercurial temperament, reveals mixed feelings about this grandiose display. On his second visit, on a rainy day in November 1857, he concluded that 'I have not much enjoyed the Crystal Palace, but think it a great and admirable achievement.'

I was not purposing to go near the Exhibition myself till I took . . . someone to see it – I had not so much as gone to view the outside since it was roofed in. But the other day . . . we went and oh how – tired I was! Not that it is not really a very beautiful sight – especially at the entrance; the three large trees, *built in, because the people objected to their being cut down*, a crystal fountain, and a large blue canopy give one a momentary impression of a Bazaar in the *Arabian Nights Entertainments* – and such a lot of things of different kinds and of well dressed people – for the tickets were still 5/- – was rather imposing for a few minutes – but when you come to look at the wares in detail – there was nothing really worth looking at. The big diamond indeed – worth a *million! that* one could not have seen at any jeweller's – but oh . . . what a disappointment! for the big diamond – unset – looked precisely like a bit of crystal the size and shape of the first joint of your thumb! and the fatigue of even the most cursory survey was indescribable and to

tell you the God's truth I would not have given the pleasure of reading a good Fairy Tale for all the pleasure to be got from that 'Fairy Scene'! I have surely a great many things to tell you *not* about the *Exhibition* – but I have only a horrid steel pen and my paper appears to be scarce.

1855. September 27th . . . went out and took a cab for the terminus of the Crystal Palace railway . . . It was a beautifully bright day . . . The Crystal Palace gleamed in the sunshine; but I do not think a very impressive edifice can be built of glass; – light and airy, to be sure, but still it will be no other than an overgrown conservatory. It is unlike anything else in England; uncongenial with the English character, without privacy, destitute of mass, weight, and shadow; unsusceptible of ivy, lichens, or any mellowness from age.

The trains of cars stop within the domain of the palace, whence there is a long ascending corridor up into the edifice. There was a very pleasant odour of heliotrope diffused through the air; and, indeed, the whole atmosphere of the Crystal Palace is sweet with various flower-scents . . . It would be a delightful climate for invalids to spend the winter in; and if all England could be roofed over with glass, it would be a great improvement on its present condition . . .

Within . . . we found abundance of refreshment-rooms, and John Bull and his wife and family at fifty little round tables, busily engaged with cold fowl, cold beef, ham, tongue, and bottles of ale and stout, and half-pint decanters of sherry . . . It is remarkable how large a feature the refreshment-rooms make, in the arrangements of the Crystal Palace.

The Crystal Palace is a gigantic toy, for the English people to play with. The design seems to be, to reproduce all past ages, by representing the features of their interior architecture, costume, religion, domestic life, and everything that can be expressed by paint and plaster; and likewise to bring all climates and regions of the earth within these enchanted precincts . . . The Indian, the Egyptian, and especially the Arabic courts are admirably done . . . There is nothing gorgeous now. We live a very naked life. This was the only reflection I remember making, as we passed from century to century through the succession of classic, oriental, and mediaeval courts.

1852

Wandering lonely

London in the mid-nineteenth century became a refuge for a wide range of political refugees, who were mostly from Europe. In the anonymity of the vast city, people who had been forced to leave their home countries could disappear into the crowd and pursue their own interests without disturbance. Karl Marx was one, the Muscovite Alexander Herzen another. Herzen arrived in Paris in 1847 and moved to London in 1852. Loneliness was a penalty that exiles paid, but he learned to love London, although as a socialist he was deeply disturbed by the overt misery of many of its citizens.

I began by taking a house in one of the remotest parts of the town, beyond Regent's Park, near Primrose Hill . . . London life was very favourable for such a break. There is no town in the world which is more adapted for training one away from people and training one into solitude than London. The manner of life, the distances, the climate, the very multitude of the population . . . all this together with the absence of Continental diversion conduces to the same effect . . . The life here, like the air here, is bad for the weak, for the frail, for one who seeks a prop outside himself, for one who seeks welcome, sympathy, attention; the moral lungs here must be as strong as the physical lungs, whose task it is to separate oxygen from the smoky fog. The masses are saved by battling for their daily bread, the commercial classes by their absorption in heaping up wealth, and all by the bustle of business; but nervous and romantic temperaments, fond of living among people, fond of

intellectual sloth and of idly luxuriating in emotion, are bored to death here and fall into despair.

Wandering lonely about London, through its stony lanes and stifling passages, sometimes not seeing a step before me for the thick, opaline fog, and colliding with shadows running – I lived through a great deal.

In the evening, when my son had gone to bed, I usually went out for a walk . . . I read the newspapers and stared in taverns at the alien race, and lingered on the bridges across the Thames.

On one side the stalactites of the Houses of Parliament would loom through the darkness, ready to vanish again; on the other, the inverted bowl of St Paul's . . . and street lamps . . . street lamps . . . street lamps without end in both directions . . . nothing could be heard but the measured tread of the policeman with his lantern . . . And so for all this I came to love this fearful ant-heap, where every night a hundred thousand men know not where they will lay their heads, and the police often find women and children dead of hunger beside hotels where one cannot dine for less than two pounds.

1852

Cricket at the Oval

Victorian London was full of popular entertainment, including a wide range of sporting activities. A German novelist, Theodore Fontane, was attracted by an advertisement he spotted in the omnibus on the way home from the Dulwich Gallery. The Oval Cricket Ground was formed from a nursery garden in 1845, considerably after the exclusive Lord's Cricket Ground (1814), the home of the Marylebone Cricket Club. For most of the nineteenth century the Oval also served as a rugby and football ground.

'Cricket match' proclaimed the red and blue letters, 'between one-armed Greenwich pensioners and one-legged Chelsea pensioners. Eleven-a-side. Sixpence at Kennington Oval.' Here was something for me. I no longer felt a trace of tiredness. I got off at Vauxhall Bridge, only worried that I would be too late, for the sun was already high . . . One look at the game and any doubts were dispelled. This was no child's play, no strange joke, but serious business, made for heroes. The ground had the look of an amphitheatre, the first row formed by chairs and benches which enclosed the players in a huge circle and were occupied by over a thousand well-groomed people. A wooden fence

Cricketers gamely pressing on despite their handicaps in the annual veterans' cricket match at the Oval.

formed the gallery behind, which the arch-enemies of entry fees sat astride, ready to disappear if necessary. Finally, as a backdrop to everything, were the houses and balconies on which the ladies stood, looking in turns at the game and the setting sun ...

Such was the scene. What about the game and the players? The result was near. The next minutes would show who had won – Greenwich or Chelsea. The Chelsea team in the long red-cloth jackets were three runs ahead, but Greenwich, in marine-blue jackets and three-cornered hats, were in, and one good shot could bring them victory. Many players had thrown their hats on the ground; much thin grey hair blew in the wind. Almost all the players were in their seventies, old salts from Trafalgar and even Abukir; those who lost an arm at Navarino must have been among the youngest. There they stood, old defenders of British glory ... Sailors and soldiers who had often shared the victory wreath now stood eye-to-eye fighting for it for themselves. As I mentioned, Greenwich were in, and an old man with one arm and one leg (a total cripple but a whole man) stood, bat firmly in hand and eyes ablaze, at the wicket and defended it from the oncoming ball with a determined look and a strong arm. He had hit it back three times, but not far enough to risk running with his wooden leg. But now, with his fourth hit, luck was with him ... and, quickly reckoning that he could manage the three runs, he started running up and down as fast as

he could. Victory hung on a thread! Before he could reach the wicket for the third time, his opponent (whom he must have underestimated) was closer to it than he was. What to do? Greenwich seemed lost. But, no! With utmost presence of mind, the old man flung himself to the ground. As he fell he stretched out his bat and immediately covered the eight feet separating him from the wicket. Not he but the tip of his bat was there. A storm of applause broke out all around the ground. The ladies on the balconies waved white handkerchiefs; the trumpets sounded a flourish. The game was over and Greenwich were the victors.

But poor would be an English celebration without a feast. Busy hands dragged out oak tables, waiters and maids carried beef and pudding in steaming dishes, and within ten minutes the opposing sides sat in neat rows at the tables, chatting as if round a campfire after a battle ... in the neighbouring Vauxhall Gardens three rockets hissed into the sky. My eyes had hardly recovered from the shock before the whole garden was ablaze with fireworks.

1855

Cholera in the West End

The terrible scourge of cholera, the most deadly of the epidemics, was a constant background to life in the slums. As population densities grew even higher, public health grew ever worse. The misunderstanding of the nature of infection meant that sanitary reformers spent wasted energies on combating contagion by miasma, while the true explanation, a water supply infected by sewage, was under everybody's noses. John Hollingshead was a campaigning journalist whose *Ragged London in 1861* was, like Henry Mayhew's, a vivid account of life in London's underside. In the 1860s Hollingshead became a highly successful theatre manager, first of the Alhambra, then of the Gaiety. In his autobiography he describes the cholera plague of 1855.

In and about Poland Street, Broad Street, Wardour Street, and that neighbourhood, the scenes for me – a latent 'graphic reporter' – were most dramatic. The gutters were flowing with a thick liquid, partly water and partly chloride of lime; blinds were drawn down in nearly all the houses; men, women and children stood in groups in the middle of the road as if they thought there was safety in the warm and heavy summer air. They talked in low tones and pointed ominously to houses where the plague had made itself felt . . . 'front parlours' were taken by dozens in every old and stuffy street for the preparation of coffins that could not be supplied fast enough, and the peculiar sharp tap of the undertaker's hammer could be heard above the muffled sound of voices. The most impressive sign of the pestilence was the 'silencing' of public-houses. Most of these thickly planted convivial resorts were closed, and if their owners were not dead, and they were not closed for conventional decency, they were closed because their business had deserted them.

1859

London clerks

George Augustus Sala was a journalist and regular contributor to Dickens's *Household Words*. His report of the hour-by-hour life of London was written in bombastic, satirical style but conveyed the essential strands of the city, as it worked, played and was serviced. His contrasting accounts of the arrival of the government clerks in Whitehall and the clerks in the City of London is a cheerfully overblown piece of writing.

There are some of these gay clerks who go down to their offices with roses at their button-holes, and with cigars in their mouths. There are some who wear peg-top trousers, chin-tufts, eye-glasses, and varnished boots. These mostly turn off in the Strand, and are in the Admiralty or Somerset House. As for the govern-

ment clerks of the extreme West-End – the patricians of the Home and Foreign Offices – the bureaucrats of the Circumlocution Office, in a word – *they* ride down to Whitehall or Downing Street in broughams or on park hacks. Catch them in omnibuses, or walking on the vulgar pavement, forsooth! . . . I observe – to return to the clerks who are bending citywards – that the most luxuriant whiskers belong to the Bank of England . . .

'Every road,' says the proverb, 'leads to Rome'; every commercial way leads to the Bank of England. And there, in the midst of that heterogeneous architectural jumble between the Bank of England itself, the Royal Exchange, the Poultry, Cornhill, and the Globe Insurance Office, the vast train of omnibuses . . . with another great army of clerk martyrs outside and inside, their knees drawn up to their chins, and their chins resting on their umbrella handles, set down their loads of cash-book and ledger fillers. What an incalculable mass of figures must there be collected in those commercial heads! . . . They file off to their several avocations, to spin money for others, often, poor fellows, while they themselves are blest with but meagre stipends. They plod away to their gloomy wharves and hard-hearted counting-houses . . . Upon my word, I think if I were doomed to clerkdom, that I should run away and enlist.

1861

Fire in Tooley Street

Another agent of physical change in London remained fire. The Tooley Street fire that Arthur Munby describes so colourfully in the first extract led to the tragic death of James Braidwood, the superintendent of the London Fire Engine Establishment, which then numbered just eighty full-time firemen using old-fashioned machinery. The conflagration, largely of warehouses filled with highly inflammable materials and built within the last twenty years, shocked the capital and ensured that the fire service was modernized. In 1866 it became the Metropolitan Fire Brigade, with a full complement of professional firemen and steam fire-engines.

Saturday, 22 June [1861] . . . Between Epsom and Cheam, we saw from the train a great fire in the direction of London. A pyramid of red flame on the horizon, sending up a column of smoke that rose high in air and then spread . . . At Carshalton, where the villagers were gazing in crowds, as at all the stations, we heard that it was by London Bridge, at Cotton's Wharf. At New

Cross the reflection of the firelight on houses & walls began to be visible; & as we drove along the arched way into town, the whole of Bermondsey was in a blaze of light . . .

The fire was close to the station: dull brickred fumes & showers of sparks rose high between it and the river. The station yard, which was as light as day, was crammed with people: railings, lamp posts, every high spot, was alive with climbers. Against the dark sky southwards, the facade of S. Thomas's Hospital and the

smouldered & steamed here, & there, sent up sheets of savage intolerable flame a hundred feet high. At intervals a dull thunder was heard through the roar of fire – an explosion of saltpetre in the vaults, which sent up a pulse of flame higher than before. Burning barges lined the shore; burning oil & tallow poured in cascades from the wharfs . . . And all this glowing hell of destruction was backed by enormous volumes of lurid smoke, that rolled sullenly across the river and shut out all beyond . . . The river too, which shone like molten

The dramatic conflagration of the Tooley Street warehouses in Southwark, 1861, a scene witnessed in person by Arthur Munby.

tower of S. Saviour's stood out white and brilliant; and both were fringed atop with lookers on.

A few of the regular omnibuses had got, but hardly, into the station: men were struggling for places on them, offering three & four times the fare for standing room on the roofs, to cross London Bridge.

I achieved a box seat on one, and we moved off towards the Bridge, but with the greatest difficulty. The roadway was blocked up with omnibuses, whose passengers stood on the roofs in crowds; with cabs and hansoms, also loaded *outside*, with waggons pleasure vans & carts, brought out for the occasion and full of people; and amongst all these, struggling screaming & fighting for a view, was a dense illimitable crowd, which even surged in heaps, as it were, over the parapet of the bridge . . . For near a quarter of a mile, the south bank of the Thames was on fire: a long line of what had been warehouses, their roofs and fronts all gone . . . a mountainous desert of red & black ruin, which

gold except where the deep black shadows were, was covered with little boats full of spectators, rowing up & down in the overwhelming light.

So, through the trampling multitude, shouts and cries — roaring flame and ominous thunder, the air full of sparks and the night in a blaze of light, our omnibus moved slowly on, and in *half an hour* we gained the other end of the Bridge . . .

No such fire has been known in London since *the* Fire of 1666: which, by the way, began at a spot exactly opposite this. Two millions, at least, of property destroyed: near eleven acres of ruin: many lives lost, among them the chief of the Fire Brigade.

———

This calamitous event, moreover, has suddenly deprived us of one of our most useful public servants – a man who was by name familiar to the whole community, and who for many years past has bravely done his duty in saving life and property . . . Mr Braidwood . . .

met his death, by the falling of one of the external walls, while kindly encouraging a party of his men. At this time the scene which was presented from several points was grand and terrible beyond expression.

From The Builder, *29 June 1861*

1861

Tolstoy visits London schools

Education in mid-Victorian London remained a patchwork of private enterprises and philanthropic and charitable efforts. The young writer Leo Tolstoy visited London for some days in March 1861 and, given his particular interest in education, was presented with a letter of introduction to a number of schools – presumably the best of their kind – from the poet Matthew Arnold, a senior official at the Department of Education. Tolstoy also visited the College of St Mark in Chelsea, an early teacher training establishment.

Education Department,
Council Office,
Downing Street, London.

March 11th 1861

1. Abbey Street British School, Bethnal Green.
2. British School, Brentford, Middlesex.
3. Jews' Free School, Bell Lane, Spitalfields.
4. Minton Street Wesleyan School, Hoxton.
5. Perry Street British School, Somers Town.
6. British School, Stratford, Essex.
7. Wesleyan Practising School, Horseferry Road, Westminster.

I shall feel much obliged to the teachers of the above named schools, if they will kindly enable the bearer of this, Count Leon Tolstoy, a Russian gentleman interested in public education, to see their schools, and if they will give him, as far as they can, all the explanations and information which he may desire.

Count Leon Tolstoy is particularly anxious to make himself acquainted with the mode of teaching Natural Science in those schools where it is taught.

Matthew Arnold

1863

The opening of the Underground

The coming of the first underground railway to London was an event of enormous moment. After the official opening of the Metropolitan Railway in 1863, as recorded in the first extract by the *Annual Register*, the public rushed to

try the new conveyance. Thomas Hardy, then a 22-year-old architectural apprentice living in Kilburn, wrote home to Dorset (19 February), 'I tried the Underground Railway one day – Everything is excellently arranged.' Another writer, 'CLE', gave a graphic account of his journey from the Edgware Road to Farringdon Road, the eastern terminus, and back to Paddington, the western terminus. Soon after this, the line was extended to become the Circle line.

Opening of the Metropolitan railway

It is now eight years ago since the first practical steps towards the realization of the idea … The early struggles of the company were enormous, and more than once the scheme was almost abandoned as hopeless. Perhaps it would have been abandoned for ever had it not been for the well-founded and universal outcry at the impediments to circulation in London arising from the mighty tide of traffic passing through it … There remained the great and novel task of burrowing under ground for between three and four miles, of undermining streets and houses, of working in the midst of water-pipes, gas-pipes, sewers, mains, and ditches. Those who may use the line will never be able to appreciate, from what they see, the vast labour and the stupendous resources which were exerted in this part of the undertaking …

Trains, bearing about 650 invited passengers, started from Paddington about one o'clock and proceeded along the line to Farringdon-street, inspecting the various stations on the way.

At Farringdon -street terminus a banquet had been prepared and was partaken of by the guests …

The line was opened to the public on the 10th and it was calculated that more than 30,000 persons were carried over the line in the course of the day. Indeed, the desire to travel by this line on the opening day was more than the directors had provided for: and from nine o'clock in the morning till past midday it was impossible to obtain a place in the up or cityward line at any of the mid stations. In the evening the tide turned … Notwithstanding the throng, no accident occurred, and the report of the passengers was unanimous in favour of the smoothness and comfort of the line.

Whether owing to modern apathy or accident, I had not yet travelled by [the Metropolitan Railway], and determined to make my journey …

They are queer little buildings, those offices on the Metropolitan line … For the most part they resemble

Trial trip on the Metropolitan Underground Railway, passing through Portland Road station. From The Illustrated London News, *13 September 1862.*

isolated police-stations, or half an establishment for baths and wash-houses ... On entering the door, however, these doubts are dispelled. There are the traditional pigeon-holes, labelled respectively '1st class,' and '2nd and 3rd Class,' between which, on the occasion of my visit, a youthful railway official was dividing as much of his attention as could be spared from a round of bread and butter in his hand ... How many hundred different faces must peep in daily at those little windows! ... 'What d'ye say? one second return to Gower Street? Sixpence.' Click, click, goes that awful machine; the change is banged on the counter; Viator seizes his ticket, and passes on to make room for the next man.

I descend the broad stone staircase which leads some thirty feet below, and as I do so, leaving the genial morning air outside, become aware of a certain chill, which creeps upon me like the change one experiences in entering a cathedral on a summer's day. There is an unmistakeable smell, too, of railway steam, which increases as I proceed; and having at length reached the platform of the subterranean station, I am free to confess it is *not* a very cheerful place ... A roof of corrugated iron and glass, columns and tie-rods of the same material, walls decorated with that species of light literature which sets forth the merits of cutlery, sixteen-shilling trousers, and restorative elixir, is not calculated to cheer the heart of man above ground ... The family vault on a large scale ... is perhaps the nearest description I can give as to the general aspect of the

place ... A dense fog filled the place when I was there ...

On it came – the long flat engine puffing at its head with subdued snorts, and glaring out of the dark abyss behind with two great fiery eyes ... The carriage doors are flung open, and I have no sooner popped in and seated myself than they are shut again, and the train is in motion. One last gleam of daylight enters at the window, and then we plunge into the tunnel. Not into darkness, though – there is a good steady light from the gas-burner above, which enables you to read ... as easily as you could by your moderator lamp at home; or you may lean back in the well-cushioned, comfortable seat of the most roomy railway carriage in England, and, forgetting that you have twenty feet of earth above you, contemplate your opposite neighbours ...

When we arrived at the Farringdon Street terminus, I felt rather ashamed at seeing every one hurrying off to his or her destination in the City, while I had really none ... I had simply travelled over the ground to see what this new Metropolitan line was like ...

I determined to return by the next train; and ... took a second-class ticket half the way back, determining to complete my journey by the third ...

The guard had no sooner shut our door than the train was off. At full speed there is a peculiar vibration noticeable on the underground rail. The carriages are too wide and heavy to sway much from side to side, but there is a sort of undulating motion which is due either to the unevenness of the ground or to springs ...

When I entered the third-class carriage, I found it occupied by a man in a very loose overcoat and very tight trousers ... After these details, I need scarcely add that he was an omnibus driver, and, indeed, one by whose side it had often been my lot to sit when he was

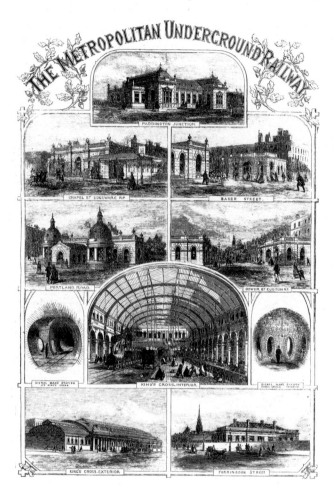

professionally employed in Oxford Street ... he touched his hat and wished me good morning. I immediately ... commented on the state of the weather.

'Well, it *is* a fine day, sir,' he answered; 'but law bless you, what's the use o' fine days down 'ere? One day's as good as another for the matter of that ...'

Presuming that this was a metaphorical way of expressing his contempt for the Metropolitan line, I ventured to ask him whether he found it interfered with his business.

'Interferes! in course it interferes,' says the charioteer, somewhat testily; 'interferes with every-think ...'

Here I made bold to suggest ... that the population of London was quite sufficient to support both modes of transit ...

At this juncture the train luckily stopped, and I hear the welcome shout of 'Pedding-*ton*, Pedding-*ton*,' which announced our arrival at the West End terminus.

1864/5

A new sewage and waterworks system

The setting up of the Metropolitan Board of Works in 1855 meant that finally the desperate public health problem in London could be addressed. Joseph Bazalgette was Engineer to the Metropolitan Board of Works throughout the life of the body from 1856 until 1889. He and his team undertook the stupendous task of first planning a system that would separate sewage from fresh water and then laying underground sewers and constructing pumping stations, reservoirs and embankments. He was required to continually report progress.

July 1864 Fair progress has been made in the construction of the Main Drainage Lines of Sewers ... Pumping Stations, Reservoirs, Outlets &c. during the past year ... It is also satisfactory to me to be able to state that, whilst a large amount of tunnelling has been completed on the south side of the river, under canals, railways, houses, and through treacherous soils, filled with water ... no one section of these works has failed, whilst the damage to property ... has been unimportant, and the casualties to the workmen not numerous, and with but few of a fatal character.

He summarized the completed scheme, which opened in April 1865.

There are about 1,300 miles of sewers in London, and eighty-two miles of main intercepting sewers. Three-hundred-and-eighteen millions of bricks, and 880,000 cubic yards of earth have been excavated in the execution of the Main Drainage works. The total pumping power employed is about 2,380 nominal H.P.

1864/8

The Thames Embankments

As if the enormous accomplishment of supplying a mains sewage and fresh water system to the city within ten years was not enough, Bazalgette also set to work on the three Thames Embankments – the Victoria, Albert and Chelsea Embankments. The project was watched closely by Arthur Munby, barrister, poet and social observer, through his window in the Inner Temple looking towards the Thames.

After the disruption was over, he surprised himself by enjoying the benefits of the new thoroughfare, which initially carried little traffic.

Friday, 15 April [1864] ... On my way home, went to look at the great mound of earth, now an acre in extent, which carts are outpouring on Thames shore at the foot of Norfolk Street, for the Embankment.

Tuesday, 31 May [1864] ... Today I finally lost my view of the Temple Gardens and the Thames ... now it is gone for ever, not from me only but from all the Temple. For the Embankment is coming.

Tuesday, 10 November [1868] ... To Westminster along the Thames Embankment, as usual. Here, for a time,

OPPOSITE *A compilation of the architectural features of the Metropolitan Underground Railway, including the signalman's position, exposed to all the fumes and smuts of the trains. From* The Illustrated London News, *27 December 1862.*

RIGHT *Joseph Bazalgette (standing top right) proudly surveys work on the sewer below Abbey Mills pumping station, 1862.*

Beginning of a new chapter in London history. So I went by it, at 4.40. Temporary stairs, a temporary platform: the great building in the Strand being yet unroofed, yet unmasked by stucco.

Our train went out of what lately was Hungerford market, over what was Hungerford Bridge: instead of the graceful curves of that, we have now a horizontal line of huge gratings, between the bars of which the folks on the footway stood to gaze at us. All the rest of the way, our Asmodeus-machine looks over the roofs of poor men's houses which it has made horrible to live in, and passes across the sites of infinite dwellings destroyed ... then we stare impudently *down* upon the glorious old church of S Saviour, lying in the pit which we have made for it: and finally crawl into the miserable makeshift station at London Bridge. No words are

there is a sort of quiet ... there is the river below the granite wall ... on it the brown sails of stately sliding barges, as well as the vulgar hurry of the steamers. It is better than nothing; a faint and languid reflex of the pure pleasures of a country walk.

1864

The Charing Cross Railway

Munby also took a close interest in the development of the railway system out towards south London. However, he was horrified to witness the destruction that came with it.

Monday, 11 January, 1864 ... The new Railway from Charing Cross to London Bridge was opened today.

strong enough to condemn the scandalous & irretrievable ugliness which has spoilt the old Station & the entrance to the Borough. Leasehold houses are ugly, but they are built to fall down at the end of the lease, so their baseness will at least have a speedy end: but these railways are meant to last; and who are we, that we should decimate the population and defile our children's minds with the sight of these monstrous and horrible forms, for the sake of gaining half an hour on the way to our work or our dinner? ... I walked back through the crowds, passing on my way another tremendous excavation on each side of Ludgate Hill ...

Friday, 22 January ... Last night and tonight I have observed for the first time the noise of the new Charing Cross Railway. Even as I write the dull wearing hum of trains upon the Surrey side is going on: it goes on far into the night, with every now & then the bitter shriek of some accursed engine.

1859

Bethnal Green churches

The multiplicity of places of worship in Victorian London was endless. However, the established church had not kept up with the physical expansion of London, so Bishop Blomfield, Bishop of London between 1828 and 1856, initiated a campaign to build churches where they were lacking. He founded the Metropolitan Churches Extension Fund in 1836 to induce private donors to contribute towards the costs of his programme for fifty new churches. Far fewer were actually built, but a number appeared in one area, Bethnal Green, largely through the good offices of William Cotton, banker and cordage manufacturer. Blomfield and Cotton set up a separate fund for Bethnal Green and built ten churches. Difficulty in finding suitably committed incumbents was a major factor in the failure of this earliest attempt at social and moral intervention in the East End.

In 1859 the Vicar of St Matthews in Bethnal Green, the Revd Gibson, described the state of affairs in some of the new churches in a letter to the secretary of the Bethnal Green Fund.

St. Andrews . . . The present incumbent Mr. Parker . . . has become a great Politician and tells the very few people who attend him – that they should read nothing but the Bible and the newspaper – the destinies of the French Empire form the perpetual theme of his Sermons . . . His schools are shut up – his Church almost empty.

St. Philip . . . was for years, the scene of Mr. Alston's vagaries, who annoyed the Bishop – and tormented and defrauded the Clergy by marrying for 2s.6d. (including all charges) thus he brought people from all parts of London to be married at his Church – and used frequently to join together 50 couples per diem. Mr. Trevitt, his successor, is a most amiable man . . . very lax and liberal in his Notions – stating that being obliged to sign and swear conformity to – or agreement with – the Articles and Liturgy is one of the greatest curses of our Church . . . his Church is very poorly attended.

St. James the Less, Victoria Park, has proved a uniform failure till recently . . . Mr. Coghlan left over head and ears in debt . . . he was succeeded by a Mr. Haughton . . . he had an aversion to coming in contact with poor

St Andrew's Church, Bethnal Green – one of the newly built churches in the area, described as 'almost empty' by the Revd Gibson in 1859.

people . . . he would have no schools built . . . he was a sort of perpetual blister to good Mr Cotton and to our late good Bishop.

St. Simon Zelotes had for the first Incumbent, Mr. Ansted – a truly excellent man – but he was so out of health – that for the most part he was compelled to be from home – and when in residence his illness destroyed all his energies – and his wife was a forward, meddling and quarrelsome person . . . the present Incumbent Mr. Christie is only a slug in the Lord's Vineyard.

1864

Garibaldi at Crystal Palace

Garibaldi's visit to London was an extraordinarily popular occasion. The liberator of Sicily and Naples had become a British hero, even inspiring a small band of young British followers who dressed in 'loose scarlet blouses' and wore the Italian tricolour. Arthur Munby was in the crowd in central London to welcome him; a week later there was an equally enthusiastic gathering at the Crystal Palace.

Monday, 11 April, 1864 Bright warm spring day. All the afternoon, the neighbourhood of Whitehall was in a bustle; bells ringing, music playing, every one getting ready to witness the entry of Garibaldi into London . . .

Scotland Yard was full of . . . mounted police from the country, in felt helmets, riding in to reinforce the native peelers . . .

By four o'clock the crowd was impassably dense as far as one could see, from Trafalgar Square to Parliament Street. It was a crowd composed mainly of the lowest classes; a very shabby and foul smelling crowd . . .

Yet for three hours . . . this coarse mob behaved with the utmost good humour and peacefulness, though

Garibaldi receiving a rapturous welcome at the Crystal Palace, Sydenham, April 1864.

their patience must have been taxed to the utmost. They had come to see what was worth seeing . . . not merely as sightseers. The procession . . . came in sight at 5, and went on continuously till 5.50. Then it suddenly ended . . . No one could tell . . . what was become of Garibaldi himself or why he did not appear . . . Then at last the rest of the procession struggled up: more banners of Odd Fellows and the like, more carriages and cabs, filled with working men and foreigners, who looked all unused to the luxury of riding; more trades unions on foot, from all parts of London, a young lady on horseback (who was she?) riding calmly alone; a small bodyguard of Garibaldians; and the General himself,

seated on the box of a barouche, in brown wideawake and what looked like a blue blouse. The excitement had been rapidly rising, and now, when this supreme moment came, it resulted in such a scene as can hardly be witnessed twice in a lifetime. That vast multitude rose as one man from their level attitude of expectation: they leapt into the air, they waved their arms and hats aloft, they surged and struggled round the carriage, they shouted with a mighty shout of enthusiasm that took one's breath away to hear it: and above them on both sides thousands of white kerchiefs were waving from every window and housetop . . .

No soldier was there, no official person: no King nor government nor public body got it up or managed it: it was devised & carried out spontaneously by men and women simply as such . . . How rare . . . to see hundreds of thousands of common folks brought together by motives absolutely pure, to do homage to one who is transcendently worthy!

1865

Lord Palmerston's funeral

For newcomers to London, as for residents, the great State occasions seemed to punctuate the year. Thomas Hardy's letters home were full of descriptions of such events, which were sometimes royal, like the marriage of the Prince of Wales in 1863. Hardy, an assistant to the architect Arthur Blomfield since 1862, noted the incredible preparations, which had begun almost a month before. There were also State ceremonies, which the population attended in vast numbers. The best way of gaining a first-hand picture of these events, however, was to be there in person, as Hardy wrote to his sister.

Saturday Oct. 28 [1865] . . . Yesterday Lord Palmerston was buried – the Prime Minister. I & the Lees got tickets . . . & we went of course. Our tickets admitted to the triforium, or monk's walk, of Westminster Abbey, & we got from there a complete view of the ceremony. You will know wh part of the Abbey I mean if you think of Salisbury Cathedral & of the row of small arches over the large arches, wh throw open the space between the roof of the aisles & the vaulting.

Where I have put the X in the section is where I stood. The mark shows where the grave is, between Pitt's & Fox's & close by Canning's. All the Cabinet ministers were there as pall bearers. The burial service was Purcell's . . . Beethoven's Funeral March was played as they went from the choir to the vault, & the

Dead March in Saul was played at the close. I think I was never so much impressed with a ceremony in my life before, & I wd not have missed it for anything . . .

Only fancy, LdP has been connected with the govt off and on for the last 60 years, & that he was contemporaneous with Pitt, Fox, Sheridan, Burke &c. I mean to say his life overlapped theirs so to speak. I sent father a newspaper containing an account of his life, & to day one with an account of the funeral. As you are not a politician I didn't send you one, but since father has taken to reading newspapers these things interest him.

1866

Bank crash

Because the City of London was the nerve centre of the financial markets, one shudder there caused tremors to be felt at the extremities of the country. The crash of Overend and Gurney, established bankers, as reported in the *Annual Register*, 1866, had terrible repercussions and brought down countless enterprises behind it, including Sir Samuel Morton Peto's firm, Peto & Betts, the leading railway engineers and contractors.

Extraordinary monetary panic in London

The announcement of the stoppage of the great establishment of Gurney, Overend, and Co., whose business as bill-discounters had been transfered in the preceding year to a Joint-Stock Company with limited liability, produced a panic of extraordinary severity in the city, and extended to all the great commercial centres of the country. There has probably been nothing like it within living memory . . . The general appearance of the streets, especially in the banking quarters of the city, was remarkable. From about ten o'clock in the morning, by which time the failures of Messrs. Overend, Gurney and Co. had become widely known, there was a marked influx of people, far beyond the ordinary community of business men of all classes, and in . . . the neighbourhood of the Royal Exchange, restless crowds were collected during the whole day. For some hours in the height of the day, Lombard-street and Birchin-lane, from both of which the premises of Overend, Gurney and Co. have an entrance, were all but impassable and the services of an additional body of policemen were brought into requisition to facilitate the traffic and to maintain order. The prevailing excitement greatly increased when it became

known that the English Joint-Stock Bank in Clement's Lane had temporarily suspended payment . . . for many reasons, the day will be long remembered in the city of London as the 'Black Friday'.

1870

The University Boat Race

Popular amusements in London consisted of a vast range of hole-in-the-wall gambling and informal entertainments, from the curious fancy-dress affair that Arthur Munby

FUN.—May 26, 1866.

A BANK STOCK(ING).

The Old Lady of Threadneedle Street:—"NOW, MY YOUNG FRIENDS, LET THIS BE A WARNING TO YOU AGAINST RASH SPECULATION. WHAT WOULD YOU HAVE DONE BUT FOR MY LITTLE SAVINGS!"

encountered one night – women dressed as men, men dressed as women – to the two enormous annual popular attractions – the Derby, held outside London at Epsom, and, surprisingly enough, the University Boat Race. First held on the current course from Putney to Mortlake in 1845, it became an annual event in 1856. Gustave Doré and Blanchard Jerrold, better known as chroniclers of London's underside, gave considerable space to an account of the preparations, undeterred by a 'completely representative London fog'. Along the way they note the habits of an English popular holiday, before giving a report of the 1870 race between the light blues (Cambridge) and the dark blues

(Oxford), although Jerrold omits to tell the reader who won. Their description brings to mind a modern football Cup Final.

Chapter V. All London at a Boat-race

Let us remember the Chinese proverb: 'What is the glory of having fine clothes, if you cannot go to your own village to wear them?' In this spirit London must have turned out of bed on the foggy morning of the 6th of April, 1870. Every man shook out his finest suit: every woman drew forth her dress, that to her mind, best became her ... The fresh University colours

looked very harsh and odd in the lowlier neighbourhoods through which the mighty tide of holiday London rushed. The blue, pale or deep, was tied to a stick, crowning ginger-beer barrows, flaunting from broken whips, about the fantail of a dustman, nodding over the noses of costermongers' donkeys, and stuck amid the tatters of 'gutter children' perched aloft in the river-side trees.

But the holiday was for all London: Parliament and people, for the Heir Apparent planted in the Umpire's boat, and for the workfolk lining the sylvan shores ... From Hampstead to Sydenham, from Islington to

Brompton, London was covered with the blues ... the English way of making holiday ...

While breakfast proceeded the yellow curtains of fog swayed and tumbled, and began to show streaks of lighter finery beyond ...

The towing paths presented ... a mixed population that, in its holiday guise, showed marks of the fierce London struggle ... Every lane, alley, and road through which the human river, broken into streams, tended to the scene of the day, was gay with the happy spirits of the travellers to the race ...

At the same time the popular gipsy tribes, and the poor coster-mongers trotted forth, to let out chairs and forms; tell fortunes, and offer the fair-games upon the open spaces which are dear to the mass bent on amusement. The public-houses played their usual part ... The frothing pots were everywhere handing to pyramids of drinkers upon the tops of omnibuses: to buxom women crowded by the half dozen, by a most incomprehensible economy of space, into spring carts, and to the flaunting, impudent roughs perched upon costers' barrows. Authority, in the shape of the police – was alone solemn and stolid ...

There was an electric current over all the course ... the race of life, in little – or expressed in a happy, festive manner.

Chapter VI. The Race!

Listen! The Gun! There is a heaving of the entire mass: a low, full murmur rolls along the river banks. A spasm of intense excitement passes through the two or three hundred thousand people who have packed themselves along the shores to see the prowess of a few University lads ...

THEY ARE COMING!

Far away in the distance we catch the cheering ... beyond the bridge, roll waving echoes of the wild agitation ...

THEY COME!

Amid frantic shouting, amid a snow-storm of pocket handkerchiefs and delirious ravings of purple-faced betting men, two lithe, trim, swift boats, dipping one dip and feathering one flame of light – skim along the shining way ...

THEY PASS!

And then a white ocean of faces bursts upon us. Helter skelter at fullest speed, hidden under their human burden and gay with bunting, the steamers, serried like guardsmen ... close behind the fighting crews. The roar dies out slowly, and with expiring bursts, like a nearly spent storm; and then rises and rumbles away from us to the winning post.

The first gun: a second's pause, and then another gun ... news of the battle has taken wing ... Features relax, and settle back to the everyday expression.

1871

The Royal Albert Hall

Lady Eastlake, wife of Sir Charles Eastlake, director of the National Gallery from 1855, was ready with her opinions on London artistic matters. She reported unsettling rumours in

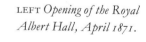

LEFT *Opening of the Royal Albert Hall, April 1871.*

OPPOSITE *The Royal Albert Hall photographed under construction.*

1863 that the Albert Memorial was to be 300 feet high, but she did not agree with Mark Twain that it was 'the most genuinely humorous idea I have met with in this grave land' and found much to criticize in its mere 175 feet, an elaborate incrustation of ornament and sculpture. The Albert Hall was originally planned as part of the complex to be built with the profits from the Great Exhibition. Eventually it was paid for by public subscription in memory of the Prince Consort, who died in 1861. Lady Eastlake was at the opening in April 1871 and viewed the new building in a slightly more positive light than his memorial.

The Hall looks ill at a distance, being low and formless in outline; but, seen near, it has much to recommend it, and is both sumptuous and elegant. Much depends on its keeping its agreeable colour, which I believe is warranted by Mr. Cole, whose latest offer is to pull down all London and build it again in his particular terracotta.

1872

A wet Sunday in London

The French royalist historian Hippolyte Taine was no Anglophile, and his account of London on a Sunday is something of an antidote to the description of the University Boat Race on the preceding pages. The weather is simply a reflection of the atmosphere, which Taine sees as repressively, and depressingly, Puritan. After visiting a handful of churches, he passes the day noting the hyppocrisy of Sunday observance.

Sunday in London in the rain: the shops are shut, the streets almost deserted; the aspect is that of an immense and a well-ordered cemetery. The few passers-by under their umbrellas, in the desert of squares and streets, have the look of uneasy spirits who have risen from their graves; it is appalling.

I had no conception of such a spectacle, which is said to be frequent in London. The rain is small, compact, pitiless ... one's feet churn water, there is water everywhere, filthy water impregnated with an odour of soot. A yellow, dense fog fills the air, sweeps down to the ground; at thirty paces a house, a steam-boat appear as spots upon blotting-paper ...

It seems as if the livid and sooty fog had even befouled the verdure of the parks. But what most offends the eyes are the colonnades, peristyles, Grecian ornaments, mouldings ... of the houses, all bathed in soot; poor antique architecture – what is it doing in such a climate? The flutings and columns in front of the British Museum are begrimed as if liquid mud had been poured over them. St Paul's a kind of Pantheon, has two ranges of columns, the lower range is entirely black, the upper range, recently scraped, is still white, but the white is offensive, coal smoke has already [covered] it with its leprosy ...

What is to be done on the day of rest? There is the church or the pot-house, intoxication or a sermon, insensibility or reflection, but no other way of spending a Sunday such as this ... Let us visit the churches.

I visited four, and I heard two sermons, the first in a church in the Strand. A naked, cold and unornamented structure ... large wooden pews in which one is ensconced up to the neck. The congregation which fills it is ... the respectable middle class, very well dressed, and with serious and sensible physiognomies.

On returning to my hotel I read the following proclamation in Friday's *Gazette*: – 'Victoria R ... we do hereby strictly enjoin and prohibit all our loving subjects, of what degree or quality soever, from playing on the Lord's-day, at dice, cards, or any other game whatsoever, either in public or private houses.'

In this passage Taine, allowing himself to be slightly impressed, describes the recently built, architecturally eclectic suburbs of south-west London and notes the changing pattern from terraces to villas, as well as the smart terrace houses around Hyde Park.

From London Bridge to Hampton Court are eight miles, that is, nearly three leagues of buildings. After the streets and quarters erected together, as one piece ... come the countless pleasure retreats, cottages surrounded with verdure and trees in all styles – Gothic, Grecian, Byzantine, Italian, of the Middle Age, or the Revival, with every mixture and every shade of style, generally in lines or clusters of five, ten, twenty of the same sort, apparently the handiwork of the same builder, like so many specimens of the same vase or the same bronze. They deal in houses as we deal in Parisian articles. What a multitude of well-to-do, comfortable, and rich existences! ... The most humble, in brown brick, and pretty by dint of tidiness; the window panes sparkle like mirrors; there is nearly always a green and flowery patch; the front is covered with ivy, honeysuckle, and nasturtiums.

The entire circumference of Hyde Park is covered with houses of this sort, but finer, and these in the midst of London retain a country look; each stands detached in its square of turf and shrubs, has two stories in the most perfect order and condition, a portico, a bell for the tradespeople, a bell for the visitors, with a flight of steps for the service; very few mouldings and ornaments; no outside sun-shutters; large, clear windows, which let in plenty of light; flowers on the sills and at the portico; stables in a mews apart, in order that their odours and sight may be kept at a distance; all the external surface covered with white, shining, and varnished stucco; not a speck of mud or dust; the trees, the turf, the flowers, the servants prepared as if for an exhibition of prize products ... even in London [the Englishman] plans his house as a small castle, independent and enclosed ... The number of such houses at the West-end is astonishing! The rent is nearly £500; from five to seven servants are kept; the master expends from twelve to twenty-four hundred pounds a year ...

Hyde Park ... [resembles] a pleasure park suddenly transported to the centre of a capital. About two o'clock the principal alley is a riding-ground ... Looking at this crowd of persons on horseback one comes to the same conclusion as after seeing the houses and the staff of servants. The wealthy class is much more numerous in England than in France. Another index is the outlay in linen, clothes, gloves, and dresses always new. The climate dirties everything rapidly; they must be continually renovated. In every newspaper I find the addresses of dealers who come to the house and buy slightly soiled clothes; the obligation of a gentleman is to be always irreproachably well dressed; his coat when shabby is handed over to a man of the lower class, ends in rags on the back of a beggar ...

Imagine the evening dress of a man of fashion or the rose-coloured bonnet of a lady; you will find the former again on a miserable wretch squatting on one of the stairs of the Thames, and the latter at Shadwell on the head of an old woman groping amidst rubbish.

1877

Chinese visitors

If London through a Frenchman's eyes sometimes seemed a very distant city, it was considerably more so to the Chinese ministers who came to set up their mission in February 1877. According to the *Annual Register*, 'Kuo-Ta-jen is accompanied by Lady Kuo, who may be said to be the first lady of position who has ever ventured beyond the shores of the Central Kingdom.' Throughout her stay in London she remained in strict seclusion, 'visiting and receiving persons only of her own sex'. Liu Hsi-hung, another member of the mission, was able to visit London, but he saw it almost as if he were from another planet. He was much taken by the railway system, both above ground and below ground, and visited Brunel's Thames Tunnel, which was by then converted to a railway tunnel.

[5 February 1877] London has no city wall, but the bridges over which the trains pass are strong as city walls. Since the population is so dense that the trains cannot pass through the streets, bridges are made from huge stones, high over the tops of thousands of houses and chimneys. On these iron plates are laid, and sand and earth piles between them, in order that the trains may travel to and fro. Even when sleeping in a building a hundred feet high, one can often hear the ceaseless thunder overhead made by passing trains. Sitting in the train and looking into the distance, you see from afar the pedestrians below moving about as though on a loom. The city streets and alleys seem small and abysmal, so that you almost begin to wonder whether you are looking into a pit dug into the earth, forgetting that you are up on a bridge. You also pass high above the tops of towers and can almost bend down and touch the tops of the masts of boats. When I first came to this place, I was frightened at heart by all that I saw, for everything was strange ...

[30 March – 1 April] On 1st April 1877 I visited the Tower [of London] and then went to the Thames to see the railway underneath the river. One goes underground, down some eighty-seven stone steps to reach it. The walls on the left and right are made of huge rocks, and iron pieces are used on the top to keep away

the river water, so that it resembles the courtyard between the inner and outer gates of a city. Trains run underneath the river, with coal-gas lamps illuminating the whole place. This is certainly a clever construction, but far from indispensable.

1887

An appeal for open space

Octavia Hill's work as a housing reformer gave her wide insights into the social conditions of the poor. One aspect of their lives that she felt passionately about was lack of open space. This article, written in 1875 to raise funds for the attempted purchase of Swiss Cottage Fields, was her eloquent testament on the subject. It also refers to her ideas about disused burial grounds, a movement that in the 1880s was to prove highly successful as a way of ensuring small open spaces, 'outdoor sitting rooms' as she termed them. Despite the failure to save Swiss Cottage Fields from development, she later fought successfully to save Parliament Hill Fields. All these concerns came together in the National Trust of which she was a co-founder in 1895, formed in large part to allow access to the open countryside for city dwellers.

There is perhaps no need of the poor of London which more prominently forces itself on the notice of any one working among them than that of space . . .

It is strange to think [space] must be a gift recovered for Londoners with such difficulty . . . where it is not

easily inherited it seems to me it may be given by the state, the city, the millionaire . . . the park or the common, which a man shares with his neighbours . . . a common inheritance from generation to generation, surely this may be given . . .

I think we want four things. Places to sit in, places to play in, places to stroll in, and places to spend a day in. The preservation of Wimbledon and Epping shows that the need is increasingly recognised. But a visit to Wimbledon, Epping or Windsor, means for the work-

ABOVE *The homes of the London poor. The images of the old houses, desperately overcrowded and completely unmaintained, was typical of many areas of London. The explosion in population was not matched by any housing made available to the poor, except on the most exploitative basis. From* The Builder, *1854.*

LEFT *Children finding street amusements of a traditional type. Photograph by Paul Martin, 1892.*

LEFT *Path over the Swiss Cottage Fields which became Fitzjohns Avenue, following the failure of Octavia Hill's rescue attempt.*

OPPOSITE *The Lord Mayor's Show, c.1880. With the exception of the exotic animals, the parade differs little today from the contemporary annual show. Coloured woodcut drawn by W. Kelly.*

man not only the cost of the journey, but the loss of a whole day's wages . . .

First, then, as to places to sit in. These should be very near the homes of the poor, and might be really very small but they ought to be well distributed and abundant. The most easily available places would be our disused churchyards . . . There is a small, square, green churchyard in Drury Lane, and even the sight of its fresh bright verdure through the railings is a blessing; but if the gates could be opened on a hot summer evening, and seats placed there for the people, I am sure the dwellers about Drury Lane would be all the better for it . . .

Secondly, the children want playgrounds. I am glad the Board Schools are providing these, and wish they would arrange to have them rendered available after school hours . . .

And, thirdly, we come to the places to stroll in. We could not have a better instance than the Embankment . . . But many . . . never find their way to these open spaces . . . they burrow in courts and alleys out of sight, when they might well avail themselves of park and embankment . . . happy outdoor amusement, within short distance of their homes, for those who have no gardens, no back-yards – rarely a second room.

There are a few fields just north of this parish of Marylebone . . . the nearest fields on our side of London; and there on a summer Sunday or Saturday evening you might see hundreds of working people, who have walked up there from the populous and very poor neighbourhood of Lisson grove and Portland Town . . . perhaps they go on up to Hampstead Heath, to which these fields lead, which many could not reach,

if these acres were covered with villas . . . the fields will be built over, if they cannot be saved. They are now like a green hilly peninsula or headland, stretching out into the sea of houses . . . The houses have crept round their feet, and left them till now for us . . .

Our lives in London are over-crowded, over-excited, over-strained. This is true of all classes; we all want quiet; we all want beauty for the refreshment of our souls.

1878

City churches under threat

In 1877 William Morris founded the Society for the Protection of Ancient Buildings, as Hon. Secretary of which he wrote this letter to *The Times* in April 1878. Encouraged by Thomas Carlyle, Morris had widened his concern for Gothic architecture to cover Wren's City churches, under threat from development. Of the four mentioned, St Margaret Pattens is the only modern survivor.

Sir,

The question asked by Lord Houghton in the House of Lords on Thursday elicited from the Bishop of London an acknowledgement that the scheme proposed some few years back for the wholesale removal of the City churches is continuing its destructive course unimpeded. Four more churches are to be sacrificed to the Mammon-worship and want of taste of this great city. Last year witnessed the destruction of the fine church of St. Michael's, Queenhithe, and All Hallows, Bread-street, which bore upon its walls the inscription stating that Milton had been baptized there. St. Dion's Backchurch, a remarkable building by Wren, is now in course of destruction while within the last ten years the beautiful church of St. Antholia, with its charming spire, and the skilfully designed little church of St. Mildred in the Poultry, All Hallows, Staining (except its tower), St. James's, Duke-place, St Bennet, Grace-church, with its picturesque steeple, the tower and vestibule of All Hallows-the-Great, Thames-street, have all disappeared. Those for the removal of which a Commission has been now issued are as follows: – St.

1881/4
The Lord Mayor's Show

An annual festivity held in the bleak season of early November was the Lord Mayor's Show. Back in 1849 American writer Herman Melville pronounced it 'a most bloated pomp, to be sure'. Ernest Baker, a London schoolboy, recorded his visit in 1881, while in 1884 Melville's compatriot, poet James Russell Lowell, found little improvement.

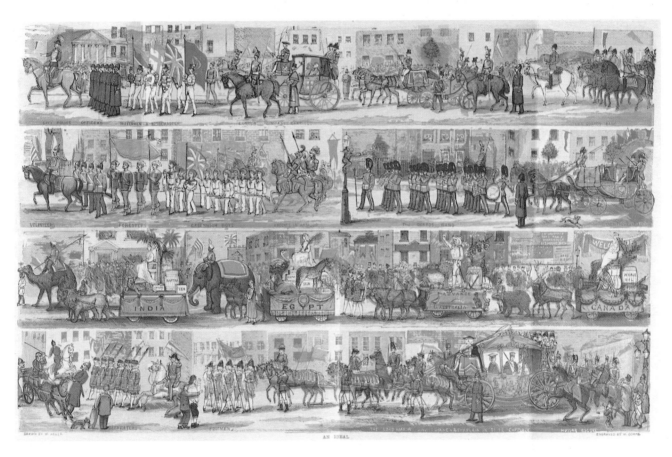

Margaret Pattens, Roodlane; St. George, Botolph-lane, St. Matthew, Friday-street; and St. Mildred, Bread-street, all works of Wren ... It must not be supposed that these are the only churches which are in danger, but their proposed destruction serves to show the fate which sooner or later is in store for the whole of Wren's churches in this city, unless Englishmen can be awakened, and by strong and earnest protest show the ecclesiastical authorities that they will not tamely submit to this outrageous and monstrous barbarity ... alas for those who come after us, whom we shall have robbed of works of art which it was our duty to hand down to them.

Wednesday November 9th 1881 Mine, and the Prince of Wale's birthday, I aged 15 ... Left for the Lord Mayors Show at 1/2 past 10, the streets were rather crowded. When we arrived at Mr Muir's office we were (Mama, Papa, Grace, Seppy, Cecil and I) ushered into a bare room with nought but a tabel and chaire in it ... The next 1/4 of an hour saw us all perched up with a stuffy lot behind us before a window that would not open. Every one (except us) was trying to be so pleased and happy, even Mr. Muir who perched himself up on the top of a great bookcase, with his legs dangling down, declared he saw splendidly, but he was really in agonies of fallings. At last when the windows were stained with the breaths of the stuffy lookers on, and we nearly losing our patience the show appeared, fire men, engines, salvage corps, soldiers, sailors, City dinner eaters, Companys and Lord Mayors etc, helped to enlargen the processions ... After the show had passed we all went into another room to have sandwiches, and warm claret. The sandwiches were not bad, but the warm claret unnatural.'

31, Lowndes Square, S W Nov.9, 1884 ... the Lord Mayor's Show was pure circus and poor circus at that. It was cheap, and the other adjective that begins with n. 'Twas an attempt to make poetry out of commonplace by contract ... Why, I saw the bottoms of a Norman knight's trousers where they had been hitched up into a tell-tale welt round the ankle by his chain armour! There was no pretence at illusion; nay, every elephant, every camel, every chariot was laden with disillusion. It was worth seeing once, to learn how dreary prose can contrive to be when it has full swing.

1870s/80s

Lighting by electricity

In 1878 electric light was installed along the Embankment and John Hollingshead pioneered its use in the West End at his Gaiety Theatre; a description in the *Morning Post* of the equipment illustrates the shortcomings of the system.

Passengers along the Strand last evening were interested and astonished at the dazzling brilliancy all around the Gaiety Theatre ... the generator ... has now been placed in a neighbouring newspaper office, and is worked by a steam-engine there. The wires are carried underground ... and then to the several lamps.

The young Sebastian de Ferranti's invention of the dynamo was an important technical advance towards the commercial production and supply of electricity. His work as engineer for the Grosvenor Gallery in 1886–7 led to the setting up of the London Electricity Supply Company.

I must say that I have got a most fortunate place ... Our work is to try all the experiments for the Electric Light Department; also all the new machines and different combinations of different lamps; to measure the strengths of currents given out and Horse-power absorbed by the same etc. etc. ...

As I am now writing I see that the lights which light up the works during the whole of the night have just started and I suppose that the twenty-one lights which light up three miles of the Victoria Docks over the water will start soon. The lights at Siemens shine into my window and when I am lying in bed I see their light on the wall ... I think this is rather different to gas.

The 1st Duke of Westminster expressed his delight at the novelty in a letter to his daughter-in-law, January 1882.

Edison's electric lighting is the best thing out, and apparently perfect for house lighting *everywhere*, I mean for rooms, passages, everywhere, no more lamps nor candles nor steam no nothing! and all perfectly safe you may lay hold of the wires with perfect impunity – *delightful*!

A report in the *Kensington News*, 4 October 1882.

The Kensington Vestry is being drawn into the question of electric lighting; and the whole subject of electric lighting is in a state of utter confusion, and may be revolutionized at any moment by such inventions as that of the Ferranti Dynamo.

1874/83

East End poverty

In 1889 Jane Addams founded Hull House in Chicago, the pioneer American settlement house. Her travels in Europe in 1883 after a long illness reinforced her resolve to take action in the cause of the underclass in one of the fastest growing American cities. Looking back at her first impressions of East End poverty, however, she remembers her horror at the social divide that had opened up in mid-Victorian London. She is also struck by the depth of political concern for social conditions, which led to the foundation of the London County Council, municipal housing programmes, education and health reform. The first extract is a paper written in a very different moral climate by the Revd (later Canon) Samuel Barnett, vicar of St Jude's Whitechapel and founder of Toynbee Hall in the East End. Barnett, whom Jane Addams met on her London visits, was to soften his views during a lifetime of working with the poor, but in 1874 he was still a firm adherent of the Charity Organisation Society and the ethos of self-help.

1874 The relief of the poor is a matter which I hold to be of the greatest importance. Indiscriminate charity is among the curses of London ... The people of this parish live in rooms the state of which is a disgrace to us as a nation ... Alms are given them – a shilling by one, a sixpence by another, a dinner here and some clothing there; the gift is not sufficient if they are really struggling, the care is not sufficient if they are thriftless or wicked ...

I will tell you our plan. When someone comes begging, I myself see him, talk to him and send him to the Charity Organisation Society, who investigate the case, not so much with a view to finding out the applicant's deserts as to show us, from his past life, the best means of helping him in the present. A committee ... meet on Friday evenings, before which the man is summoned to appear. Perhaps it proves to be the best plan to give him efficient assistance in the shape of a substantial gift, or a loan; perhaps the most hopeful way of helping him will be by a stern refusal. In neither case does our watchful care cease ... we have seen success attend our efforts – the family has commenced to save; the children sent to school; the girls to service; but when visitors, no less kind, but less wise, have come in with ... their promise of help, we have seen the chains of idleness, carelessness, and despair fall again around the family ... Money pauperises the people; time, given as a child of God to those who, if degraded, are still our brothers, will ennoble and strengthen them.

On a Saturday night ... I received an ineradicable impression of the wretchedness of East London, and also saw for the first time the over-crowded quarters of a great city at midnight. A small party of tourists were taken to the East End by a city missionary to witness the Saturday night sale of decaying vegetable and fruit, which, owing to the Sunday laws in London, could not be sold until Monday, and, as they were beyond safe keeping, were disposed of at auction as late as possible on Saturday night. On Mile End Road, from the top of an omnibus which paused at the end of a dingy street lighted by only occasional flares of gas, we saw two huge masses of ill-clad people clamoring around two hucksters' carts. They were bidding their farthings and ha'pennies for a vegetable held up by the auctioneer, which he at last scornfully flung, with a gibe for its cheapness, to the successful bidder. In the momentary pause only one man detached himself from the groups. He had bidden on a cabbage, and when it struck his hand, he instantly sat down on the curb, tore it with his teeth, and hastily devoured it, unwashed and uncooked as it was. He and his fellows were types of the 'submerged tenth' as our missionary guide told us ... of

myriads of hands, empty, pathetic, nerveless and workworn, showing white in the uncertain light of the street, and clutching forward for food which was already unfit to eat ...

Nothing among the beggars of South Italy nor among the saltminers of Austria carried with it the same conviction of human wretchedness which was conveyed by this momentary glimpse of an East London street ...

Our visit was made in November, 1883, the very year when the *Pall Mall Gazette* exposure started 'The Bitter Cry of Outcast London' and the conscience of England

A typical back alley, photographed in the 1890s, with its water butts, costermongers' barrow and forest of overhead drying lines. A large percentage of London's population was crammed into small terraced houses.

was stirred as never before over this joyless city in the East End of its capital. Even then, vigorous and drastic plans were being discussed, and a splendid program of municipal reforms was already dimly outlined. Of all these, however, I had heard nothing but the vaguest rumour.

1884

Terrorist attacks

One concern that has strong contemporary echoes was with the programme of Fenian terrorism – focusing on many of the same targets as the IRA today. A report in the *Annual Register* in 1884 relates one incident.

On February 26 a plot was arranged to blow up four of the principal railway stations of the metropolis – Victoria, Paddington, Charing Cross, and Ludgate Hill. In each case the same method was adopted. A quantity of 'atlas' dynamite of American manufacture was concealed in a portmanteau, with an American clock so arranged that at a certain hour it would let fall a detonator and explode the charge. The portmanteau was then deposited in the cloak-room, the bearer having full time to escape. The machine, which was of necessity complicated, seems to have been disarranged in all cases but one – but at the Victoria Station, shortly after midnight, a terrific explosion took place, shattering the luggage-room and a waiting-room, seriously injuring the booking office, and very nearly causing a fire by the bursting of a gaspipe. Luckily there were no passengers about the station, whilst by the presence of mind of the company's officials the fire was promptly extinguished ... The Government at once offered a reward of 1,000L., to which the railway companies added a like sum ... The only information which the police were able to obtain ... was that, February 20, about half-an-hour after the time at which the express

from Liverpool was due at Euston, a hansom cab drove up to the Waverley Hotel in Great Portland Street. A middle-aged man (about forty) alighted there, whose luggage consisted of a portmanteau of black American leather ... On February 23 another stranger arrived, apparently an acquaintance of the first, and also took lodgings. The new comer's luggage consisted of a portmanteau similar ... to that described above ... The two following days the two men were together all day. Between six and seven on the evening of the 25th the second comer sent for a hansom, and left with his luggage ... [his friend] went a few minutes later, also in a hansom, taking with his portmanteau ... These facts were brought on when the prisoners were tried for treason-felony ... having been found guilty, Daly was sentenced to penal servitude for life, Egan for twenty years.

1880s

Artists' studios

The late 1870s and early 1880s saw a reaction against the portentous historicism of Victorian architecture. An amalgam of vernacular materials and techniques with early-eighteenth-century classicism produced a 'Queen Anne' Revival that soon percolated from being the chosen style for the new houses of artists and thinkers into mainstream commercial developments.

Progressive figures in the arts were setting new standards of elegance and simplicity in their domestic surroundings – and sometimes extravagance. Edward W. Godwin was the

original architect for Bedford Park and designed many of the fashionable studios in Tite Street, Chelsea. In an entertaining talk delivered at the Architectural Association in 1879 he recounts his troubles to persuade officialdom (the forerunners of modern planners) of the strengths of his design. The second extract refers to his work in the Aesthetic style for Whistler's neighbour, Oscar Wilde and his new wife, Constance. As Wilde's letters show, Godwin is a patient intermediary over problems over payment with successive builders (one, Green, seized Wilde's Japanese furniture as it arrived). Client and architect remained on good terms, Godwin being enthusiastically engaged in theatre design at the time, shortly before his early death.

Gentlemen, I stand here in a very awkward predicament. I have lost my lecture! (Great laughter) . . . Here I am . . . simply to talk to you about a few studios . . . I have lately built . . . On the wall are a series of plans and designs relating to a house I have carried out for my old friend Mr. Whistler (applause) . . . Whistler moved to Chelsea, to a very different house in Cheyne Walk, built by Sir Christopher Wren . . . looking nearly west with a light somewhat vague and foggy – just the terms in which the Attorney-General was pleased to describe his pictures the other day. I thought he was working under studio disadvantages, and on my suggestion he took two plots of ground in Tite-street . . . The Metropolitan Board of Works, having let us proceed, at last objected to the design. Of what they said about it in council assembled, things were repeated to me which were positively shocking to one's morality. (Laughter). They specially objected, I found, to my roof, which was at two different angles . . . is architecture a matter of string-courses and parapets, and of following out to the letter every detail to which the provisions of the Building Act apply? Because I chose to do something different to the conventional, because I was not in the fashion, and because the Board and its officers knew nothing by experience of the nature of my work, the Board refused to let my design [for Frank Miles's studio, also in Tite Street] be carried out . . . And who are they who dare to sit in judgment on my work? What 'judgment' have retired farriers and cheesemongers, who never drew a line nor saw a drawing till yesterday?

[Bristol]
October 14, 1884
Dear Godwin,

I write to you . . . to say that Allport [the surveyor] estimates work to be done by Green at £72!!! Amazing: now let us for heaven's sake [get a] move on. Is Sharpe in?

December 17, 1884
My dear Godwin,

I cannot understand Sharpe's account . . . I thought the £120 was for everything . . .

The house must be a success – do just add the bloom of colour to it in curtains and cushions.

To E. W. Godwin, April 1885 from 16 Tite Street

I am glad you are resting – Nature is a foolish place to look for inspiration in, but a charming one in which to forget one ever had any. Of course we miss you, but the white furniture reminds us of you daily, and we find that a rose leaf can be laid on the ivory table without scratching it.

To W A S Benson 16 May 1885, from 16 Tite Street

I am surprised to find we are at such variance on the question of the value of pure colour on the walls of a room ... I have for instance a dining-room done in

think Morris himself sets the exaggerated value on wallpapers which you do.

1884–5

H. G. Wells at the Royal College of Science

Another self-contained world within London was that of academics, in particular the world of science. H. G. Wells was a student of Professor Thomas Huxley at the Royal

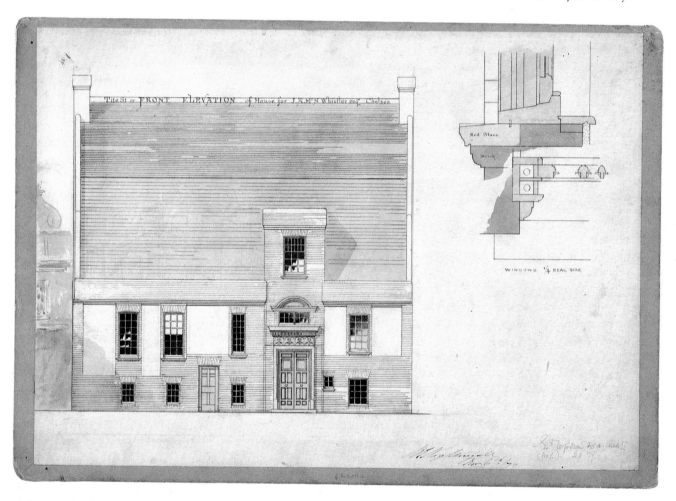

different shades of white, with white curtains embroidered in yellow silk: the effect is absolutely delightful, and the room is beautiful.

I have seen far more rooms spoiled by wallpapers than by anything else: when everything is covered with a design the room is restless and the eye disturbed ...

Some day if you do us the pleasure of calling I will show you a little room with blue ceiling and frieze (distemper), yellow (oil) walls, and white woodwork and fittings, which is joyous and exquisite, the only piece of design being the Morris blue-and-white curtains, and a white-and-yellow silk coverlet ... I do not

ABOVE *E. W. Godwin's signed watercolour drawings of September 1877, showing the front elevation of his house and studio for James Whistler in Tite Street, Chelsea.*

OPPOSITE *H. G. Wells whilst studying biology, imitating T. H. Huxley, his revered professor. Bad health forced Huxley to give up his lectures at the School of Science during 1885 and Wells lost his inspiration.*

College of Science (to become part of the Imperial College of Science and Technology established in 1907). The college was one of a group of institutions for the arts and sciences built on almost 100 acres of land bought by the Commissioners for the Great Exhibition of 1851 with the profits of the exhibition and sale of the building. Wells recalled his impressions of an intellectual powerhouse.

The day when I walked from my lodging in West-

bourne Park across Kensington Gardens to the Normal School of Science, signed on at the entrance to that burly red-brick and terra-cotta building and went up by the lift to the biological laboratory was one of the great days of my life. All my science hitherto had been second-hand – or third or fourth hand; I had read about it, crammed textbooks, passed written examinations with a sense of being a long way off from the concrete facts and still further off from the living observations, thoughts, qualifications and first-hand theorizing that constitute the scientific reality ... Now by a conspiracy of happy accidents I had got right through to contact

with all that I had been just hearing about. Here were microscopes, dissections, models, diagrams close to the objects they elucidated, specimens, museums, ready answers to questions, explanations, discussions. Here I was under the shadow of Huxley, the acutest observer, the ablest generalizer, the great teacher, the most lucid and valiant of controversialists. I had been assigned to his course in Elementary Biology and afterwards I was to go on with Zoology under him ...

The study of zoology ... was an acute, delicate, rigorous and sweepingly magnificent series of exercises. It was a grammar of form and a criticism of fact. That year I spent in Huxley's class was, beyond all question, the most educational year of my life.

1886

Deptford riots

Octavia Hill, the housing reformer, had set up her projects in many of the most desperate areas of the capital. At a time of political upheaval she wrote to her sister to reassure her of the situation in London, particularly in Deptford, her most problematic housing scheme of all. Characteristically, Miss Hill was sanguine about her tenants and their response to the current political upheavals.

To Mrs Edmund Maurice, January 1886

I knew you would hear some report of the riots, and would be anxious for news ... You need not be anxious about Deptford. Of course, after such a breakdown of police administration, one feels as if one *might* meet violence *any* where; but I think of all places I should feel, if it came, safest in Deptford ... At least I know they [the tenants] would stand by us. *No* one thinks the outbreak came from workmen; *no* one thinks it was excited by Socialists. It was just thieves and vagabonds; and the amount of excitement from the Socialists is also clear. I was interested to hear ... that it has been the custom of late years to enter into communication with the promoters of working men's gathering; and, if they themselves considered they could keep order, to leave it to them; and you would notice the workmen mentioned having told off 500 marshals, as if they felt themselves in charge; and from the very first they warned Hyndman and Co. [of the Social Democratic Federation] off the ground ... I hear from others that a force of police *is* always ready, or I conclude ought to be; but it is nice to feel what way the working men themselves are trusted ... It has seemed a very strange week in London.

1887–1914

IMPERIAL
LONDON

Queen Victoria's Golden Jubilee year was, paradoxically, a particularly unhappy one for London. In many ways London was paying for the mistakes of the Queen's reign. A chronic state of unemployment, together with exploitation of cheap sweated labour exacerbated by a series of harsh winters, led to working-class discontent that boiled over in a succession of spectacular incidents and demonstrations – Bloody Sunday, the Bryant & May strike, and the Dock Strike.

The metropolis had already absorbed a vast population from Ireland, and now the influx from Eastern Europe of Jews fleeing pogroms and religious persecution swelled the numbers of those seeking work at any price and led to tension and anti-Semitism. Even the Jack the Ripper murders, which terrified the East End in 1888, were laid at the immigrants' door.

London was becoming physically and socially stratified in a potentially disastrous fashion. The efforts of the Metropolitan Board of Works and the local vestries to sustain and improve the urban infrastructure had limited effect, especially on public health, and hardly impinged on the wider social problems. The city had long outgrown its organizational framework.

The establishment of the London County Council in 1889 augured well for a fresh start, in which *ad hoc* charity and so-called '5% philanthropy' would be replaced by municipal action on a much broader scale. Over these early years the LCC created a formidable building programme for schools, technical colleges, fire stations and particularly housing, following the Housing of the Working Classes Act of 1890, which mandated local authority action in this area. The LCC began work with the Boundary Street estate in Shoreditch. In the early 1900s the emphasis shifted to cottage estates further from the centre of town and proved that municipal housing could be well designed. The LCC estates were regarded as models, both at home and abroad.

While the contact between the world of large, well-staffed houses in Bayswater or Kensington and that of the slum courts of Marylebone or

ABOVE *Queen Victoria passing through the City of London during the celebration of her Diamond Jubilee in 1897.*

OPPOSITE *Victoria station, by Eugenio Alvarez Dumont. With its hurrying commuters, shops and speak-your-weight machine, the station of a century ago is a recognizable enough scene.*

Whitechapel was negligible, there were those who passed between. These years saw a shift from the philanthropic amateur to the social-reform professional. The university settlement movement brought protected young men and women into contact with the ghettos of London, while social reformers, such as Charles Booth and Beatrice Webb, were observing and publishing the lives and routines of the poor. The London School of Economics, with its first chairman Sidney Webb, was founded in 1895, offering courses for those wanting a professional start in the world of social reform.

Despite municipal reform, the stirrings of socialism, and campaigns for universal suffrage, as well as the rise of a confident plutocracy, London remained incorrigibly class-ridden. The Notetaker in George Bernard Shaw's *Pygmalion* says: 'Men begin in Kentish Town with £80 a year, and end in Park Lane with a hundred thousand. They want to drop Kentish Town; but they give themselves away every time they open their mouths.'

For social aspirants, as for those already arrived, an arduous programme of social events made up the season. The very rich or aristocratic simply came to London at given times of the year, dividing the other months between a country house and foreign travel. The Prince of Wales helped to set the pace. Immense hotels were built in London to provide a fully serviced version of the grand town house for wealthy overseas visitors, though the most luxurious, such as the Savoy (opened in 1889), offered modern amenities – bathrooms close to bedrooms, electric lights and lifts – that few great houses could boast.

London also offered a wide range of pleasures for anyone on a modest salary. The hero of *The Diary of a Nobody*, Mr Pooter, of 'The Laurels', Brickfield Terrace, Holloway, takes in both professional and amateur theatre, a firework display, even a ball at the Mansion House, as well as regularly dining with friends in Peckham and Sutton.

As the city became more physically extended, the West End drew in enormous crowds nightly to enjoy metropolitan entertainment. London was

Horse-drawn traffic meets early motorized transport in a full-scale traffic jam around the Royal Exchange in the City of London.

alive and, superficially at least, awash with wealth. Occasionally dark shadows crossed the horizon: the desperate imperial war being fought in South Africa came home with a jolt with the Siege of Mafeking in 1900. The Relief of Mafeking was one of those moments in London's history when the city rejoiced as one. The year after, Queen Victoria died, and her playboy son became king.

The principal shopping streets were being transformed by the development of department stores from family concerns into limited companies, attended by the remodelling and expansion of premises. Harrods tended to break all the records; the company installed the first escalator in London in 1898, and by the time of a major rebuilding in 1901–5 it boasted 80 departments on a 36-acre shopping floor.

The 1890s were a gigantist decade for the confident capital of the British Empire. New landmarks appeared – Eros in the middle of Piccadilly Circus and the memorable outline of Tower Bridge. So constant was traffic on the Thames that the bridge opened fifty times a day in its first year. The Victoria and Albert Museum, one

product of the 1851 Exhibition, announced a competition for its new building in 1890, but no one could have guessed that by the time Aston Webb's winning design was completed and opened to the public, Queen Victoria's son would have been some years on the throne.

The institutions of state around Whitehall were also inflating at a spectacular rate; civil servants were becoming a major sector in London's workforce. The War Office, later incorporated within the Ministry of Defence, was built between 1899 and 1907 and boasted some one thousand rooms. Its full-bottomed Baroque style mirrored the overconfident imperial mood that the Edwardian architects of London felt obliged to reflect.

With the inexorable growth of the city ever outwards along suburban railway lines into the formerly agricultural areas of Kent, Surrey, Middlesex and Essex, there seemed no limit to London. As its tentacles spread, villages and even small towns were swallowed up, leaving surprising relics of rural and traditional architecture and sometimes occasional precious acres of green common space, adrift in the urban fabric.

Only the City boundaries were fixed. A tight cummerbund encircled the commercial heart of the empire, where trade between the outposts and the centre was at its height. In central London, in complete contrast to the rest of the metropolis, the population was shrinking rapidly. The LCC served a population of 4.5 million, of whom fewer than 30,000 lived in the City. Typically, Walthamstow to the north east of London, was both densely built up and heavily industrial by the end of the century. No one worried unduly about the separation of manufacturing and residential areas into distinct zones, and it was there that the first British car, the Brewer, was built in the early 1890s.

The early 1900s brought genuine mobility to the population of London and its suburbs. Electricity was coming into its own in public transport, powering trams and, more significantly, providing a new soot-free underground train system. On the roads, still mostly lit by gas, the first motor bus was licensed in 1897, it co-existing for many years with its horse-drawn predecessor. Metered taxi-cabs made their appearance soon after; by 1914 there were over 8,000 on the roads of the city, and little by little the private car was cropping up on the streets.

As E. M. Forster in *Howards End* (1910) put it: 'the city . . . rose and fell in a continual flux, while her shallows washed more widely against the hills of Surrey and over the fields of Hertfordshire. This famous building had arisen, that was doomed. Today Whitehall had been transformed; it would be the turn of Regent Street tomorrow. And month by month the roads smelt more strongly of petrol, and were more difficult to cross, and human beings heard each other speak with greater difficulty, breathed less of the air, and saw less of the sky.'

1887

Queen Victoria's Golden Jubilee

Inevitably, London was the focus for the principal events in Queen Victoria's reign. The Golden Jubilee for an elderly queen, who had become rather more visible lately than in her prolonged mourning, was whole-hearted and a necessary respite from the troubles of that year. George Gissing, with his journalist's ear, caught in this fictionalized account a sense of suburban Londoners coming up to 'Town' for a carefree evening of festivity in the West End.

At Camberwell Green they mingled with a confused rush of hilarious crowds, amid a clattering of cabs and omnibuses, a jingling of tram-car bells. Public-houses sent forth their alcoholic odours upon the hot air. Samuel Barmby, joyous in his protectorship of two young ladies ... bustled about them whilst they stood waiting for the Westminster car ...

'You would rather be outside, wouldn't you, Miss Lord? Here it comes: charge!'

But the charge was ineffectual for their purpose. A throng of far more resolute and more sinewy people swept them aside, and seized every vacant place on the top of the vehicle. Only with much struggle did they obtain places within ...

A woman near her talked loudly about the procession, with special reference to a personage whom she called 'Prince of Wiles.' This enthusiast declared with pride that she had stood at a certain street corner for several hours, accompanied by a child of five years old, the same who now sat on her lap, nodding in utter weariness; together they were going to see the illuminations, and walk about ... for several hours more. Beyond sat a working-man, overtaken with liquor who railed vehemently at the Jubilee, and in no measured terms gave his opinion of our Sovereign Lady ... half a million of money, wheedled most of it, from the imbecile poor. 'Shut up!' roared a loyalist, whose patience could endure no longer ... Thereupon, retort of insult, challenge to combat, clamour from many throats, deep and shrill ...

At Westminster Bridge all jumped confusedly into the street and ran for the pavement ...

Twilight began to obscure the distance. Here and there a house-front slowly marked itself with points of flame, shaping to wreath, festoon, or initials of Royalty ...

Along the main thoroughfares of mid-London, wheel-traffic was now suspended; between the houses moved a double current of humanity, this way and that, filling the whole space, so that no vehicle could possibly have made its way ... At junctions, pickets of police directed progress; the slowly advancing masses wheeled to left or right at word of command, carelessly obedient. But for an occasional bellow of hilarious blackguardism, or for a song uplifted by strident voices, or a cheer at some flaring symbol that pleased the passers, there was little noise; only a thud, thud of

footfalls numberless, and the low, unvarying sound that suggested some huge beast purring to itself in stupid contentment.

1887

Bloody Sunday

Annie Besant was a radical socialist at the time of the events that led to Bloody Sunday, a debacle not of her making. The march to Trafalgar Square on Sunday, 13 November 1887, was seen as a crucial test of free speech. Sir Charles Warren, chief of the Metropolitan Police, had thrown down the gauntlet by closing the square to public assembly a week earlier. The confrontation between almost 2,000 police and troops and the demonstrators, mostly working people orchestrated by the Social Democratic Federation, culminated in the death of one man – who was accorded an impressive public funeral. Walking alongside Annie Besant from Clerkenwell Green was George Bernard Shaw, who also recorded events on the march, which soon enough disintegrated into tragic farce. If Shaw's role was minor, Annie Besant was in the forefront, attempting to set up a line of defence against the troops.

In ... October the unemployed began walking in procession through the streets, and harshness on the part of the police led to some rioting ... At last we formed a Socialist Defence Association, in order to help poor workmen brought up and sentenced on police evidence only, without any chance being given them of proper legal defence, and I organised a band of well-to-do men and women, who promised to obey a telegraphic summons, night or day, and to bail out any prisoner arrested for exercising the ancient right of walking in procession and speaking.

Then came the closing of Trafalgar Square, and the unexpected and high-handed order that cost some men their lives, many their liberty, and hundreds the most serious injuries ... It was finally decided to go to the Square as arranged, and, if challenged by the police, to protest formally against the illegal interference, then to break up the processions and leave the members to find their own way to the Square. It was also decided to go Sunday after Sunday to the Square, until the right of public meetings was vindicated.

The procession I was in started from Clerkenwell Green, and walked with its banner in front, and the chosen speakers, including myself, immediately behind the flag. As we were moving slowly and quietly along one of the narrow streets debouching on Trafalgar

Lifeguards defending Trafalgar Square on Bloody Sunday, 13 November 1887. The use of soldiers as well as the police, seen in the foreground, whipped up the level of violence and embittered all concerned.

Square, wondering whether we should be challenged, there was a sudden charge, and without a word the police were upon us with uplifted truncheons; the banner was struck down, and men and women were falling under a hail of blows. There was no attempt at resistance, the people were too much astounded at the unprepared attack. They scattered, leaving some of their number on the ground too much injured to move, and then made their way in twos and threes to the Square. It was garrisoned by police, drawn up in serried rows, that could only have been broken by a deliberate charge. Our orders were to attempt no violence, and we attempted none. Mr Cunninghame Graham and Mr John Burns, arm-in-arm, tried to pass through the police, and were savagely cut about the head and arrested. Then ensued a scene to be remembered; the horse police charged in squadrons at a hand-gallop, rolling men and women over like ninepins, while the foot police struck recklessly with their truncheons, cutting a road through the crowd that closed immedi-

ately behind them. I got on a waggonette and tried to persuade the driver to pull his trap across one of the roads, and to get others in line, so as to break the charges of the mounted police; but he was afraid, and drove away to the Embankment, so I jumped out and went back to the Square. At last a rattle of cavalry, and up came the Life Guards, cleverly handled but hurting none, trotting their horses gently and shouldering the crowd apart; and then the Scots Guards with bayonets fixed marched through and occupied the north of the Square. Then the people retreated as we passed round the word, 'Go home, go home.' The soldiers were ready to fire, the people unarmed; it would have been but a massacre. Slowly the Square emptied and all was still . . . the injuries inflicted were terrible. Peaceable, law-abiding workmen, who had never dreamed of rioting were left with broken legs, broken arms, wounds of every description. One man, Linnell, died almost immediately, others from the effect of their injuries . . . we gave poor Linnell . . . a public funeral. Sir Charles

Warren forbade the passing of the hearse through any of the main thoroughfares west of Waterloo Bridge, so the processions waited there for it . . . From Wellington Street to Bow Cemetery the road was one mass of human beings, who uncovered reverently as the slain man went by; at Aldgate the procession took three-quarters of an hour to pass one spot, and thus we bore Linnell to his grave, symbol of a cruel wrong, the vast, orderly, silent crowd, bareheaded, making mute protest against the outrage wrought.

George Bernard Shaw to E. T. Cook

I am an ordinary coward myself, and can sympathize with the white feather, but the cowardice of the people was stupendous. Nobody asked them to stand the charges – only to run away down the side streets and get to the square one by one how they could. But ninety percent of them simply turned tail and fled to the extremity of the four mile radius at the first sign of opposition. There was practically nobody in the square when I got there except sightseers [and] the few hundreds of us who had carried out the plan and come on.

1887

The High Life

While some pursued social action, others pursued social life. Sir Edward Hamilton was a Treasury civil servant and man about town and made sure he went where it mattered: in the summer of 1887 that entailed dinners, balls (which rarely started 'much before midnight'), a Buckingham Palace Garden Party, and, finally, a spot of fashionable sport.

Tuesday, 24 May. Dined last night at the George Bentincks – a well arranged dinner of 24 at two tables – afterwards to a ball given by Mrs Oppenheim, whose entertainments are always most pleasant & well done. The Prince of Wales was there (one might add, as usual); for there is hardly a Ball now with any pretentions [sic] to smartness which he not only attends but at which he remains till a very late hour. This is scarcely dignified at his age. His capacity for amusing himself is extraordinary.

Saturday, 2 July Yesterday afternoon I went and experimented on the new Lawn Tennis Club at West Kensington – the Queen's Club. It is a splendid flat piece of ground; & the Courts are of the very best. If the Club were a little less distant, it would be a great success.

1888

Gandhi stays at the Victoria Hotel

The young Mahatma Gandhi, visiting London for the first time, was wide-eyed at the appointments of the new Victoria Hotel on Northumberland Avenue, opened the year before. Despite its luxury, there were only four bathrooms for 500 guests.

28th October, 1888. Saturday Mr. Mazmudar, Mr. Abdul Majid and I reached the Victoria Hotel. Mr. Abdul Majid told in a dignified air to the porter of the Victoria Hotel to give our cabman the proper fare. Mr. Abdul Majid thought very highly of himself, but let me write here that the dress which he had put on was perhaps worse than that of the porter . . . I was quite dazzled by the splendour of the hotel. I had never in my life seen such a pomp. My business was simply to follow the two friends in silence. There was all over electric lights. We

The manager receives guests at the Victoria Hotel. From Living in London *(vol 2) by G. R. Sims.*

were admitted into a room. There Mr. Majid at once went. The Manager at once asked him whether he would choose second floor or not. Mr. Majid thinking it below his dignity to inquire about the daily rent said yes. The Manager at once gave us a bill of 6s. each per day and a boy was sent with us. I was all the while smiling within myself. Then we were to go to the second floor by a lift. I did not know what it was. The boy at once touched something which I thought was lock of the door. But as I afterwards came to know it was the bell and he rang in order to tell the waiter to bring the lift. The doors were opened and I thought that was a room in which we were to sit for some time. But to my great surprise we were brought to the second floor.

1888/9

Deptford works

The advent of an efficient electricity supply in London came about through private initiative, assisted by rapid improvements in technology. Beginning sporadically, the trend was for individual operators to join forces and expand. The London Electricity Supply Company, a development from the pioneering Grosvenor Gallery scheme, sited its impressive works in Deptford, a riverside location that provided water for cooling and easy unloading for coal barges. It was planned to supply energy for two million incandescent lamps – a gigantic leap into the future. By 1900 there were 30 power stations in London. Reports from the *Electrical Engineer* 26 October 1888 and *London Daily News* 23 September 1889 chart the progress.

The designer of the great Deptford installation was laughingly dubbed the Michael Angelo of that installation, because from first to last, from foundation to top of highest turret, architecture, materials, foundations, and machines, all were specified or designed by one man ... Ferranti ... It required some courage to jump from supplying tens to supplying hundreds of thousands of lamps, to put electric lighting upon the same footing as gas lighting, to supply an area as large as that supplied by the largest gas company ...

Mr Ferranti, who is a young man, made some of his most striking inventions while he was still in his teens. Even the architectural plans of the Deptford works are Mr. Ferranti's. The Ferranti 'mains' are believed to be one of the most valuable discoveries yet made in electric lighting ... The 'mains' thus completed, are laid down in lengths of twenty feet each. They now extend from Deptford, through Charing Cross to the distributing station at Maiden Lane. This is the section which will be ready to supply some twenty thousand glow lamps of ten-candle power each on the 1st October.

1888

Starting out

Starting out on life in a great city is always alarming. London was overwhelming. H. G. Wells returned to

London in 1888 after his student years at South Kensington. He found the solitary enjoyment of watching the crowds easily dissolved into the misery of loneliness, particularly on Sundays when street life was suspended.

I arrived ... at St Pancras and found a lodging that night in Judd Street, which I considered to be just within my means; a rather disconcerting lodging. The room had three beds and one of my fellow occupants, the lodging-house keeper told me, was 'a most respectable young man who worked at a butcher's' ... I went to bed early because the journey up had tired me. The next morning I breakfasted in a coffee house – one could get a big cup of coffee, a thick slice of bread and butter and a boiled or fried egg for fourpence or fivepence – and then set out to find a room of my own in the streets between Gray's Inn Road and the British Museum.

I got one for four shillings a week, in Theobald's Road. It was not really a whole room but a partitioned-off part of an attic; it had no fireplace, and it was furnished simply with a truckle bed, a wash-hand-stand, a chair and a small chest of drawers carrying a looking-glass. The partition was so thin, that audibly I was, so to speak, in the next room.

In this lair I tried to do some writing ... and from it sallied out to find that job that was to carry me ... until I had really mastered this writing business ... I put myself on the lists of any employment agency that did not attempt to exact a fee for registration ... I ate at irregular intervals and economically. There were good little individual shops where sausages or fish sizzled attractively over gas jets in the windows; the chops in chop houses were not bad, tea shops were multiplying ... My first substantial employer was my old fellow-student Jennings.

Jennings was trying to build up a position as a biological coach ... he needed a collection of wall diagrams and ... he commissioned me, so soon as he learnt I was in want of work, to make him a set. His idea was to have these copied from textbooks and high priced series of diagrams, mostly German, which I could sketch in the British Museum Reading Room. He bought a piece of calico and paints for me, I procured one of those ... reader's tickets of very soft card, which lasted a lifetime, or until they fell to pieces, and I made my sketches under the Bloomsbury dome and enlarged them as diagrams in a small laboratory ... in 27 Chancery Lane ...

My week-days during that period of stress were fully

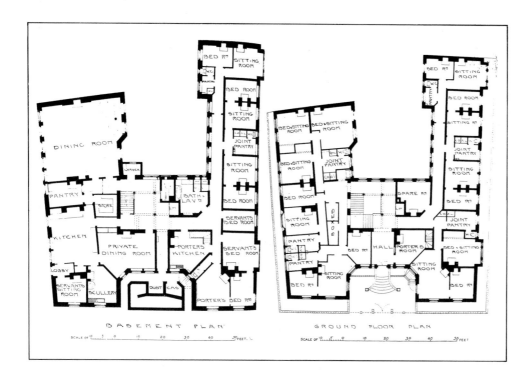

BASEMENT PLAN

GROUND FLOOR PLAN

LEFT *Plan of accommodation in the Ladies' Residential Chambers in York Street, Marylebone. Note the communal dining room and servants' premises in the basement. From* Residential Flats *by Sydney Perks.*

BELOW *'Call on' at London Dock, 1902. Gangers going to choose the men required for the day's casual labour – the dispiriting lottery of dockland labour supply and demand in action.*

occupied by small activities. The British Museum Reading Room and the Education Library at South Kensington were good places for light, shelter and comfort. You could sit in them indefinitely so long as they were open. And the streets and shops were endlessly interesting. I loitered and watched the crowds ... I found the Sundays terrible. They were vast, lonely days. The shuttered streets were endless and they led nowhere but to chapels and churches which took you in and turned you out at inconvenient hours. Except in St Paul's Cathedral there was nowhere to sit and think. In the smaller places of worship one had to be sitting down or standing up or kneeling and pretending to participate. Loneliness weighed upon me more and more.

1892

Ladies' Residential Chambers

In 1892 Molly Hughes, embarking as a lecturer on a teacher training course at Bedford College, London, and paying £100 per annum non-resident, had to find lodgings. First she shared a tiny flat with a fellow teacher, and then they heard of something more suitable – the Ladies' Residential Chambers, one of several set up for independent working women in London.

One day Miss Rogers came in with the exciting news that a grand building had been opened quite near, called the Ladies' Residential Chambers. We hurried off to see it and make inquiries, full of rosy visions of being free of landladies for ever ... We found a dignified Lady Superintendent, who informed us that every applicant must have references and must agree to certain regulations, of which the chief seemed to be that no nail must be driven into the walls. There was a flat available on the top floor, containing two rooms and a third little

place, half kitchen, half scullery. One bathroom, charged extra, had to serve all the flats on one floor. There were six stories and no lift ... The rent was high and we had no furniture, but we reckoned that in the long run we should spend less than in our lodgings, and get infinitely more comfort. And I reflected that any furniture I bought would come in useful when I was married. How we enjoyed prowling round the little back streets in search of bargains – chairs, a gaunt table 'salvaged' from a fire, and a rickety writing-desk ... One looking-glass we bought was so vile that it discouraged vanity ... Meals gave us no trouble, for a good dinner was served in the common dining-room, lunch was either a picnic affair at home or else taken at a tea-shop, and our gas-ring was enough for breakfast requirements ...

The evening dinner was always a pleasant interlude, for we met a variety of interesting women, all of them at work of some kind – artists, authors, political workers, and so on.

1887/9

Life in the docks

Beatrice Webb was asked by Charles Booth (her cousin by marriage) to research life in the docks, as well as tailoring and the Jewish community in the East End, for his forthcoming publication *The Labour and Life of People in London* (the first volume of which was published in 1889 –

the title was inverted in later editions). Her diary entries include both her own observations and conversations with those immersed in the situation. From time to time a patrician disdain creeps through the social concern. However, her research on life in the docks, as published in the periodical *Nineteenth Century* in 1887 and later as a chapter in Booth's great social survey, was a spirited account of what she had seen and heard.

8 May [London] Kerrigan, amusing Irish School Board visitor, Limehouse district (Stepney). Describes his casuals (about 900) as 'hereditary casuals' ... The worse scoundrel is the Cockney-born Irishman. The woman is the Chinaman of the place, and drudges as the women of the savage races. She slaves all day and all night. Describes the communism of this class. They do not migrate out of the district, they are constantly changing their lodgings, but if they like the circle of their friends they go round and round within a certain area. They work for each other – hence low ideal of work. Never see excellence ... From the dock gates they lounge back to the street – 'treating' or being 'treated' according to as they have earned a few pence. Live chiefly on 'tobacco' which is a compound of sugar, vinegar, brown paper and German nicotine. The teapot is constantly going – bread and a supply of dried haddock which goes through a domestic preparation, dried in the chimney and acquiring a delicate flavour by lying between the mattresses of the beds. They never read; and, except the Catholics, never go to church. On the Bank Holiday the whole family will go to Victoria Park.

12 May [London] Docks early morning. Permanent men respectable and clean. Casuals low-looking – bestial, content with their condition. Brutal fight and struggle. (As a few men are given work for the day.) Sudden dissolution of the crowd, with coarse jokes and loud laughs. Look of utter indifference on their faces. Among them are one or two who have fallen from better things. Abject misery and hopeless determination to struggle on. The mass of rejected lounge down to another dock or spread over the entrances to the various wharves ... Some hundred of the lowest will congregate, waiting on the chance of a foreman needing an odd man. If a man weary with the *ennui* of an empty stomach drops asleep, his companions will promptly search his pockets for the haphazard penny.

13 May [London] Most amusing afternoon with Kerrigan, in Victoria Park. Victoria Park lies in the extreme east of London. It is surrounded by streets of small two-storied houses of the genteel type; a porch and one bow-window, venetian blinds and a lace curtain. These are inhabited by the lower middle class. Now and again there is a row of more modest little dwellings, without the bow or the porch . . . the abode of the aristocrats of the working class, mechanics or permanent labourers.

In truth the work of the docks is typical of the life of a great city. Extremes meet, and contrasts are intense. There is magnificence in the variety and costliness of the multitudinous wares handled by the most decrepit and poverty-stricken worker – a hidden irony in his fate, touching all things and enjoying none . . .

The two big dock companies employ three classes of workers – permanent, preference, and casual . . .

The foreman is distinctly the official. Directly the day's work is over he hurries from a disreputable neighbourhood back into the odour of respectability which permeates a middle-class suburb. There, in one of those irreproachable houses furnished with the inevitable bow window, and perchance with a garden . . . he leads the most estimable life. Doubtless he is surrounded by a wife and family, perhaps keeps a maid-of-all-work, and has a few selected friends. He meddles little with the public business of the district, leaving that to retail tradesmen: he belongs to no political, and frequently to no religious organization . . .

But the foremen and permanent men are, after all, the upper ten of dock life, and our interest is naturally centred in the large mass of labour struggling for a livelihood . . . the irregular hands employed by the docks, warehouses, and wharves of East London . . .

Now, we believe . . . that there are 10,000 casual labourers, exclusive of waterside labourers, resident in the Tower Hamlets, employed principally at the docks . . .

At the West and East India, and at most of the wharves and warehouses, there are a certain number of men who are usually secure of work if there be any. They are for the most part an honest, hard-working set, who have established themselves by their regular attendance and honesty in the confidence of their employers. These men, together with the more constant of the casuals, are to my mind the real victims of irregular trade . . . Physically they suffer from the alternation of heavy work for long hours, and the unfed and uninterested leisure of slack seasons . . . not only are they and their families subject to the low moral tone of the neighbourhood in which they pass their days and nights, but they habitually associate with the lower class of casuals . . . Many of the professional dock labourers

live in common lodging-houses of the more reputable kind. If married they must submit to the dreariness of a one-roomed home which . . . costs them from 3s to 4s 6d out of their scanty earning . . .

The casual by misfortune tends to become the casual by inclination . . . Sections of them are hereditary casuals . . . They have a constitutional hatred to regularity and forethought, a need for paltry excitement. They are late risers, sharp-witted talkers, and, above all, they have that agreeable tolerance for their own and each other's vices which seems characteristic of a purely leisure class, whether it lies at the top or the bottom of society.

The London Dock Strike lasted over a month during August and September 1889. Like Annie Besant's successful efforts for the Bryant & May matchgirls in 1888, the Dock Strike legitimized the claims of the workers and led to the formation of a mass membership union. From the countryside, Beatrice Webb followed the events with excitement, while London, haunted by the spectre of revolution, discovered peaceful protest. Their leader, John Burns's achievement was a daily march that wended from the East End through the City and that helped to bring the justice of the cause home to the middle classes, who collected large sums of money for their support. As things

LEFT *The Dock Strike, September 1889. A meeting of the striking workers at the West India Dock gates.*

RIGHT Punch *magazine offers its epitaph to the Metropolitan Board of Works, replaced by the London County Council.*

became more desperate, Cardinal Manning intervened as official mediator, supported by the Lord Mayor and the Bishop of London. The final act, before agreement was reached on 16 September, was a march by 7,000.

29 August [1889] The Argoed The dock strike becoming more and more exciting – even watched at a distance. Originally 500 casuals marched out of the West and East India Docks – in another day the strike spread to the neighbouring docks – in a week half East London was out. For the first time a *general* strike of labour, not on account of the vast majority of strikers, but to enforce the claims to a decent livelihood of some 3000 men. The hero of the scene, John Burns the socialist, who seems for the time to have the East End working man at his feet ... The men's demands: 6d an hour, to be taken on at fixed intervals of four hours, and a revision of the contract system or a minimum wage of 8d an hour under it, are just – that is to say they ask for only the possibility of a decent existence ... The dock companies maintain the trade of London will not stand it, the public of all classes declare that it must ...

The 'solidarity of labour' at the East End is a new thought to me ... the dock labourers ... have shown the capacity for common action, of temperate and reasonable action ... commercially and financially an

extended labour disturbance in London is far more disastrous than in any other part of England.

1889

The London County Council

The institution of the London County Council, replacing the Metropolitan Board of Works with an elected body but covering the identical area, was a delicate and complex task. Lady Eastlake simply hoped it would deal with the problem of poverty.

January 18, 1889, from a letter

The chief excitement of late has been the elections for the County Council. I was sore pressed to go and put my X at a house, up high steps and down a dirty narrow lane, in order to help to bring in two gentlemen,

PEACE
TO ITS
HASHES

Obiit, March 21, 1889.

TO THE MELANCHOLY MEMORY OF
THE METROPOLITAN BOARD OF WORKS.
IT WAS AN UNFORTUNATE INSTITUTION.
FLUSHED, IN THE EARLIER YEARS OF ITS EXISTENCE,
WITH A LAUDABLE AMBITION
TO COMMAND THE RESPECT AND ADMIRATION OF THE RATEPAYERS
IT GAVE AN EMBANKMENT TO THE THAMES,
DRAINED LONDON,
AND SUDDENLY SHOWED THE WORLD
HOW JOBBERY COULD BE ELEVATED TO THE LEVEL OF THE
FINE ARTS;
THEN FIGHTING TO THE END, IT WAS MORE ANXIOUS
TO LEAVE AN INHERITANCE OF SPITE TO ITS SUCCESSOR,
THAN TO RETIRE FROM THE SCENE OF ITS LATE LABOURS WITH
DIGNITY TO ITSELF.
UNWEPT, UNREPENTANT, YET UNHUNG,
IT HAS PASSED FOR GOOD AND AYE TO THAT OBLIVION
FROM WHICH IT IS POSSIBLE THE MORE THOUGHTFUL AND
PHILOSOPHICAL RATEPAYER
MAY THINK IT WOULD HAVE BEEN AS WELL,
FOR THE INTERESTS OF MUNICIPAL HONESTY,
THAT IT HAD NEVER EMERGED.

The first meeting of the London County Council in its temporary home in Spring Gardens off Trafalgar Square in 1889. Painting by Henry Jamyn Brooke.

who were opposed by a billiard-ball maker and a green-grocer; and I am happy to say the two gentlemen were returned by a large majority. I hope they may help to solve the pauperising problem in London, which puzzles me more and more, and which, apparently, one cannot justly judge without a certain hardening of the heart. My hard-hearted opinion is, that the evil will not be met until the Poor of London bring up and treat their children better.

John Burns was an eloquent and radical proponent of the new civic organization, standing successfully for election in Battersea. Candidates were elected for three years. The vestries were the tier of local government that remained unchanged, looking after the daily, domestic business of the city. Looking back in 1907, Burns writes about the LCC's beginnings and its Progressive administration, while George Bernard Shaw, who refused the chance of standing for Deptford in 1889, was later to spend six years as a maverick local councillor, elected as a Progressive to an

uncontested seat in 1897 on Ward 7 of St Pancras Vestry. He relates some of his impressions in the second passage. In 1899 the London Government Act amalgamated the 44 vestries into 28 boroughs. Women, who had been active in the vestries, were initially excluded.

We were composed of statesmen and labour leaders, a banker and a shopkeeper, a poet and a philosopher, and of all sorts and conditions of men who had been hungering through the generations for something that would give to London the true civic freedom. We met within a small hall, and we had for our Chairman an ex-Premier, a statesman and a good counsellor Lord Rosebery ... It has been charged against us that some of us were idealists. A public body without idealism is indifferent. A public body without imagination converts high duty into dull routine ... What was our work? It was to efface the heritage of neglect that had accumulated not only through the generations but through the centuries.

I was expected to answer them in council with a collection of local shopkeepers, licensed victuallers (publicans), builders, auctioneers, and the like, with an occasional doctor or two and a Methodist minister, I being a playwright. Our ablest leaders were a greengrocer and a bootmaker, both of them much more capable than most members of Parliament; for it needs considerable character and ability to succeed as a shopkeeper, especially as a publican, whereas persons with unearned money enough can easily get into Parliament without having ever succeeded in anything. I found them excellent company, and liked and respected them for their personal qualities ... but in the effective lump we were as ignorantly helpless politically as the mob of ratepayers who elected us, and who would never have elected me had they had the faintest suspicion of my ultimate political views.

1889

Tchaikovsky in London

In a visit to London, Tchaikovsky initially had formed a rather negative impression. He missed the qualities of Paris – 'what a lovely, jolly, dear town it is compared to London'. In 1889 he expressed his views with firmness: 'London is a loathsome town; I can never find anything here. No men's lavatories; no money exchange office; it was with difficulty I found a hat to fit my head.' Four years later he returned to give his first London performance of Symphony No 4. Saint-Saens's Piano Concerto No 2 was in the same programme, with the composer as soloist. This time Tchaikovsky was a little more impressed by the warmth of his welcome but, typically, prone to exhaustion.

London 3 June 1893, to Modest Tchaikovsky

The concert was brilliant, ie according to general opinion. I enjoyed a real triumph, so that Saint-Saens who appeared after me rather suffered from my extraordinary success. This, of course, is very nice but what a punishment the life here is during the 'Season'! All my lunches and dinners are booked and everything takes so much time. Yesterday the Directors gave a dinner to Saint-Saens and myself at the Westminster Club. The opulence and elegance were extraordinary, but we sat down at 7 and got up at 11.30 (without exaggeration). Besides all this, every day one has to be at afternoon concerts, for which they come and invite you, and it is difficult to refuse ...

It is difficult to give an idea about the traffic on the London streets. Last time I came here it was bad weather and I could not get any real idea of it. The devil only knows what it is like – with all the beautiful harnesses and trappings – and one does not know where to look ... what crowds of people I have to meet here. And how all this tires me!! Every morning I wake up suffering and unhappy, then get into a hazy state with only one thought in my mind, that all this should end as soon as possible!!

1897

Queen Victoria's Diamond Jubilee

Queen Victoria's journal entries for her Diamond Jubilee are touchingly appreciative of her subjects' enthusiasm. Interestingly, in the midst of all the pomp, she found a moment to note the changes in London streets, especially the absence of Temple Bar, removed in 1870 and re-erected years later in Theobalds Park in Hertfordshire.

20 June 1897 Felt rather nervous about the coming days, and that all should go off well.

21 June 1897 The 10th anniversary of the celebration of my fifty years Jubilee [her Golden Jubilee of 1887] ... Passed through dense crowds [from Paddington station to Buckingham Palace], who gave me a most enthusiastic reception. It was like a triumphal entry ... The windows, the roofs of the houses, were one mass of beaming faces, and the cheers never ceased. On entering the park, through the Marble Arch, the crowd was even greater, carriages were drawn up amongst the people on foot, even on the pretty little lodges well-dressed people were perched. Hyde Park Corner and Constitution Hill were densely crowded. All vied with one another to give me a heartfelt, loyal, and affectionate welcome. I was deeply touched and gratified ...

A never-to-be-forgotten day. No one ever, I believe, has met with such an ovation as was given to me, passing through those six miles of streets ...

The denseness of the crowds was immense, but the order maintained wonderful. The streets in the Strand are now quite wide, but one misses Temple Bar ... As we neared St Paul's the procession was often stopped, and the crowds broke out into singing 'God save the Queen' ...

In front of the Cathedral the scene was most impressive. All the Colonial troops, on foot, were drawn up round the Square. My carriage, surrounded by all the Royal Princes, was drawn up close to the steps, where the Clergy were assembled, the Bishops in rich copes, with their croziers, the Archbishop of Canterbury and the Bishop of London each holding a very fine one. A *Te deum* was sung.

1896–7

Mark Twain moves to Chelsea

Mark Twain was a frequent visitor to London, but his months there in 1896–7, when he came to write *Following the Equator*, were overshadowed by the death of his daughter Susan in America, just after the family had arrived in England. Like Emerson, his comments, apart from a discursion on the private water companies, tend to be epigrammatic, but none the less observant. His rented house was 23 Chedworth Square.

Monday, Sept. 21 [1896] Day after tomorrow the queen will have achieved the longest reign in the history of the English throne.

Sept. 22 House-hunting again. England is the land of neat and pretty and shapely and polite housemaids. An ugly or ill-dressed or unpolished one is rare.

Chelsea. Oct. '96 In London it takes five weeks to find a house (furnished) that will suit both your convenience and your means ... it takes the former occupant nine weeks to persuade the postmaster to respect his new address. We already had maids or maybe it would have taken eleven weeks to get them. Got a good man the first day to do odd jobs – carry up coal, black boots, scour knives, etc. He is the authorized messenger of the block and has to show a good character before the police authorities will appoint him.

More hugging and kissing by boys and girls and young men and maids in the streets at night and parks by day! And no chaffing them by anybody.

London is a collection of villages. When you live in one of them with its quiet back streets (Chelsea) and its one street of stores and shops (Kings road) little bits of stores and shops like those of any other village, it is not possible for you to realize that you are in the heart of the greatest city in the world.

The Water Co. has sent *me* no bill, but here is a notice requiring me to pay up at once ... if I didn't pay the water would be cut off ...

Well, you see, they decline to know anybody in the matter but the *house* ... They know you will pay G's bill and take it out of rent rather than have your water cut off ...

Their charters are as old as the time of the Stuarts – a time when the king had a finger in every pie ... The rest of those big monopolies have gone the way of all things perishable, but a water company is not perishable. A king's share in one of these old water companies, that was worth twenty pounds originally, is thrown on the market about once in a generation and it makes a mighty stir ...

The dividends are incredible, and one wouldn't mind it so much if this surplus went to support the government, but it hurts when you know it goes to private pockets ... Did you see the proposition the other day that London buy out the companies for £40,000,000? One million of that represents plant, no doubt, – represents pipes and reservoir and water, the other 39 represent 'water'. They charge for water not by any rule, but to value the building.

I wish the Lord would disguise Himself in citizens clothing and make a personal examination of the

sufferings of the poor in London. He would be moved, and would do something for them Himself.

April 13, '97 Boys whipping tops – never saw it in my life till in London, this time – yet was raised on books with woodcuts of boys doing it.

1900

Mafeking Night

The Relief of Mafeking on 17 May 1900 was a symbolic moment in which the hidden pressures of the Boer War on the British people could be expressed in national exultation. For more than 200 days Major-General Baden-Powell and 700 men, few of them soldiers, had withstood a concerted attack by a company of 4,000 Boers backed by artillery. And London celebrated. As the old Queen put it, 'The people are quite mad with delight and London is said to be indescribable.' Bernard Allen, head of the Higher Education board of the London County Council, was spending an evening at home in Hampstead with his informal classical

Greek study circle, reading 'The Seven Against Thebes', when the news came.

Suddenly we were interrupted in our reading by a loud knock at the front door. I went to open it, whereupon our nephew, Stuart Garnett, a youth of eighteen, flung himself forward, called out, 'Mafeking is relieved,' and dashed off again ... Immediately, with one accord, we broke off our reading, put on our outdoor things, and hurried along Well Walk to the main High Street. The old Hampstead 'bus was just passing along the road on its way into town. We hailed it, and ... climbed up to the seats beside the driver ... Hardly had the 'bus gone 100 yards when people were seen on every side streaming from their homes into the street and jumping on to any vehicle that came along. All were cheering wildly, and a supply of flags was produced mysteriously from somewhere and passed up to us ... On we went down through Camden Town, past General Gordon's Turkish Baths, waving our flags and cheering ourselves hoarse. At every window as we went by people were waving flags, and the noise of the cheers grew mightier and mightier as we drove down Tottenham Court Road and into the centre of London. The outburst was absolutely spontaneous ... It has long been the fashion to speak disparagingly of Mafeking night, and the word 'Mafficking' has been coined with a sinister implication. But it took something more than an ordinary wave of

OPPOSITE *The Kings Road, Chelsea, the main street through what remained a village within south west London.*

RIGHT *Crowds outside the Mansion House on Mafeking Day, 19 May 1900.*

patriotic feeling to snatch three serious-minded people from their Greek reading and carry them in a tumultuous flood of emotion . . . into the heart of a cheering, flag-waving crowd of fellow-citizens.

1902

The Season

The social side of London had its own ritual character, an inexorable round of pleasure seeking that was dictated initially by the movements of royalty and aristocracy. By the turn of the century, as Robert Machray wrote, 'Blue blood or new blood matters not at all – rich blood is the thing.'

The pursuit of pleasure, like death, claims all seasons for its own, but London has ear-marked, so to say, two of them. There is the season proper, *the* season, which begins after Easter and lasts till well into July or the beginning of August. Then there is the 'little season' in October and November, after the cream of the shooting has been skimmed and before the hunting has commenced. As an institution the 'little season' is growing in popularity, but it does not begin to compare with the other. All the greater social functions take place during the course of the latter. Royalty is in town, and this is a prime factor. *The* season is distinguished by 'Levees' and 'Drawing-Rooms' at the Palace – also by balls, garden-parties, and concerts there. In this year, 1902, the day Drawing-Rooms have been abandoned, and evening courts have taken their place; thus a novel feature ... has been introduced. People whose state is little less than royal are also in town. If the Duchess of Blankshire is going to give a ball, you may be sure it will come off about the end of May or some time in June; but it must be remembered 1902 is an exceptional year – the year of the Coronation. Also, of course, Parliament is in session during this period. An all-night sitting is one of the sights you may wish to see in your round-up of the town's Night Side, but you will find it much better fun to be in bed.

London, besides, attracts at the time vast numbers of people from all quarters of the globe ... Foremost amongst the elements which go to swell the already-gorged city is the ever-enlarging 'Amurrican' invasion each spring, and at the head of the invaders is the pretty, brilliant, perplexing, distracting, American 'gal' ... She is indefatigably pleasure-loving ... She comes, she is seen, she conquers. And at the end of each season her native newspapers recount with no inconsiderable pride the number of dukes and other big game she has 'bagged'.

1900s
The suburban public house

The London public house had exploded in Queen Victoria's reign. The Beer Act of 1830 took duty off beer and relaxed the licensing system, setting in motion the building of gin palaces, replacing the traditional tavern. The numbers of licensed houses spiralled. In reaction, licensing went back to the magistrates with the Beer Act of 1869, finally signalling a slowdown. However, as this acerbic extract illustrates, every expanding 1900s suburb could boast a generous scattering of architecturally ambitious public houses.

[In the suburbs] the one feature that takes the traveller's eye continuously, and perhaps not unpleasantly, is the public-houses. The miles and miles of villas with bay-windows and little backyards to them, the rows on rows of indifferent shops ... the squads of dilapidated 'family residences' that have never been inhabited by a single family any time these fifty years, the hideous Board Schools, the still more hideous railway-stations, the idiotic free libraries – all these things fill the heart with sadness, and the mind with the bitterest reflections.

But the public-houses are distinctly and indubitably another pair of horses. I suppose that Suburbia's drink bill is scandalously large. Your true suburban, of course, is most justly described as a moderate drinker. It is obvious, however, that this kind of drinker is precisely the kind of drinker whom the brewers, distillers and publicans have reason to love . . .

It is the shining virtue of the drink trade that it looks well after its customers. 'You treat me decently and I'll treat you handsomely' is the workaday motto of the Imperial Majesty King Swipes. And in the matter of his suburban palaces, wherein he keeps revel and open house from six o'clock in the morning till half-past twelve o'clock next morning, there can be no doubt that he has been lavish and imperial. As mere buildings, these establishments stand out amid Suburbia's villas and cabbage-shops like oases in the desert. Architects of parts, builders whose name is not Jerry, reputable upholsterers and decorators, have clearly been employed in the erection and fitting of these mammoth houses. Costly marbles, honest building-stone, teak, oak, and mahogany of the soundest, fine plate-glass, solid brass and iron work, the chastest wall-coverings . . .

Literally, the suburban public-house is the one thing about Suburbia which is eminently not suburban. That it should be so is, perhaps, a thousand pities. It makes

the heart bleed when one reflects that in all this region of residences the finest, most palatial, and most artistic of houses are the public-houses. That the weary, soulless, overwrought denizens of villas, half-houses, maisonettes, cheap flats, and furnished apartments should resort to them assiduously for a little light and warmth and cheerfulness is not exactly astounding. They have their purpose; otherwise they would not exist.

1909

Homes for the working classes

When John Burns accompanied the distinguished black American Booker T. Washington around London in 1909, he proudly showed him examples of new London County Council housing, including the Millbank Estate. The cottage estate mentioned by Washington later in the extract below is Totterdown Fields, Tooting. Against this proud achievement, the description of life around Kennington Lane in the second excerpt, published by Maud Pember Reeves, a leading member of the Fabian Women's Group, stands as a reminder of what had yet to be done.

Mr Burns has promised to show me, within the space of a few hours, examples of the sort of work which is now going on in every part of London. A few years ago, on

A royal visit to the new estate at Totterdown Fields, Tooting, south west London, 1903.

the site of an ancient prison, the London County Council erected several blocks of workingmen's tenements. These were, I believe, the first, or nearly the first, of the tenements erected by the city in the work of clearing away unsanitary areas and providing decent homes for the working classes.

It was to these buildings, in which a population of about 4,000 persons live, that we went first. The buildings are handsome brick structures, well lighted, with wide, open, brick-paved courts between the rows of houses, so that each block looked like a gigantic letter H with the horizontal connecting line left out.

Of course, these buildings were, as some one said, little more than barracks compared with the houses that are now being erected for labouring people in some of the London suburbs, but they are clean and wholesome and, to any one familiar with the narrow, grimy streets in the East End of London, it was hard to believe that they stood in the midst of a region which a few years ago had been a typical London slum . . .

A little farther on we crossed the river and entered what Mr Burns referred to as 'my own district', Battersea . . .

Not far from Battersea Park, and in a part of the city which was formerly inhabited almost wholly by the very poor, we visited the public baths and a public washhouse where, during the course of a year, 42,000 women come to wash their clothes, paying at the rate of three cents an hour for the use of the municipal tubs and hot water. Children pay a penny or two cents for the use of the public baths.

The building is also provided with a gymnasium for the use of the children in winter, and contains a hall which is rented to a workingmen's club at a nominal price.

At Lower Tooting, an estate of some thirty-eight acres, the London County Council is building outright a city of something like 5,000 inhabitants, laying out the streets, building the houses, even putting a tidy little flower garden in each separate front door yard. It was as if the London County Council had gone to playing dolls, so completely planned and perfectly carried out in every detail is this little garden city.

Mr Burns, who has all his life been an advocate of temperance . . . pointed out here, as he did elsewhere, that there was no public house.

In the building of this little paradise all the architectural and engineering problems had indeed been solved. There remained, however, the problem of human nature, and the question that I asked myself was:

Will these people be able to live up to their surroundings?

The people whose lives form the subject of this book . . . are not the poorest people of the district . . . They are . . . some of the more enviable and settled inhabitants of this part of the world. The poorest people – the riverside casual, the workhouse in-and-out, the bar-room loafer – are anxiously ignored by these respectable persons whose work is permanent, as permanency goes in Lambeth, and whose wages range from 18s.. to 30s. a week . . .

They are respectable men in full work . . . Their wives are quiet, decent . . . women, and the children are the punctual and regular scholars . . . of the poorer schools . . .

The streets they live in are monotonously and drearily decent . . .

A working man's wife in receipt of a regular allowance divides it as follows: Rent; burial insurance; coal and light; cleaning materials; clothing; food.

The chief item in every poor budget is rent, and . . . it is safe to say that a family with three or more children is likely to be spending between 7s. and 8s. a week on rent alone.

It is obvious that, in London at any rate, the wretched housing, which is at the same time more than they can afford, has as bad an influence on the health of the poor as any other of their miserable conditions . . . The London poor are driven to pay one-third of their income for dark, damp rooms which are too small and too few in houses which are ill-built and overcrowded.

1902/6

Evening entertainment

London's flourishing theatres brought in an audience from the suburbs to see the major West End attractions. As one account shows, their arrival gave an air of spectacle to the railway stations into which they came, dressed up for the evening. By contrast, Virginia Woolf, aged twenty, enjoyed sitting on the fringes of the Royal Academy Annual Reception and a few weeks later threw herself into a more whole-hearted evening at Earls Court.

Trains disgorge hundreds and thousands of fair ladies elegantly attired, accompanied by their well-groomed male escorts. Beneath the lofty, massive and gloomy station roof, between the slimy blackened walls, among the tireless, panting engines ... through the foul, smoky suffocating atmosphere of the station they thread their way – delicate visions of white, pale blue, or pink, in hoods or wraps of Japanese silk, embroidered slippers and fancy boas, wrapped in their brocaded opera cloaks, beneath which stray glimpses are caught of the lace and chiffon of evening bodices – or they flit, with a fantastic shimmer of pearls and diamonds, with a soft rustle of silks, satins and tulle.

---

1 July [1902] Again we took [a] cab tonight & drove through the populous streets which look their gayest about this hour. We had four large cards for the Academy Soirée – an entertainment unique, I should think, of its kind.

The courtyard in which Edward the Black Prince stands was packed with carriages cabs & motor cars so that it was almost difficult to get in & find one's way round the edge to the large door.

The Academy is a gloomy great place, even on its festive nights; you take off your cloak in a kind of catacomb, damp, with stone arches. The little urbane President [Sir Edward Poynter], already looking a trifle bored, pressed our hands perfunctorily & we passed on

into the great rooms. This crowd, I say, has a character of its own. Every other person you feel must be distinguished: the men wear a surprising number of decorations ...

The women, as though to atone for their want of definite orders, dress up in the oddest ways. We found some queer specimens. Here was a stuffy black dress, somehow suggestive of high tea & bugles; here the artistic temperament had gone to the other extreme, and left bare a good deal of the person which is usually covered ... I could have been well content to take my evening's pleasure in observation merely ...

It is not a party at which one talks. The conditions are somehow adverse. The great rooms indeed are full, but you never rid your mind of the public gallery feeling – & certainly the light & space are not becoming. The crowd as a whole looks badly dressed, & moves awkwardly ... We drifted about, gazing at human pictures mostly, with snatches of desultory talk. We looked with admiration at those ladies ... who know the President & all the more distinguished academicians ... Exquisite in old lace & most refined evening gowns, they know well that they are the Queens of the gathering ...

LEFT *Leaving His Majesty's Theatre, a scene of nightlife from 1907. Theatre-going was a formal, full-dress occasion and the West End flourished in the Edwardian period.*

RIGHT *The water chute at Earls Court around 1904. Virginia Woolf describes how the same features resurfaced, thinly disguised, year after year.*

A cab home again! Down the brilliant charging Piccadilly, now thoroughly awake, as though it had slept all day. The wood pavement in the heat gets beaten to a shiny hard surface, which at night reflects the lamplight almost as though it were wet.

———————

22 July We go once a year to Earls Court. I do not know that I want to go oftener – but I enjoy that one visit. This evening it was a little suddenly decided that the three of us should go … We raked together the most miscellaneous garments, which had to be evening, & outdoor & waterproof at once. In the end we compromised: our shoes were indoor … only our hats could rightly be called out of doors. But it didn't matter. Earls Court is one of those places where you can wear exactly what you like. The first thing we made for was the Chute. The exhibition is supposed to have something to do with fire engines; but really the name of the show is the only thing that changes; all else remains the same … one can think oneself in Venice … or Constantinople which was last years name, I think … The Chute is unfailing … last year I made six descents running … this year I didn't mind stopping after the third … There

he Chute, Earl's Court.

was some difficulty in deciding what to do after this – but 'The River of Lava' written in twinkling lamps attracted Adrian & me so much that we paid our sixpences & took our seats in the boat. It was a horrid fraud; I travelled that river when it was the Styx; when it was a Venetian Canal – & under some other disguise. The point is that you are floated along a kind of drain which is worked by electricity so that the current floats you without oars. The way is variegated with grottos & sunsets & effects of light upon the water … As we left a man came up & entreated us to laugh a hundred times for sixpence … we accepted. Inside we found ourselves in a tent lined with looking glasses, of all conceivable curves & hollows: we grew long – & lop sided & gigantic and dwarfed … When we felt we had secured as many of our 100 laughs as were forthcoming we left … We shall not go to Earls Court again for another year.

1907

Golders Green by Tube

Virginia Woolf's description of the march of urbanization over the farmland at Golders Green could have fitted the scene on any of London's extremities. She was an early passenger on the just opened (22 June 1907) Northern Line to Golders Green, tunnelled below Hampstead Heath and a spur to development on that side of London.

July [1907] Last Sunday, the 6th, to be precise I made an expedition which seems to me to deserve commemoration. The Twopenny Tube has now burrowed as far as Golders Green; so that sinking into an earth laid with pavement & houses at one end, you rise to soft green fields at the other; the ashen dark & the chill & cold glitter of electricity is replaced by the more benignant illumination of daylight. Indeed on Sunday there was a sky & a sun; & the exuberant holiday making of the crowd had some excuse. Well, we all of us got out at Golders Green; which term I take to apply to a dusky triangle between cross roads, which was now occupied by a cluster of idle people … Their little island was a refuge from motor cars which shot past constantly almost shaving slices from the edge … [we] chose one of the four roads as our way into the country. But no real country road, as I could not but remember, is raked so persistently by huge barrelled motor cars; nor do strings & knots & couples of brightly dressed people fill all the way, so that you must steer to get past them. But there were fields on either side though one had to

OPPOSITE *A promotional image of Selfridges department store in Oxford Street, opened 1909. Shorn of the dome that Gordon Selfridge has planned, it still aimed to outshine its competitors.*

ABOVE *The new Golders Green station, and onward public transport, seen shortly after its opening in 1907.*

RIGHT *The march of development. Houses are let as fast as they are built.*

violate some instinct which held them forbidden before one crept under the paling. It seems so natural that all open spaces should be hedged off, or only available on payment; & half the people I think kept to the road in obedience to this traditional belief . . .

It is hard to describe the view, for it was indeed of a most singular kind. Golders Green is all red brick; huge factories or railway buildings are specially prominent; then to the North (perhaps) there was another separate hamlet, grouped as real villages are up a hill which was pointed by a Church spire. And between them there was this soft land, undulating with long grass . . . Old lichen crusted palings, & streamlets & fields with cows in them, all seemed ready to prove that they were part of the neglected world, & then the tail of your eye was caught by a line of villas, like a block of childrens bricks set on end. A line of moving heads at a little distance

showed me that there was . . . a regular channel up to Hampstead, along which one might legitimately walk. The walk which I took afterwards through the fields lacked somehow the stimulus of walks through real fields. I fancied dust & fatigue & a thousand annoyances; & found myself gravitating, half sulkily, towards that cut in the land where I should find a real road, & people.

1900s

Selfridges department store

The opening of the great department stores dramatically changed London's shopping habits. None was more spectacular than the store of the American Gordon Selfridge on Oxford Street, which opened in 1909. Although the great dome that was planned to crown the building never

materialized, the store has remained a major London attraction ever since. The following accounts are by two customers and a member of staff.

I was at Selfridges the day they opened. I was living at Maida Vale and I paid a penny to get to the store. Everyone was given a hyacinth and made very welcome.
MRS D. YATES

I can remember my mother taking my sister and I up to Selfridges very often, from Finchley. I can remember Mr Selfridge walking around the store, which he did every day, wearing a top hat. I also remember Bleriot's aeroplane there. It was ringed off with white rope, but we were so thrilled when a man in charge said, 'Let the little girls go in!'
GLADYS PARRY

I joined the staff of Selfridges in 1909 at the age of fifteen years ... I was the lowest form of animal life, a junior to wait on the seniors and hopefully learn salesmanship. This could be a dog's life, and very often was. My wages were 2s. 6d. per week with dinner and tea thrown in, and if by any wonderful chance I made a sale of the goods the department stocked – corset – which I never did, commission was 3d. in the pound. Later on, dinner and tea were discontinued and I then received 15s. per week ...

On the death of Edward VII, the whole store plunged into mourning; all displays as far as possible were black; everyone wore as much black as they could afford and most of us looked like a lot of black crows.

In the year 1911 we experienced the hottest summer anyone could remember – over 90 degrees in the shade, day after day. During this heat I wore a black serge, long-sleeved, high-necked dress, black woollen stockings and sturdy black shoes, and the appropriate underwear. When the store closed at 6.30 p.m., we had

to go into the Bathing Dress Department to restore order out of chaos, as these garments were in the main two-piece and we had to make the garments match. This took some time, with nothing extra to eat or drink and no money for overtime.
MRS ADELA HILL (ADELA PRATT)

1908/12

Suffragettes

The suffragette campaign was nation wide, as was that of the non-militant suffragists, but inevitably its focus was London, as the home of the legislature. Numerous campaigns were mounted, such as that in 1912 which involved the systematic breaking of window panes, beginning with No. 10 Downing Street, then areas all over the West End, Haymarket and Piccadilly, Regent Street and the Strand, Oxford Circus and Bond Street. Imprisonment followed for the women. In her autobiography Mrs Pankhurst looked back upon her campaigns.

The largest number of people ever gathered in Hyde Park was said to have approximated 72,000. We determined to organise a Hyde Park demonstration of at least 250,000 people. Sunday, June 21, 1908, was fixed for the date of this demonstration ...

London, of course, was thoroughly organised. For weeks a small army of women was busy chalking announcements on sidewalks, distributing handbills, canvassing from house to house, advertising the demonstration by posters and sandwich boards carried through the streets ... Mrs Drummond and a number of other women hired and decorated a launch and sailed up the Thames to the Houses of Parliament, arriving at the hour when members entertain their women friends at tea on the terrace ... 'Come to the park on Sunday,' she cried ... An alarmed someone telephoned for the police boats, but as they appeared, the women's boat steamed away.

What a day was Sunday, June 21st – clear, radiant, filled with golden sunshine! ... When I mounted my platform in Hyde Park, and surveyed the mighty throngs that waited there and the endless crowds that were still pouring into the park from all directions, I was filled with amazement not unmixed with awe ... It was a gay and beautiful ... spectacle, for the white gowns and flower-trimmed hats of the women, against the background of ancient trees, gave the park the appearance of a vast garden in full flower ...

At five o'clock the bugles sounded again, the

speaking ceased, and the resolution calling upon the Government to bring in an official woman-suffrage bill without delay was carried at every platform, often without a dissenting vote. Then, with a three-times-repeated cry of 'Votes for Women!' from the assembled multitude, the great meeting dispersed.

Late in the afternoon of Friday, March 1st, 1912 I drove in a taxicab, accompanied by the Hon. Secretary of the Union, Mrs Tuke and another of our members, to No. 10 Downing Street ... It was exactly half past five when we alighted from the cab and threw our stones, four of them, through the window panes. As we expected we were promptly arrested and taken to Cannon Row police station. The hour that followed will long be remembered in London. At intervals of fifteen minutes relays of women who had volunteered for the demonstration did their work ... The demonstration ended for the day at half past six with the breaking of many windows in the Strand. The *Daily Mail* gave this graphic account of the demonstration:

From every part of the crowded and brilliantly lighted streets came the crash of splintered glass. People started as a window shattered at their side; suddenly there was another crash in front of them; on the other side of the street; behind – everywhere.

Scared shop assistants came running out to the pavements; traffic stopped; policemen sprang this way and that; five minutes later the streets were a procession of excited groups, each surrounding a woman wrecker being led in custody to the nearest police station. Meanwhile the shopping quarter of London had plunged itself into a sudden twilight. Shutters were hurriedly fitted; the rattle of iron curtains being drawn came from every side. Guards of commissionaires and shopmen were quickly mounted, and any unaccompanied lady in sight, especially if she carried a hand bag, became an object of menacing suspicion.

1909

Junior clerks

Richard Church joined the ranks of the junior clerks, aged sixteen, with his mind filled with vivid Dickensian imagery. Despite his early misgivings, Church remained a civil servant for the next twenty-four years. The routine, and in particular the lunch place, are familiar enough to any modern office worker.

In the April of 1909 I was instructed to report to an office called the Land Registry, of which I had never heard. It was in Lincoln's Inn Fields, and at once I thought of the scenes in Dickens's *Bleak House* and the death of the solicitor Mr Tulkinghorn. I pictured the Land Registry as an establishment similar to that of the sinister lawyer, where I should be employed as a junior at a high desk in a little ante-room . . .

I entered Herne Hill station, and as I walked through the subway to the up-platform, a spasm of dismay shook me. I saw myself imprisoned for life in a job in which I was likely to have no aptitude and no interest . . .

To my dismay, I found the Land Registry anything but a Dickensian lawyer's office. It was a red-brick, modern institution, standing at the corner of Lincoln's Inn Fields, just outside the great gateway into Lincoln's Inn proper. I have not yet discovered how I found my way to it, for I knew nothing about London, other than the two suburbs where I had spent my sixteen years . . .

I was carried to the first floor and deposited in a vast room filled with bound volumes of property titles – the registry; and there, under the direction of a pale little man with a cripple's face and curved spine, I was seated in a bay window overlooking the Gothic gateway of the Inn, my table surrounded by card-index cabinets, which it would be my duty to keep up to date, hour by hour, as the documents of land and house property registration flowed through the department.

Another new boy was installed with me . . . When the lunch-hour came, he and I went out together to seek a meal . . . We found a little eating-house in Clements Inn, next door to the vicarage of St. Clement Dane's Church. It had back-to-back settles, and the customers had to slide themselves into the cubicles. A small, elderly woman waited on the diners, appeared to know most of them by their Christian names, greeting them with a fretful cheerfulness, as of a mother of a large and noisy brood.

1913

The sweated women's conference

The sweated women's conference held at Marlborough House in November 1913 achieved enormous publicity, mainly because of the unlikely surroundings in which it was held and the unusual figure of the hostess. In her autobiography Consuelo Balsan, as the former Duchess of Marlborough became, quoted a contemporary report of it.

It is evident that the Duchess of Marlborough understands the British public. She is in closer touch with the thrifty spirit of the nation, which abhors the house-burning and window-breaking methods of illuminating grievances, than any of her radical co-workers. Quite lately she convened a conference of sweated women at Sunderland House, and secured the presence there of the Press and of representative leaders of every section of society. We must take leave to doubt that a soul would have attended had the British public suspected the noble lady's little game.

In all probability the great array of bishops, politicians, butterflies of fashion, industrial captains and bigwigs that assembled went to Sunderland House in the expectation of passing a pleasant hour or two exchanging trite moral reflections over tea and strawberries and gratuitous champagne. We can picture their discomfiture, their horror, on discovering that the Duchess had successfully arranged a trap for the capture and destruction of the national complacency . . . When the conference was opened they found they were to listen, not to talk. Twelve old women occupied the stage . . . poor but respectable old women . . . They did all the talking. One after another they came forward and related the stories of their miserably cramped and sweated lives. One was a shirt maker. She showed her gilded audience a shirt she had made . . . 'Last week me and my husband sat from 5.30 till 11 at night and made fourteen dozen shirts, which came to ten shillings, and ten pence for cotton.' And such had been her daily grind for more than twenty years. A widow in the confectionery trade had worked for twenty years in a factory for eight shillings a week, out of which she had had to provide for the support and education of her child. For twenty years she had never eaten a dinner costing more than a penny. And thus ran all the tales the silent and confounded conference was forced to hear.

1914–1945

LONDON

at

WAR

Proclamations of war and peace had an immediacy in London that they could not command elsewhere. When the unexpected but longed-for announcement came that World War I had ended, the London crowds went to Whitehall and stood outside the War Office – where else?

War had been highly visible in the capital. The coming and going of troops through the main-line railway stations, a melancholy succession of trains bearing the wounded, the survivors and tales of the dead brought the unexpurgated truth home. The streets were full of ambulance traffic conveying men to and from the hospitals, convalescent homes and places for incurables. Any crowd would include a number of maimed men, no longer fighting at the front. London was, in its way, a front-line in both World Wars.

The physical menace of both wars, whether threatened or real, was a direct introduction to the battle zone. If the scale of destruction in London in World War I was little compared to that in World War II, the toll on the nerves of those who stayed put was much the same.

Peacetime sent the new working woman back home and, if she was over thirty, finally enfranchised her. It saw Homes for Heroes, which in London terms meant the cottage estates built by the LCC on an increasing scale, extending ever further away from the heart of London. Slum clearance was seen as imperative and the Prince of Wales took the issue as a personal crusade, endorsing 1930s campaigns such as New Homes for Old.

Private development went unchecked and the spread of the car did its work. Arterial roads pushed on outwards, pulling new urban and suburban development with them. Inter-war London had become a major modern industrial city. Munitions factories were taken over by civilian manufacturers while heavy industry and large-scale enterprises sprang up in a wide belt around London. Not surprisingly, the capital was viewed

ABOVE *The wounded arriving at Charing Cross station. Painting by J. Hodgson-Lobley, 1916.*

OPPOSITE *A newspaper seller on 3 September 1939. The threat of war becomes reality.*

as a consuming monster before which the country-side was lost. Only the tightening of the Green Belt, with legislation in 1938, served to reassure the public. Local authorities were even urged to buy open land to hold the capital back.

Civil aerodromes, industrial estates and an efficient integrated public transport system were part of a new London with a taste for the modern. Yet, rebuilding at the commercial heart of London was retrospective in style. Truly modern buildings were hard to find – save at the Zoo or in enclaves such as Highgate and Hampstead, where *émigrés* from Europe brought new approaches that had hitherto found no foothold in London. London took on the 'machine age' second-hand but no less enthusiastically for that. The private car was, if not the streamlined beast of American manufacture, as dominant a presence in the city as in the suburbs. The citizen on foot had to be protected, and the first pedestrian crossings, known as 'Sanctuary lanes', were introduced in 1934.

The coronation of Queen Elizabeth II may be generally known as the first to be shown on television, yet 50,000 viewers in and around London had watched her father being crowned in 1937, broadcast from Alexander Palace. The wireless was already a feature in many living rooms.

Out in the suburban boroughs, in the residential estates glorying in their hyperbolic names ('the Arcadia Wonder House') with a comfortable life-style underpinned by the novel Hire Purchase system, central London began to seem about as distant as Paris.

In the East End and elsewhere, the picture was little changed. Poverty tended to breed xenophobia and anti-Semitism. The Depression took its toll both economically and politically. Fascism spread insidiously and by 1936 rallies and marches were being held at the Royal Albert Hall and in Trafalgar Square. Seen against the weakening of the League of Nations and the strengthening of Fascism and Nazism in Europe, London's position as the capital of continental Europe's off-shore island became a crucial one.

At the same time, all was not well with the Empire. The blithe assumptions of the 1924 Wembley Exhibition did not stand close examination, and by the 1930s the cracks were becoming gulfs. Mahatma Gandhi's campaigns of civil disobedience in India were difficult to handle and introduced doubts about colonialism at home as well as abroad.

But London was hardly joyless. Londoners embraced the cinema; the Art Deco super-cinemas of the early 1930s were the most flamboyant of the almost 300 cinemas in the capital – one for every suburban high street and dozens in the West End. Hollywood was just one strand of a pervasive American influence.

For all that, London was at its best in the tea-shops, in its efficient and truly modern underground system, in its ceremonial for monarchy's rites of passage. As ever, London demonstrated a maddening mixture of resistance to change and civilized modern metropolitan living.

With World War II, London became for a time a battlefield. The behaviour of the population astounded the watching world; it drew both on those reserves of bloody-minded conservatism and the decency upon which the city has always depended.

1915/17

Zeppelin raids

The atmosphere in London during the early months of World War I was full of rumours and reports both from utterly sound and highly dubious sources. War was declared on 4 August, but for a while London remained an unattainable object given the many known defects of the Zeppelin (which had been in civilian use before the war). However, in early June 1915 the Zeppelin arrived. *The Times* reported every move.

MAY 17, 1915
Fog Bombs for London
The coming invasion
(by a neutral)

Germany is talking of the coming invasion of London by a fleet of Zeppelins possibly accompanied by other forms of aircraft. Some people there have even gone so far as to predict a date for the destruction of London, so confident are they in the power of the latest creations of Count Zeppelin, aided by a highly trained staff of scientists...

An expressionist cover design for a triumphant account of the Zeppelin attacks on England, of which London took the brunt.

The latest production of these highly skilled scientists is directly aimed at England. It is the Nebelbomben (the fog bomb), to be used 'when the big attack on London' takes place. Workers in the factories, who are usually so secretive are as enthusiastic as schoolboys over the successful experiments made with the new contrivance, which explodes in the air and sheds over a large area a fog-like cloud sufficiently dense to obscure the airship from the rays of the most powerful searchlights. The new invention can also be used in daylight.

GREAT THINGS IN PREPARATION

This information I gained while travelling through Germany during the last ten days ... The threats of a Zeppelin raid on London during the first months of the war had remained boastful threats, and the Zeppelins had not shown themselves capable of inflicting any damage of military value. They had only killed some innocent civilians and caused meaningless destruction of property. There was, of course, always a possibilty that Zeppelins would reach London ...

Later I was told by a friend that 5 or 6 new Zeppelins had been constructed at Fredrickshafen, specially intended to be used on an air raid on London. It would not be a question of any isolated airship dropping one or two bombs but of a fleet of dirigibles. The journeys already made to the neighbourhood of London had given evidence of the feasibility of such a plan and the Hoechst and Badensche chemical factories, the most proficient in the world, were hard at work for some purpose in connection with a plan of that kind.

WEDNESDAY JUNE 2, 1915
The Zeppelin raiders
About 90 bombs drop
Some fires but few casualties

The Secretary to the Admiralty made the following announcement yesterday: – 5pm. In amplification of the information which appeared in this morning's papers the following particulars of last night's Zeppelin raid in the metropolitan area are now available for publication. Late last night about 90 bombs mostly of an incendiary character, were dropped from hostile aircraft on various localities not far distant from each other. A number of fires (of which only three were large enough to require the services of fire engines) broke out. All fires were promptly and effectively dealt with; only one of these fires necessitated a district call ... No public building was injured, but a number of private premises were damaged by fire or water.

The number of casualties is small. So far as at present ascertained, one infant, one boy, one man and one woman were killed, and another woman is so seriously injured that her life is despaired of. A few other private citizens were seriously injured. The precise numbers are not yet ascertained.

Adequate police arrangements including the calling out of special constables, enabled the situation to be kept thoroughly in hand throughout.
Amsterdam June 1st Official communique issued in Berlin today says: – as a reprisal for the bombardment of the open town of Ludwigshafen, we last night threw numerous bombs on the wharves and docks of London. (Reuters)

War-time raids made Londoners more than usually obsessed with the condition of the weather. Rain and high winds were the best insurance against the Zeppelin; clear, still weather with a full moon the worst conditions of all. There were fifty-two airship raids between January 1915 and August 1918, and ten Zeppelins were brought down. Virginia Woolf and Mrs C. S. Peel give their impressions.

Monday 22 October [1917] The moon grows full, & the evening trains are packed with people leaving London. We saw the hole in Piccadilly this afternoon. Traffic has been stopped, & the public slowly tramps past the place, which workmen are mending, though they look small in comparison with it. Swan & Edgar has every window covered with sacking or planks; you see shop women looking out from behind; not a glimpse of stuffs, but 'business goes on as usual' so they say. Windows are broken according to no rule; some intact, some this side, some that. Our London Library stands whole, however, & we found our books, & came home in the tube, standing the whole way to Hammersmith. *Sunday 28 October* Still no raids, presumably the haze at evening keeps them off, though it is still, & the moon perfectly clear. The numbers who have gone out of London this week must feel a little foolish . . .

The difficulty was to make people take shelter. They would rush into the streets and stand gazing up at the intruder. 'Never shall I forget' says a woman, speaking of those days, 'hearing an odd chunkety, chunkety noise. It sounded as if a train with rusty wheels were travelling through the sky. I ran out on to the balcony and saw something which looked like a large silver cigar away to my left, and I realized it was a Zeppelin. Almost immediately it burst into flames and the sky turned red. Then came the sound of cheering. It seemed as if the whole of a rather far-away London was cheering, and almost unconsciously I began to cry, 'Hooray, horray!' too. But suddenly I stopped. We were cheering whilst men who were after all very bravely doing what they thought it their duty to do were being burned to death . . . later I was told that when a car reached the scene of its fall . . . of a crew of forty only fourteen were found on the ship. These were in a standing position grasping the steel struts of the machine . . . How *loathsome* war is!'

1915

Women in wartime

Life was turned upside-down by war. While social life carried on, with a degree of bravado, the remorseless drain on the young men of the country was soon evident – as much in the streets as in the hospitals. Women were pitched

into action, and for the first time they gained responsible positions in the Civil Service as well as in the more conventional roles of nursing and ambulance driving. Vera Brittain was twenty, well below the minimum age for service in an army hospital, when she came from Derbyshire to be a VAD in a south London hospital.

The next morning, soberly equipped in my new VAD uniform, I took for the last time the early train to London, and turned my back for ever upon my provincial young-ladyhood.

After the solid, old-fashioned comfort of the Buxton house, it seemed strange to be the quarter-possessor of a bare-boarded room divided into cubicles by much-washed curtains of no recognisable colour, with only a bed, a wash-stand and a tiny chest of drawers to represent one's earthly possessions. There was not, I

Recruitment poster for some of the more conventional of women's occupations during the war, emphasizing their role overseas as at home.

noticed with dismay, so much as a shelf or a mantelpiece capable of holding two or three books ...

Now two insignificant units at the 1st London General Hospital, Camberwell – the military extension of St Bartholomew's Hospital – Betty and I had reported to the Matron that afternoon. We were among the youngest members of the staff, we learnt later, only two of the other V.A.D.'s being 'under age'. The nucleus of the hospital, a large college, red, gabled, creeper-covered, is still one of the few dignified buildings in the dismal, dreary, dirty wilderness of south-east London, with its paper-strewn pavements, its little mean streets, and its old, ugly houses tumbling into squalid decay. Formerly – and now again – a training centre for teachers, it was commandeered for use as a hospital early in the War, together with some adjacent elementary schools, the open park-space opposite, and its satellite hostel nearly two miles away on Champion Hill.

To this hostel, as soon as we had reported ... [we] were dispatched with our belongings. Our taxicab ... deposited us before a square, solid building of dirty grey stone, with gaping uncurtained windows. Closely surrounded by elms and chestnuts, tall, ancient and sooty, it looked gloomy and smelt rather dank ...

Each morning at 7 am we were due at the hospital, where we breakfasted, and went on duty at 7.30. Theoretically we travelled down by the workmen's trams which ran over Champion Hill from Dulwich, but in practice these trams were so full that we were seldom able to use them, and were obliged to walk, frequently in pouring rain ... the mile and a half from the hostel to the hospital. As the trams were equally full in the evenings, the journey on foot had often to be repeated at the end of the day.

Whatever the weather, we were expected to appear punctually on duty looking clean, tidy and cheerful ... as we struggled up or down Denmark Hill in the blustering darkness all through that wet autumn, Betty and I encouraged each other with the thought that we were at last beginning to understand just a little of what winter meant to the men in the trenches ...

Every task from the dressing of a dangerous wound to the scrubbing of a bed-mackintosh, had for us in those early days a sacred glamour which redeemed it equally from tedium and disgust. Our one fear was to be found wanting in the smallest respect; no conceivable fate seemed more humiliating than that of being returned to Devonshire House as 'unsuitable' after a month's probation.

1914–18

Life on the Home Front

Nothing in daily life escaped the effects of the war, and yet life went on as usual. In 1915 philosopher and thinker Bertrand Russell met and fell in love with Lady Constance Malleson, an actress known by her stage name Colette O'Neil, an ardent pacifist like himself. In the second passage novelist Robert Graves's wedding to the daughter of the painter William Nicholson combined the conventions of a smart West End wedding with the peculiarities of wartime.

Robert Graves and his wife, Nancy Nicholson, some months after their marriage. He wears army uniform while she is dressed in the land-girl uniform she donned at the end of her wedding ceremony.

The War was bound into the texture of this love from first to last. The first time that I was ever in bed with her ... we heard suddenly a shout of bestial triumph in the street. I leapt out of bed and saw a Zeppelin falling in flames. The thought of brave men dying in agony was what caused the triumph in the street ...

After the night in which the Zeppelin fell I left her in the early morning to return to my brother's house in Gordon Square where I was living. I met on the way an old man selling flowers, who was calling out: 'Sweet lovely roses!' I bought a bunch of roses, paid him for them, and told him to deliver them in Bernard Street. Everyone would suppose that he would have kept the money and not delivered the roses, but it was not so, and I knew it would not be so.

———————

Nancy and I were married in January 1918 at St. James's Church, Piccadilly . . .

Then the reception. At this stage of the war, sugar could not be got except in the form of rations. There was a three-tiered wedding-cake and the Nicholsons had been saving up their sugar and butter cards for a month to make it taste like a real one; but when George Mallory lifted off the plaster-case of imitation icing, a sigh of disappointment rose from the guests. However, champagne was another scarce commodity, and the guests made a rush for the dozen bottles on the table . . . After three or four glasses [Nancy] went off and changed back into her land-girl's costume of breeches and smock . . . The embarrassments of our wedding night . . . were somewhat eased by an air-raid: Zeppelin bombs dropping not far off set the hotel in an uproar.

was just as concerned with the rigours and pleasures in wartime London as with the dramatic events like the Zeppelin raids.

December 16 1914 The 'Die-Hards' who regard as slackers those who attend any form of public entertainment, and hate them as bitterly as they hate German spies, are making a dead set on Saturday evening football, led on by *The Globe* newspaper. Rugby has cancelled its matches . . . Association football being professional and requiring 'gates' carry on to meet its financial obligations. On a Saturday recently I saw a match between Chelsea and Arsenal at the Chelsea ground. There was as big an attendance as I had ever seen there before the War. This shows how popular the game is as a spectacle and the relaxation it affords to workers . . .

Going to football matches in the old days we used to be confronted with evangelical posters greatly

At the outbreak of war Michael MacDonagh had already worked for *The Times* for twenty years, a journalist covering 'parliamentary and general'. As staff members of military age were enlisted, MacDonagh found himself with increasingly onerous responsibilities, reporting the war from London. Owing to heavy censorship, much of what a journalist observed went unprinted, but MacDonagh kept a journal and published it upon his retirement. MacDonagh

concerned for our eternal welfare, asking us, among other questions, 'Are you prepared to meet your God?' . . . In these days the posters carried by a line of sandwich-men . . . ask the crowds such questions as: 'Are you forgetting that there's a War on?' 'Your Country Needs You', 'Be Ready to Defend your Home and Women from the German Huns'. So far as I could notice, little attention was given to these skeletons at the feast. Inside the ground there was excitement and uproar. What a picture! The rosettes of the supporters of the rival clubs; the rattles and horns; the frenzied cheers, and the shouts of welcome when the teams came running on to the field!

1918

The National Kitchen and Eating House

By late 1917 the food situation was becoming acute. MacDonagh saw food queues everywhere: 'It is becoming a regular daily thing in all parts of London to see long lines of people outside provision shops waiting to be served and doubtful whether anything will be left when their turn comes.' National rationing was introduced shortly after. MacDonagh quoted from a Lyons's teashop menu: 'Half a coupon is required for one sausage; half veal and ham pie; or egg and bacon. A whole coupon is required for two sausages; plate of cold ham or tongue; or stewed steak and

carrots.' The National Kitchen and Eating House that he describes below was the first of a number opened in 1918, an attempt to deal with the health of the poorer Londoners at a time of severe food shortages. His account also added a futuristic glimpse towards the world of self-service.

May 22 [1918] To-day I lunched at the National Kitchen and Eating-House opened at Poplar by the Food Ministry. Its purpose is to show how, by proper cooking meals can be appetisingly served at low charges, and, at the same time, commodities which are scarce made to go a long way. More than that, poor housewives can obtain cooked meals more nourishing and at less cost than they could themselves provide at home. My meal, consisting of vegetable soup, fish, pie and baked rice, was quite satisfying and cost only sixpence. What a contrast to the Mansion House dinner [for delegates to the Inter-Allied Conference for the aftercare of permanently wounded service men] last

OPPOSITE *Chelsea Football Club, posing for a club portrait in the months before the war.*

RIGHT *Lady Rhondda opens the communal kitchen at Poplar, East London, a government initiative to improve nutrition standards in wartime.*

night, though that was necessarily limited in courses and wines! Thus frequently does the newspaper reporter touch life at both extremes within twenty-four hours!

At the eating-house (notice how the French word, 'restaurant' is ignored!) expenses are reduced by a new system of service. You buy tickets for the meal on entering, and, in exchange for them, obtain the food at a long counter and bring it with knife and fork and spoon to the table yourself. There are no waiters and only a few women to clear away the soiled plates and cups. The place, I was told, is run at a profit. An eating-house of the same kind is to be opened in New Bridge Street, Blackfriars.

1917

Life in an internment camp

The plight of German nationals as enemy aliens came to a head in the late months of the war. Alexandra Palace was the main internment camp, along with the Islington Workhouse. Around 6,000 men, many of whom were long resident in the country, some with British wives and even sons fighting for Britain, became the target of a campaign to intern every enemy alien, without distinction. The intern whose memoirs are quoted below had been transferred in February 1917 from an inferior camp at Stratford East.

It seemed like a new life as the place is beautifully situated on a hill surrounded by nice grounds and lovely trees ... here in this large building were 3000 Germans interned, mostly all men with English wifes, divided into Battalions A.B.C. After I was registered at the main office I was handed over to B. Battalion, right in the centre of the main building, the place made a most peculiar impression, the Hall was about 90 feet high, on the further end a large organ, right round the whole Hall all the figures of the Kings of England since Cromwells time, and in the middle about a thousand strawsacks all more or less surrounded by blankets, canvas or other fancy material put up on four sticks like huts, it seemed like a Oriental Bazaar ... I received the No 12640 and was placed with the 12th Company on table 26. But there was one great evil, utensils for cleanliness seemed very scarce, the very buckets in which the soup was served were used for washing up, and on most instances for washing the floor, and the atmosphere was at times unbearable. The wash and bath arrangement very bad, it was very difficult to get warm water, and to dry the washing, but we had to do

somehow. In foggy days sometimes, the doors were not opened for four days the stench became unbearable ... outside ... we could see all over London ... There was also a garden plot set apart, for those who took interest in gardening, each battalion also had a skittle ally, the time seemed to go very quickly ... there is also a large theatre in which we had regular concerts and cinemato-

graph, and every week we had some lectures on Political and Worldly matters.

Also the visits were each one allowed once a week, two hours at the time, here we could for the first time sit side by side with our wifes ... there was not very much to complain of in comparison to other camps.

1918

'Digging for Victory'

One feature common to both World Wars was the conversion of London's parks and commons to places for vegetable growing. MacDonagh describes the success of the campaign to divert people's energies from cultivating flowers to the essential business of producing foodstuffs.

[April 1, 1918] 'No flowers, by request.' This is the Order of the Day for Easter. It means, in the first place, that the very domesticated, stay-at-home Londoner, of whom there are hundreds of thousands, instead of

devoting the holiday to planting bulbs in his back garden, as is traditional with him at Easter, should ... extend his sphere of vegetable-growing by taking a plot or allotment in the nearest open space. An example has been set by the King. His Majesty has directed that the flower-beds surrounding the Queen Victoria Memorial at Buckingham Palace are not to present this year the

'servants' peace is partly a recunciation of the event but also a reflection of the public's growing conviction of the ghastly futility of that war, so mishandled and resulting in such a devastating loss of life. With her usual honesty, Virginia Woolf admits distaste for the gradual pull of the celebrations, seen from Richmond. Her account of the day ends on a poignant note, with the occupants of the Star and

OPPOSITE *King George V encourages the wartime vegetable growing effort, visiting allotments on Clapham Common in 1918 – evidently fertile soil for prize cabbages.*

RIGHT *Londoners celebrate Peace Day, 11 November 1918.*

customary blaze of scarlet geraniums, but ... the sight of potatoes, cabbages, parsnips and carrots all a-blooming!

My heart filled with satisfaction on visiting the Commons in my own neighbourhood, Clapham, Tooting and Wandsworth, and also Battersea Park – all under the London County Council – where I saw hundreds of men and women cheerfully and healthily employed on their plots, making the potato and the cabbage grow where only the grass grew before in London's open spaces.

1918/19

Celebrating peace

Armistice Day was 11 November 1918. In London the still unexpected end of the terrible war was met with an ecstatic sense of relief. The peace celebrations of 19 and 20 July 1919 were the official marker and took place in a changed climate, as Mrs C. S. Peel tells in the first extract. Virginia Woolf's

Garter Home (founded in 1915) on the top of Richmond Hill – men whose lives had been wrecked in the Great War, unable and unwilling to celebrate anything.

As if by magic London has become a city of flags. From Heaven knows where the toy squib and the paper streamers come out of their long hiding. One sees a stout, elderly Colonel on the top of a taxi beating violently a dinner gong. Presently, because the crowds are so dense, all traffic is stopped, and then in the afternoon the rain comes down. It needs more than rain to damp our spirits ... The restaurants are stormed, the supply of food runs out, but somehow more is obtained ... Strangers join hands and sing ... Out in Trafalgar Square the crowd is dancing, singing again the songs of the war.

The experiences of a young girl then working in the War Office are typical.

'Though everyone knew that in all probability the Germans *must* agree to the Armistice terms, yet no one seemed to have realized that peace would come so soon – at any rate, everyone arrived as usual, and there was no sign of any excitement for about half an hour after we started work. Then my chief, Major ––– … marched up to me saying "Shake hands with me, and I'll tell you some good news." Then he wrung my hand and said, "Germany signed the Armistice at five o'clock this morning" … on the stroke of eleven the maroons thundered out their message … that "fighting had ceased on all fronts". … The windows opposite had filled with people, who began to cheer wildly. In a few moments there came from Trafalgar Square, that wonderful sound of a deep, roaring cheer issuing from thousands of throats. There's something extraordinary about the roar of a crowd, something terrifying and yet inspiring … Major ––– said that we would go into the Mall and then to Buckingham Palace and see the King, so we turned into Whitehall … the grey old War Office looked as if it had suddenly been lighted up with a torch of many colours, for along one floor every balcony held a "bouquet" of staff officers, khaki-clad and red-tabbed against the grey …

On the Horse Guards Parade we … all followed the crowd that was pouring down the Mall, between the captured German guns (dozens of which have been ranged there for some little time now), in motors or on foot, to the Palace. We learnt that the King had just been out on the balcony and had gone in again … It was a very long time before the King came out …

I thought of the night we were at the Palace at the beginning of the war … we should have rubbed our eyes in 1914 if we had seen some of those who mingled in the 1918 crowd – munition girls in bright overalls, who arrived in large lorries, shouting and shrieking with joy; girl messengers in brown overalls, beating tin tea-trays and waving flags, staff officers in cars driven by smart khaki girls, and cars from the Admiralty with the even smarter "WREN" chauffeuses, and everywhere men in hospital blue …

Then at last the windows of the centre balcony were flung open, and the King, Queen, Princess Mary, the Duke of Connaught, and Princess Patricia appeared, to the accompaniment of a cheer that seemed as if it would lift the sky …'

Saturday 19 July [1919] One ought to say something about Peace day, I suppose … Rain held off till some half hour ago. The servants had a triumphant morning. They stood on Vauxhall Bridge & saw everything. Generals & soldiers & tanks & nurses & bands took 2 hours in passing. It was they said the most splendid sight of their lives. Together with the Zeppelin raid it will play a great part in the history of the Boxall family. But I don't know – it seems to me a servants' festival; some thing got up to pacify & placate 'the people' – & now the rain's spoiling it … There's something calculated & politic & insincere about these peace rejoicings. Moreover they are carried out with no beauty, & not much spontaneity … Yesterday in London the usual sticky stodgy conglomerations of people, sleepy & torpid as a cluster of drenched bees, were crawling over Trafalgar Square, & rocking about the pavements in the neighbourhood. The one pleasant sight I saw … some long tongue shaped streamers attached to the top of the Nelson column licked the air, furled & unfurled, like the gigantic tongues of dragons … I can't deny that I feel a little mean at writing so lugubriously; since we're all supposed to keep up the belief that we're glad & enjoying ourselves.

Sunday 20 July [1919] Perhaps I will finish the account of the peace celebrations. What herd animals we are after all! – even the most disillusioned. At any rate, after sitting through the procession & the peace bells unmoved, I began … to feel that if something was going on, perhaps one had better be in it … First lighting a row of glass lamps, & seeing that the rain was stopped, we went out just before ten. Explosions had for some time promised fireworks. The doors of the public house at the corner were open, & the room crowded; couples waltzing; songs being shouted, waveringly, as if one must be drunk to sing. A troop of little boys with lanterns were parading the Green, beating sticks. Not many shops went to the expense of electric light. A woman of the upper classes was supported dead drunk between two men partially drunk. We followed a moderate stream flowing up the Hill. Illuminations were almost extinct half way up, but we kept on till we reached the terrace. And then we did see something – not much indeed, for the damp had deadened the chemicals. Red & green & yellow & blue balls rose slowly into the air, burst, flowered into an oval of light, which dropped in minute grains & expired. There were hazes of light at different points. Rising over the Thames, among trees, these rockets were beautiful; the light on the faces of the crowd was strange; yet of course there was grey mist muffling everything, & taking the blaze off the fire. It was a melancholy thing to see the incurable soldiers lying in bed at the Star & Garter with their backs to us, smoking cigarettes, & waiting for the noise to be over.

1915–30

Avant-garde interiors

Post-war fashions in interior design were generally a radical departure from what had gone before. Dora Black, soon to be Bertrand Russell's second wife, was an emancipated woman. She lived, after 1915, at Cheyne Walk, Chelsea, and later on the fringes of Bloomsbury – bohemian London.

I went to live in Cheyne Walk, Chelsea, at the shabby end, then the home of working artists. From here I looked out on to the power station chimneys and Turner sunsets ... the first real place of my own.

Life in Chelsea suited me. I had begun to abandon bourgeois styles of dress ... it has always been customary for 'arty' people to dress for beauty or bizarre effect rather than for fashion. We made our own clothes, at this time peasant-style pinafore dresses of vivid cretonne, over a very bright, coloured blouse. Bright colours in furnishings and decoration were replacing the patterned chintzes and soft hues of the ornate Edwardian period, rooms were no longer cluttered up with all sorts of bric-a-brac, Roger Fry's Omega workshops made amazing carpets, Heals were there with new style painted furniture, ornamented with a characteristic bright blue, red, green or orange.

The next thing was to find a place ... where I could stay in vacations [she had a Fellowship at Girton]. Obviously this had to be near the British Museum, in that part of London which was a sort of Mecca or Holy of Holies to intellectuals, Bloomsbury ...

In 1919 I had the luck to find a top-floor flat at 24, John Street in a row of good Georgian houses ... I had the flat decorated in the bright, fashionable colours ... for a wide Heal divan I incurred my first debt – of £10 – for which I had to save; I explored the second-hand labyrinths of Tottenham Court Road ... most of the furniture is still with me; I write now seated on an old upright Heal painted chair.

Another avant-garde aesthetic trend of the 1920s was jazz-modern, exemplified in the fictional account of a smart flat in Gordon Square, Bloomsbury – thought to be based upon that of Lady Rhondda, founder of *Time and Tide* magazine.

Joan was surprised at the starkness of Helen's own [flat]. The room was a study in silver and red. The walls and ceiling were covered in dull silver. The woodwork was quite straight, no mouldings, no curves anywhere, and painted a bright red. The chairs were of ebony and upholstered in silver-grey, and the table had a top of hammered silver. Dulled white glass with geometrical black and red lines drawn on it make curious lampshades. Against this background a vivid primitive with a gold sky shone like a jewel in a case.

Generally, however, the preferred architectural style of the late 1920s was neo-Georgian. Architect Philip Tilden described his decorative scheme for his house in Pelham Crescent, South Kensington.

I took my tempera paint and started to decorate the whole house. Structurally we had done little or nothing save to rip out the Victorian grates and mantles, substituting open fireplaces lined with grey narrow brick, with surrounds of marble bolection mouldings. It is astonishing how this innovation from the end of the seventeenth century ... gives a gentlemanly air of stabilized taste to any room ... nearly all my friends at that time insisted upon doing the same thing ... by the use of a pleasant fancy in paint I tried to knit it all together. I pillared the hall ... The dining room was simple, with its marbled walls ... The banisters of the stairs were vivid red, and ... giant painted figures on the walls processed with one ... we put colour or brilliance where we thought it was needed most.

1920s/30s

The East End Jewish community

By the inter-war years the East End was in some areas almost entirely settled by Jews – mostly those who had left Russia before 1914 to escape the Tsarist pogroms. Emanuel Litvinoff's memories were of life at the poorest extreme of that community, for his anarchist father had gone back to

full of synagogues, backroom factories and little grocery stores reeking of pickled herring, garlic sausage and onion bread ...

My first coherent memory [was] of moving to our two-roomed flat and tiny kitchen in Fuller Street Buildings, Bethnal Green; with us were our sewing-machine and a cartload of second-hand furniture ... furniture was arranged, a kettle went on the gas and the women of the tenement came in to welcome us in a chatter of excited Yiddish ...

The tenement was a village in miniature, a place of ingathered exiles who supplemented their Jewish speech with phrases in Russian, Polish or Lithuanian. We sang songs of the ghettoes or folk-tunes of the old Russian Empire and ate the traditional dishes of its countryside ...

People spoke of Warsaw, Kishinev, Kiev, Kharkov, Odessa as if they were neighbouring suburbs.

LEFT *The East End garment trade, since the 1880s a predominantly Jewish business.*

Russia, leaving his seamstress mother pregnant with her fourth child. Typical of new immigrant communities, life in the East End held tightly to memories of Eastern Europe.

Until I was sixteen I lived in the East London borough of Bethnal Green, in a small street ... part of a district populated by persecuted Jews from the Russian empire and transformed into a crowded East European ghetto

OPPOSITE *Granville Square, c.1920, less down-at-heel than Arnold Bennett described it.*

1923

Clerkenwell: fact and fiction

Arnold Bennett's journey to Clerkenwell, presumably misdated in the published journal, was to confirm the physical background for his novel *Riceyman Steps* (1923).

Tuesday, January 15th 1924 [?] Yesterday afternoon I

suddenly decided that I couldn't proceed with my story about Elsie until I had been up to Clerkenwell again. So at 4.50 I got a taxi and went up Myddleton [sic] Square. Just before turning to the left into this Square I saw a blaze of light with the sacred name of Lyons at the top in fire, far higher than anything else; also a cinema sign, etc., making a glaring centre of pleasure. I said, surely that can't be the Angel, Islington, and I hoped that it might be some centre that I had never heard of or didn't know of. Certainly its sudden appearance over roofs was very dramatic. However, the old chauffeur said of course it was Islington. Rather a disappointment.

Myddleton Sq. with its Norman windows of its 4-storey houses, and church nearly in middle, with clock damnably striking the quarters, was very romantic. I had to correct several of my memories of the architecture. I walked round the Square gazing, and going up to front-doors and examining door plates and making

notes under gas lamps (very damp and chilly) while the taxi followed me slowly in the mud. Then I drove up to the Angel and saw that it had truly been conquered and annexed by the Lyons ideals. Still, it was doing good up in Islington, much good. Compare its brightness and space to the old Angel's dark stuffiness. Then I drove to Dr Griffin's to get information about the organisation of the life of panel doctors. I got home at 6.30 and I had been in other worlds, though less than two hours away in all.

Riceyman Steps is set in a miser's second-hand bookshop on the King's Cross Road, on the tram-car route to the West End. The confectioner's shop was across the road. Riceyman Square was Granville Square. Although he had

lived in London since 1888, Bennett rarely set his novels there. In the extracts from the novel he conveys the sense of the different worlds to be found a stone's throw apart.

The girl usually began half-holidays by helping her friends ... in Riceyman Square, whether by skilled cleansing in the unclean dirty house or ... by taking children out for an excursion into the more romantic leafy regions of Clerkenwell up towards the north-east, such as Myddelton Square, where there was room to play and opportunity for tumbling about in pleasant outdoor dirt ... The doctor's house – or, rather, the house of which he occupied the lower part – was one of the larger houses in the historic Myddelton Square, and stood at the corner of the Square and New River Street. The clock of St Mark's showed two minutes to the hour, but already patients had collected in the ante-room to the surgery in the side-street.

Mrs Arb's shop was the sole building illuminated in Riceyman Steps ... it attracted. The church rose darkly, a formidable mass, in the opening at the top of the steps. The little group of dwelling-houses next to his own establishment showed not a sign of life; they seldom did; he knew nothing of their tenants, and felt absolutely no curiosity concerning them. His little yard abutted on the yard of the nearest house, but the wall between them was seven feet high; no sound ever came over it ...

There were dozens of such little shops in and near King's Cross Road. The stock, and also the ornamentation of the shop came chiefly from the wholesalers of advertised goods made up into universally recognizable packets. Several kinds of tea in large quantities, and picturesque, bright tea-signs all around the shop. Several kinds of chocolate, in several kinds of fancy polished-wood glazed stands ... All manner of patent foods, liquid and solid, each guaranteed to give strength. Two competitors in margarine. Scores of paper bags of flour. Some loaves; two hams, cut into. A milk-churn in the middle of the shop ... And in the linoleum-lined window the cakes and bon-bons which entitled the shop to style itself 'confectioner's'.

1924–5

The British Empire Exhibition

The British Empire Exhibition of 1924–5 was held in the new Wembley Stadium, completed the year before. (Later the stadium, designed to hold 120,000 spectators, housed the 1948 Olympic Games.) The exhibition, a revival of plans that had to be abandoned in 1915, was both innovative and hidebound. The concrete and steel structures for the Palaces of Engineering and Industry, albeit dressed in classical fashion, and the stadium designed by engineer Owen Williams were modern in concept, if not in technology or detail. Cheerful kiosks designed by Joseph Emberton introduced advertising and memorable graphics to the showground. The roads inside were named by Rudyard Kipling, while the big popular attraction was the Amusement Park, featuring the same Water Chute that had entertained Virginia Woolf twenty years earlier at Earl's Court. Karel Capek, the Czech satirist, was amused by it all but also struck by the one-sided nature of the exhibition, emphasized by, as he puts it; 'the terrible silence of the four hundred million', the people of the British Empire.

'The Biggest Samples Fair; or The British Empire Exhibition.' If I am to tell you at the outset what there is most of at the Wembley Exhibition, then decidedly it is the people and the parties of school-children ... From time to time, by dint of infinite patience, I managed to

The Indian section of the Wembley International Exhibition, one of the commercial swansongs of the British Empire.

reach a stand ... I even had the luck to behold a statue of the Prince of Wales, made of Canadian butter ...

Powerlessly I abandon the intention of producing an illustrated guide to the Wembley Exhibition. How am I to portray this commercial cornucopia? ... it is a regular tour round the world, or rather a trip through an overgrown bazaar.

The Palace of Engineering is magnificent; and the finest works of English plastic art are locomotives, ships, boilers, turbines, transformers, queer machines with two horns at the top, machines for all sorts of rotating, shaking and banging ... I do not know what they are called and what they are used for, but they are superb ...

Besides the machines, the exhibition at Wembley displays a twofold spectacle: raw materials and products. The raw materials are usually more attractive and interesting. An ingot of pure tin has something more perfect about it than an engraved and hammered tin dish ...

The British Empire Exhibition is huge and full to overflowing; everything is here, including the stuffed lion and the extinct emu ... The Wembley Exhibition shows what four hundred million people are doing for Europe, and partly also what Europe is doing for them.

1926

The General Strike

The General Strike of 1926 was a nine-day staged withdrawal of virtually all working-class labour. Ostensibly in support of the miners, it also saw the testing of the new Labour party's muscle. Workers in power, transportation, and printing were solidly out, and the famous single page edition of *The Times* was put on to the page by, among others, the young Graham Greene. The General Strike brought out London's 'war-time spirit'; middle-class professionals, in particular, rose to the occasion with all kinds of resourcefulness. The strike was the first such confrontation with unionized labour, and the strikers were the losers. The issue of *The Times* published on Wednesday, 5 May was simply a replicated typewritten page – a unique edition of 'The Thunderer' (see illustration opposite).

THURSDAY MAY 6
The paper resumes normal appearance
Friday May 7 Society Column. Courts postponed. The Lord Chamberlain announces that the Courts arranged

The Times

No. 44263 London Wednesday, May 5, 1926. Price 2d

WEATHER ORECAST. Wind N.E.; fair to dull; risk of rain.

THE GENERAL STRIKE.

A wide response was made yesterday throughout the country to the call of those Unions which had been ordered by the T.U.C. to bring out their members Railway workers stopped generally, though at Hull railway clerks are reported to have resumed duty, confining themselves to their ordinary work, and protested against the strike. Commercial road transport was only partially suspended. In London the tramways and L.G.O.C. services were stopped. The printing industry is practically at a standstill, but lithographers have not been withdrawn, and compositors in London have not received instructions to strike. Large numbers of building operatives, other than those working on housing, came out.

The situation in the engineering trades was confused; men in some districts stopped while in others they continued at work: There was no interference with new construction in the ship building yards, but in one or two districts some of the men engaged on repair work joined in the strike with the dockers.

Food – Supplies of milk and fish brought into Kings Cross, Euston and Paddington were successfully distributed from the Hyde Park Depot and stations. The Milk & Food Controller expects it will be possible to maintain a satisfactory supply of milk to hospitals, institutions, schools, hotels, restaurants and private consumers. Milk will be 6d. per gallon dearer wholesale and 2d. per quart retail today. Smithfield market has distributed 5,000 tons of meat since Monday

Mails – Efforts will be made to forward by means of road transport the mails already shown as due to be dispatched shortly from London. The position is uncertain and the facilities may have to be limited to mails for America, India and Africa.

At Bow Street Mr. Saklatvala, M.P., who was requred asa result of his Hyde Park speech on Saturday to give sureties to abstain rrom making violent and inflammatory speeches, was remanded for two days on bail.

Full tram and (or) bus services were running yesteday at Bristol, Lincoln, Southampton, Aldershot, Bournemouth and Isle-of-Wight, and partial services in Edinburgh, Glasgow, Liverpool, Leeds, Northampton, Cardiff, Portsmouth, Dover

N. Derbyshire and Monmouthshire. Evening papers appeared at Bristol, Southampton, several Lancashire towns and Edinburgh, and typescript issues at Manchester, Birmingham and Aberdeen.

The Atlantic Fleet did not sail on its summer cruise at Portsmouth yesterday. The men went on shore duty.

Road and Rail Transport – There was no railway passenger transport in London yesterday except a few suburban trains. Every available form of transport was used. A few independent omnibuses were running, but by the evening the railway companies, except the District and Tubes, had an improvised service.

Among the railway services to-day will be 6.30 a.m. Manchester to Marylebone; 6.30 a.m. Marylebone to Manchester; 10.10 a.m. Marylebone to Newcastle; 9 a.m. Norwich to London; 9 a.m. King's Cross to York; 3 p.m. King's Cross to Peterborough; 9 p.m. Peterborough to King's Cross. L.M.S. Electric trains will maintain a 40 minutes service. On all sections of the Metropolitan Railway except Moorgate to Finsbury Park, a good service will run to-day from 6.40 a.m.

The Underground hope to work a six minutes service on the Central London Line today from 8 a.m. to 8 p.m. between Wood Lane and Liverpool Street. The following stations only will be open:- Shepherds Bush, Lancaster Gate, Oxford Circus, Tottenham Court Road, Bank, Liverpool Street. A flat fare of 3d will be charged

The Prime Minister had an audience of the King yesteday morning.

There was no indication last night of any attempt to resume negotiations between the Prime Minister and the T.U.C.

The Government is printing an official newspaper, "The British Gazette" which will appear today, price 1d. It will be distributed throughout the London area. Volunteers for the London Underground Railways and for L.G.O.C. omnibuses should communicate with the Commercial Manager's Department. 55 Broadway, S.W.

The Prince of Wales returned to London from Biarritz last night travelling from Paris by air.

for May 13th and 14th have been postponed until further notice.

Many theatres not to close
A false telephone message

Telephone messages were received at many London theatres on Wednesday morning to the effect that the Ministry of Labour desired that they close immediately and that formal confirmation would follow. Upon communication with the Ministry of Labour it was learned that there was not a word of truth in the statement.

Despite all difficulties many theatres are determined to carry on as usual, and there have been good audiences at Drury Lane, the Empire, Hippodrome, London Pavilion, Lyric, Palace, Palladium, Queens, Victoria Palace, and other houses.

The managements of *Rose Marie* and *Lady, be Good*, have arranged a service of motor transport in order to take their employees home after the show.

Eight London theatres – the Apollo, Shaftesbury, His Majesty's, Winter Garden, St Martins, Adelphi, Gaiety and Savoy – have, however, closed.

The Stoll Picture Theatre announces that it will not close down under any circumstances.

MAY 7
Tramcars mobbed

Attempt to run Camberwell service.

The London County Council Tramways Department attempted to provide a service from Camberwell on Wednesday and six cars were brought out from the Camberwell depot. They were manned by volunteers and also by employees of the department. Police officers were on the cars as a guard and one policeman stood by the side of each driver. The attempt produced a storm of opposition on the part of an angry crowd on the Walworth Road. Efforts were made to stop the vehicles and one was considerably damaged by stones. One of the cars succeeded in reaching Westminster, but the others did not proceed. Some of the more violent members of the crowd endeavoured to attack the drivers of the cars. Blows were exchanged and it became necessary for the police to use their truncheons. Eventually the cars returned to the depot.

Seven persons received attention at the Kings College Hospital suffering from cuts and other injuries, one being detained.

Attempts were also made to disorganise the emergency service provided by the London General Omnibus Company at Hammersmith. In some areas a hostile crowd attacked the drivers and conductors, but no serious injuries were inflicted. Efforts were made to damage the engines and cut the petrol pipes.

LETTER FROM 7 MAY ISSUE
May 4 1926
To the Editor,

May I suggest that motorists having room in their cars, and willing to give a lift to anyone needing it should carry a notice on the windscreen stating their destination.

I have today been taking business girls home from

their work in my car, and displayed a notice saying: 'Going in the direction of Camden Town. Ladies can ask for a lift.' I always have my car overflowing, and both men and women stopped and congratulated me on the idea. Several business girls told me that they had to walk very long distances in the morning, although many nearly empty cars passed them. Doubtless the drivers of these cars would have been only too glad to give one or more of them a lift but as the girls pointed out, they could not hail every car to ask in what direction it was going.

Yours faithfully,
Ethel M. Copeman
76 Regents Park Road

Virginia Woolf describes the odd sight of London without public transportation, with uncertainties about the supply of gas or electricity, with non-unionized workers desperate for work and settlement of the dispute. When her friends the Marshalls are injured in a train crash caused by a novice undergraduate driver, the nearness of tragedy to farce becomes apparent.

Wednesday 5 May [1926] An exact diary of the Strike would be interesting. For instance, it is now a 1/4 to 2: there is a brown fog; nobody is building; it is drizzling. The first thing in the morning we stand at the window & watch the traffic in Southampton Row. This is incessant. Everyone is bicycling; motor cars are huddled up with extra people. There are no buses. No placards. No newspapers. The men are at work in the road; water, gas & electricity are allowed; but at 11 the light was turned off.

Thursday 6 May (one of the curious effects of the Strike is that it is difficult to remember the day of the week). Everything is the same, but unreasonably, or because of the weather, or habit, we are more cheerful, take less notice & occasionally think of other things. The taxis are out today. There are various skeleton papers being sold. One believes nothing ...

We get no news from abroad; neither can send it. No parcels. Pence have been added to milk, vegetables &c. And Karin has bought 4 joints.

Friday 7 May No change ... Girl came to make chair covers, having walked from Shoreditch but enjoyed it.

Monday 10 May Yesterday Ralph & Frances Marshall were in a railway accident. She had her teeth jangled. One man was killed; another had his leg broken – the result of driving a train without signals, by the efforts of ardent optimistic undergraduates ...

Tuesday 11 May The Strike was settled about 1.15 – or it was then broadcast ... Message from 10 Downing Street. The T.U.C. leaders have agreed that Strike shall be withdrawn ... I saw this morning 5 or 6 armoured cars slowly going along Oxford Street; on each two soldiers sat in tin helmets, & one stood with his hand at the gun which was pointed straight ahead ready to fire. But I also noticed on one a policeman smoking a cigarette. Such sights I dare say I shall never see again; & dont in the least wish to.

1920s/30s

Working on the River

Even the most skilled workers had little job security in the inter-war period. Alfred Dedman's account of life as a lighterman on the river chronicles his job with its periods of slack and regular searches for piece work to cover the quiet times. He retired as a foreman lighterman on the River Lea in 1975, becoming a messenger for a firm of accountants.

I cannot remember the first day I went to work, but I know I was very nervous ... My father had to sign papers to allow me to be apprenticed ... The company I worked for was J J Smith, whose nickname was Captain Kettle. They called him that because, I was told, he had had a sailing barge of that name that sailed across to France in the First World War. It was a very small firm, only about a dozen barges. We had about four steel barges. The rest were old wooden ones. They used to leak – you would be rowing with one hand and pumping with the other. In those days there was no electric pump – you did it by hand. The freemen who worked for him taught me everything. They were the most skilled men I have met. And they taught me thoroughly, there is no doubt about that. They used to do the most impossible tasks. It was unbelievable to see them drive a barge up river.

I was 14 when I first went on the water. You had to be apprenticed for seven years, which you served in two periods. You worked for two years and then you went up to be tested by a court at the Waterman's Hall. If you passed that you were a licensed lighterman. After seven years you were tested again to become a freeman ... When I started work, all the craft were rowed. There was tug power, but it was in its infancy ... Rowing was done until you reached high water. Then you stopped and waited until the next flood ... You would have two men rowing a barge with a capacity of about 150 tons ...

A lighterman rowing his barge upriver. Beyond is the temporary Waterloo Bridge and the South Bank, including the Shot Tower (demolished in the 1960s). Painting by C. R. W. Nevinson, 1938.

It was a hard life, I can tell you ... I used to do only about six months out of twelve lightering work. To start with I got half a crown a day and sixpence an hour overtime – but you were allowed very little overtime ... When I got my licence it went up considerably, but ... invariably you spent as much time out of work as you did in work ... When I was out of work ... I used to sometimes get jobs as a docker when the docks were very busy ... I've pulled beef out of the freezerboats at Victoria Dock – it took the skin off my shoulders, 180 lb of chilled beef ... I have unloaded mutton down a refrigerator ship. I have done oranges out of the Jarl Line boats down the East India Docks – we used to empty them in about half a day ...

I have walked about for weeks when I have been out of work – in my young days it was the Depression. I have drawn my labour money at Freemason's Road Custom house, given it to the wife to pay the rent and housekeeping and walked about with a halfpenny in my pocket until the next labour money ...

In those days of occasional labour, you got a job like this. There was a place called Poverty Corner, a stretch of pavement outside Mark Lane Tube [now Tower Hill] station ... there were other places like it, but this was the main one. All the out of work lightermen used to go up there and stand on Poverty Corner. The various firms used to come out, take a list of names and then go back into their office. You would wait and they would come back perhaps ten minutes later ... perhaps an hour and pick about five or six out of a hundred men ... You took your chance, just like the docker ... Work was so fluctuating ... that you would get a bunch of ships come in one day and then a period of slackness while the ships turned round. They would all discharge together and all load together ... when those ships sailed together ... everyone would be out of work.

1920s

The social scene

In addition to having an acute eye for social realism, Arnold Bennett was a crisp observer of the London social scene in the late 1920s. American amusements were the rage, whether in the shape of the cinema or the cocktail. He considers the cocktail, and in strong contrast revels in the prim pleasures of the London teashop and finds himself drawn into the premiere of an early 'talkie'.

London, New Year's Day I resolved not to drink cocktails any more. So in the late afternoon I went to a cocktail party. It was convened in the sacred cause of dramatic art. The party had to be serious, but also it had to be smart; it was both. Half the highbrows in London were there. I tried conscientiously to be serious about dramatic art (British variety), and succeeded fairly well ... Very many cocktails were consumed.

Up to a few years ago you could not advance the cause of anything without a banquet more or less expensive. Nowadays you do it to cocktails. The change is for the better. The new method takes a shorter time, and less alcohol is swallowed. I am not in favour of cocktails; but the harm of them is exaggerated by the godly. The amount of spiritous liquid in a cocktail is trifling. The mischief is that people – especially the young – do not confine themselves to one cocktail ...

The cocktail craze will pass. And perhaps by the time it has passed we shall know the origin of the word ...

By how many inches per cocktail consumed the sacred cause of dramatic art was pushed forward at the cocktail party I cannot say. My own personal consumption of nourishment was as follows: Olives, one. Cocktails, none.

Some people have odd notions of romance. I have. When the dailiness of the domestic atmosphere oppresses me in the afternoon, and what I am writing seems flat and getting flatter, I sneak out of the house and go to a Dairy Company's tea-shop in King's Road, and order a pot of China tea ... and ... furtively ... watch my fellow-wassailers. A tea-shop is a wonderful place, in a high degree romantic. The people who come in and go out. The girls together, feminine. The men together, masculine. The men who would no more think of taking their hats off in a tea-shop than in a railway station ... The staid supervisors. The slatternly dish-washers peeping forth now and then. The cash-girl eternally in her cage, and in the draught from the ever-opening and ever-shutting door. One talks of the romantic quality of Paris cafés. They are prose compared to the free-verse of a London tea-shop.

London, September I went by invitation to the 'world-premiere' of an English-written and English-directed talking film, in which Gloria Swanson was the star. The film was apparently made in America. My opinion of Gloria Swanson's gifts as an actress in silent films is very high indeed. I was bidden for nine o'clock, and at nine o'clock I arrived.

The street in front of the theatre was crowded with sightseers, some of whom were perched on the tops of lorries used as grandstands. A broad path across the pavement was kept clear by the united efforts of policemen and theatre officials ... The big theatre was crowded, except in the best seats round about me, which had been reserved for guests whose names have a publicity value ... A silent film was already in progress, and it continued ... for an hour or so ... it did at length finish. Then a gentleman came in front of the curtain and said ... 'Miss Gloria Swanson is in the audience and if you will kindly remain in your seats for one minute after the conclusion of the new film, you will see her.' At these words there was a great noise from the audience – a curious kind of clapping not intended to signify approval. The talking film began. The noise increased. So much so that the film, though it could be seen, could not be heard at all. The film-operator and the audience were equally obstinate ... The audience won. Gloria Swanson, who was seated a few rows behind me, stood up in the gangway and bowed. Useless! Half the audience could not see her. The audience grew still more restive. The noise was resentful and imperious ...

She left the circle, and was presently seen walking up the centre aisle of the floor, well escorted. Then she came before the curtain, obviously in a highly nervous condition, and made a little speech, which was almost inaudible. As soon as she had retired, at least two-thirds of the huge audience on the floor stood up and hurried from the theatre. They had come to see, not the film, but Gloria Swanson ...

The film started again ... I could discover ... no merit except the striking merit of Gloria Swanson's performance ... She proved that a great star of the silent can be equally great as a star of the talking ... She even sang. The songs were her one mistake ...

I left the theatre saddened by this spectacle of the waste of a first-rate artist. The space across the pavement was still being kept by policemen and commissionaires . . . suddenly order vanished . . . Gloria Swanson had appeared in the entrance-hall. She fled back . . . Order was restored and Gloria Swanson slipped into the film-star's immense and luxurious automobile which was waiting . . . What an evening! What a light thrown on the mentality of the film fan!

1930s

Two French views

London's continued status as a tourist attraction, from the nineteenth century onwards, ensured the city's cosmopolitanism as well as providing a useful source of foreign currency. Two indefatigable visitors who approached London from rather different viewpoints were the French philosopher Jean Paul Sartre and his companion, writer Simone de Beauvoir. When they came for twelve days in the early 1930s, she recorded her impressions.

We spent our Easter vacation in London. Here was a city that was bigger than Paris and quite new to us. We sallied forth into the streets, and walked for hours on end. Piccadilly, the City, Hampstead, Putney, Greenwich: we were determined to see everything. We would clamber up to the deck of a big red bus, drive out to the suburbs, and make our way back on foot. We would have lunch in a Lyons or a Soho restaurant or one of the old chophouses of the Strand, and set out once more. Sometimes it rained, and we didn't know where to take shelter: the absence of cafés disconcerted us. One afternoon the only refuge we could find was in the Underground.

We amused ourselves by observing the conventions of English life. When women came down to breakfast in our hotel dining room they wore astonishing garments somewhere between a tea gown and an evening dress. Men really did wear bowler hats and carry umbrellas in the afternoon. Soapbox orators *did* hold forth every evening at Hyde Park Corner. The shabby taxis and peeling posters and teashops and ugly window-dressing all disorientated us. We spent hours in the National Gallery, and stayed behind in the Tate to stare at Van Gogh's yellow chair and sunflowers. In the evenings we went to the cinema . . .

I had to admit that despite our private entente certain discrepancies of outlook existed between Sartre and myself. I went to the heart of London looking for traces of Shakespeare and Dickens: I explored the byways of Old Chiswick with a sense of rapturous discovery: I

dragged Sartre around all the London parks, to Kew Gardens and even as far as Hampton Court. He lingered in lower-class districts, trying to guess at the lives and thoughts of the thousands of unemployed persons who dwelt in these joyless streets.

1933

Down and out

With *Down and Out in Paris and London* (1933) George Orwell took advantage of a dip in his fortunes to observe the condition of the poor. He wanted to see how a penniless, homeless man arriving in the city would fare. With ten shillings and twopence for the month (but acknowledging he could borrow more) he set out, first pawning his clothes. He explored sleeping on the streets, in Rowton Houses (one shilling a night) and Salvation Army hostels. As he concluded: 'here is the world that awaits you if you are ever penniless.'

My new clothes had put me instantly into a new world . . . Dressed in a tramp's clothes it is very difficult, at any rate for the first day, not to feel that you are genuinely degraded . . .

At about eleven I began looking for a bed. I had read about doss-houses . . . and I supposed that one could get a bed for fourpence or thereabouts. Seeing a man, a navvy or something of the kind, standing . . . in the Waterloo Road I stopped and questioned him. I said that I was stony broke and wanted the cheapest bed I could get.

'Oh' said he, 'you go to that 'ouse across the street there, with the sign "Good Beds for Single Men." . . . I bin there myself on and off. You'll find it cheap *and* clean.' . . .

I paid the shilling, and the boy led me up a rickety unlighted staircase to a bedroom . . . the windows seemed to be tight shut, and the air was almost suffocating at first. There was a candle burning, and I saw that the room measured fifteen feet square by eight high, and had eight beds in it. Already six lodgers were in bed, queer lumpy shapes with all their own clothes, even their boots, piled on top of them. Someone was coughing in a loathsome manner in one corner . . .

I had about an hour's sleep in all . . . The walls were leprous, and the sheets, three weeks from the wash, were almost raw umber colour . . . I was going to wash, when I noticed that every basin was streaked with grime . . . I went out unwashed . . . Altogether, the lodging-house had not come up to its description . . . It was however, as I found later, a fairly representative lodging-house.

All day I loafed in the streets, east as far as Wapping, west as far as Whitechapel. It was queer after Paris; everything was so much cleaner and quieter and drearier ... It was the land of the tea urn and the Labour Exchange, as Paris is the land of the *bistro* and the sweatshop.

1934

A countryman's view

The attraction of London for those born and brought up in the countryside never fades. In 1934 Laurie Lee set off from his Gloucestershire village to walk to London.

Coming out of a wood near Beaconsfield, I suddenly saw London at last – a long smoky skyline hazed by the morning sun and filling the whole of the eastern horizon ... emitting a faint, metallic roar.

No architectural glories, no towers or palaces, just a creeping insidious presence, its vast horizontal broken here and there by a gasholder or factory chimney. Even so, I could already feel its intense radiation – an electric charge in the sky – that rose from its million roofs in a quivering mirage, magnetically, almost visibly dilating.

Cleo, my girl-friend, was somewhere out there ... Also mystery, promise, chance, and fortune – all I had come to this city to find. I hurried towards it, impatient now, its sulphur stinging my nostrils. I had been a month on the road, and the suburbs were long and empty. In the end I took a tube.

Working on a building site and moving from one set of lodgings to another, Laurie Lee tried to come to terms with the scale of London.

As for the great spread of London, which I'd come to discover, I don't think I even began to get the feel of it then. Its dimensions were all wrong for my country-grown mind, too out-of-scale for my experience to cope with. In any case I was twenty, when environment plays tricks ... I just floated around in a capsule of self-absorption ...

But I can remember the presence of London, its physical toughness at that time, its homespun, knock-about air. There was more life in the streets (it cost money inside) and people thronged outdoors in the evenings. One saw them standing on corners, in the doorways of pubs, talking in groups, eating from paper bags. And the streets themselves had an almost rustic confusion – Edwardian transport in all its last-ditch vigour: rattling old buses, coster ponies and traps, prim little taxis like upright pianos, and huge dray wagons laden with beer and flour and drawn by teams of magnificent horses ... Private cars were few, and were often a sign of ill-omen, particularly when parked in a side street, where the sight of a car outside a terraced house might well mean the doctor or death ...

After paying for my lodgings I had £1 to spend, which could be broken up in a hundred ways. A tot of whisky cost sixpence, a pint of beer fourpence-halfpenny, cigarettes were elevenpence for twenty. The best seats in the cinema cost ninepence to a shilling, or I could climb to the gallery for threepence. Then there were fairs and music halls, Russian ballet at the Alhambra, Queen's Hall concerts – seldom more than a shilling ...

It was a time of rootless enjoyment.

1930s

A reluctant debutante

Some aspects of life in London had changed little despite the cataclysm of the Great War. Social life readjusted its balance, and society went about its business. Jessica Mitford's family, the Redesdales, lived the traditional life of the aristocracy, moving between the country and the city in a manner scarcely altered from a century before. She describes the Kensington town house to which the family adjourned at certain fixed times of year and her own experience in the early 1930s of being a debutante who did not fit the mould.

The West End of London was in those days partitioned into a number of distinct residential districts, with nothing haphazard or fortuitous about them ... The very rich and fashionable lived in Mayfair, Belgravia, Park Lane; the artistic, literary and bohemian gravitated towards Chelsea or even Bloomsbury; Hampstead, Hammersmith and St. John's Wood were middle-class; while the substantial London houses of run-of-the-mill squires, knights, baronets and barons were found in Kensington, Paddington, Marylebone and Pimlico.

We were in the last category. Our huge, seven-storey house at 26, Rutland Gate in Kensington reflected comfort and serviceability rather than elegance. There was even a passenger lift which my father had installed and of which he was immensely proud ...

A bevy of debutantes – most of whom look quite as out of place as Jessica Mitford found herself at Queen Charlotte's Ball, the highspot of the season. From The Tatler, *28 May 1930.*

We used the house in Rutland Gate only occasionally for the London season. Most of the time it was either let or stood unoccupied; then, very, very rarely, one or two of us were allowed to stay for a few days with Nanny in the Mews, a tiny flat, formerly chauffeur's quarters, at the back of the house over the garage. We considered this a tremendous treat. Life in the Mews had the quality of camping out. There was no cook there, so Nanny did the cooking . . . Even having one's bath was an adventure at the Mews. The Bathroom, with its ancient, claw-foot bath, was dominated by a big, round, evil-smelling water-heater called The Amberley. Lighting it was an action fraught with danger . . .

A move up to the big house at Rutland Gate was a very different matter, resembling the evacuation of a small army . . . The sleeping furniture seemed to come slowly back to life as the dust-sheets were removed one by one; familiar objects, half-forgotten since the last time we stayed in London, were exposed to view to be examined and fingered.

Tediously angelic were the forms and faces of the hundreds of seventeen-to-twenty-one-year-old Anglo-Saxons who frequented the deb dances.

Conversation wasn't much of a clue to identity. After initial introductions, one would stumble on to the dance floor in the arms of one of the Australian sheep.

Opening gambits were generally restricted to two or three subjects: 'D'you do much riding?' 'Do you get up to Scotland much?' 'Care for night-clubs?' . . .

The London season lasts for about three months in the summer; to me, it seemed to drag on for ever . . .

As the season drew to an end, it became cruelly evident that it had been a complete waste of time. I had made no friends, had learned nothing, was no further advanced in planning my life.

1928

An architect's view

Steen Eiler Rasmussen's classic account of London conveyed the perceptions of both the overseas visitor and the professional. Architect, town planner, and social observer he brilliantly characterized the form and development of London, while recognizing what was new and best in the London he had first visited and written about in 1928. He mourned the loss of the Regent Street Quadrant and disliked the florid commercial buildings rising in the City and elsewhere, 'covered with columns and cornices and innumerable traditional details . . . details which have lost all interest hundreds of years ago, and are now merely repeated mechanically to suit the taste of some mercantile magnate'. He did, however, find style in two aspects of contemporary London – advertising hoardings and London Transport, in which he preferred the new Holden-designed stations to the Victorian railway termini.

For the past three months I have been trying to

understand London's architecture – not just by looking at buildings, but also by spending time every day with London architects and talking the subject over with them ...

How promising the early stages of new buildings in London seem to be! Rows of old houses disappear, high hoardings go up and are covered with enormous and colourful posters. In reality, this is the best stage of the building process: darkness has yielded to light, and England's colourful hoardings are much preferred to the pictures at its annual Royal Academy Exhibition. The mighty cranes, too, are beautiful. They rear into the sky upon three towering legs of steel ... Respect for the authority of the engineer catches our imagination ... In time, the elevations are covered with wooden scaffolding, and a new architecture takes shape ... Then, one fine day, the building stands before us in all

I hoped to find modern architecture in London. I found only Lutyens – who is not modern. The only true modern construction is, taken as a whole, not architecture: the Underground. But this is more important for London than all the works of Lutyens and England's other famous architects put together. It is also very well managed. When it rains in London, posters rapidly appear saying 'If you want to miss the rain, take the Underground'. If you want to miss the chaos of London's architecture, take the Underground too.

At Piccadilly Circus there is an excellent illustration of what the Underground has done for modern civilization. After experiencing annoyance at the bad taste shown by prominent architects in the rebuilding of the Quadrant, one need only vanish down the stairways leading to the Underground and one finds oneself

LEFT *Turnpike Lane Underground station, one of the series designed by Charles Holden on the northern section of the Piccadilly line, photographed shortly after its opening.*

OPPOSITE *Fascists stepping out with Sir Oswald Mosely and his Blackshirts in the East End, 4 October 1936.*

its stone-clad, frozen unimaginativeness. It may, like the new Liberty's, be a historical fake in Elizabethan half-timberwork; it may be in the Beaux-Arts style and sport giant columns in front of its steel frame, like Selfridge's ... or it may look like an Italian villa blown up to grotesque size, like Devonshire House, Piccadilly. Perhaps it will be 'modern' and turn out even worse ... Whichever, it will be coarse and disrespectful in scale, an unfeeling essay in the styles, slapped on to its steel frame ...

amidst surroundings which are different and far more refined ... the Underground Railway Station ... is planned as a large oval with exits and entrances all round it leading to the street ... This subterranean station is a thoroughfare ... In the morning it is like a turbine grinding out human beings on all sides. In the evening it sucks them in again, through the circle and down the escalators to the rushing stream of trains. The architects who have designed it have done the right thing in the right way. Everything is made of a smooth material easy to clean and always looking neat and orderly ... it is a pleasure to go down into the stations of the Underground, bright clean and orderly as they are ... Here, there, and everywhere, posters and signboards are the only decoration. And the signboards are many. It is never necessary to ask the way, the stranger finds his way about on the Underground as easily as the Londoner ... In 1916 the Company communicated with an expert in lettering, Edward Johnston ... He designed a really first-rate alphabet ... the very quintessence of the Roman lettering. One can look at it year after year without growing tired of it. It is now used for the names of all the stations and for all the signboards of the stations.

1934–6

Fascist marches and Jubilee celebrations

Kingsley Martin's regular pieces in the *New Statesman*, of which he was editor, from 1931 are a chronicle of London seen from the Left. Here, Martin observes the menacing events of the mid-1930s, which were to culminate in the battle of Cable Street in October 1936 between Oswald Mosley's Blackshirts and his opponents. Against the background of this increasingly disturbing atmosphere came the innocuous celebration of the Silver Jubilee of George V and Queen Mary.

15 September, 1934 I spent a pleasant Sunday afternoon in Hyde Park studying the broad backs of London policemen and listening to the remarks of an almost universally anti-Fascist crowd. When I arrived the counter-demonstration was in full swing. There were four entirely orderly mass meetings at which, I think, the general non-political public was scarcely represented at all. How large this counter-demonstration was, I cannot tell ... I noticed that *The Times* in an admirably objective report said that the anti-Fascist processions 'which came from all parts of London, took nearly an hour to enter the park' ... The Fascist lines marched in while the counter-demonstration was still proceeding. The Blackshirts were carefully counted and numbered about 2,500. They found waiting for them (several hundred yards away from the counter-demonstration) a large oblong enclosure created by a tight cordon of police. Inside it there were mounted police, four fascist wagons and platforms for the press. The Blackshirts were received within this *cordon sanitaire*, and that was very nearly all that anyone saw of them for the rest of the afternoon. Over the heads of the police one could

see gesticulating blackshirted figures ... trying to make speeches against the noise of the crowd and of the autogyro which hovered overhead. But I do not think that any single person, except a policeman or a Blackshirt, heard a single word that came from a Fascist platform. As for the display, unless one used a looking-glass as a periscope, the only glimpses one got of the Blackshirts were through the legs of policemen. It was rather like trying to get near the cages at the Zoo on a Bank Holiday.

11 May, 1935 The most hard-boiled critics have been pleasantly surprised by the Silver Jubilee celebrations ... I got, indeed, the impression that the occasion was answering an acute need – the crowd devoured the colour and the music and the pageantry and the bright lights like starving men falling upon food. It is seventeen years since London's last Bacchanalia, far too

long a time. The autocrats have learnt that men require collective rejoicings, and it is essential that the democracies bestow upon themselves the same opportunities for pleasure. It is notorious that Louis Napoleon became an Emperor because under a constitutional monarchy France was bored.

18 May, 1935 It was on the Saturday night that the Jubilatory excitement reached its most delirious point. The invaders turned Trafalgar Square, Piccadilly Circus and Regent Street into ballrooms; they perched themselves on the running-boards and luggage-carriers of every private car which tried to nose its way through them, and outside the Piccadilly Hotel they were calling obstinately for the dance band which plays there to come out and play for them: 'We want Sidney Kite, we want Sidney Kite!' Mounted police, who were controlling the situation with remarkable tact, found themselves slightly embarrassed when the crowd, instead of dispersing in front of them, insisted upon patting their horses ... The final word on the whole business lies perhaps with a banner in an East End slum dwelling – 'Lousy, but Loyal.'

24 October, 1936 I have this week talked to several people who live in the East End and have intimate knowledge of recent events. They agree that Mosley's march was deliberate provocation; it was to go through almost wholly Jewish streets where Fascism could win no adherents. 'We've gotta get rid of the Yids' was the mildest and most printable of the insults flung ... Mosley is rapidly making converts for Communism and mobilizing some anti-Semitism to his side. Dr Harry Roberts, who knows the East End as only a popular doctor who has worked there for many years can know it, tells me that most of the victims of the riot who have come to his surgery have been silly youths of from fifteen to eighteen years of age who have been induced to shout with the Fascists. They have no political opinions, but are merely budding Jew-baiters. On the other side, he quotes a woman whom he heard say to her child: 'Stop your grizzling or I'll give you to the Blackshirts!'

1936

Abdication crisis

Because of its constitutional implications, the abdication crisis was played out in the House of Commons. In his diary Harold Nicolson watches events inside and outside the House, while Kingsley Martin observes reaction by Londoners.

30th November, 1936 I go to see Ramsay MacDonald. He talks to me in deep sorrow about the King. 'That man', he says, 'has done more harm to this country than any man in history.' It seems that the Cabinet are determined that he shall abdicate. So are the Privy Council. But he imagines that the country, the great warm heart of the people, are with him. I do not think so. The upper classes mind her being an American more than they mind her being divorced. The lower classes do not

mind her being an American but loathe the idea that she has had two husbands already.

3rd December, 1936 I dash off without dinner to Islington. There I find the Rev. Paxton much disturbed at the King crisis. The streets flame with posters, 'King and Mrs Simpson'. I gave my address on biography ... At the end Paxton asked them to sing the National Anthem 'as a hymn'. They all stand up ... but only about ten people out of 400 join in the singing. Poor Paxton is much upset ...

I do not find people angry with Mrs Simpson. But I

do find a deep and enraged fury against the King himself ...

10th December, 1936 The House is crowded and rather nervous and noisy ...

The [Speaker] rises and reads out the message of Abdication in a quavering voice. The feeling that any moment he may break down from emotion increases our own emotion. I have never known in any assemblage such accumulation of pity and terror.

On Thursday morning when it was said that the King was to abdicate one heard nothing among poor people but sorrow. The King was as popular with the working class as he had become unpopular with the well-to-do.

This tolerant attitude is, if reports are true, almost confined to London.

1937–9

The spread of suburbia

By the mid-1930s the spread of suburbia was an increasing concern. Municipal housing had been beaten back into the city, where the LCC were building solid six- and seven-storey blocks, but the developers continued with their work on the edges of town. Conservationists were up in arms as the first extract, Howard Marshall's outburst in *Britain and the Beast,* demonstrates. Between 1937 and 1939 Doris Scott lived in Dagenham, where the Becontree 'cottage estate' had

OPPOSITE *News-stands in Parliament Square announce the, by then, expected abdication of Edward VIII on 10 December 1936.*

RIGHT *Aerial photograph over Hendon, 1939, showing the Great North Road and the recently built developments, both factories and housing, reaching out into the countryside conducted by the building of roads.*

this new method of planning homes in mile-long ribbons along the arterial roads ... Behind the noisy roads ... lie patches and spaces apparently unused by man; for the people who inhabit these ribboned roads have no contact with the land.

I hated it, living out there altered your whole way of life, really. The streets were very long and you had to trek half a mile or a mile to the nearest shops. Well, I didn't approve of that, that was too far for my liking. Especially after I'd been used to living quite close to a

taken 18 years to complete and housed over 100,000 people. Mrs Scott fled back to the comforting and familiar networks of the East End.

To realize the muddling and blundering that is going on ... you must get up into the air and see what combined greed and lack of design may do to make the world ugly ...

A glance at Barnet by-pass on its way from Finchley to Hatfield ... As soon as this road leaves the dense suburban belt that extends to Mill Hill, this dreary trimming of its edges by little houses begins and continues for miles; one comes to realize the extent of

market in Canning Town, that was much cheaper and more convenient. And it was terribly lonely and boring, it seemed so dead. I was used to being with people all the time, and I used to know most of the people in our street. But out on the estate the lights seemed to go out at eight o'clock everywhere and there was nothing to do. Another thing was you spent so much time travelling and it took your husband so long to get home, that by then it was too late to do much, like ... going out for a drink. In any case the pubs out there were very few and far between.

And where I'd lived before, Mother was on hand to babysit. I remember I spent so much time going back on the bus to see mother and my old friends that she said 'you might as well live here.' So that's what we did, we went back to rooms in Canning Town. I wasn't the only one that did, lots couldn't settle, droves of us went back. We were glad to get back to civilization.

1930s

Working for the movies

During the 1930s the British film industry succeeded (with the help of favourable legislation) in beating back the tide of Hollywood. Since the best actors liked to divide their time between stage and screen, the British studios were tied to London – generally on suburban or industral sites. Within London itself, the Ealing Film Studios became the best-known enterprise. All the studios needed the services of what in modern terminology would be called post-production facilities. Quentin Crisp was one toiler in this world, albeit briefly, typically attracted by the phoney glamour that soon fell away on closer examination.

While I had been living the furnished life in Chelsea, among the inmates of the house ... had been the secretary of a film producer. As well as she could she had explained me to her employer. Without seeing one of the dingy letterheads and layouts of advertisements in such papers as the *Fur Times* and the *Cactus Journal* which were pasted into my book of specimens, he had offered me the job of lettering the titles of a number of travelogues he had made ...

I could hardly keep pace with the work, partly because there was so much of it and partly because the lettering of a film was never commissioned until a few days before the trade show. The movie business has a genius for bringing some kind of chaos out of order.

Of course lettering credits was only another form of commercial art. It required the speed, the high gloss that I had always lacked, but because it was connected with the movies, for me it had glamour. I flailed my limbs so wildly in my efforts to cling on that at one moment I caught hold, by accident, of an art director-ship ...

Working for the movies was the first job I ever wanted to do for reasons other than to show I could ... I applied for and, to my amazement, obtained a job in Studio Film Laboratories. This was a mistake. I was not able to flit from room to room learning the secret of the celluloid universe. I was confined to the art department where, even if my ineptitude had not almost immedi-

ately been unmasked, I do not think I would have lasted long ...

I became a model.

1939

War declared

If World War I had left London relatively unscathed, the capital became a prime target in World War II with the development of effective air power. The threat of a concerted air attack by a deadly force of bomber aircraft was profoundly alarming. Radar, becoming sophisticated by the late 1930s, offered an important line of defence but was not infallible. By the time war was declared on 3 September 1939 the country and above all London feared the very worst from Hitler's Luftwaffe. Prime Minister Neville Chamberlain broadcast to the nation at 11.15 a.m. At 11.40 Harold Nicolson, assiduous diarist and MP for West Leicester, walked over to the House of Commons with colleagues Leo Amery, Anthony Eden and Duff Cooper.

Hardly have we left 28 Queen Anne's Gate when a siren blows. Amery says, 'They ought not to do that after what we have heard on the wireless. People will think it is an air-raid warning.' Hardly has he said these words when another siren takes it up. 'My God!' I say 'it *is* an air-raid warning!' ... We walk on trying to make casual conversation. The sirens scream all around us and policemen wave at us ... We reach Parliament Square. As we enter it the crowd, which had massed itself against the railings, breaks up like a flock of pigeons. They run away towards Westminster Hospital. They cut across the grass plot where the statues are ... The police there [in the House] are in steel helmets and tell us to go down to the air-raid refuge. I do so, and find the corridor towards the Harcourt Room blocked by all manner of people from Cabinet Ministers to cooks. It is very hot. People chat to each other with forced geniality. After ten minutes we are released and go on to the terrace. People assert that they heard gunfire and bombs dropping. I suggest that it was merely the carpenters nailing in the asbestos lining to the windows ... we watch with disapproval the slow movements of people at Lambeth trying to get a [barrage] balloon to rise. It has been dampened by last night's rain.

At noon we return to the Chamber. The Speaker takes his seat with the usual calm procedure. We have prayers. The Prime Minister then makes a speech which is restrained and therefore effective. He looks very ill ...

The sirens continue during the debate ... We learn afterwards that the whole raid-warning was a mistake.

The pattern of false alarms, massive evacuation, resentment, and confusion marked the early months of the war in London, the 'phoney war'. Schools closed, lest they become targets. Many women and children who had left on the declaration of war with Germany were back within the year. The psychological strain of preparing for attacks that never came was intense for Londoners. Harold Nicolson, with a discernible curl of the lip, records concerns voiced in the House regarding the evacuation programme.

14th September, 1939 The House is mainly concerned with the evacuation of children. It seems that where children have been evacuated along with their school-

between the urban and the rural poor. This is a perplexing social event. One thing that they say is that these children were evacuated at the end of the holidays and were therefore more verminous and undisciplined than if they had been taken in the middle of the term. But the effect will be to demonstrate to people how deplorable is the standard of life and civilization among the urban poor.

1939/40

The war takes hold

Long before the Blitz, Hitler was working hard at sapping civilian morale. A few islands of calm remained: one such event was the famous lunchtime recital given by Myra Hess at the National Gallery (by then emptied of its treasures),

Mothers anxiously watch their children leave Waterloo station under the evacuation scheme set up in the early months of the war.

teachers everything has gone well. But when the mothers have come, there has been trouble. Many of the children are verminous and have disgusting habits. This horrifies the cottagers upon whom they have been billeted. Moreover, the mothers refuse to help, grumble dreadfully, and are pathetically homesick and bored. Many of them have drifted back to London. Much ill feeling has been caused. But the interesting thing is that this feeling is not between the rich and the poor but

here commented on by Kingsley Martin. On a less happy note, George Orwell saw the wave of anti-Italian feeling that followed Mussolini's declaration of war.

14 October, 1939 Here is a stroke of imagination in high places! At one o'clock every day, except Saturdays and Sundays, and at 4.30 on Tuesdays and Fridays there is now music at the National Gallery. Miss Myra Hess, who has organized these concerts, and Sir Kenneth

Clark, who has given them a home, deserve every congratulation ... at the first concert – though there had been little publicity – there was an audience of a thousand. I found the occasion deeply moving. On the walls the carved frames, emptied of their altarpieces, bore witness to the ravages of a war that is aimed at

Dame Myra Hess keeps warm in fur as she gives her regular lunchtime piano recital at the National Gallery, empty of its pictures, during wartime.

every token of civilization. But as the first bars of Scarlatti sounded under Miss Hess's fingers, they seemed to reconstruct the exiled paintings ... One's belief in the worth of man was thus restored – at the cost of a shilling.

12 June [1940] I last night walked through Soho to see whether the damage to Italian shops etc was as reported. It seemed to have been exaggerated in the newspapers, but we did see, I think, 3 shops which had had their windows smashed. The majority had hurriedly labelled themselves 'British'. Gennari's, the Italian grocer's, was plastered over with printed placards saying 'This establishment is entirely British'. The Spaghetti House, a shop specialising in Italian food-

stuffs, had renamed itself 'British Food Shop'. Another shop proclaimed itself Swiss, and even a French restaurant had labelled itself British. The interesting thing is that all these placards must evidently have been printed beforehand and kept in readiness.

1940–41

The Blitz

On 10 May 1940 Winston Churchill became Prime Minister and Minister of Defence. The Battle of Britain began in July, and in August the first German bombers were seen flying over London on reconnaissance missions. Later in the month bombing began in the suburbs. As George Orwell points out in the first excerpt, people were not yet schooled in the proper actions in the face of a raid. The bombing continued to affect every kind of public building in the capital, as Kingsley Martin records in the second passage. The climax came on Saturday, 7 September 1940 – the first day of the Blitz, Hitler's strike against the morale of the civilian population. For fifty-seven continuous nights and days London was subjected to a terrible bombardment. The damage began in the east, in the working class streets of the East End, where the destruction was intended for industry around the Docks. For a further six months the raids continued intermittently. The Germans dropped 18,000 tons of bombs upon London. The effect on the city and its population was devastating, both psychologically and physically. Of 90,000 casualties, 20,000 were fatal: 300 people died that first night.

16 August The people in inner London could do with one real raid to teach them how to behave. At present everyone's behaviour is foolish in the extreme, everything except transport being held up but no precautions taken. For the first 15 seconds there is great alarm, blowing of whistles and shouts to children to go indoors, then people begin to congregate on the streets and gaze expectantly at the sky. In the daytime people are apparently ashamed to go into the shelters till they hear the bombs.

7 September, 1940 I was in the British Museum library when one daylight air-raid warning was given, and nothing could have been more instant and military than the way in which the whole body of readers, marshalled by the staff, marched off through long galleries, past the Assyrian bulls, who seemed to behold the spectacle with a cynical eye, past the finger-rings and pottery and terracottas, or such of them as remain, into a quite

Extensive bomb damage along Cannon Street with St Paul's Cathedral miraculously left standing amongst the ruins. Photographed on 28 October 1941.

spacious hall reinforced as a shelter. One hardly recognized the pleasant attendants in their grim-looking tin-hats and with their armlets, but one generous provision was made in this British Museum shelter in the shape of tables with chairs at them so that the student of hieroglyphics could still pursue them. It is true that no reader was allowed to take a book from the dome, but many of them took their own manuscripts, and it was very reassuring to see them immediately begin upon their interrupted work as though nothing out of the ordinary had happened. At the shelter under Lincoln's Inn Chapel, too, a table is provided where the legal gentlemen from the surrounding chambers can get on with their work. From Whitehall, however, there are complaints that it is compulsory to go to the shelter and that the light there is so bad that one cannot continue to read or dictate.

A woman ambulance conductress remembered her journey – a literal baptism of fire – to Oriental Road in Silvertown, a heavily industrial Thames-side area of West Ham on the night of 7 September. Fortunately, the ambulance driver had done the same job in the First World War and was cool and collected.

We went off and we weren't allowed any lights at all, and the streets were absolutely pitch-black except when we got the full glare of the copper-coloured fire ... I met a man, and I said – is this right for Silvertown? And he said – Oh, that's about two miles further on – no good going there, it's entirely ablaze from end to end. Well, we went on and now we found we were completely alone, there wasn't a soul in any street ... eventually we came to a sort of swing bridge into the

Victoria Docks ... As far as we could see everything was on fire – great, red flames were going up and down the brick walls, piles of houses all collapsed or on fire, warehouses like blazing cathedrals standing up and then falling down ... everything reflected in the water.

There wasn't a single house standing – there was nothing, nothing at all except holes. Out of several of these holes little people popped their heads – exactly like a Chinese war film. I said – Is this Oriental Road? And they shouted – The ambulance? ... I just filled the ambulance with as many people as I could cram in, about fifteen or sixteen. Still nobody spoke, it was all the most deathly silence, and I got in beside them this time, not beside the driver, and drew the curtains to shut out the ghastly glow, and deafen the noise a bit, and we drove off. We got them all back and we got them all to hospital and we got back to our station, I suppose, about half-past one in the morning.

Ralph Ingersoll was an American journalist, the editor of *PM*, a radical and short-lived New York newspaper, who wrote a graphic account of his visit to London in the early days of the Blitz.

On my first morning in London it was not the extent of damage to any one place that surprised or shocked me – because I couldn't take it in ... It was simply the fact that having counted only thirteen bomb incidents in over a hundred miles I now counted thirty in half a mile.

Bomb damage is freakish in the extreme ... Here where a house stood, its rooms furnished, its walls prepared, and its plumbing intact, clothes in its closets and carpets on its floors, cooking utensils in the kitchen and toothbrushes in its bathrooms, shades on its windows, and a roof overhead – here where all these things were, there is but nothing ... There is no pile of ruins. Underneath the nothing it is flat. It is a filled-in hole in which what was this house is pulverized into such small pieces that the pieces are indistinguishable ...

I had always thought of it [the balloon barrage] as a ring of balloons around the outskirts of the city. In London it is no ring at all. Balloons shoot up all over the city like stalks of a badly planted asparagus bed ... I guessed they were about 4,000 feet up – three Empire State Building-lengths ... When you see them go up in the morning ... they wobble and yaw on their lines as they go up. As they get higher they settle down and the pressure of the air becomes less and the back-of-the-

pants part inflates until, at full altitude, it stands out, awkward but stiff. It acts as a kind of rudder and all the balloons point in the same direction, as cows do in a field on a windy day ... the balloons ... go up from trucks which move about, so that the incoming dive bombers will not know where to expect them.

With Ed Murrow, the distinguished American broadcaster, Ingersoll set out on a tour of shelters. First he visited Broadcasting House, where the BBC concert hall provided refuge. Then he visited a shelter in the Isle of Dogs intended for 4,000 people but being used by twice that number. Their next call was Liverpool Street tube station shelter, sixty feet underground. Finally, back at the Dorchester, where he was staying (resolutely on the seventh floor), Ingersoll decided to complete his survey by observing the hotel's own arrangements.

This [the BBC Concert Hall] was really the first big shelter I saw. The seats were out of it and the whole floor and the whole stage were carpeted solid with human figures ... It's a strange feeling to be standing in the

doorway and looking into a concert hall in which people are not listening to a concert but sleeping on the floor *en masse*. My first surprise was at how tight they were packed ... In all but the swankiest and daintiest shelters in London people sleep packed tightly. Face against face. Elbows overlapping.

We walked on and on, up one row and down another. It took the conversation and the questioning out of us ... In this shelter of 8,000 people [in the Isle of Dogs] there were six ... burlap-screened conveniences for men, six for women ... The whole experience shocked so that it numbed.

An escalator runs down to it [Liverpool Street station] in a single long, straight descent. We came in out of the dark into the lighted station and found ourselves standing at the top of it ... The entire length of this long stairway ... was packed – *two* people to a stair – with sleeping men ... contorted into unimaginable discomfort ... Finally we picked our way down. The escalator opened on a tube platform. Along this platform, heads to the wall, feet toward the tracks, was another carpet of

sleepers, absolutely solid ... There was a train in the station, brightly lighted, with its doors open. In startling contrast to the packed horizontal humanity on the platform, only two or three people were sitting in the cars. I was about to say 'But why don't they go in the cars?' when its doors closed and it moved off away into the tunnel.

We went past the empty kitchen and around a corner into what were once the Turkish baths. And there they were, the sleepers in the Dorchester shelter. A neat row of cots, spaced about 2 feet apart, each one covered with a lovely fluffy eiderdown ... Behind each cot hung the negligee, the dressing gown. By each cot the mules and the slippers. Alongside, the little table with the alligator-skin dressing case ... Even though it was 3 am and we tiptoed, most of them raised off the pillows and eyed us defensively. There was a little sign pinned to one of the Turkish-bath curtains. It said, 'Reserved for Lord Halifax.'

By the middle of October the Germans had targeted Whitehall and the effects of their raids were felt at No. 10

LEFT & ABOVE *Londoners prepare for the night packed into Aldwych Tube station, 8 October 1940. A similar scene drawn by Henry Moore in 1941.*

Downing Street itself, as Winston Churchill remembers.

Another evening (October 14) stands out in my mind. We were dining in the garden-room of No. 10 when the usual night raid began ... Suddenly I had a providential impulse. The kitchen at No 10 Downing Street is lofty and spacious, and looks out through a large plate-glass window about twenty-five feet high. The butler and parlourmaid continued to serve the dinner with complete detachment, but I became acutely aware of this big window, behind which Mrs Landemare, the cook, and the kitchen-maid, never turning a hair, were at work. I got up abruptly, went into the kitchen, told the butler to put the dinner on the hot plate in the dining-room, and ordered the cook and the other servants into the shelter, such as it was. I had been seated again at table only about three minutes when a really very loud crash, close at hand, and a violent shock showed that the house had been struck. My detective came into the room and said much damage had been done ... We went into the kitchen to view the scene. The devastation was complete. The bomb had fallen fifty yards away on the Treasury, and the blast had smitten the large, tidy kitchen, with all its bright saucepans and crockery, into a heap of black dust and rubble.

The last day of the London Blitz was 11 May 1941. The day before the House of Commons had been bombed and the Chamber gutted by fire. Harold Nicolson visited it a week later.

It is impossible to get through the Members' Lobby which is a mass of twisted girders. So I went up by the staircase to the Ladies' Gallery and then suddenly, when I turned the corridor, there was the open air and a sort of Tintern Abbey gaping before me. The little Ministers' rooms to right and left of the Speaker's Lobby were still intact, but from there onwards there was absolutely nothing.

Whatever damage London sustained during the harsh months of late 1940 and early 1941, the city continued to function. The West End had weathered the early months of war without too much difficulty. Theatres closed, then reopened. Although a number of leading Italian restaurateurs were interned on the Isle of Man, the great Mayfair hotels were busier than ever. Even high fashion adapted to the times. Elizabeth Arden's Bond Street salon suggested 'Burnt Sugar' as a suitable lipstick to wear with khaki. Society magazines altered their focus suitably. 'Unable to photograph peers on shooting sticks, they get along as best they can, peeresses driving ambulances, debutantes trundling fire hose', as Mollie Panter-Downes described the scene in her 'Letter from London' in the *New Yorker*. It was still possible for those sitting out the war in the countryside to come into town for the day. The devastation struck such visitors all the

more forcibly. Nan Fairbrother put it thus in *An English Year*: 'Crumbling stone and hollow shells of brick, no more solid against the next bombing than the children's sandpies. The willow-herb is bright on the summer hills, but brighter on the ruins of the city. Fireweed they call it, for it follows destruction.'

The letter that Ralph Ingersoll reprinted, however, to a customer from Selfridge & Co., the Oxford Street department store, demonstrates the remarkable phlegm that Londoners brought to life during the Blitz.

Dear Madam:

As you have doubtless read in the Press, on the night of the 18th inst. we were selected by enemy raiders as a 'Military Objective', but fortunately the Store only received slight damage and had it not been for the delayed action bombs in the neighbourhood we should have opened as usual the following morning.

The fact that the authorities prevented us from opening caused a certain amount of inconvenience to our customers, which is much regretted, although in co-operation with our associate House, William Whiteley, we endeavoured to fulfill all Provision orders and to deliver on time all rationed food stuffs.

If by chance you were put to any inconvenience, we feel sure you will appreciate that the circumstances were entirely beyond our control, but we are happy to inform you that every department in the Store (including the Provision Section) is now functioning quite normally.

With compliments,
Yours faithfully,
SELFRIDGE & CO., LTD.

Volunteers were pulled in for every kind of duty but the night-time fire-watchers at St Paul's were a very specialized group, chosen for their ability to explain the complex plans of the hidden parts of the cathedral to the fire-brigade should it be needed. The editor of the *Architectural Review* was one of the regular team.

Many of the members were architects. Godfrey Allen [Surveyor to the Fabric] who was given charge of the Night Watch ... realized that an architect's experience of reading plans would be invaluable ... My night was Monday ... I came to look forward to my night at St Paul's, beginning with the walk through empty City streets with the dome faintly visible, or silhouetted against the play of searchlights, at the top of Ludgate Hill. Pushing open a door in the north wall of the bell-tower, I would descend a flight of steps into the cold

W. Godfrey Allen and R. M. Wakelin in the fire-watching control room at St Paul's Cathedral.

stone smell of the crypt, where a perspective of round arches could be felt as much as seen disappearing into the gloom; then open another door into the brightly-lit mess-room which was our headquarters ... Our routine during the first few months – those of the 'phony war' – was this. Having dressed ourselves in blue overalls, steel helmets and webbing belts which held a tool for turning on fire-hydrants and an electric torch ... we began our nightly training ... The exercises began with the first pair of volunteers setting off to explore the roof-spaces until they found a lighted hurricane-lamp ... placed there beforehand to represent a burning bomb or some other sort of fire. Then the telephone would ring at Advanced Headquarters and ... A second pair would be despatched to deal with it ... So the exercise went on.

There was no end to the variety and the visual excitements offered to us during our explorations of the upper levels of the building. At triforium level one would suddenly find oneself emerging on top of the main cornice with views through a bronze railing down on to the floor of the choir fifty feet below, its patterned pavement glowing faintly in the light that came through the clerestory windows. Then one's route might take one back ... into one of the dusty roof-spaces. Here we had to beware of the rows of shallow mounds protruding from the floor – the upper surfaces of the saucer domes of the aisles beneath ... I looked forward to ... this

curiously self-contained life-within-a-life that membership of the Night Watch provided. Its oddity came back ... when I found in a drawer a pocket engagement diary for 1940 in which frequent Monday evenings had the entry – 'Midnight. The Crypt. Chess with the Dean.'

Enough time had elapsed between the Blitz and the arrival of the V1 and V2 missiles (doodle-bugs) for Londoners to have almost forgotten the drill. The stealthy new arrivals, sinister aerial presences without a pilot, were, as Evelyn Waugh described them, 'impersonal as a plague, as though the city were infested with enormous venomous insects'. Harold Nicolson noted the first arrivals in his diary entry for 16 June 1944.

They are illuminated like little launches at a regatta. They fly slowly and low ... make a terrific noise like an express train with a curious hidden undertone. In a week or so we shall have learnt how to deal with them. The Germans, of course, have boosted the thing immeasurably and tried to raise the spirits of their people by claiming that this secret weapon can really destroy London. In fact Goebbels says that London is 'paralysed'. This is absurd. There was not a sign of anything yesterday and the traffic continued just as usual.

1941

The railings return

Gradually London returned to an appearance of its old self. Even before the end of the war, the railings were replaced, in George Orwell's view, to keep the populace out of select neighbourhoods.

I see that the railings are returning – only wooden ones, it is true, but still railings – in one London square after another ...

When the railings round the parks and squares were removed, the object was partly to accumulate scrap-iron, but the removal was also felt to be a democratic gesture. Many more green spaces were now open to the public, and you could stay in the parks till all hours instead of being hounded out at closing time by grim-faced keepers ... the parks were improved out of recognition by being laid open, acquiring a friendly, almost rural look that they had never had before. And had the railings vanished permanently, another improvement would probably have followed. The dreary shrubberies of laurel and privet – plants not suited to England and always dusty, at any rate in London – would probably have been grubbed

up and replaced by flower beds. Like the railings, they were merely put there to keep the populace out.

1945

Victory Day

Inevitably, the comparison between Armistice Day and VE-Day flashed into many minds. In the first passage, Orwell remembered the atmosphere in 1918 and felt that this time, with things not quite resolved, the end of war would be anticlimactic. On the day of the unconditional surrender, Harold Nicolson heard Churchill speak in the House earlier – 'He was short and effective ... "The evil-doers", he intoned, "now lie prostrate before us"'. Outside the House, Nicolson felt reassured by the scene in Trafalgar Square.

7 April 1945 V-Day with its two Bank Holidays, will not be at all like Armistice Day, 1918 ... I was in London on the 12th and the celebrations resembled nothing that I have seen or heard of since. London was just carnival ... quite drunk with happiness. I remember best Trafalgar Square, where thousands of people were dancing on the pavements, singing ... linking up and merry-making with other groups of people they had never met before and would never see again ... This time, I fancy, there will be more drink and hooliganism, and less sponta-

*Piccadilly Circus on VE Day
– relief and delight on every
face.*

neous happiness. The Day will be 'stage' and has been too long expected . . . When V-Day does come, it will be a day of wonderful release from tension. The killing in Europe will be over, or nearly over . . . It will mean the end of rockets, and no more blackout; most important of all, it will mean family reunions and a rest and a holiday . . . what could be better than that?

_____

The National Gallery was alive with every stone outlined

in flood-lighting, and down there was Big Ben with a grin upon his illumined face. The statue of Nelson was picked out by a searchlight, and there was the smell of distant bonfires in the air. I walked to the Temple and beyond. Looking down Fleet Street one saw the best sight of all – the dome of St Paul's rather dim-lit, and then above it a concentration of search-lights upon the huge golden cross. So I went to bed. That was my victory day.

1945–1965

LONDON

in the

POST-WAR
WORLD

attered, both physically and mentally, London and its population were in poor shape after the war. Not surprisingly, the only way forward was to look towards the new. The early post-war years were frugal in material terms, with stiffer rationing even than in the war. Food apart, goods in the shops were few and had become far more expensive. Fuel shortages were exacerbated by the grim winter of 1946–7. The worst of the century, it brought transport into and within London to a standstill for weeks. In March terrible storms flooded the Underground. The elements seemed to offer a grim portent for the peace. If the 1945 Labour government had tapped into a spirit of aspirational euphoria – victory behind and social reform with the implementation of the Welfare State ahead – the realities of that winter ground everybody down. In 1949 the lights came back on in London, but there was little brightness otherwise.

The Festival of Britain was a watershed that performed two functions. It had a serious side: the London County Council contributed a major new concert hall, the Royal Festival Hall, and in the East End at Poplar, the first phase of a giant model housing scheme, the Lansbury neighbourhood. But the festival also hosted a gigantic fun fair along the south side of the Thames, which with the futuristic Skylon and the Dome of Discovery was a cheerful mêlée of colour, fantasy, and frivolity to which people flocked. Change was abroad. In the autumn general election the Conservatives regained power.

Celebration in the form of historic ritual brushed up for the new age of television was again the mood when the young Queen Elizabeth II was crowned in June 1953, with her first Trooping the Colour just nine days later. The occasion was marked by a special issue of four ounces of butter above the ration.

Physical change in London had been largely incremental since the mid-Victorian upheavals, but the severity of bomb damage ensured that the shape of the city would be transformed over these

ABOVE *The Dome of Discovery at the Festival of Britain, 1951.*

OPPOSITE *The South Bank of the Thames during clearance of the Festival of Britain site in 1949. Watercolour by Laurence Wright.*

decades. Over one third of the City was destroyed; some 250 million square feet had to be rebuilt. In the East End the damage was as heavy, but the devastation was in residential areas. In addition to the massive need for rebuilding, the Abercrombie Plan suggested satellite New Towns for London's 'overspill', and this plan was pursued – a phased relocation of hundreds of thousands of Londoners far away from home. The change of government from Labour to the Conservative administration in 1951 hardly affected these plans.

By 1963 all the taboos were broken. The skyline was rising in every direction. Public housing, much of it in factory-made, systems-built form, was being rapidly built in an attempt to reach a government target of 400,000 units a year. Whether built as tower blocks or slab blocks, new estates were transforming residential London. Anonymous office blocks were produced by enormous architectural practices. Occasionally a renowned figure such as Walter Gropius or Mies van der Rohe was asked to tweak at a design, but to little avail. The Hilton Hotel, one of a new generation of (mostly American) hotel chains putting down their roots in London, peered over Hyde Park and cheekily into the gardens of Buckingham Palace. Conveniently enough, the air had cleared – the last smog was in 1962 – largely as a result of the Clean Air Act.

London was re-establishing itself as the hub of transport in the era of motorways and airports. The first motorway, the M1, was opened in 1959 and ran between London and Birmingham – just as the first train had done. Overhead droned the growing fleets of commercial aircraft taking thousands away on business and pleasure. The parking meter was introduced to control city centre traffic. For all this, the Thames river still held its place. After bomb damage the post-war docks saw enormous investment, and 1961 was the busiest year ever – 60 million tonnes of goods passed through.

All these pressures added to the ceaseless development of greater London. Public dismay with the failure of planning safeguards was considerable. Schemes for Piccadilly Circus – especially Jack Cotton's Monico site – or Paternoster Square around St Paul's, were chewed over, sent to Public Inquiry, redesigned and either postponed indefinitely or built in amended form. In 1964 one of Richard Crossman's first acts within the new Labour administration was to put a stop to London office development. The relocation of commercial development outside central London was pursued with renewed vigour.

The administrative shape of London was also changing. When the London Government Bill went before the House of Commons in 1963, the prospect of enlarged boroughs with wider responsibilities was seen to be more workable; in 1965 the Greater London Council replaced the London County Council.

People left, people came. Commonwealth immigration, largely Indian, West Indian, Cypriot and Maltese, increased during the 1950s. Despite being invited by industries that needed labour, such as London Transport, the newcomers were treated shabbily. The culmination of bad race relations in London was the Notting Hill riots of 1958, a chilling reminder of East End fascism.

Meanwhile, a new teenage (the word itself was an American import) generation, consciously apolitical and with spending power, appeared, an affluent society in the making. There was no time for nostalgia. These were patently better times, and London was the place to celebrate the fact. Youth had an image, but it also had a voice. The anarchic, the angry, the off-beat were all acceptable after the prim years of self-restraint. Music and the visual arts, with one eye over the shoulder to the USA, celebrated the rougher side of life. Artists took up an imagery of change – and its concomitant, detritus – as well as speed and wit. London was well placed to sustain an alternative arts culture and to provide the stimulus of rich subject matter. Advertising became an art form.

Novelists and playwrights, young and outspoken, John Osborne, Colin Wilson, Nell Dunn, and Colin MacInnes among them, used slang and street *argot* to give documentary immediacy to their subjects – young people on the down-side of the capital. Just a fraction away, the worlds of vice

Beatlemania: police control a crowd of screaming teenagers waiting for The Beatles *outside the Palladium theatre, 13 October 1963.*

and racketeering seemed more visible than ever before; the name of Peter Rachman, infamous London slum landlord, entered the dictionary.

Drawn by a rumour of London's vitality and dominant youth culture, a new breed of tourist poured into the city. If Teddy boys had faded out of metropolitan life and fashion, to be found hanging around in small provincial towns for years after, the visitors on their package deals did not notice that they had gone to be replaced by Mods and Rockers. They loved the contrast between the seasoned historic attractions, the Tower of London, Hampton Court or the British Museum, and the unpredictable eccentricities on the streets.

The dramatic change between the grey world of immediate post-war London and the devil-take-the-hindmost atmosphere of 1960s London was captured by Christopher Booker in the introduction to a reissue of *The Neophiliacs*.

When I first came to London in my teens in 1956 – the year of *Look Back in Anger* and the Suez crisis – I spent evenings at the two little Soho coffee bars

which were producing Britain's first crop of homegrown rock'n'roll singers. In 1960 I remember driving round London in search of the first of those startling new buildings in glass, steel and concrete which seemed as symbolic of the new age as the election of John Kennedy ... In 1961, in the dawn of the satire boom, I became the first editor of *Private Eye* ... As a satirist I relished the almost unbroken stream of hysteria which raged through that extraordinary year, 1963, as one sensation followed another, from the Profumo scandal to the fall of Macmillan, from the Great Train Robbery to the rise of Beatlemania ... but in 1964 and 1965, as London became what *Time* was to call 'the most swinging city in the world', I began to view this great avalanche of nervous excitement which was sweeping us all along in rather a different light.

The announcement of Sir Winston Churchill's death momentarily brought the population up short. As with Nelson or Wellington, the ceremonial that attended Churchill's lying-in-state and funeral served as a kind of national pageant of remembrance – a pause before the capital spun away into the mid-1960s and the hyperbole of Swinging London.

1945

A return to normal

The end of the war coincided with a General Election, which Labour won by a majority of 180 seats. Polling day was on 5 July, but because of the numbers of servicemen remaining overseas, votes were sealed and the count made on 26 July. Harold Nicolson was fully prepared for his own defeat at Leicester West but happily celebrated London coming back to life.

For years I have crept out of the Club with my torch, seeking and peering for the little step on the threshold. Tonight I emerged into a London coruscating with lights like Stockholm. My old way along the Embankment … was lit up by a thousand arc-lights. All these were turned up on 15th July when double-summer-time ended … Meanwhile all the sticky stuff has been removed from the windows of the buses and under-

grounds, and we shall no longer remember how we used to peep out through a little diamond slit in the texture to read the names of the stations as they flashed by.

1943–7

Plans for Rebuilding

Throughout the later war years intense thought was given to the rebuilding and replanning of London. Some documents were unofficial, such as the report of the Royal Academy Planning Committee, to which architect RAs, their chairman Sir Edwin Lutyens, and other invited specialists contributed in Lutyens's words 'an ideal possibility'. *The County of London Plan*, 1943, prepared by Professor Patrick Abercrombie and J. H. Forshaw and illustrated with William Walcot's superb perspectives, was with Abercrombie's *Greater London Plan* of 1944 the most official and far-reaching of the planning proposals. Another plan of 1947, the work of Charles Holden and William Holford, concentrated on the City. The preamble to the 1943 plan foresaw the difficulties, the decisions that needed to be taken, and among immediate post-war works identified the LCC's contribution to the Festival of Britain, the Festival Hall, and the Lansbury neighbourhood in Poplar.

Remedies proposed

It is comparatively easy to point to the defects of London; it is less simple to try to suggest remedies. There can be no town which presents a more complex background, nor one in which interaction is more intense and interpenetrating. A balance has to be struck between contending interests, between different aspects of town activity, no less than between the needs and functions of different sections of the community, different public authorities and corporations and even Ministries. Are there to be flats or houses; high densities or low; open space or loose texture within or compactness and playing fields far off; industry decentralised with population or one taken out and the other left behind; tube extension to the country or electrified suburban lines; high level roads or tunnels; fruit markets or opera houses; centralised or dispersed hospitals? These and many more questions have to be answered … all of which have here an urgency and an extreme complication, heightened by high values and the existence of historic landmarks.

The time factor

One of the chief difficulties of every constructive

scheme of any degree of boldness is that it shows a vision of the future assembled in a single Report and group of maps. It appears as though the whole were to be carried out at once, with a corresponding shock to the uninformed who are led to imagine that it is much more ambitious than is really the case and even chimerical.

Works for the immediate post-war period

The works to be carried out ... must be prepared and ready to be put in hand as soon as labour and materials are available after the cessation of hostilities. Here is the chance to show London on a grand scale what her reconstruction really means. In three directions there are immediate opportunities, corresponding to the three major aspects: the provision of new housing and open spaces in the damaged industrial boroughs; the creation of the southern embankment and cultural centre; and the construction of new roads.

1948

Snow, streets and the Olympics

Dramatic weather effects always have a curious effect in city conditions, and London is no exception. Daily life becomes abnormal, its sights and atmosphere heightened by the extremes of temperature or elements. Heat waves or fierce winters are recorded down the years, but the winter of 1947 and to lesser extent that of 1948 produced famously severe conditions that tended to emphasize post-war privations. The theatre critic J. C. Trewin wrote a series of letters that year, covering topics such as the severe weather, the distinctions between one neighbouring corner of central London and the next, and the London Olympics, a low-key affair after the frenzy and menace of the Berlin Games of 1936.

We've been living, until the last day or two, in a snow-dazzle – almost incandescent it seemed up here on Sunday, under that queerly bright, blind sky that should have been granite-grey and wasn't. They say that in town at one period on Saturday, it was impossible to see St Paul's from Ludgate Circus through the snow curtain ... I don't know about that, though the blizzard was heavy enough in Tudor Street, not stealthily, silently sifting, but lumping, flopping, down – a clumsy ham-fisted snowstorm, if there can be such a thing ... Still it was pleasant – pleasant, that is, to watch from the other side of a thick sheet of glass ...

The city has recovered now from slushy convalescence, and a theme for small talk is scotched.

OPPOSITE *Workmen preparing to change the lights of Fleet Street from 'moonlighting' to normal standards. Photographed 5 May 1945.*

RIGHT *London in the hardest winter of the century. Painting by Ruskin Spear.*

6 April 1948

On the whole, I think the Strand, Oxford Street, and Caledonian Road are my special metropolitan hates. I could linger for hours in Piccadilly, which has a graciousness and airiness, and I am fond of the sedate streets at the back of Burlington House. I used to be fond, too, of wandering in remoter Finsbury and in the little-known squares of Clerkenwell. Before the war there was one with symmetrical houses of darkened brick, dull yellow paint and classic pediments, and a central garden with close-bit turf and a society of flowers: an early Victorian print 'skied' as it were, on the wall of Finsbury's parlour. And there used to be in Clerkenwell a delightful circus, painted in light brown and cream, and standing on its head upon a steep incline. I have not been to Finsbury for years but . . . I get quite often to Kensington, a borough of many faces. Kensington High Street is spruce and well-ordered. The sea-coast of Bohemia is far away; no sound of breaking surf penetrates those tall flats. There, you feel, is the borough's midday, just as South Kensington has a sense of afternoon . . . Campden Hill of a fresh morning, the Addison Road district of an early autumn evening, Brompton Road of mid-morning about the coffee-hour, and parts of North Kensington and Notting Dale of a murky night. There are at least a dozen towns between Brompton Oratory and Wormwood Scrubs.

28 July 1948

We returned in an unkind blaze of sunshine to a London planted with the interlinked rings of the Olympic Games – the flags I saw last in Berlin during those queer weeks of July and early August, 1936, when the Nazis were out to present a shop-window to the world . . . But all that . . . is a long way from Wembley, and it seems to me uncommonly long ago – much longer than twelve years. For my part I have been less excited over the present Olympics than over the Covent Garden production of *The Pilgrim's Progress*, a play by Hugh Ross Williamson, after Bunyan, to celebrate the 250th anniversary of the S.P.C.K. I believe 200 bishops, in town for the Lambeth Conference, were present on the first night, but I missed this rather alarming episcopal jamboree.

1949

London renewed

Post-war London was creeping back into the light. The late Forties were hard times, but Kingsley Martin observed the preparations for the Festival of Britain, in particular the building of the Festival Hall, and the cheering signs of normality in the West End shops on Christmas Eve.

[12 November, 1949] In Sunday's sunshine I walked over Hungerford Bridge to watch the progress of the new concert hall. I fell into conversation with a workman on the bridge. He said he had been six years in the Army and could not get a house . . . what did the Government want to go putting up a concert hall for when a worker and ex-soldier couldn't get a house? These Exhibition buildings were using enough material and timber for hundreds of houses, and so on. A little elderly man, also taking a Sunday constitutional, joined in . . . But the young worker . . . is well aware how much better off he is than he would have been after the First World War. At least he has a job. He agreed that it might be necessary to build some things apart from houses. If the Exhibition brought in dollars, it would be justified. He was just browned off because he was still living in lodgings five years after he came out of the Army.

A bird's-eye impression of the Festival of Britain site. From The Illustrated London News, *12 May 1951.*

[24 December, 1949] London looks pre-war. To come down Regent Street, positively riotous in colour, into Trafalgar Square, with the Christmas-tree and the silver fountains and the streamers and bunting – why ... you might even kid yourself that England was capable this year of having a merry Christmas. The shops perpetrate the illusion of jollity. Certainly it's eleven years since they looked like this ... It's not only that you can get all the fruit, including pineapples and such-like, that you want, but that you have only to dip, somewhat deeply, into your pocket to buy gorgeous luxuries like *marrons glacés* and even chow-chow, lichees, and cumquats ... I've not yet heard a Hungarian band ... but I have seen a barrow of coconuts. As for poultry, you can only get into the butchers' shops by clambering over mountains of it ... Sugar is still short, but that complaint is lessened by the fact that you can buy all the plum puddings and sweet cakes you want. You can get drunk on anything but whisky. Those who still grumble complain that there are no dried eggs or only one egg on this week's ration book ... When you come to clothes and toys the situation is very much the same. Small toys have multiplied out of all memory and some are not dear. Big toys are expensive ... good mechanical toys, the trains and boats, not to speak of the children's tricycles, are all available again; but their price ... is double or sometimes treble what it was in pre-war days. For the first time I hear of well-to-do parents buying refurbished, second-hand toys. On the other hand, if you want to give your girl or your wife gloves or a scarf or a pair of bedroom slippers you'll pay less than last year. Add all this up and it's a pretty good and jolly picture.

1951

The Festival of Britain

The Festival of Britain was dreamt up as a reminder of the hugely popular 1851 Great Exhibition and an optimistic curtain raiser to a better decade. As Evelyn Waugh put it sardonically, 'the Government decreed a Festival. Monstrous constructions appeared on the south bank of the

Thames'. Although the festival was decidedly a good thing, it never had a mission in the manner of the Prince Consort's Exhibition. But, like Noël Coward in his 'Don't Make Fun of the Fair', people did not mind. Once the festival had opened and could allay doubts and criticism of the seeming extravagance of it all, over eight million people came to look on the bright side of life and to celebrate, as Herbert Morrison said afterwards, 'the British giving themselves a pat on the back'.

Verse 1   We're proud to say
In every way
We're ordinary folk,
But please to observe
We still preserve
Our sturdy hearts of oak.
Although as servants of the state
We may have been coerced,
As we've been told to celebrate
We'll celebrate or burst.
Though while we brag
Our shoulders sag
Beneath a heavy yoke
We all get terribly heated
If it's treated
As a joke. So:

Refrain 1   Don't make fun of the festival,
Don't make fun of the fair,
We down-trodden British must learn to be
    skittish
And give an impression of devil-may-care
To the wide wide world,
We'll sing 'God for Harry',
And if it turns out all right
Knight Gerald Barry,
Clear the national decks, my lads,
Everyone of us counts,
Grab the traveller's cheques, my lads,
And pray that none of them bounce.
Boys and Girls come out to play,
Every day in every way
Help the tourist to defray
All that's underwritten.
Sell your rations and overcharge,
And don't let anyone sabotage
Our own dear Festival of Britain.

Verse 2   ...We know we're caught
And must support

This patriotric prank
And though we'd rather have shot ourselves
We've got ourselves
To thank. So:

Refrain 2   Don't make fun of the festival,
Don't make fun of the fair,
We must pull together in spite of the
    weather
That dampens our spirits and straightens
    our hair.
Let the people sing
Even though they shiver
Roses red and noses mauve
Over the river.
Though the area's fairly small,
Climb Discovery's Dome,
Take a snooze in the concert hall,
At least it's warmer than home.
March about in funny hats,
Show the foreign diplomats
That our proletariat's
Milder than a kitten.
We believe in the right to strike,
But now we've bloody well got to like
Our own dear Festival of Britain.

Refrain 4   Don't make fun of the festival,
Don't make fun of the fair.
We mustn't look glum when the visitors
    come
And discover our cupboard is ever so bare.
We must cheer, boys, cheer,
Look as though we love it
And if it should be a bust
Just rise above it.
Take a nip from your brandy flask,
Scream and caper and shout,
Don't give anyone time to ask
What the Hell it's about...

The editor of the *Architectural Review*, J. M. Richards, took a very different, rather solemn, view. His belief was that the festival was a much-needed symbol of modernity.

The Prince Consort, were he to visit the South Bank this summer, would immediately recognize the fulfilment at last, after a whole century of gestation, of the project he and Henry Cole dreamed of...

    Britain has for the first time this summer instead of a

few freakish examples of a modern style, a whole quarter where the twentieth century Englishman can wander about in a world of his own making . . .

The South Bank exhibition – together with its adjuncts at Battersea and Poplar – is clearly destined to be a triumphant success . . . the mere fact that it has been conceived and built in a contemporary spirit, with no sign of the compromise usually thought necessary in order to placate conservative and official taste, is sufficient triumph in itself . . . [we] salute the efforts of Gerald Barry, director-general, and Hugh Casson, director of architecture, and to state that . . . the exhibition is in the literal sense epoch-making.

1952/3

Negative impressions

London in the immediate post-war period could offer surprising pockets of prosperity. Raymond Chandler, who had not visited England since 1918, was surprised by the affluence he found in the autumn of 1952. London seen from the Connaught Hotel had its share of pleasures and penances.

To Paul Brooks, September 28

Thanks for your letter . . . Today is an English Sunday and by God it's gloomy enough for a crossing of the Styx. I thought England was broke but the whole damn

Affluent London comes back to life. The scene in Bond Street in the early 1950s.

city is crawling with Rolls Royces, Bentleys, Daimlers and expensive blondes.

Never thought I'd get sick of the sight of a grouse on toast or a partridge, but God I am.

To Hamish Hamilton

Try to understand that I think you and yours were all utterly kind and charming to us, and that even though certain things about our stay in London were a little annoying at the time, they are all very pleasant in retrospect. The annoying things were mostly things that could not be avoided. There was the desperate struggle on Cissy's part . . . to find something to wear, and not merely something to wear to a dinner party but things which she badly needed and things which she simply could not find in the West End of London. She couldn't even find a decent pair of shoes to put on. At fantastic prices they were selling what we should over here regard as quite second-rate English goods. Of course I do understand why, but it was annoying just the same. I couldn't find a decent pair of woollen socks . . . But . . . compared with New York, which is an abominable place in far too many ways, I think London is a paradise of charm and good manners.

To Dale Warren, November 13

I see in the current *New Yorker* that Sacheverell Sitwell, that visiting virtuoso of the quill pen, remarks that New York traffic is better managed than that in London, about as idiotic a remark as I have ever heard or read. New York traffic . . . is absolute chaos. London traffic, generally speaking and considering the fantastic pattern of the streets, is superbly managed. Of course the system wouldn't work in New York because it depends on a certain element of decency and obedience to the law. The only real fault I found with the London traffic system was their allowing left turns from places like Oxford Circus during rush hours. With which gripe I conclude.

A year later S. J. Perelman was staying at Brown's Hotel and wrote home with his negative impressions, intensified, as he himself acknowledged, by the lack of company: 'I must be more gregarious than I'd supposed.' By the next letter all was well, and he was caught up in a social round amidst the literati of London.

December 13, 1953
Dear Laura . . .

London is in the grip of a smog attack . . . breathing is like burying your head in a smokestack . . .

Life in the ubiquitous London teashop – the English equivalent of the continental café, with its own particular atmosphere.

everybody here has a pinched, gray look, but it's probably a combination of weather and the grisly food.

Arriving as I did on a Friday, I was just in time for the weekend ... The whole city shut down with a snap Friday night; yesterday (Saturday) the place looked as if it were striken with pestilence, all the shops closed and many of the restaurants, and today absolutely nothing was open.

The most parlous aspect, as always here, is the feeding arrangements. The whole god-damned city seems to be made up of nothing but snack bars and bottle clubs ... It's all teashops, with dainty little sandwiches of Spam, cream gateaux, and savories – nothing to put your teeth into. (Not because of rationing, either; plenty of food, apparently, but I suspect the English have got out of the habit of eating after all the years of austerity.) The only half-way decent meal I had was night before last in a dickty Italian place, all rose boudoir lamps and waiters in tails, in Wardour Street. I was the only occupant in a room about seventy feet long, and I had four waiters hovering about me ... Fortunately, there is no danger of my getting scurvy, as I have to consume at least two gin-and-limes every evening to keep the cold out.

December 23, 1953 (from Paris)
Dear Laura ...

London got real busy right after I wrote you that first letter ...

1953

The coronation

The coronation of Queen Elizabeth II was the celebration that London and the nation needed. Fleur Cowles was invited as the official 'American Ambassador' to the event. Her rather quaint and breathless account catches the scene through the eyes of a foreign visitor overwhelmed by the ceremonial and delighted by proximity to the monarchy.

I was utterly conquered by what I saw and did ... The experience was unforgettable ... I saw a beautifully embroidered pageant. For once, and for good, blood-less history. Ancient ritual, reaffirming its place in a modern world; gilt and plumage instead of aluminium and helmets. Length and ceremony instead of brevity and dispatch, happiness instead of despair.

Rain did pour down on millions standing on wet streets; cold winds chilled bones, blew hair, went through heavily wetted clothes (June was like Novem-ber) but never were the English enveloped in so large a smile.

Art Buchwald called it 'England's wettest hour' ...

Three faces ... stand out ... [one] was a *very* old lady, who parked her little stool on the pavement in Park Lane facing Hyde Park twenty-four hours before the great morning ... 'This will be my fourth Coronation, and the most important one of all,' she told me ...

Just outside the Abbey, there was a last memorable face of the tiny little boy perched on his father's shoulder, one arm around his father's neck, the other one holding on for dear life to his father's nose. Children were everywhere (schools were given a place of honour on the route), but this little boy and his patient father stand out. They were still there, in the same place, and in the same position, many hours later when we returned from the 'Queen's Luncheon'.

The Queen, though hostess, was absent, riding in the State Coach through the crowds, to be seen with her new crown. After the ceremony her guests dined in

The coronation of Queen Elizabeth II, a wet day in June 1953.

Westminster Hall. The dark stone walls were hung with huge pink and orange garlands . . . pink and orange is an unremarkable twosome today but Constance Spry seemed to have invented it then, working through the night on flowers which had been flown in from Africa.

The most colourful sight of all, to me, were the Zulus, Arabs, Indians, Chinese, Nepalese, Germans, tribesmen, Russians and coroneted English nobility – mixed like tossed confetti, side by side, in a never-to-be-repeated tableau. Wrapped turbans, tropical plumage and emerald beacons punctuated a sea of conventional tiaras and veils. The view along the aisles in the Abbey was staggering . . .

1950s
Milk delivery modernized

Kingsley Martin remarks on another break with Victorian London as the Express Dairy moved with the times.

Until the other day we . . . enjoyed the chance to pat the pony which pulled the Express Dairy van. For half an hour you could hear from our windows the pleasant chink of milk bottles and the Edwardian cloppety-clop

of the pony as he went from street to street. The milkman's pride in his sleek pony was a fine thing to see . . . Some six weeks ago the company decided that the pony should work a less exacting round on the edge of South London. The milkman is broken-hearted; he pays the pony occasional visits, but in Charing Cross he has to put up with an electric van which, in unhappy contrast to his pony, is apt to break down. Now that there is no pony to munch a lump of sugar, most of the charm of fetching our morning milk has gone.

1950s
Different corners of London

Many of the best descriptions of London in the post-war years are in fiction. In her first novel, *Under the Net* (1954), Iris Murdoch wittily captures the different corners of London, including bomb-damage, as seen through the eyes of her peripatetic hero, Jake, a feckless artist.

There are some parts of London which are necessary and others which are contingent. Everywhere west of Earls Court is contingent, except for a few places along the river. I hate contingency.

I usually keep clear of Soho, partly because it's so bad for the nerves and partly because it's so expensive. It's expensive not so much because the nervous tension makes one drink continually as because of the people who come and take one's money away. I am very bad at refusing people who ask me for money . . . By the time I had worked my way along Brewer Street and Old Compton Street and up Greek Street as far as the Pillars of Hercules most of the money in my pocket had been taken away by various acquaintances.

LEFT *An Express Dairy woman in wartime, showing a method of delivery which came to an end in central London in the 1950s.*

RIGHT *Street scene in Soho, London's bohemia – home to artist and petty villain alike.*

The taxi stopped and we got out ... Hugo lived, it appeared, right up above Holborn Viaduct in a flat perched on top of some office buildings ... The taxi drove off and left us standing alone on the Viaduct. If you have ever visited the City of London in the evening you will know what an uncanny loneliness possesses those streets which during the day are so busy and noisy. The Viaduct is a dramatic viewpoint. But although we could see for a long way, not only towards Holborn and Newgate Street, but also along Farringdon Street, which swept below us like a dried-up river, we could see no living being. Not a cat, not a copper. It was a warm evening, cloudlessly and brilliantly blue, and the place was mute around us, walled in by a distant murmur which may have been the sound of traffic or else the summery sigh of the declining sun. We stood still.

The evening was by now well advanced. The darkness hung in the air ... The zenith was a strong blue, the horizon a radiant amethyst. From the darkness and shade of St Paul's Churchyard we came into Cheapside as into a bright arena, and saw framed in the gap of a ruin the pale neat rectangles of St Nicholas Cole Abbey,

standing alone away to the south of us on the other side of Cannon Street. In between the willow herb waved over what remained of streets. In this desolation the coloured shells of houses still raised up filled and blank squares of wall and window. The declining sun struck on glowing bricks and flashing tiles and warmed the stone of an occasional fallen pillar.

Contrary to external impressions London was still an intricate web of small manufacturing industries and artisan workshops – on the Victorian model. Every mainstream activity was backed up by dozens of tiny specialist firms. The poet P. J. Kavanagh fell upon one such secret place.

I was sent to the East End of London to learn about colour-printing. Wandering round Cheapside one afternoon, not far from the Tower of London, I caught through the open doorway of a little tumbledown house a glimpse of a furnace. I went in and found two lugubrious young men dressed like pastry-cooks, with round brimless caps on their heads, pulling out from an oven tiny rolls of metal type. What made the scene extraordinary, even hellish, like the Witch's Transformation scene in a pantomime, was that everything was bright red – their clothes, their faces, the walls, even the ceiling, glowed the colour of blood in the light of the furnace; it was as if the spectrum had gone wrong. They sadly explained that this was due to a powder they used in their work, called, incredibly, Dragon's Blood. They were making the type that goes inside a bus-conductor's ticket machine. That was all they did, the two of them, and they did it for the whole world: Glasgow, Saigon, Tokyo, London. Every so often these towns would obligingly raise their fares, or change their fare-stages or do something which caused the whole business to be done again; they were set up for life, but one of them had doubts: 'I mean, you never really look at your ticket, do you – read it, I mean.' They devoted such care to their type-setting and their casting, these two brilliantly encardadined figures, it seemed a pity.

Brought up in an orphanage, Frank Norman was one of those enterprising cockney spirits who made rumbustious prose out of the seamier side of London in the 1950s and 1960s. In this piece Norman compares Soho in 1958 with its later manifestations.

One time I used to lay about round Soho nearly all the time ... In my opinion Soho is double overrated these days, because all the best tealeaves etc. live not in Soho but in places like the Elephant, Hoxton and the Angel ... But I don't want anyone to get the idea that I don't like Soho ... I love the smells that come from the kayfs, and it often reminds me of the days I used to walk the streets of Soho dead skint and starving hungry, and nowhere to live ... The boozers are still full of tortured intellectuals who just sit around and wait for God knows what, and they are not sure about anything, which is the sign of a true intellectual ... In recent years Soho has taken up the coffee-house craze, and I should think that there is now about a hundred of them scattered all over the place ... They bring a different character to Soho, they are the teenagers and skiffle merchants; the old Soho characters don't have nothing to do with the teenagers, because most of them are not as young as they was and all that energy makes them feel dead uncomfortable.

My London is Soho, that square mile which has by turns destroyed and enriched my soul and pocket. I have walked its streets without food for three days or proper sleep for a week. I have trod the same pavements with several hundred pounds in my pocket and the future as bright as a newly minted sixpence. I have been chased by the police around Soho Square and cried for loss of a lover in Italian restaurants. Twenty years and many crates of whisky ago I arrived in Dean Street a beautiful and naive boy of sixteen years, had a light ale in the French Pub under-age and have remained under-age ever since ... I perpetually complain about how much the old place has changed in recent years, but hardly a week passes without my visiting Muriel Belcher at the Colony Room in Dean Street and Gaston Berlemont at the French Pub further down. Like a junkie I must have my fix. I get stoned on drink and the atmosphere of Soho combined.

A seasoned observer of another underside of London in the pages of his novels was Colin MacInnes. Through the medium of the wide-boy photographer hero of *Absolute Beginners* (1959), he describes down-at-heel west London and sets the scene for the Notting Hill race riots, which he sees as they are brewing.

I'd like to explain this district where I live, because it's quite a curiosity, being one of the few that's got left behind by the Welfare era *and* the Property-owning whatsit, both of them, and is, in fact, nothing more than a stagnating slum. It's dying, this bit of London, and

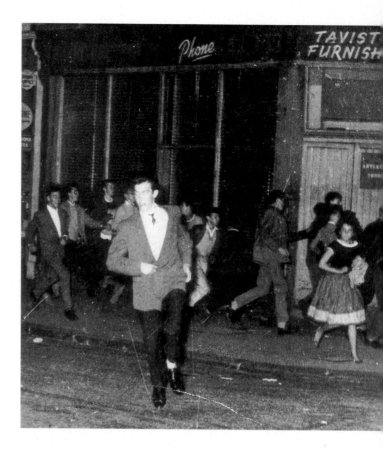

that's the most important thing to remember about what goes on there. To the north of it, there run, in parallel, the Harrow road I've mentioned, which you'd hurry through even if you were in a car, and a canal, called the Grand Union that nothing floats on except cats and contraceptives, and the main railway track that takes you from London to the swede counties of the West of England. These three escape routes, which are all at different heights and levels, cut across one another at different points, making crazy little islands of slum habitation shut off from the world by concrete precipices, and linked by metal bridges. I need hardly mention that on this north side there's a hospital, a gasworks ... and a very ancient cemetery with the pretty country name of Kensal Green.

On the east side, still in the W10 bit, there's another railway, and a park with a name only Satan in all his splendour could have thought up, namely Wormwood Scrubs, which has a prison near it, and another hospital, and a sports arena, and the new telly barracks of the BBC, and with a long, lean road called Latimer road which I particularly want you to remember, because ... of what I think must really be the sinisterest highway in our city, well, just listen to the names: Blechynden, Silchester, Walmer, Testerton and Bramley – can't you

Notting Hill Gate, race riot country.

just smell them, as you hurry to get through the cats-cradle of these blocks? ...

On the south side of this area, down by the W11, things are a little different, but in a way that somehow makes them worse, and that is, owing to a freak of fortune, and some smart work by the estate agents too, I shouldn't be surprised, there are one or two sections that are positively posh: not *fashionable*, mind you, but quite graded, with their big back gardens and that absolute silence which in London is the top sign of a respectable location. You walk in these bits ... when – wham! suddenly you're back in the slum area again – honest, it's really startling.

In September.
As soon as you passed into the area, you could sense that there was something on. The sun was well up now, and the streets were normal ... until suddenly you realized that they *weren't* ... you could feel a *hole*: as if some kind of life was draining out of it, leaving a sort of vacuum in the streets and terraces ...

Standing about on corners, and outside their houses, there were Teds: groups of them, not *doing* anything, but standing in circles, with their heads just a bit bent down. There were motor-bikes about, as well, and the

kids had often got them out there at angles on the roadway ... As for the Spades, they seemed to creep a bit, and keep in bunches. And although they often did this anyway, a great number of them were hanging out of windows and speaking to each other loud across the streets ...

Then I saw my first 'incident' ...

As the riots worsened, people came from elsewhere in London, just to look. Colin MacInnes continues.

There's no doubt night favours wickedness ... I went down by Westbourne Park station, and took a ride along the scenic railway to the Bush. The train was packed with sightseers from the West, who hopped out at different stations for the free display. From the height between the stops, you could see the odd fire and firemen and, at sudden glimpses as the train rocked by a street at right angles, the crowds, and law cars prowling, or standing parked with cowboys packed in them, waiting for action ... And when the train halted, at Ladbroke and by Latimer, you could hear loud-speakers blaring something harsh and meaningless, like at Battersea pleasure gardens, in the funfair there. And all along the ride there were patches of blue-black darkness, then sudden glares and flares of dazzling light.

But at the Bush, I was amazed. Because when I crossed over, beyond the Green, to the middle-class section outside our area – all was peace and quiet and calm and as-you-were-before ... Inside the two square miles ... there was blood and thunder, but just outside it – only across one single road, like some national frontier – you were back in the world of Mrs Dale and *What's my line?* and England's green and pleasant land.

1960/4

Architectural controversy

As the economy recovered, development pressures built up to boiling point. Piccadilly Circus was one focus of attention. Jack Cotton's scheme for the Monico site, a triangular block to the north of the circus, attracted widespread opprobrium. After the rejection of the proposals in 1960 he turned to Walter Gropius to improve the design, but with no success. In the *Spectator*, Bernard Levin's celebratory piece at the demise of the development, following a public inquiry, mirrored public opinion.

The grapevine had been saying for some time that the Minister of Housing, Mr. Henry Brooke, would give

Mr. Jack Cotton and the Legal and General Assurance Society permission to put up their monster in Piccadilly Circus, though he might insist on a few comparatively trivial alterations first. As usual, the grapevine was wrong ... not only has the Monster of Piccadilly Circus been conquered; it has been beaten with the right weapons and for the right reasons.

... If it had not been for Mr. Cotton's over-confident action in calling the press conference at which he showed the photographs that finally gave the game away, 'it is a fair guess,' as Mr. Buchanan put it, 'that the building would now be in course of erection.' The outcry which followed Mr. Cotton's revelation of exactly what it was that he proposed to do to and in Piccadilly Circus (an outcry in which I am happy to recall the *Spectator* joined at the top of my lungs) made much of the singularly idiotic imaginary advertising slogan with which Mr. Cotton's designer (we will come to *him* in a minute) had seen fit to decorate the model of the proposed building ...

The second, and even more disturbing fact that emerges clearly from Mr. Buchanan's report (it was beginning to emerge from the evidence at the inquiry itself) is that nobody in fact designed the Monster at all. We know the name of the firm responsible – Messrs. Cotton, Ballard & Blow – and we know also that Mr. Frank Booth was called in as consultant architect for the

elevations as late as March, 1958. We know, too, that Mr. Bennett, Architect to the London County Council, had suggestions to make after the initial plans were submitted, and thereafter kept in close touch with the developers. But there the trail disappears into the sand. Mr. Bennett was at some pains during the inquiry to deny that he had designed the Monster (as well he might have been), and no person, or group of people, was willing to admit fatherhood of the puking babe, or to accuse anybody else of the offence. It seems strange, and worse than strange, that a building 172 feet high, of almost uniquely hideous aspect, covered with slabs of advertising visible over huge distances, could be submitted *and approved* without anybody knowing who actually designed it. (It is true that we do not know the name of the architect who designed Salisbury Cathedral. But I doubt if Mr. Cotton would maintain that the Monster of Piccadilly Circus was designed for the greater glory of God.)

In the City, much redevelopment was on sites bombed during the Blitz and the scheme for the area around St Paul's, Paternoster Square, was for psychological reasons one of the first to be considered. Planned by Lord Holford, co-author of the 1947 City plan, it was designed by the developers' architects and resulted in a pale imitation of his original ideas. As can be seen in the two views from the

OPPOSITE *The redevelopment of London. An illustration by BATT from* How Should We Rebuild London? *by C.B. Purdom.*

LEFT *Paternoster Square, beside St Paul's, in its immediate post-war state.*

Spectator, below, from May and October 1964, the site and its buildings were as controversial then as now, when redevelopment is once again proposed – this time in neoclassical dress.

Sir, . . . It is difficult to believe that any responsible and competent public body could have planned and supported the erection of the building at present under construction and at a time when all thinking people are becoming increasingly concerned about vandalism throughout the country.

In our view no effort should be spared to stop this outrage to history and good taste. It is a national disgrace that St. Paul's Cathedral should be desecrated by an unlet office block the result of which will be to deny to millions a beautiful setting and vista for Sir Christopher Wren's great masterpiece. The danger and impending disaster is far worse than we have seen so far. The developers intend, it appears to erect more buildings and even closer to the Cathedral . . .

Letters of protest and the fact that public opinion is overwhelmingly against further building around St. Paul's will not be sufficient to move those who have in effect placed office accommodation and profit before the future enjoyment of millions of people throughout the world. (The fact that the considerable correspondence received by one national newspaper alone has been almost entirely strongly against the projected buildings illustrates the extent of public feeling about this.) . . .

There is no tenable argument in favour of further construction closer to St. Paul's than the existing buildings. There are vast areas only five minutes from the Cathedral which badly require development, which are a disgrace to the City, and which have adequate space for those who for profit are prepared to ignore the further congestion in London their plans will entail.

Set one architect to master-plan for a second architect and the result is likely to be third-rate architecture. Yet the practice has the complete confidence of most local authorities and, as things are, it seems set to be widely used in the immense task of rebuilding Britain's cities.

The latest product of master planning is the huge Paternoster development to the north of St. Paul's Cathedral. It is the work first of Sir William Holford and then of Trehearne & Norman Preston and Partners. Sir William was asked by the City Corporation to prepare a design for the blitzed area around Paternoster Row in the early Fifties and in the idiom of the day he deployed a pattern of slabs and towers as a child might blocks. He also, to his credit, pushed cars down below and made the surface of the whole area over to pedestrians. His plan was published in 1956 amid applause from the architectural profession and screams of pain from fundamentalists who wanted to go back to the precincts of Wren. Trehearne and Co. were subsequently brought in by the Church Commissioners, the owners of the site, to design buildings with the positions and sizes fixed by Sir William. (The tallest of Sir William's towers had been forced to bow its head by the Royal Fine Art Commission in deference to St. Paul's, in fact making it appear squatter, fatter and more assertive, but despite this and other changes the neighbourhood as built conforms roughly to the Holford plan.)

The outcome is worth a visit . . . And when visiting it, it is necessary to remember that an integral part of the Paternoster design is a new forecourt for the cathedral. This will be irregular in shape, free of vehicles, and partially enclosed on the west side to allow the same view of Wren's west front from Ludgate Hill as at present. It was the creation of this framed view, or more particularly the building that will form the north side of the frame, that recently roused the *Daily Telegraph* to apoplexy. Framed views happen to be an English townscape tradition which was the reason Sir William

Holford used one, but the *Telegraph* with customary daring advocated a sweeping vista *à la* Versailles...

Once one is up among the office courtyards and walking about on the honey-coloured York stone paving, the cathedral soars up excitedly – first, the western cupolas, then half of the dome, then all of it. This is excellent because it focuses attention on the intricacy of the parts of the building instead of dulling the appetite with an overpowering view of the whole. Sir William's skill lay in his ability to look at the cathedral's huge, sculptured shape from an open bomb site and realise that it would be best revealed by such a series of snapshot views. The only snap he seems to have overlooked is a thin vertical one. There used to be such a squinch in an alley running from Paternoster Row to St. Paul's churchyard. As one turned into it the other end was blocked by a glacier of cornices topped by the great black dome. It will be a pity if, when the last of the new buildings is in place, a similar architectural peepshow cannot be found.

Yet a lack of slits and slots notwithstanding, Sir William Holford has given Londoners their most extensive series of new outdoor spaces to walk about in since the Festival of Britain and for this he must be congratulated... The trouble comes when one starts to look not outwards at St. Paul's but inwards at the faceless flanks of commerce. The mediocrity of the architecture that gives body to Sir William's master plan then becomes horrifyingly apparent. At the corner of Newgate Street and Warwick Lane there is a long corrugated box of Portland stone that appears about to crush the glasshouse it rests on. Next to it is a tower where a pretence has been made at distinguishing the base from the upper part – by changing the window design and tossing in a spandrel of Portland stone. But there is no point in going on. As architecture the Paternoster area is a complete flop. It has neither richness nor the good manners to act as a subdued foil to Wren's baroque *tour de force* in the manner of the Georgian houses surrounding Thomas Archer's church of St. John in Smith Square.

Master planning must bear the responsibility for this failure. I do not mean by this to condemn Sir William Holford. He probably did as well as a man could designing buildings for unknown people doing unknown jobs. The City Corporation asked him to do the impossible. The practice of commissioning prominent experts to master plan large city neighbourhoods was prompted by good intentions. It was a device for curbing commercial developers (with whom must be lumped the Church Commissioners) who could not be trusted to prepare enlightened layouts. But all it does is split the process of design unreasonably into two parts. This is as absurd as asking two men to cook a soufflé.

How far the division of design responsibility at new Paternoster resulted in the banality of the architecture, and how far it is the result of other factors is of course arguable, but the immeasurably better results of a unified design process can be seen in Alison and Peter Smithson's new cluster of towers for the *Economist* and Boodles' Club in St. James's Street. Because the architects had to think the whole problem through, and because they are skilled designers, both the towers and their intertwining spaces are magnetically bound together. Sooner or later local authorities must scrap the half-solution of master planning and accept that they have a responsibility to patronise, and encourage the patronage of, architects capable of work of this quality. At the same time they will have to devise methods for defining in writing what they expect to be provided in an area – safety for pedestrians, sunny spaces for sitting and feeding pigeons in, deference to historic buildings and so on. Plans will then be needed to show only the major and distributive road networks and the scale of permitted development. New Paternoster is a warning of the urgent need for a change of approach. Replicas of it could too easily deaden the individuality of town after town all over the land.

1960

De Gaulle's state visit

In other areas of life, existence went on as before. On becoming President of the Fifth Republic Charles de Gaulle chose to pay his first state visit to England, on 5 April 1960. Despite his Anglophobia, his admiration for British institutions and ceremonial remained (and was revived when he returned for Churchill's funeral in 1965). He was overwhelmed by his welcome, although such was his egotism that he seems to have imagined that a state visit of such splendour was accorded to him alone.

Queen Elizabeth set the tone. On our arrival, she came to Victoria Station with Prince Philip to welcome me and my wife and those who accompanied us, and as we drove through London side by side in her open carriage, the Sovereign went out of her way to encourage with gestures and smiles the enthusiasm of the crowd massed along the route. To give an exceptional cachet to the dinner and reception at Buck-

ingham Palace, she arranged for the first time a glittering firework display around the Palace, and in the midst of the illumination stood for a long time on the balcony by my side acknowledging the cheers of the vast crowd below. For the gala performance at Covent Garden, the Opera House was garlanded from top to bottom with carnations. At the dinner which I gave at the French Embassy, the entire royal family was present with the Queen. At her invitation, I had the unusual honour of reviewing the Household troops, with the Duke of Edinburgh at my side.

1961

A 'sit-down' protest

The Committee of 100 was a splinter group of the Campaign for Nuclear Disarmament (CND), which was founded in 1958. Their 'sit-down' protest outside the Ministry of Defence was a new kind of peaceful demonstration that took the government by surprise. The purpose was to show opposition to the plans for the American Polaris Base on Holy Loch. Bertrand Russell, almost ninety, was to publish his apocalyptic *Has man a future?* the same year.

The morning of February 18th [1961] was dark and drizzly and cold, and our spirits plummeted ... But when we assembled in Trafalgar Square there was a great crowd ... the Committee made it about 20,000. The speeches went well and quickly. Then began the march up Whitehall preceded by a large banner ... It

comprised a surging but calm and serious crowd of somewhat over 5,000 of those who had been in the Square ... Finally, over 5,000 people were sitting or lying on the pavement surrounding the Ministry. And there we sat for about two hours till darkness had fallen, a very solid and quiet, if not entirely mute, protest against government nuclear policies. A good many people joined us during this time, and more came to have a look at us, and, of course, the press and TV people flocked about asking their questions ... We learned that the Government had asked the Fire Department to use their hoses upon us. Luckily the Fire Department refused.

1960s

Spitalfields

The East End seems to have remained untouched by the fluctuations of fortune that affected other districts on the margins of central London (in this case, the City). There

worlds. Raphael Samuel remembers the transformation of the area, at the tail-end of its life as a Jewish ghetto, before its imminent change into the centre of the Bengali garment trade.

Spitalfields, when I first came to live here in 1962, seemed to be caught in a time warp. The district had miraculously escaped the war time bombing, perhaps because of its distance from the docks, and was as closely built over, if not inhabited, as it had been in the 19th century, when Christ Church, Spitalfields, was the most crowded parish in the metropolis. It was neglected by the local council. It was untouched by the developer's hand ... The Georgian streets – or 'Queen Anne houses' as they were then generally called – had been preserved by their poverty from improvement ... The 'Dickensian' tenements, such as the Industrial Dwellings in and about Flower and Dean Street (my mother spent the first eight years of her life in them), were also still in their original state ...

LEFT *Decayed fine houses in Fournier Street, Spitalfields, c. 1960, then mostly divided into small-scale garment workshops.*

OPPOSITE *Henry Cooper in the ascendancy during his fight against Cassius Clay (later known as Muhammad Ali) on 18 June 1963.*

was a constant flow of immigrant groups, starting with the eighteenth-century Huguenot weavers who were replaced by the Eastern European Jews arriving from the 1880s, then by the Bengalis. Spitalfields, the western fringe of the East End, has been a quite remarkable palimpsest of other

Economically, Spitalfields was still, as it always had been, a home of the textile trades. The weavers' attics no longer echoed to the clack of the loom, as they had done in the days when silk was the staple industry of the district, but the whirr of the sewing machine and the hiss of the pressing iron could still be heard from upstairs windows ... In Fashion Street ... a forest of trade signs testified to the multiplicity of garment makers; the same was true of Hanbury Street, where tailors' workrooms competed for space with the fruit merchants, and Fournier Street, where Queen Anne houses, infinitely sub-divided, served as owner-occupied industrial premises for the fur trade ... Umbrella makers, a last vestige of the Spitalfields silk industry, were still to be found in obscure courtyards ...

Spitalfields was still a ghetto, albeit one in an advanced state of decay. The Jews had mainly departed, but the streets were full of their businesses ...

The word 'conservationist' enjoyed no currency when I bought my house ... and I would scarcely have known what it meant ...

Spitalfields has been under threat from the developers for as long as I have lived here. In the 1960s, it seemed, there was no one to oppose them.

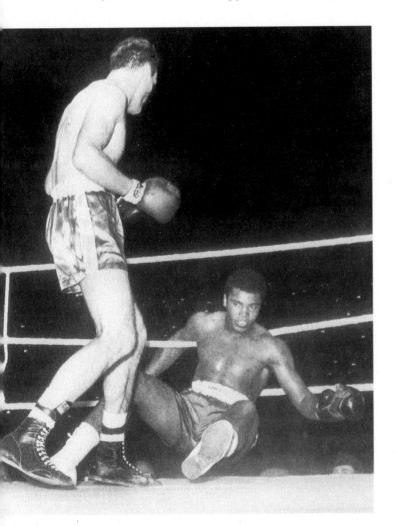

1963

Henry Cooper v Cassius Clay

Every so often a sporting personality steps outside the confines of their professional world and becomes a national figure. The south London boxer Henry Cooper, 'Our 'Enery' was one such. Here he recounts his first encounter with the then Cassius Clay, number two heavyweight in the world. Clay himself, through his antics on television as much as by his remarkable skills, was a public figure.

When Cassius Clay came to England to fight me at Wembley Football Stadium on Jun 18, 1963, some of the press here tended to write him down ... We knew he was a flashy type of fighter with an enormous reach, and we'd heard about his ranting and his raving and his prediction lark. But raw? To my mind he'd beaten some useful boys on the way up, and in the next fight after me he won the world title.

Directly he got here he was up to his games. It was Cooper for the chop in round five. And he would hold up his hand with the fingers and thumb spread out just to make sure the photographers got the message. Friends kept asking me, 'Are you worried by all that talk?' I'd been too long a professional. 'No, let him carry on,' I'd say ... It was all a gimmick ... he'd go into the ring shouting 'I'm the prettiest. I'm the greatest.' ...

Although it was only a ten-round fight it meant a lot to my world standing. We trained for this at the Fellowship Inn, a big pub on the Bellingham estate [Catford] run by good friends of ours ... They had a big ballroom at the back of the pub, and we transformed this into a gymnasium ... We lived in rooms at the front of the pub, away from any noise, and I suppose about a hundred to a hundred and fifty people would come most days to watch us in training ... Someone would take a box round and we'd get quite a useful sum for the old age pensioners or some other charity. It was quite an event in Bellingham ...

We had a strategy worked out. We knew he was going to be fast, but it's not until you are in there with him that you realise just how fast he really is. In the first round my problem was to try and get in distance to land my punches ... We were pleased with the way it was going ... But in the third round I hit trouble, with my eye starting to bleed ... in the fourth I knew the eye was bad and it was now or never ... Jim was going to stop the fight at the end of the third, but after all this he had to let me come out again for the fifth round just in case

Clay was still a little groggy . . . I could feel it . . . like a tap pouring on to my chest. I thought, this is bad, and then Clay started to come forward . . . slinging punches as hard as he could . . . Jim shouted 'Stop it, ref!' and was up on the apron of the ring before the referee had actually done so. It was that bad.

1963

A night out in Battersea

One novel that captures London with extraordinary immediacy is Nell Dunn's *Up the Junction* (1963). A series of linked stories set in and around Battersea, her gang of girls inhabits a world of likely lads and roller-coaster attachments. She accurately pinpoints the south London settings of the period – the bowling alleys, clubs and pubs, scrap-yards and public laundries, as well as the day-to-day background of petty crime and racial prejudice.

We are at a party in a block of LCC flats: plates of ham sandwiches, crates of brown ale and Babycham, the radiogram in the lounge, pop-song oblivion with the volume turned to full . . .

Out on the concrete balcony dusky Fulham stretches away.

ABOVE *Illustration by Susan Benson from Nell Dunn's* Up the Junction.

RIGHT *Centrepoint, architect Richard Seifert, looming over the West End,* c.*1964.*

'My wife went for me this morning when I was lying in bed, hit me on the back of the neck,' says Dave. The lights of Stamford Bridge Saturday-night football. Little rows of houses cluster round the gasworks. 'I should never have got married, I'm not the marrying sort.' ...

'You girls like to come over the One-O-One?'

Out in the road the six of us pile into the beat-up Buick ...

The car slows to a stop. Dave lifts me off the back. We go through a bricklayers' yard and down some filthy stone steps. The club is an old cellar poshed up with hardboard and flashy paper. 'Got two thousand pound' worth of gear in 'ere. There's that one-armed bandit ... Them pin tables ... And that new American-style juke-box.' ... 'Let's go. It's dead in here.' ...

We pile into the Buick and cruise through the park ... Then among the houses the car stops ...

'Let's get out' says Dave, 'I can't take you home because me Mum's pawned all the furniture.' ... We walk across a chaos of grass and rubble to a row of deserted houses. 'This is where we lived till it got demolished – slum clearance. They moved us out to lousy Roehampton.' ... Outside the dawn slides over the gasworks, slips over the rubble through the window.

1964

War declared on office building

The office boom continued in London. Harry Hyams, one of the most reclusive of the post-war developers, built Centrepoint. Across London numerous office blocks rose – undistinguished but for their names. Astronaut House, Space House, Orbit House, Planet House, and Telstar House were from the age of the moon shot. They were also the last of their kind. In 1964 the newly elected Labour government's Secretary of State for Housing and Local Government, Richard Crossman, put an end to it all as he remembers in his diary.

Tuesday, November 3rd Cabinet was almost entirely devoted to the secret plan George Brown [at the Department of Economic Affairs] and I had worked out for stopping all office building in London. This was suddenly presented to Cabinet. George spoke. I gave details on the factual case for doing it, and despite the predictions in my Ministry that there would be tremendous opposition there was none at all. Nobody in a Labour Cabinet is going to object to an action which is

LEFT & OPPOSITE *Winston Churchill's funeral, January 1965. The end of an era.*

extremely popular outside London and which will only ruin property speculators; actually, it probably won't even do that because a lot of them will make money out of the rising rents paid now for offices already in existence. It all went with a bang...

Wednesday, November 4th Today we suddenly found George Brown was to speak this afternoon and not on Thursday and everything had to be prepared for the great declaration on office building... this was a terrific success. It gave a tremendous sense of the Hundred Days [the Wilson government's action plan].

1965

Winston Churchill's funeral

In strange and sombre contrast to the youth culture of the early 1960s, the funeral of Sir Winston Churchill on Saturday, 30 January 1965, marked the end of the post-war chapter. The close of that immense life, the death of a single figure whose courage was perceived to have kept the country free from Nazism, was marked by the stupendous crowds who came, and queued, to pay their last respects to Sir Winston as he lay in state. As Richard Crossman records in his diary on the day of the funeral London stopped to pay respect.

[Saturday, January 30th] Winston's funeral. All through the week London had been working itself up for the great day. The lying-in-state in Westminster Hall had taken place on Wednesday, Thursday and Friday. I went on all three evenings, taking Molly and our doorman, Arthur, on one night, and Anne and Tommy Balogh the second night, and then on the third night Mr Large who cuts my hair. Each time one saw, even at one o'clock in the morning, the stream of people pouring down the steps of Westminster Hall towards the catafalque. Outside the column wound through the garden at Millbank, then stretched over Lambeth Bridge, right round the corner to St Thomas's Hospital. As one walked through the streets one felt the hush and one noticed the cars stopping suddenly and the people stepping out into the quietness and walking across to Westminster Hall. We as Members of Parliament could just step into the Hall through our side door.

I really hadn't wanted to go to the funeral ... My chief memory is of the pall-bearers, in particular poor Anthony Eden, literally ashen grey, looking as old as Clement Attlee. And then of the coffin being carried up the steps by those poor perspiring privates of the Guards, sweat streaming down their faces, each clutching the next in order to sustain the sheer weight ... My other chief memory was the superb way the trumpets sounded the Last Post and the Reveille. The trumpeters were right up in the Whispering Gallery, round the inside of the dome, and for the first time a trumpet had room to sound in a dimension, a hemisphere of its own. But, oh, what a faded, declining establishment surrounded me. Aged marshals, grey, dreary ladies, decadent Marlboroughs and Churchills. It was a dying congregation gathered there and I am afraid the Labour Cabinet didn't look too distinguished either. It felt like the end of an epoch, possibly even the end of a nation.

SOURCES

ROMAN *and* SAXON LONDON, *43–1066*

pages
13–14 Tacitus, *Annals*, Book 14
14–15 Inscriptions:
 (a) Julius Classicianus: tomb in British Museum
 (b) others from Royal Commission on the Historical Monuments of England, *London, vol. III: Roman London*, 1928, Appendix II
16 Eumenius, *Panegyricus Constantio Caesari*
16–17 Ammianus Marcellinus, *Rerum Gestarum Libri*, Book XX, 1
17 *Bede's Ecclesiastical History*, ed. Bertram Colgrave and R.A.B. Mynors, 1969
17–19 *English Historical Documents, vol. 1, c.500–1042*, ed. Dorothy Whitelock, 1979
19–20 Margaret Ashdown, *English and Norse Documents Relating to the Reign of Ethelred the Unready*, 1930
20–1 *English Historical Documents, vol. 1, ut supra*
22–3 *Vita Aedwardi Regis*, ed. Frank Barlow, 1962

MEDIEVAL LONDON, *1066–1485*

27–8 W. de Gray Birch, *The Historical Charters and Constitutional Documents of the City of London*, 1884
28–9 *Gesta Stephani*, ed. K. R. Potter, 1976
29–30 Christopher Brooke and Gillian Keir, *London 800–1216*, 1975
30 *Ibid.*
30 Birch, *op. cit.*
31 Matthew Paris, *English History*, ed. J. A. Giles, vol. I, 1852
31–2 W. Taylor, *Annals of Saint Mary Overy*, 1833 (translation adapted)
32 E. Williams, *Early Holborn and the Legal Quarter of London*, 1927
32–3 *London Assize of Nuisance 1301–1431*, ed. Helena Chew and William Kellaway, 1973
33–4 *Calendar of Select Pleas and Memoranda of the City of London 1381–1412*, ed. A. H. Thoms, 1932
34 *Ibid.*
34–5 L. F. Salzman, *Building in England down to 1540*, 1952
35–6 *Munimenta Gildhallae Londoniensis, vol. III: Liber Albus, Liber Custumarum et Liber Horn*, ed. Henry Thomas Riley, 1862
36 *The Westminster Chronicle 1381–1394*, ed. L. C. Hector and Barbara F. Harvey, 1982
36–8 *The Chronicles of Froissart*,

translated by Sir John Bourchier, Lord Berners, vol. 3, 1901
38–9 *Survey of London, vol. 9, St Helen's Bishopsgate*, 1924
39–40 *Chronicles of London*, ed. Charles Lethbridge Kingsford, 1905: Julius B II
40–1 *The Historical Collections of A Citizen of London*, ed. James Gairdner, 1876
41 *Chronicles of London*, ed. Charles Lethbridge Kingsford, 1905: Vitellius A XVI
41–2 Sir John Fortescue, *De Laudibus Legum Angliae*, ed. S. B. Chrimes, 1949
42 George D. Painter, *William Caxton: A Quincentary Biography*, 1976
43–5 Sir Thomas More, *History of King Richard III*, 1883 edn

LONDON *under the* EARLY TUDORS, *1485–1558*

49–50 *Relation or rather a True Account of the Island of England*, ed. C. A. Sneyd, 1847
50–1 *Chronicles of London*, ed. Charles Lethbridge Kingsford, 1905: Vitellius A XVI
51–2 *Ibid.*
53 Edward Hall, *The Triumphant Reign of Henry VIII*, ed. Charles Whibley, vol. 1, 1904
53–6 George Cavendish, *The Life and Death of Cardinal Wolsey*, ed. Richard S. Sylvester, 1959
56 John Stow, *The Annals or General Chronicle of England*, 1615 edn
56–8 *The Medieval Records of a London City Church, St Mary at Hill*, ed. Henry Littlehales, vol. 2, 1905
58 John Stow, *Survey of London*, ed. C. L. Kingsford, 1908
58–60 *Chronicle of the Grey Friars of London*, ed. J. G. Nichols, 1852
60–2 *The Journal of the King Edward's Reign, written with his own hand*, 1884 edn
62–3 *Narratives of the Reformation*, ed. J. G. Nichols, 1859
63–4 *Ibid.*
64–5 *The Acts and Monuments of John Foxe*, ed. S. R. Cattley, vol. 8, 1839

ELIZABETHAN *and* JACOBEAN LONDON, *1558–1625*

71–2 W. Sparrow Simpson, *Documents Illustrating the History of St Paul's Cathedral*, 1880
72–3 Edward Murray Tomlinson, *A*

History of the Minories, London, 1907
73–4 John Stow, *A Survey of London*, 1615 edn; *The Annals or General Chronicle of England*, 1615 edn
74–5 Raymond Needham and Alexander Webster, *Somerset House Past and Present*, 1905
75–6 Giordano Bruno, *The Ash Wednesday Supper*, ed. Edward A. Gosselin and Lawrence S. Lerner, 1977 (translation adapted)
76–7 E.K. Chambers, *The Elizabethan Stage*, vol. 2, 1923
77–8 *Ibid.*
78–9 *Ibid.*, vol. 4
79–81 Leslie Hotson, *The Death of Christopher Marlowe*, 1925
81–2 *Diary of John Manningham of the Middle Temple*, ed. John Bruce, 1868
82–3 *The Plague Pamphlets of Thomas Dekker*, ed. F. P. Wilson, 1925
83–4 *Trial of Guy Fawkes and Others*, ed. Donald Craswell, 1934
84–5 Bernard Rudden, *The New River, A Legal History*, 1985
86 C. M. Clode, *Memorials of the Guild of Merchant Taylors*, 1875
86–7 *Ibid.*
87 Sir George Buck, *The Third Universitie of England*, 1615
88–9 *Acts of the Privy Council, January 1618 to June 1619*, 1929
89 Thomas Mun, *A Discourse of Trade from England unto East-Indies*, 1621

LONDON *between* KING *and* PARLIAMENT, *1625–1660*

92–4 *Memoirs of the Embassy of the Marshal de Bassompierre*, ed. J. W. Croker, 1819
94 *Camden Miscellany*, ed. John Gough Nichols, vol. 55, 1853
94–5 *The Travels of Peter Mundy, in Europe and Asia, 1608–1667*, vol. 3, Hakluyt Society, 1919
95–6 Mis-Amaxias [Henry Peacham], *Coach and Sedan*, 1636
96–7 W. Sparrow Simpson, *Documents Illustrating the History of St Paul's Cathedral*, 1880
97–8 *The Autobiography of Dr William Laud*, 1839 edn
98–9 *The Manuscripts of the House of Lords*, vol. 11, 1962
99–100 *Clarendon's History of the Great Rebellion*, ed. Roger Lockyer, 1967
100 William Lithgow, *The Present Surveigh of London and England's State*, 1643

101–2 *A Letter from Mercurius Civicus to Mercurius Rusticus . . .*, 1643
102–3 *The Clarke Papers*, vol. 1, Camden Society n.s., vol. 53, 1894
103 *Clarendon's History, ut supra*
103–4 *The Clarke Papers, ut supra*
105 *Diaries and Letters of Philip Henry, M.A.*, ed. Matthew Henry Lee, 1882
106 Henry Robinson, *The Office of Addresses and Encounters*, 1658
106–7 Stephen Wren, *Parentalia*, 1750

LONDON *under the* LATER STUARTS, *1660–1714*

111–12 *The Diary of John Evelyn*, ed. E. S. de Beer, 1959
112–15 Evelyn, *op. cit.*
The Diary of Samuel Pepys, ed. Robert Latham and William Matthews, vol. 6, 1972
[Allin] Walter George Bell, *The Great Plague in London in 1665*, 1924
115–17 Evelyn, *op. cit.*
Pepys, *op. cit.*, vol. 7
117–19 Henry Thomas, *The Wards of London*, 1828
119–21 Wren, *op. cit.*
121–2 Evelyn, *op. cit.*
122–3 Narcissus Luttrell, *A Brief Historical Relation of State Affairs*, vol. 1, 1857
Evelyn, *op. cit.*
123–4 *Correspondence of the Family of Hatton*, ed. E. M. Thompson, vol. 2, 1878
124–5 Samuel Jeake, *An Astrological Diary of the Seventeenth Century*, ed. Michael Hunter and Annabel Gregory, 1988
125–7 Ned Ward, *The London Spy*, 1704 edn
127–8 [Edward Hatton] *A New View of London*, 1709
129 Richard D. Altick, *The Shows of London*, 1978

HANOVERIAN LONDON, *1714–1789*

132–4 Daniel Defoe, *A Tour through the Whole Island of Great Britain*, 1927 edn
134–5 Bedford Estate Papers, Greater London Record Office, E/BER/CG/E8/10/1
136–7 Hogarth's *'Apology for Painters'*, ed. Michael Kitson, Walpole Society, vol. 41, 1968
137 *Vertue Notebooks Vol. III*, Walpole Society, vol. 22, 1934
137–8 [James Ralph], *A Critical Review of the Publick Buildings, Statues and Ornaments in and about London and Westminster*, 1734
138–40 Desmond Fitzgerald, *The Norfolk House Music Room* 1973, Appendix A
140–1 *The Official Diary of Lieutenant-General Adam Williamson, Deputy-Lieutenant of the Tower of London 1722–1747*, ed. J. C. Fox, Camden Society 3rd series, vol. 22, 1912
141–2 *Peter Kalm's Account of his Visit to England in 1748*, 1892
142–3 P. J. Grosley, *A Tour to London*, vol. 1, 1772
143–4 *Collected Works of Oliver Goldsmith*, ed. Arthur Friedman, vol. 2, 1966
144–5 *Boswell's London Journal 1762–1763*, ed. Frederick A. Pottle, 1950
145 *Memoirs of William Hickey*, ed. Alfred Spencer, vol. 1 [n.d.]
145–6 *Horace Walpole's Correspondence*, ed. W. S. Lewis, vol. 25, 1971
146–7 *Boswell's Life of Johnson*, ed. R. W. Chambers, 1957 edn
147 *John Wesley's Journal*, abridged edn, 1903
148–50 R. Leslie-Melville, *The Life and Work of Sir John Fielding*, 1934
150 John Howard, *An Account of the Principal Lazarettos in Europe*, 1789
150–1 *Sophie in London 1786*, ed. Clare Williams, 1933
151 *The Journal of Mary Frampton*, ed. Harriet Mundy, 1885

LONDON *in the* ERA *of* REVOLUTION, *1789–1837*

155–7 H. C. Robbins Landon, *The Collected Correspondence and London Notebooks of Joseph Haydn*, 1959
157–8 William Wordsworth, *The Prelude*, Book VII, 1805 edn
158 *Everybody's Lamb*, ed. A. C. Ward, 1933
158–60 *Selections from the Papers of the London Corresponding Society 1792–1799*, 1983
160–1 Hackney Vestry Minutes, January 1795, Greater London Record Office, P79/JN1/157
161–2 P. Colquhoun, *A Treatise on the Commerce and Police of the River Thames*, 1800
162–3 Leigh Hunt, *The Old Court Suburb*, 1851
163–5 *Extracts of the Journals and Correspondence of Miss Berry*, ed. Lady Theresa Lewis, vol. 2, 1865
165–6 Benjamin Silliman, *A Journal of Travels in England, Holland and Scotland*, 1820
166–7 *The Diary of Joseph Farington*, ed. Kathryn Cave, vol. 13, 1984
167–8 *A Portion of the Journal Kept by Thomas Raikes*, vol. 3, 1857
168–9 John Gore, *Creevey*, 1948
169–70 Marquis de Vermont and Sir Charles Darnley, *London and Paris, or Comparative Sketches*, 1823
170–1 *Life and Struggles of William Lovett*, 1967
171–3 Karl Friedrich Schinkel, *The English Journey*, ed. David Bindman and Gottfried Riemann, 1993
173–5 John Thomas Pocock, *The Diary of A London Schoolboy 1826–1830*, 1980
175–6 *The New Moral World*, 7 November 1840
176 E. M. Forster, *Marianne Thornton*, 1956
176–7 Francis T. Buckland, *Curiosities of Natural History*, 3rd series, 2nd edn., vol. 1, 1868.
177–8 Najaf Koolee Merza, *Journal of a Residence in England*, vol. 2 [n.d.]
178–9 *The London Journal of Flora Tristan*, translated, annotated and introduced by Jean Hawkes, 1982
179 *The Diary of Benjamin Robert Haydon*, ed. W. B. Pope, vol. 4 (1832–40), 1963

FIFTY YEARS OF VICTORIAN LONDON, *1837–1887*

184–5 Louisa Twining, *Recollections of Life and Work*, 1893
185 *Ibid.*
185–6 *Felix Mendelssohn: Letters*, ed. G. Selden-Goth, 1945
186 *Mary Taylor: friend of Charlotte Bronte*, ed. Joan Stevens, 1972
186–7 Charles Dickens, *Sketches by Boz*, 1836, enlarged edition 1839 [quoted, John Lehmann, *Holborn*, 1970]
187 *The London Journal of Flora Tristan*, 1842, translated, annotated and introduced by Jean Hawkes, 1982
188 James Cornish, *Royal Magazine*, XXIII, no. 138, April 1910 [quoted, David Goodway, *London Chartism 1838–1848*, 1982]
188 Dr. C. G. Carus, *The King of Saxony's journey through England and Scotland in the year 1844*, 1846
188 William Cullen Bryant, *Letters of a Traveller*, 1850 [Walter Allen, *Transatlantic Crossing*, 1971]
188 Goodway, *op. cit.*
188–9 *Northern Star*, May 1842
189 *Northern Star*, 15 April 1848
189 Cornish, *op. cit.*

189–90 Henry Mayhew, *London Labour and the London Poor*, ed. Victor Neuburg, 1865, 1985
190–1 quoted Allen, *op. cit.*
191–2 Carus, *op. cit.*
192 Emerson, *op. cit.*
192–3 Nathaniel Hawthorne, *English Notebooks*, ed. Randall Stewart, 1941
193 Carus, *op. cit.*
194 Hawthorne, *op. cit.*
194 quoted C. H. Gibbs-Smith, *The Great Exhibition of 1851*, 1950
194 *Queen Victoria in her Letters and Journals*, selected by Christopher Hibbert, 1984
195 *Jane Welsh Carlyle, letters to her family 1839–1863*, ed. Leonard Huxley, 1924
195–6 Hawthorne, *op. cit.*
196 Herzen, *Ends and Beginnings*, ed. Aileen Kelly, translated by C. Garnett, 1985
196–7 *Preussische Zeitung*, 12 November 1852, translation by Nicholas Jacobs as 'Old Heroes, New Victories'
197–8 John Hollingshead, *My Lifetime*, vol. I, 1895
198 George Augustus Sala, *Twice around the Clock*, 1859
198–9 [Arthur Munby] from Derek Hudson, *Man of Two Worlds*, 1972
199–200 *The Builder*, 29 June 1861
200 Victor Lewis, *Tolstoy in London*, 1979
200 *Annual Register*, 9 January 1863
200–1 'London Society Underground', *London Society*, vol. III, 1863
202 *Sir Joseph Bazalgette*, exhibition catalogue, Institution of Civil Engineers, 1991
202–3 Munby, *op. cit.*
204 Revd Gibson's letter to the secretary of the Bethnal Green Fund, copy in Tower Hamlets Local History Library, 1859
204–5 Munby, *op. cit.*
205–6 *The Collected Letters of Thomas Hardy*, ed. Richard Little Purdy and Michael Millgate, vol. I, 1840–1892, 1978
206 *The Annual Register*, 1866
206–7 Gustave Doré and Blanchard Jerrold, *London, a Pilgrimage*, 1872
208–9 *Journals and Correspondence of Lady Eastlake*, ed. Charles Eastlake Smith, 1895
209–10 H. Taine, *Notes on England*, 1872
210–11 *The First Chinese Embassy to the West*, translated and annotated J. D. Frodsham, 1974
211–12 Octavia Hill, *Homes of the London Poor*, 1875; originally published as

'Space for the People', *Macmillan's Magazine*, August 1875
212–13 *The Collected Letters of William Morris*, vol. I, ed. Norman Kelvin, 1984
213–14 *A Victorian Schoolboy in London, the diary of Ernest Baker 1881–2*, ed. David Rodgers, 1989
214 quoted Allen, *op. cit.*
214 *The Morning Post*, 3 August 1878
214 Gertrude Ziani de Ferranti and Richard Ince, *The Life and Letters of Sebastian de Ferranti*, 1934
214 *Survey of London*, vol. 40, 1980
214 *Kensington News*, 4 October 1882
214–15 *Canon Barnett, his life, work and friends*, vol. I, by his wife, 1918
215 Jane Addams, *Twenty Years at Hull-house*, 1910
216 *Annual Register*, 1884
217 *Building News*, 7 March 1879
217–18 Montgomery Hyde, 'Oscar Wilde and his architect', *Architectural Review*, June 1951
218 *The Letters of Oscar Wilde*, ed. Rupert Hart-Davis, 1962
219 H. G. Wells, *An Experiment in Autobiography*, vol. I, 1937
219 *Life of Octavia Hill, as told in her letters*, ed. C. Edmund Maurice, 1913

IMPERIAL LONDON, *1887–1914*

224 George Gissing, *In the Year of Jubilee*, 1892
224–6 Annie Besant, *An Autobiography*, 1893
226 Michael Holroyd, *Bernard Shaw*, vol. I, 1856–1898, 1988
226 Pamela Horn, *High Society*, 1992, Appendix B
226–7 *The Collected Works of Mahatma Gandhi*, vol. I, 1884–1896, 1958
227 *Electrical Engineer*, 26 October 1888
227 *London Daily News*, 23 September 1889
227–8 H. G. Wells, *Experiment in Autobiography*, vol. I, 1937
228–9 Molly Hughes, *A London Home in the Nineties*, 1937
229–30 Beatrice Webb, *Diary*, vol. I, 1873–92 ed. Norman and Jeanne MacKenzie, 1982
230–1 Beatrice Webb, 'The Docks', from C. Booth, *Labour and Life of the People of London*, vol. I, 1889
231 Webb, *Diary, op. cit.*
231–2 *Memoirs of Lady Eastlake, op. cit.*
232 Arthur Page Grubb, *The Life Story of the Right Hon. John Burns*, 1908

232–3 Holroyd, *op. cit.*
233 Piotr Ilyich Tchaikovsky, *Letters to his Family: an Autobiography*, translated G. von Meck, 1981
233 *Queen Victoria in her Letters and Journals*, selected by Christopher Hibbert, 1984
234 *Mark Twain's Notebook*, ed. Albert Bigelow Paine, 1935
235–6 Bernard M. Allen, *Down the Stream of Life*, 1948
236–7 Robert Machray, *The Night Side of London*, c.1902
237–8 T. W. H. Crosland, *The Suburbans*, 1905
238–9 Booker T. Washington, 'London Through the Eyes of John Burns', from Walter Allen, *Transatlantic Crossing*, 1971
239 Maud Pember Reeves, *Round About a Pound a Week*, 1913
239–40 Mario Borsa, *The English Stage of Today*, 1906 [quoted, Gavin Weightman, *Bright Lights, Big City*, 1992]
240–1 Virginia Woolf, *A Passionate Apprentice, The Early Journals 1897–1909*, ed. Mitchell A. Leaska, 1990
241–2 *Ibid.*
243 Gordon Honeycombe, *Selfridges*, 1984
243–4 Emmeline Pankhurst, *My Own Story*, 1914
244–5 Richard Church, *Over the Bridge*, 1956
245–6 Consuelo Vanderbilt Balsan, *The Glitter and the Gold*, 1953

LONDON AT WAR, *1914–1945*

248–9 *The Times*, 17 May 1915
249 *The Times*, 2 June 1915
250 *The Diary of Virginia Woolf*, vol. I, 1915–1919, ed. Anne Olivier Bell, 1977
250 Mrs C. S. Peel, *How We Lived Then, 1914–1918*, 1929
250–1 Vera Brittain, *Testament of Youth*, 1933
251–2 *The Autobiography of Bertrand Russell*, vol. I, 1967
252 Robert Graves, *Goodbye to all that*, 1929
252–3 Michael MacDonagh, *In London During the Great War*, 1935
253–4 *Ibid.*
254 From leaflet accompanying exhibition at the Fine Art Society, quoting MSS memoirs of Richard Roschke from Records Department, Imperial War Museum, 1993
254–5 MacDonagh, *op. cit.*

255–6 Peel, *op. cit.*

256 Woolf, *op. cit.*

257 Dora Russell, *The Tamarisk Tree*, vol. 1, 1975

257 Ellen Wilkinson, *Clash*, 1929

257–8 Philip Tilden, *True Remembrances: The Memoirs of an Architect*, 1954

258 Emmanuel Litvinoff, *Journey Through a Small Planet*, 1972

258–9 *The Journals of Arnold Bennett, 1921–1928*, ed. Newman Flower, 1933

259 Arnold Bennett, *Riceyman Steps*, 1923

260 Karel Capek, *Letters from England*, translated Paul Salver, 1925

260–1 *The Times*, 6 May 1926

261 *The Times*, 7 May 1926

262 *The Diary of Virginia Woolf*, vol. III, 1925–1930, ed. Anne Olivier Bell, 1980

262–3 Alfred Dedman, from *Working Lives*, vol. 1, 1905–45, 1975

264–5 Arnold Bennett, *Journal, 1929*, 1930

265 Simone de Beauvoir, *The Prime of Life*, 1962

265–6 George Orwell, *Down and Out in Paris and London*, 1933

266 Laurie Lee, *As I Walked Out One Midsummer Morning*, 1969

266–7 Jessica Mitford, *Hons and Rebels*, 1960

267–8 Steen Eiler Rasmussen, 'First Impressions in London', *Wasmuths Monatshefte Baukunst*, 1928, translated Andrew Saint (AA Files 20)

268–9 Steen Eiler Rasmussen, *London: The Unique City*, 1934; first English edn 1937

269–70 Kingsley Martin, *Critic's London Diary*, 1960

270 Harold Nicolson, *Diaries and Letters, 1930–1939*, 1966

270 Martin, *op. cit.*

271 Howard Marshall, 'The Rake's Progress', *Britain and the Beast*, ed. Clough Williams Ellis, 1937

271–2 Gavin Weightman and Steve Humphries, *The Making of Modern London, 1914–1939*, 1984

272 Quentin Crisp, *The Naked Civil Servant*, 1968

272 Harold Nicolson, *Diaries and Letters, 1939–45*, 1967

273 *Ibid.*

273–4 Martin, *op. cit.*

274 *The Collected Essays, Journalism and Letters of George Orwell*, ed. Sonia Orwell and Ian Angus, 1968

274 *Ibid.*, vol. 11

274–5 Martin, *op. cit.*

275–6 C. Fitzgibbon, *The Blitz*, 1961

276 Ralph Ingersoll, *Report on England*, 1941

276–7 *Ibid.*

277–8 Winston Churchill, *The Second World War*, vol. II, 1949

278 Ingersoll, *op. cit.*

278–9 J. M. Richards, *Memoirs of an Unjust Fella*, 1980

279 Nicolson, *op. cit.*

279–80 Orwell, *op. cit.*

280–1 Orwell, *op. cit.*

281 Nicolson, *op. cit.*

LONDON *in the* POST-WAR WORLD, *1945–1965*

286 Harold Nicolson, *Diaries and Letters, 1939–45*, 1967

286–7 J. H. Forshaw and Patrick Abercrombie, *The County of London Plan*, 1943

287–8 J. C. Trewin and H. J. Willmott, *London–Bodmin. An Exchange of Letters*, 1950

288–9 Kingsley Martin, *Critic's London Diary*, 1960

290 Noel Coward, 'Don't Make Fun of the Fair', *The Lyric Review*, 1951

290–1 J. M. Richards, *The Architectural Review*, May 1951

291 *Selected Letters of Raymond Chandler*, ed. Frank MacShane, 1981

291–2 *Don't Tread on Me*, selected letters of S. J. Perelman, ed. Prudence Crowther, 1987

293–4 Fleur Cowles, *Friends and Memories*, 1975

294 Martin, *op. cit.*

294–5 Iris Murdoch, *Under the Net*, 1954

295 P. J. Kavanagh, *The Perfect Stranger*, 1966

295–6 Frank Norman, *Norman's London*, 1969

296–7 Colin MacInnes, *Absolute Beginners*, 1959

297–8 Bernard Levin, 'Snap Plom for Mr. Brooke', *The Spectator*, 27 May 1960

299 Letter from P. F. Carter-Ruck and J. E. Payne, *The Spectator*, 22 May 1964

299–300 Terence Bendixson, 'Pushing Out Sir William', *The Spectator*, 16 October 1964

300–1 Jean Lacouture, *De Gaulle; The Ruler (1945–1970)*, translated Alan Sheridan, 1991

301–2 *The Autobiography of Bertrand Russell*, vol. 1, 1967

302–3 'The Pathos of Conservation', *The Saving of Spitalfields*, ed. Mark Girouard *et al*, 1969

303–4 Henry Cooper, *Henry Cooper; An Autobiography*, 1972

304–5 Nell Dunn, *Up the Junction*, 1963

306–7 *The Crossman Diaries* (condensed version), ed. Anthony Howard, 1979

320

ACKNOWLEDGEMENTS

The authors and publishers would like to thank the following individuals, museums, photographers and photographic archives for permission to reproduce their material: Aerofilms 271; Apsley House London (The Bridgeman Art Library) 167; Ashmolean Museum, Oxford 53,55; Governor and Company of the Bank of England 124, 206; Bishopsgate Institute 249; Bodleian Library, Oxford 66; British Architectural Library, RIBA, London 228 (above), 268; The British Library Board 6 (above), 20, 21, 24, 26, 37, 39, 40, 43, 45, 54 (below), 75, 76, 80 (The Bridgeman Art Library), 102, 104, 109, 122; Trustees of the British Museum 14 (left), 129 (The Bridgeman Art Library), 136, 148, 159, 165, 170–1; British Railways 184; Cambridge University Library 33 (below); Camden Local Studies and Archives Centre 212; Archivist, Christ's Hospital 61; College of Arms 54 (above); Corporation of London Records Office 29, 30, 33 (above), 35, 108, 135, 137, 166, 177; The Master and Fellows of Corpus Christi College, Cambridge 28, 79; Courtauld Institute of Art 34; Dean and Chapter of Westminster 18, 22, 23, 48, 81; Drapers Company 59; Duke of Buccleuch and Queensberry 44; English Heritage Photographic Library 302; Fine Art Society 195, 282; Fotomas Index 49, 120 (below); Greater London Record Office 304–5; Guildhall Library 7 (left) (The Bridgeman Art Library), 38, 57, 62, 73, 74, 85 (The Bridgeman Art Library), 97, 118 (The Bridgeman Art Library), 119, 120 (above), 126–7, 131 (The Bridgeman Art Library), 139 (above), 144, 152 (The Bridgeman Art Library), 153 (The Bridgeman Art Library), 154 (The Bridgeman Art Library), 164 (The Bridgeman Art Library), 168–9 (The Bridgeman Art Library), 180 (The Bridgeman Art Library), 211 (above) (The Bridgeman Art Library), 213 (The Bridgeman Art Library), 232 (The Bridgeman Art Library), 298; Richard Perceval Graves 251; Houses of Parliament, Westminster (The Bridgeman Art Library) 179; Hulton-Deutsch Picture Library 10, 199, 203, 205, 207, 211 (below), 221, 225, 255, 260, 269, 270, 280 (below), 281, 283, 291, 292, 293, 296–7, 301 (above); Illustrated London News Picture Library 201, 202, 257, 267, 288–9; Imperial College Archives 219; Imperial War Museum 246, 247 (The Bridgeman Art

Library), 250, 273, 274, 276–7, 279, 280 (above), 294; Institution of Civil Engineers, *The Triumphant Bore* Exhibition (1993) 193; London Borough of Islington 215, 259; Peter Jackson Collection 242 (below); Kenwood House (The Bridgeman Art Library) 6 (below); A. F. Kersting 138; Andrew Lawson 128; London Museum of Jewish Life 258; London Transport Museum 190; MacGibbon & Kee 304; Mander & Mitchenson Theatre Collection 78, 156, 185; Mansell Collection 42, 65, 83, 113 (below), 146, 151, 160, 187, 191, 216; Mary Evans Picture Library 230–1, 235, 236, 240, 244; Marylebone Gallery 234, 252; Memories 242 (above); Museum of London 12, 13 (above and below), 14 (right), 15 (above and below), 16, 25, 67, 91, 92, 93, 101, 110, 112–13, 134, 140–1 (The Bridgeman Art Library), 143, 182–3 (The Bridgeman Art Library), 226, 228–9, 245, 263; National Maritime Museum, Greenwich 53, 88–9, 133; National Portrait Gallery, London 84, 107 (below); O'Shea Gallery (The Bridgeman Art Library) 68–9; Popperfoto 286, 294–5, 301 (below); Press Association 254, 303; Lord Primrose (Scottish National Portrait Gallery) 104–5; Private Collection 172 (The Bridgeman Art Library), 197; Royal Albert Hall 208, 209; Royal Borough, Kensington and Chelsea 163, 240–1; The Royal Collection © 1994 Her Majesty The Queen 46, 90, 189; Royal Commission on the Historical Monuments of England 32, 47, 52 (above), 169 (below); Royal Institution 165; Royal Society 107 (above); Selfridges 243; Society of Antiquaries of London 60–1, 71 (The Bridgeman Art Library); Sotheby's 114–5, 220; Staatliche Museen, Berlin 56; Syndication International 285; Tate Gallery 277, 287; Topham Picture Library 7 (right), 222–3, 306, 307; Tower Hamlets Local History Library and Archives 204, 253; Vatican Library (Weidenfeld & Nicolson Archive) 2–3; Vestry House Museum 174; By courtesy of the Board of Trustees of the Victoria & Albert Museum, London 11, 130, 139 (below), 181, 192–3 (The Bridgeman Art Library), 218; Wandsworth Library 238; Weidenfeld & Nicolson Archive endpaper (Photo. John Freeman), 51 (Photo. John Hedgecoe), 63, 82, 88 (Photo. John Freeman), 95, 217, 231, 261, 275, 299; Wesley's Chapel 147; Westminster City Archives 125, 149; Christopher Wood Gallery (The Bridgeman Art Library) 237.